Lecture Notes in Business Information Processing 55

Series Editors

Wil van der Aalst
Eindhoven Technical University, The Netherlands

John Mylopoulos
University of Trento, Italy

Michael Rosemann
Queensland University of Technology, Brisbane, Qld, Australia

Michael J. Shaw
University of Illinois, Urbana-Champaign, IL, USA

Clemens Szyperski
Microsoft Research, Redmond, WA, USA

Ilan Oshri Julia Kotlarsky (Eds.)

Global Sourcing of Information Technology and Business Processes

4th Global Sourcing Workshop 2010
Zermatt, Switzerland, March 22-25, 2010
Revised Selected Papers

Springer

Volume Editors

Ilan Oshri
Rotterdam School of Management
Rotterdam, The Netherlands
E-mail: ioshri@rsm.nl

Julia Kotlarsky
Warwick Business School
Coventry, UK
E-mail: jkotlarsky@wbs.ac.uk

Library of Congress Control Number: 2010933600

ACM Computing Classification (1998): K.6, K.4.3, D.2

ISSN 1865-1348
ISBN-10 3-642-15416-6 Springer Berlin Heidelberg New York
ISBN-13 978-3-642-15416-4 Springer Berlin Heidelberg New York

springer.com

Printed in Germany

Typesetting: Camera-ready by author, data conversion by Scientific Publishing Services, Chennai, India
Printed on acid-free paper 06/3180 5 4 3 2 1 0

Preface

This edited book is intended for use by students, academics and practitioners who take interest in outsourcing and offshoring of information technology and business processes. The book offers a review of the key topics in outsourcing and offshoring, populated with practical frameworks that serve as a tool kit to students and managers. The range of topics covered here is wide and diverse. The sourcing models available to client firms are discussed in great depth and the decision-making processes and considerations regarding the sourcing model and sourcing settings are examined. Vendor capabilities as well as client capabilities are studied in depth and links are offered to the various sourcing models. Issues pertaining to knowledge and expertise are also discussed throughout the book. Last but not least, the book examines current and future trends in outsourcing and offshoring, paying particular attention to the role that CIOs will play in shaping their sourcing strategies.

The book is based on a vast empirical base brought together through years of extensive research by the leading researchers of outsourcing and offshoring.

June 2010

Ilan Oshri
Julia Kotlarsky

Organization

Global Sourcing Workshop is an annual gathering of academics and practitioners.

Program Committee

Workshop Chair	Leslie Willcocks (London School of Economics, London, UK)
Workshop Committee	Julia Kotlarsky (Warwick Business School, Coventry, UK) Ilan Oshri (Rotterdam School of Management, Rotterdam, The Netherlands) Joseph Rottman (St. Louis University, St. Louis, USA)

Sponsoring Institution

Accenture

Table of Contents

Strategic Orientation in the Globalization of Software Firms

Jason Dedrick[1], Kenneth L. Kraemer[2,*], Erran Carmel[3], and Debora Dunkle[2]

[1] Syracuse University, 324 Hinds Hall, Syracuse, NY 13244
[2] UC Irvine, CRITO, 4100 Calit2, Bldg. 325, Irvine, CA, 92697-4650,
Tel.: (949) 824-6387
kkraemer@uci.edu
[3] American University, 4400 Massachusetts Avenue N.W., Washington, DC 20016-8044

Abstract. In the search for profits, software firms are globalizing their development activities. Some firms achieve greater profits by becoming more efficient, whereas others do so by reaching new markets; some do both. This paper creates an a priori typology of strategies based on the extent to which firms are focused on operational improvement or market access, have a dual focus or are unfocused. We find that firms with these strategies differ in degree of internationalization, organization of offshoring and performance outcomes related to offshoring. Market-oriented firms receive a greater proportion of their total revenue from sales outside the U.S., showing a greater international orientation. They keep more of their offshore development in-house via captive operations. They also are most likely to report increased non-U.S. sales as a result of offshoring. On the other hand, operations-oriented firms have lower levels of international sales, are more likely to go offshore via outsourced software development, and achieve greater costs savings and labor force flexibility as a result of offshoring. Operations-oriented firms also face more obstacles in offshoring, perhaps because of their reliance on outsourcing. Dual focus firms generally achieve some of the best of both strategies, whereas unfocused firms achieve lower cost benefits.

The research shows that it pays to have a well-defined strategy for going offshore, and that firms with an explicit strategy are more likely to achieve performance consistent with their strategy. It further shows that captive and outsourced offshoring result in different obstacles and outcomes. In general, market-oriented firms that use captive offshoring versus outsourced offshoring perform better in developing non-U.S. sales.

Keywords: Globalization, software development, offshoring strategy, captive vs. outsourced arrangements, obstacles, firm performance.

1 Introduction

The U.S. National Research Council recently noted that software is not merely an essential market commodity, but embodies the economy's production function itself,

* Corresponding author.

I. Oshri and J. Kotlarsky (Eds.): Global Sourcing 2010, LNBIP 55, pp. 1–25, 2010.

providing a platform for innovation in all sectors of the economy (NRC, 2006). This means that sustaining leadership in software is necessary if the U.S. is to compete internationally not only in the IT industry itself, but also in a wide range of leading industries from financial services to health care to automobiles. Sustaining the U.S. software industry is especially important given the globalization of the industry through the offshoring of software development. Yet, we know little about the offshoring strategies of U.S. software firms or which strategies lead to success so that business executives can manage for competitive advantage and policymakers can make decisions for country advantage.

Research has documented the large scale globalization of IT services and business process services over the last decade through surveys (Lewin and Couto, 2007) and case studies (Lacity and Rottman, 2008; Wilcocks and Lacity, 2006). However, to our knowledge, no one has empirically studied the strategy of software firms that go global. The literature on firm globalization in manufacturing indicates that organizations go offshore for different strategic reasons (Bartlett and Ghoshal, 1987a, b). One is for labor cost, availability or flexibility, which is supply side or production oriented. Another is for market access and developing products for specific customers or markets, which is demand side or market oriented. And of course, some firms might go for a mix of these reasons.

Given the importance of the software industry to national economies, it is useful to know: (1) what strategies do these firms follow in going offshore, and (2) do these globalized firms behave and perform differently based on their strategic orientation? In order to explore these relationships we conducted a telephone survey of U.S. software firms and use the data to answer these questions.

We categorize the firms in our sample according to their offshoring strategy based on the extent to which they are focused on operational improvement, market access, dual focused or unfocused, a typology developed in the context of IT investment strategy by Tallon et al. (2000), and confirmed by analysis of factors driving offshoring in our survey. Market firms are defined (using survey item labels) by the "need to be close to our customers" and "to gain access to local markets." Operations oriented firms are defined by the "need to reduce labor cost" and the "need for labor force flexibility." Dual-focus firms are defined as being both market and cost oriented, whereas unfocused firms are neither.

In this paper, we analyze how differences in strategy are related to differences in organization and management of offshoring, to obstacles faced in the offshoring process, and to performance outcomes. We find that firms with different offshoring strategies differ in degree of internationalization, organization of offshoring, and performance outcomes related to offshoring. Market-oriented firms receive a greater proportion of their total revenue from sales outside the U.S., showing a greater international orientation. They keep more of their offshore development in-house via captive operations. They also were most likely to report increased non-U.S. sales as a result of offshoring.

On the other hand, operations-oriented firms have lower levels of international sales, are more likely to go offshore via outsourced software development, and achieve greater cost savings and labor force flexibility as a result of offshoring. Operations-oriented firms also face more obstacles in offshoring, perhaps because of their reliance on outsourcing. Dual focus firms generally achieve some of the best of both strategies, whereas unfocused firms achieve lower cost benefits.

In the following sections, we first look at the 148 firms that offshore systems development and we examine their strategy, structure and performance. We further examine the firm characteristics, offshored development activities, obstacles and management practices associated with each strategy. We conclude with implications for theory and practice.

2 Literature Review

The literature on firm globalization indicates that organizations might go offshore for a number of different strategic reasons (Porter, 1986). One might be for labor cost, availability or flexibility, or to reach input markets (such as highly skilled talent), which is supply side or production oriented. Another is the need to reach new markets, including the design of new products for specific customers or markets, which is demand side or market oriented (Porter, 1986; Lewin et al., 2009). Firms may organize globally to optimize efficiency and economies of scale, increase responsiveness to national conditions, or try to achieve a combination of both (Bartlett and Ghoshal, 1987a, b).

The expanded scope and goals of offshoring have brought new organization and management challenges to all firms, including software firms. Bardhan (2006) argues that modern firms seek to tailor their organization structure to the needs of their activities, including innovation activities such as R&D and software development. "Each firm strives to build a global network of locational advantage for every activity within the business—a network which is internally consistent and compatible with the overall objectives of the firm" (Bardhan, 2006, p.104). The purpose is to match the capabilities at the home headquarters to the locational, comparative advantage of innovative activity in a different country and market in order to succeed and grow. This is a very strategic view, which might characterize more sophisticated and experienced firms, but perhaps not all firms engaged in the offshoring of innovation activities.

Whereas the offshoring of manufacturing, IT, and business processes are largely about low cost,[1] the globalization of innovative activities such as R&D and software development is likely to be driven by a combination of cost, access to new markets, and the availability of skilled, experienced talent (Bardhan, 2006; Lewin et al., 2009). We would expect that there will be differences in the offshoring strategies of software firms. Some might go offshore for cost, markets or some mix of both. Some might go for other reasons, and some might go offshore without a clear strategy.

[1] According to Bardhan, 2006, "both innovation and manufacturing are capital intensive while most services offshoring has a relatively low level of capital requirements. Manufacturing affects contiguous and similar skills and occupations from the range of blue-collar production jobs, while offshoring of services and innovation impact white collar jobs across dissimilar occupations. ...While manufacturing favored the low cost production networks of East Asia and services headed for the low cost, English speaking, institutionally compatible India, the globalization of innovation is part low cost and availability of skilled scientific talent, leading innovation offshoring to China, India and Russia."

In addition, offshoring has confronted software firms with complex issues of organizational structure and management. The structure issue is whether to offshore in-house through a U.S. subsidiary or foreign affiliate, to offshore with an outside service provider, or to offshore with some combination of both.[2] The management issues include how to manage the offshored operation and how to integrate offshore activities into a consistent corporate strategy and structure that yields successful performance (Lacity and Rottman, 2008). Success might be measured in terms of reduced costs, access to highly skilled talent, faster product development, greater international sales, more revenue from new products, or greater customer service levels.

Not all firms have handled these challenges well. Many have gone offshore in an *ad hoc* manner without any consideration of offshoring strategy (Berry, 2006). Some have gone to reduce costs only to find that the savings are not what they expected (Lacity and Rottman, 2008; Rouse, 2009). This might be due to obstacles such as cultural differences, their own institutional limitations or coordination and communication issues (Oza and Hall, 2005). Still, others have not been able to develop new products or increase international sales due to these same or other obstacles.

Yet, some firms have been successful, and have at least achieved performance consistent with their strategy. Others have achieved a consistent, unified strategy and structure and gained superior performance. Thus far, success has been documented mostly in case studies (or collections of case studies) of individual firms (Lacity and Rottman, 2008; Hirschheim et al., 2009) rather than in a broad survey of firms.

Consequently, we designed this survey research to ask four questions:

1. Do firms have different strategies for offshoring? (Tables 2-3).
2. How do differences in offshoring strategy relate to firm characteristics? (Table 4).
3. What is the relationship between offshoring strategy and the level and nature of offshoring (Tables 5-6), structural arrangements, e.g., captive vs. outsourced (Table 7), obstacles faced by firms (Table 8-9), management practices (Table 10), and offshore performance (Table 11)?
4. What is the relationship of structural arrangements to offshore performance? (Table 14).

Research framework

In order to explore the relationships between firm strategy and structure, obstacles, management practices and performance, we have developed a framework which posits that a firm's strategy is a key determinant of those outcomes. We also posit that structural arrangements may be related to obstacles and performance.

Offshoring strategies

We focus on differences in strategy as the explanation for offshoring performance, which is similar to the earlier analysis by Tallon et al., (2000) on the role of strategy in IT investment performance. In characterizing business strategy, the authors used Porter's (1996) argument that firms differentially focus on two key business

---

[2] Lacity and Rottman (2008) show that there are many variations on these options.

objectives: operational effectiveness and strategic positioning. Firms that focus on operational effectiveness "get more out of their inputs than others because they eliminate wasted effort, employ more advanced technology, motivate employees better, or have greater insights into managing particular activities… operational effectiveness includes, but is not limited to efficiency" (Porter, 1996, p. 62). Those that focus on strategic positioning attempt to differentiate their products or services from those of their rivals in the market. Such strategic or market positioning is customer dependent, and thus firms can improve their performance by closeness to customers in existing markets and extending their reach to new markets or new customers (Tallon, et al., 2000; Porter, 1996).

This distinction between operational efficiency and market positioning can be translated directly into corresponding strategies for offshoring. For example, operational efficiency is achieved by using offshoring to increase labor productivity, availability or flexibility. In contrast, market positioning involves using offshoring to extend geographic reach, customer access, or local market access.

In Figure 1, we use this association between business strategy and offshoring strategy to develop an *a priori* classification of firms based on whether they emphasize operational efficiency or market positioning, or both, as drivers of offshoring. Firms in the upper left quadrant are called "unfocused" because they do not appear to have any strategy. They are largely opportunistic and idiosyncratic in their use of offshoring.

Firms in the lower right quadrant are labeled "dual focused" because they pursue both strategies. Firms in the upper right quadrant are labeled "market focused" because they offshore software development for greater closeness to existing customers or markets and to gain access to new markets. Finally, firms in the lower left quadrant are labeled "operations focused" because they have a clearly defined strategy based on operational efficiency.

	Market focus	
	Low	**High**
Low	***Unfocused*** Offshoring is opportunistic, idiosyncratic	***Market*** Offshoring is focused on being close to customers and gaining access to local markets
Operations focus High	**Operations** Offshoring is focused on labor cost reduction, labor availability and labor flexibility	***Dual*** Offshoring is a combination of operational and market focus

Fig. 1. Typology of Offshoring Strategies

We would further expect that firms with more focused goals would be more likely to achieve higher performance on dimensions consistent with their strategies. For example, operations-focused firms should rank high on cost and labor savings, whereas market-focused firms should rank high on increased international revenues. Dual-focused firms might achieve high performance on both dimensions, but the resources required to target both operational performance and market access might dilute their efforts. Therefore, the performance of dual-focused firms compared to single-focused firms is an empirical question. We would expect unfocused firms to have the lowest performance, given the lack of strategic direction in their offshoring efforts.

Beyond strategy, we expect the organization and management of offshoring would play a significant role in offshoring performance. The literature puts particular emphasis on the structural arrangements and the management practices used by firms as factors influencing performance.

Structural Arrangements

We refer to structure (or governance structure) as the arrangements that a firm uses when it goes offshore for software development. The outsourcing literature indicates that firms can use their own in-house staff (insourcing, captive offshoring), an outside service provider (outsourcing, offshore outsourcing), or a mix of these arrangements (Dibbern et al., 2004; Dibbern et al., 2008; Dedrick et al., forthcoming; Tanriverdi et al., 2007). There are many possible variations on these options in the actual experience of firms, but analytically, they are captured by these three arrangements.

The use of outside service providers is considered superior for achieving efficiency, labor flexibility, and specialized expertise in software development, but involves control costs to ensure performance (Dibbern et al., 2008). In contrast, the use of in-house staff is considered superior for exploiting firm-specific knowledge (DiRomualdo and Gurbaxani, 1998), but setting up and maintaining a captive offshore operation can result in higher fixed costs and sacrifice labor flexibility compared to using an outside provider.

Management practices

Although there are a host of management issues in offshoring, two issues are especially important: (1) how to facilitate collaboration and knowledge sharing across teams in different geographic locations (Carmel and Tjia, 2005); and (2) how to attract and retain skilled, experienced staff both at home and abroad (Dedrick et al., forthcoming). It is now believed that collaboration and transfer of client-specific knowledge is facilitated by social practices such as locating home office managers at the offshore locations, rotating offshore managers to the home office and having home and offshore team members meet face-to-face early on in the collaboration. Team meetings facilitate sharing of tacit knowledge and help to create common understanding among team members. Offshore expats enable home office managers to better understand the capabilities of offshore resources and to better monitor offshore activities. Rotation assists offshore managers' in understanding corporate strategy and expectations as well as the client needs and environment.

The foregoing socialization practices reinforce the importance of career paths for attracting, developing and retaining staff at the home office and abroad. Retention is important to gaining value from investments in socialization. Attracting new talent via development and clear career paths is critical to achieving scale and growth in capabilities, both onshore and offshore, as well as replacing the inevitable loss of talented, experienced individuals through competition and opportunities for advancement elsewhere.

We would expect that firms will differ in their use of these management practices based on their strategies and structural arrangements. Firms with a strong market or dual focus might emphasize attracting and retaining human assets, as they are going offshore for strategic reasons and are likely to be more concerned about building offshore resources. Firms going offshore mainly to reduce costs might emphasize cost reduction more than developing resources.

3 Data and Methods

This research is based on a cross-sectional survey of U.S. software firms. Data were collected via a telephone survey conducted for us by Abt SRBI (New York) from July 29 to October 27, 2008. The respondents were selected from firms with SIC codes corresponding to computer programming services, prepackaged software and computer integrated systems design (7371, 7372, 7373, respectively). Firms in the computer services (7379) SIC code were specifically excluded as we wanted to focus on software development rather than IT services.

Most of the respondents (58.9%) were high level executives directly involved in software development (Table 1). Other executives were indirectly involved through marketing and sales, business development, operations or customer services. A few, generally from the smaller companies, were the highest level executives such as Chairman, CEO, President, GM or Principal. The others were IT executives and other functional executives.

Table 1. Respondents

Respondent category	Number	Percent
SVP, VP, Director or Manager of software/product development	136	58.9
Other Product Executive (marketing, sales, business development, innovation, operations, customer service)	55	23.8
CEO, President, GM, Principal, Chairman	19	8.2
CIO/CTO or other IT manager	15	6.5
Other C-level Executive (finance, controller, HR, legal)	6	2.6
Total	231	100

The survey resulted in 231 completed cases with a response rate of 17.1%. Of the firms surveyed, 83 had no offshore development and were asked a short set of questions to compare them with the 148 firms who did have offshore development. Firms that conduct any offshore development completed the full survey. The full telephone survey took about 20 minutes to complete. Appendix B is an abbreviation of the questionnaire survey items.

Method—A Typology of Offshoring Strategies

As indicated above, we developed a typology of offshoring strategies in order to explore the relationships between strategy, structure and performance found in the globalization and offshoring literature. The typology is derived from the results of a principal component analysis of offshore drivers. Respondents were asked to rate how important (scale ranging from 1 'unimportant' to 5 'important') in the past two years each of the items was as a business rationale for conducting software development outside the U.S. The analysis resulted in two orthogonal factors which were labeled market strategy and operational/cost strategy.

The loadings, Eigenvalues and percent variance explained are shown in Table 2 below. The two factors explain 75% of the variance in the sample and are not intercorrelated.

Table 2. Principal Components Analysis with Varimax Rotation

Questionnaire items	Market focus	Operations focus
Gain access to local markets	.917	-.015
Need to be close to our customers	.912	-.037
Need for labor flexibility	.139	.817
Reduce labor cost	-.195	.783
Eigenvalue	1.745	1.266
% of variance	43.633	31.648

Two scales (market-strategy scale and operations-strategy scale) were constructed by computing a mean of the two loading items for each factor. Both scales range in values from 1 'unimportant' to 5 'important.' The market-driven strategy scale has a median of 1.50 and a mean of 1.77; the operations-driven strategy scale has a median of 2.50 and a mean of 2.38. The Pearson correlation coefficient between the two scales is -.05.

To construct the typology, each scale was then dichotomized with scale scores less than the median scored as 'low' and scale scores at the median or higher as 'high'. Cross-tabulating the two scales resulted in a 2x2 table which was used to construct the typology. The total number of cases for each type, along with the percent of the total, is shown in Table 3 below.

Market firms are low on operations and high on market strategy. Operations firms are high on operations and low on market strategy. Dual strategy firms are high on both market- and operations-oriented strategies whereas unfocused firms are low on both. We call the low-low firms ‘unfocused’ in that they do not appear to have any clear strategy, but rather respond to offshore opportunities that come to them whether market- or operations-based. It is also possible that they are simply pursuing another strategy not captured by our typology.

Table 3. Distribution of Firms in the Typology

		Operations-driven strategy	
		Low	High
Market-driven strategy	Low	Unfocused N=26 (18%)	Market N=28 (19%)
	High	Operations N=40 (28%)	Dual N=50 (35%)

N = 144.

4 Findings

We find that different offshoring strategies are associated with different firm characteristics, with different levels and types of offshoring, and with different structural arrangements. We also find strategy is related to different perceived obstacles to offshoring, and adoption of associated management practices. Finally, we find differences in offshore performance that are consistent with the objectives of each strategy. We next present the findings along each of these dimensions.

Firm characteristics

Overall, the majority of companies in our offshoring subsample are small- and medium-sized private firms, although there are some large, public companies as well. Most firms are experienced with offshore development, as the median year they began developing offshore is 2001. However, 30% of the firms were going offshore for the first time in 2005 or later. The dominant destination for offshore systems development is India followed by Western Europe and then China/other Asia-Pacific.

There clearly are significant differences among firms with different strategies on several firm characteristics, including number of developers, international market focus, and in distribution of offshoring locations between Asia and non-Asia (Europe, Canada, Latin America) locations (Table 4).

Firms that are market-oriented have the highest number of developers in their firm or business unit, have a greater focus on international markets, and have an average of 50% of their offshoring in Asia. Operations-oriented firms are somewhat smaller, have less international market focus, and predominantly offshore to Asia, particularly India (70%). Dual-focus firms are second in number of developers, have the second-highest international market focus, and offshore mainly to Asia. Unfocused firms are small, have the lowest international revenues, have less experience offshore and have only 50% of their offshoring in Asia; they appear across the range of locations. The differences in degree of experience offshore are not statistically significant.

Table 4. Firm Characteristics

	Offshoring strategy				N	Sig.
	Unfocused	Operations	Market	Dual		
Size: Number of firms of this size						
100 employees or less	9	9	5	9	32	
101-500 employees	13	14	12	24	63	
Over 500 employees	4	17	10	17	48	
Number of firms	26	40	27	50	143	0.313[a]
Size: Median number of software developers in company	45	85	105	100	144	**0.057**[b]
International market focus: Percent of total revenue from sales outside the U.S.	17%	26%	36%	30%	134	**0.087**
Experience: Median year began developing software outside the U.S.	2002	2002	2000	2000	142	0.283[c]
Location: Mean percent offshoring in Asia (India, China or elsewhere in Asia) as compared to Europe, Canada and Latin America	50%	85%	50%	88%	144	**0.001**

[a]x^2 significance. [b]Kruskal Wallis test. [c]F-test.

Level of offshoring

We find that the firm strategy is related to the level of captive and outsourced offshoring. Looking first at captive offshoring, we find that dual firms have nearly half of their in-house developers located outside the U.S. and market firms have 38% of their developers outside the U.S. In contrast, unfocused and operations firms have only 28% and 31%, respectively, of their developers outside the U.S. (Table 5).

However, when looking at outsourced offshoring, we find that for unfocused, operations-focused and dual-focus firms, nearly 70% or more of their outsourcers' staff are located outside the U.S. For market-focused firms, only 45% of their outsourcers' staff are outside the U.S. Thus, when market-focused firms outsource they are more likely to do so within the U.S., whereas the other firms are more likely to do so outside the U.S.

It is significant to note that offshoring strategy is not simply a surrogate for firm size as Table 4 shows that there is no relationship between overall company size and the four strategies. However, it also shows that there is a relationship between size of development staff and the strategies, with unfocused firms having much smaller average development staffs.

Table 5. Offshoring Strategy and Level of Offshoring

Level of offshoring	Offshoring strategy				N	Sig.
	Unfocused	Operations	Market	Dual		
Percent in-house software developers located outside the U.S. (captive)	28	31	38	49	143	**0.023**
Percent outsourced software developers located outside the U.S. (outsourced)	68	85	45	70	80	**0.032**

Software development activities offshore

In general, there is very little difference in the development activities done offshore by firms following different strategies, except that a smaller percentage of the unfocused firms do each of the development activities offshore (Table 6). However, a significant proportion of market and dual firms (70% and 87%, respectively) do R&D offshore, in contrast to operations and unfocused firms (57% and 41%, respectively). Also, market-oriented firms are most likely to have project management done offshore (78% versus 61-62% for operations and dual-focused firms).

Table 6. Software Development Activities Offshore

Software development activity*	**Percent doing this activity offshore**				**N**	**Sig.**
	Unfocused	Operations	Market	Dual		
Analysis	50	68	78	73	132	0.166
Design	52	79	81	80	132	**0.058**
Coding	86	97	93	98	133	0.191
Testing	73	87	85	89	133	0.352
Implementation	55	68	81	73	128	0.268
Maintenance and support	59	82	88	89	132	**0.019**
Project management	38	61	78	62	132	**0.049**
R&D	41	57	70	87	131	**0.001**

*Question format: "What proportion of the following software development activities does your company/business unit do onshore or offshore? All onshore, mostly offshore, half and half, mostly offshore, all offshore." The numbers in the cells represent the percent that are "doing the activity offshore" or those that are not "All onshore."

Structural arrangements

We refer to structure as the arrangements that a firm uses when it goes offshore for software development. The literature indicates that firms can use their own in-house staff (captive offshoring), an outside service provider (outsourcer), or a mix of these arrangements (Metters, 2008). The choice of structural arrangement is likely to be influenced by some of the same factors that influence an outsourcing versus in-house decision onshore, e.g., relative operational costs, coordination costs, and risk of opportunism, (Williamson, 1975; Gurbaxani and Whang, 1991). In the offshore context, coordination costs and risks might be seen as higher, given the need to coordinate with a partner across great distance, but the cost of setting up a captive operation might increase the operational cost advantages of outsourcing.

We find that firms use a mix of in-house and outsourced arrangements, but that operations-oriented firms are more likely to outsource while market-oriented firms are more likely to keep development in-house (Table 7). For operations firms, 28% use in-house only, 25% use outsourcers only and 47% use both. In contrast, 77% of the market-oriented firms use only their in-house staff. Dual firms use either in-house staff (53%) or both in-house staff and outsourcers (40%), but few use outsourcers only. These differences might relate to the difficulty of completely outsourcing development when it has a more strategic, market-oriented element. When cost is the main concern, then outsourcing may look most attractive.

Unfocused firms are most similar to operations-oriented firms in that they are spread across all three arrangements, but their proportionate use of each arrangement is different. About 40% each use in-house staff only or both in-house staff and outsourcers; 20% use outsourcing only. As a group, they appear to be experimenting with all the different arrangements, perhaps in the hopes of discovering which works best for them.

Table 7. Offshoring Structural Arrangements

Structural arrangement	**Offshoring strategy**			
	Unfocused	Operations	Market	Dual
Percent use in-house only	41	28	77	53
Percent use outsourcers only	18	25	8	6
Percent use both in-house & outsourcers	41	47	15	40
Total	100	100	100	100

N= 135; x^2 = (p. 0.0003).

Obstacles to offshore development

The offshoring literature has identified many obstacles to offshoring, which are captured in our survey (Lacity and Rottman, 2008). Broadly, these obstacles can be described as worker capabilities, institutional barriers, or risk (Table 8). The first refers to lack of worker skills or experience, the second to various difficulties in managing the offshore relationship. Risk refers to features of the offshoring environment, such as lack of intellectual property rights protection and data security, that represent potential threats to the business as a whole.

Firms with the operations strategy generally report greater obstacles to offshoring across all categories (Table 8). Why might this be the case? Their offshoring is driven by cost pressures, whether from "spreadsheet managers" who push the activity offshore or by investors seeking to boost a balance sheet. Or perhaps they went offshore in search of cost savings without adequately considering the transactions costs involved—a common mistake that many firms make according to the IS outsourcing literature (Lacity and Rottman, 2008; Sahay et al., 2003; Willcocks and Lacity, 1995).

On the other hand, the market-focused firms tend to give a lower importance rating to most offshore obstacles. Chief obstacles for market firms include difficulty transferring necessary knowledge to offshore teams and cross-border culture and communication problems, which are obviously interrelated (correlation is 0.41). But, these obstacles are less important for market firms than for all the other categories. Market firms also are distinguished by having the lowest importance rating of worker and institutional obstacles in comparison to the other firms.

In contrast, all three kinds of obstacles are important for operations-oriented and dual firms, with cross-border culture and communications problems being highest in importance. Institutional problems are next as the firms have problems with both software documentation and knowledge transfer to offshore teams. It is likely that the foregoing obstacles are exacerbated by worker obstacles which are also rated as important.

For unfocused firms, inadequate documentation of applications and processes is the biggest obstacle. This is consistent with these firms also having difficulty transferring necessary knowledge to offshore teams.

One reason that dual firms share the same obstacles with operations firms might be that both have a higher proportion of outsourced development than captive development, and institutional/cultural problems are likely to be greater when there is also the layer of dealing with another company. This prospect is supported by the fact that market-oriented firms largely use captive offshoring and these obstacles are also ranked less important.

Table 8. Obstacles to Offshoring

Obstacles* / Offshoring strategy	Mean importance of this obstacle				N	Sig.
	Unfocused	Operations	Market	Dual		
Worker						
Offshore workers lack necessary skills	1.72	1.93	1.39	1.90	143	**0.049**
Offshore workers lack practical experience	1.72	2.00	1.39	2.06	143	**0.005**
Institutional						
Cross-border culture and communications problems	1.68	2.43	1.71	2.36	143	**0.000**
Inadequate documentation of applications and processes	2.04	1.97	1.57	2.20	143	**0.019**
Difficulty transferring necessary knowledge to offshore teams	1.92	2.28	1.96	2.26	143	**0.105**
Breaking work up across teams	1.68	1.85	1.85	1.94	141	0.681
Risk						
Intellectual property protection	1.60	1.88	1.86	1.94	143	0.493
Data security	1.72	1.75	1.71	1.78	142	0.989

*Question format: "On a scale of 1 to 5 where "1" means "unimportant" and "5" means "important", please rate how important in the past two years the following obstacles have been in affecting your company/business unit software development activities outside the U.S.?" The numbers in the cells represent the mean rank of each obstacle for each strategy.

This is confirmed by comparing firms by their offshoring structural arrangements (in-house, outsourced, both). We find that firms that use only in-house development report fewer problems in general. Moreover, the differences among firms are statistically significant for both worker and institutional obstacles (Table 9). Thus, it appears that firms are better able to hire skilled workers and manage the knowledge transfer process when they set up their own captive operations than when they outsource offshore development or do both.

Table 9. Obstacles by Structural Arrangement

Obstacles*	Mean importance of obstacle			
	In-house only	Outsourced only	Both	Sig.
Worker				
Offshore workers lack necessary skills	1.66	1.78	2.02	**0.074**
Offshore workers lack practical experience	1.72	1.94	2.09	**0.057**
Institutional				
Difficulty transferring necessary knowledge to offshore teams	2.01	2.28	2.34	**0.068**
Inadequate documentation of applications and processes	1.84	1.94	2.21	**0.056**
Cross-border culture and communications problems	2.00	2.22	2.26	0.222
Breaking work up across teams	1.76	1.83	2.00	0.308
Risk				
Intellectual property protection	1.79	1.89	1.83	0.914
Data security	1.73	1.78	1.72	0.965

*Scores range from 1 'unimportant' to 5 'important'.

Offshoring management practices

In order to deal with these obstacles, as well as implement their general strategy, software firms develop specific management practices. While some practices are equally common to all four groups of firms, others are related to the firm strategy and the particular obstacles they face or the organizational arrangements they use. What is equally common to all firms is having the onshore and offshore project team members meet face-to-face in order to facilitate collaboration and knowledge sharing (Table 10). Overall 44% of the software firms use this practice extensively.

Operations-focused firms are distinguished by their use of triage, or evaluation of new projects for their suitability for offshoring (Carmel et al., 2009). Our earlier case study research (Dedrick et al., forthcoming) indicates that triage helps to create an institutional bias towards offshoring in order to reduce cost wherever possible. Yet these firms also maintain career paths in the U.S. in order to retain their home staff. The fact that they place less emphasis on maintaining career paths outside the U.S. is consistent with their greater use of outsourced, rather than captive offshoring.

Market firms emphasize career development for technical staff. They develop career paths outside the U.S. to attract and retain staff in their offshore locations, while also maintaining career paths in the U.S. to retain staff. This might explain why lack of skills and experience among workers is not an important obstacle and why cultural obstacles are also less important than for other firms.

Table 10. Offshoring Management Practices

Offshoring management Practices* / **Offshoring strategy**	**Extent of use of this practice**				**N**	**Sig.**
	Unfocused	Operations	Market	Dual		
Socialization						
Rotate offshore managers to home office	1.46	1.93	2.07	2.45	144	**0.017**
Locate home office managers, that is, expats at the offshore location	1.46	2.00	2.04	2.28	144	**0.065**
Have U.S. and offshore project team members meet face-to-face	3.04	3.00	3.29	3.49	142	0.277
Career paths						
Develop career paths outside the U.S. to attract and retain staff	1.92	2.35	2.75	2.98	143	**0.011**
Maintain career paths in the U.S. to retain staff	2.72	3.37	3.00	3.54	141	**0.047**
Triage						
Evaluate new projects for suitability for offshoring	2.54	3.67	2.43	3.21	142	**0.000**
Compensation						
Managers' compensation is linked to performance of offshore operations	2.19	2.53	2.27	2.73	141	0.382

*Question format: "On a scale of 1 to 5 where "1" means 'never used' and "5" means 'extensively used', please indicate the extent to which your company/business unit uses each of the following software development management practices." The numbers in the cells represent the mean score of each practice for each strategy.

Dual firms emphasize socialization and career development. They are concerned about creating career paths for both U.S. staff and offshore staffs and they rotate their U.S. and offshore managers between onshore and offshore locations. More than the others, they use face-to-face meetings among project teams, and managers' compensation is linked to the performance of offshore operations. Being larger firms and having both captive and outsourced operations, it is likely that these firms need to place more emphasis on management coordination for success.

Unfocused firms emphasize maintaining career paths in the U.S. to retain their staff, but also evaluate new projects for their suitability for offshoring. They are lowest on socialization, possibly because their small scale doesn't provide the resources to employ expensive expats or pay for international travel to support face-to-face meetings.

Offshore performance

Based on their strategic focus, we would expect that operations-oriented firms would achieve the greatest cost savings from offshoring and that market firms would achieve increased revenues. And we find support for these expectations. In terms of cost savings, operations-oriented firms and dual firms report cost savings of 26% and 27%, respectively (Table 11).

In contrast, unfocused firms report lower savings (20%) and market-oriented firms report only 11% in cost savings. It seems clear that market-oriented firms are offshore for reasons other than simply cost savings. Market and dual-focus firms score highest on increasing revenues from non-U.S. markets as a result of going offshore.

These patterns are reinforced by qualitative indicators as well. Operations-oriented firms rank improvements in "access to needed skills", "labor force flexibility" and "speed of product development" highest among the qualitative performance outcomes they have experienced. In contrast, market-oriented firms rank "revenue from non-U.S. markets" and "revenue generated from new products" highest. Intrestingly, dual firms are high on all of these indicators, suggesting they are able to expand markets and improve operations at the same time. Unfocused firms are systematically the lowest in qualitative performance measures.

Table 11. Offshore Performance

Performance dimensions * / Offshoring strategy	Extent to which this dimension increased				N	Sig.
	Unfocused	Operations	Market	Dual		
Operations						
Percent cost savings from conducting software development outside U.S.	20%	26%	11%	27%	120	0.004
Access to needed skills*	3.00	3.68	3.48	3.65	140	0.031
Labor force flexibility*	3.64	4.05	3.41	3.83	140	0.041
Speed of product development*	3.32	3.63	3.07	3.63	132	0.109
Market						
Revenue from non-U.S. markets*	3.17	3.26	3.86	3.80	135	.0000
Revenue generated from new products*	3.17	3.71	3.63	3.63	137	0.091
Customer service levels*	3.20	3.08	3.57	3.16	140	0.121

*Question format: "To what extent have the following increased, decreased or stayed the same as a result of locating development outside of the U.S.? Decreased a lot, decreased a little, stayed the same, increased a little, increased a lot." The numbers in the cells represent the mean score on each performance dimension for each strategy.

Offshore performance by structural arrangement

In general, there are no significant differences among the three structural arrangements (in-house, outsourced, both) with the exception of growth in revenue from non-U.S. markets. Here, firms that rely entirely on outsourced development perform worse than those that use in-house development only, or both (Table 12). This makes sense, as it is not likely that a completely outsourced arrangement will be as useful in developing new markets as actually setting up operations in those markets.

Table 12. Performance by Structural Arrangement

Firm performance*	Extent to which this dimension increased			
	In-house only	Outsourced only	Both	Sig.
Operations				
Percent cost savings from conducting software development outside U.S.	23%	22%	25%	0.834
Access to needed skills	3.41	3.61	3.76	0.158
Labor force flexibility	3.74	3.89	3.82	0.813
Speed of product development	3.48	3.50	3.37	0.854
Market				
Revenue from non-U.S. markets	3.62	3.12	3.54	**0.071**
Revenue generated from new products	3.50	3.44	3.62	0.681
Customer service levels	3.32	3.11	3.18	0.573

*Question format: "To what extent have the following increased, decreased or stayed the same as a result of locating development outside of the U.S.? Decreased a lot, decreased a little, stayed the same, increased a little, increased a lot." The numbers in the cells represent the mean score on each performance dimension for each strategy.

5 Summary

The analysis shows that the four offshoring strategies each form a coherent and somewhat distinct pattern. It also shows that each strategy results in different outcomes, faces different obstacles and has different associated management practices (Table 13).

Operations-oriented firms focus on labor inputs, including lower cost, availability of skilled people and labor force flexibility. They are similar to other firms in the development activities they offshore, but they make higher use of outside service providers. They succeed in achieving access to needed skills, labor flexibility and cost savings (though not the highest). They tend to be medium-sized firms and locate the largest share of their offshoring activity in India. Their outsourcing providers are also mainly in India.

Market-oriented firms seek to access new markets and develop products for international markets. They make high use of captive offshoring. They tend to be medium-sized firms, and locate their offshore activities mainly in Western and Eastern Europe. They are lowest on the quantitative measure of cost savings although high on qualitative measures. They are highest on the quantitative measure of percent of revenues from outside the U.S. and they are high on the qualitative measures of growth in revenues from non-U.S. markets and revenues from new products. The primary obstacles they face are cultural, involving difficulty in transferring knowledge to offshore teams

Table 13. Summary of Strategic Models of Offshoring

Distinguishing features	Unfocused	Operations strategy	Market strategy	Dual strategy
Strategy	Ad hoc and opportunistic in approach to offshoring	Focused on labor or supply side, including cost, availability and flexibility of labor	Focused on accessing new markets, developing products for international markets	Focused on using offshore location for selling software, developing software and supporting offshore customers
Structure	About half use in-house staff and half use outsourcers	High on use of outsourcers	High on use of in-house staff (captive offshoring)	Use both in-house staff & outsourcers, but higher on outsourcers
Management practices	Use triage and maintain career paths in U.S. to retain staff	Use triage and maintain career paths in U.S. to retain staff	Develop career paths outside U.S. to attract and retain staff; Maintain career paths in U.S. to retain staff	Rotate offshore managers to home office; Locate home office manager at offshore location; Develop career paths outside U.S. to attract and retain staff; Maintain career paths in U.S. to retain staff
Performance	In the middle on cost savings, lowest in growth in international revenues	High on cost savings	Lowest on cost savings; Highest on growth in international revenues	Highest on cost savings; also high on growth in international revenues

and cross-border culture and communications problems. They are concerned with managing both onshore and offshore workers. Accordingly, they place emphasis on developing career paths outside the U.S. to attract and retain staff, while also maintaining career paths in the U.S. to retain staff at home. Their emphasis on career paths suggests that they will continue to globalize software development activities. Indeed, market firms are distinguished by the fact that they conduct R&D offshore as well as traditional software development activities—a feature they share only with dual firms (which embody a market orientation as well as a cost one).

Dual firms are focused on using offshore location for selling software, developing software and supporting offshore customers. They are motivated by both cost and market opportunities. They use both in-house staff and outsourcers, but are higher on the use of outsourcers. They are larger firms, and both they and their outsourcing providers tend to be located in India. They are highest on both quantitative and qualitative measures of cost savings and high on measures of international revenues (though not as high as market firms). The face all three types of obstacles--worker, institutional and cultural—and are similar in this regard to operations-oriented firms.

Unfocused firms are not focused, or perhaps are focused on some strategy not captured in our typology. These are generally small firms and offshore development to various locations around the world. About 40% use captive offshoring and another 40% use outside service providers. They are in the middle on costs savings and international revenues. Their chief obstacle to offshoring is the lack of documentation of applications and processes. They use triage on new projects to evaluate offshoring opportunities and maintain career paths to retain staff in the U.S. It is likely that offshoring is experimental at this stage of the firms' globalization.

Because they seemed so unusual, we further examined some firms in the unfocused category by looking at their background and history from public sources and their own websites (Appendix A). We found that they have niche products for niche markets such as a specific educational application, tax application for professional service firms, inventory management for small firms, ERP for small firms or a retail payment management application for small independent stores. Some clients are mainly located in the U.S., whereas others might be located in Europe or Asia-Pacific. Offshore development occurs at one of the offshore sites when captive, and at an outside service provider near that site when outsourced. In other words, they are largely idiosyncratic.

In summary, we have identified, through empirical analysis, four strategies that shape why and how software firms offshore development activities. These are operations, market, dual and unfocused strategies. In general, firms with more focused strategies achieve higher levels of performance than unfocused firms.

Our principal contribution is that we created an empirically driven taxonomy of the globalization characteristics of software companies. Most of the management literature focuses on either *just* the supply side or *just* the demand side of globalization. Our study attempted to combine those two views. In doing so, we also presented some interesting characteristics of each of these globalized firms.

6 Discussion and Conclusion

Implications for theory

Our empirical findings support the idea that there are two distinct reasons for internationalization, with four distinct strategic approaches to offshoring (including the dual-focus and unfocused categories). This parallels the strategy literature on strategic focus (Porter, 1986), and the IS literature on IT investment focus (Tallon et al, 2000).

We find that offshoring strategy is associated with differences on a number of dimensions of offshoring, including firm characteristics, level of offshoring, governance structures, obstacles, management practices and performance outcomes. Based on these findings, we would recommend that researchers incorporate offshoring strategy into theoretical models and empirical studies of global sourcing.

An important contribution of this research is empirical: it is the first comprehensive quantitative survey of offshoring by software firms and it presents a rich nuanced view of offshoring by firms in the software industry. It is possible that the analysis applies to other firms in the IT industry including manufacturing and IT services firms, as well as to firms in other high-technology or high-skill service industries where offshoring is common. In each of these cases, it is likely that firms will adopt different strategies for offshoring, and that those strategies will impact the nature and outcome of offshoring.

Implications for policy/practice

The study has implications for offshoring practice and for country policy. First, consistent with the many previous studies of offshoring, the research clearly shows that it pays to have a well-defined strategy if you go offshore. Unfocused firms consistently scored lowest in qualitative measures of performance, although their average cost savings of 20% was typical of the whole sample.

Second, firms that have an explicit strategy are more likely to achieve benefits consistent with their strategy. We found that operations-oriented firms generally achieved labor cost savings, labor flexibility and greater access to skilled labor. Similarly, market-oriented firms increased their revenue from non-U.S. markets and the revenue generated from new products as a result of locating development outside the U.S. And dual firms achieve both types of benefits in varying degrees. This may be a result of respondents reporting results consistent with expectations, but it is logical that firms will get the biggest results on the dimensions that they consider important; in fact, some firms are reported to pursue one benefit such as cost reduction even if it leads to other problems (such as customer dissatisfaction). This is not something we can directly measure with our data, but it should be kept in mind by practitioners as they consider and implement offshoring.

Third, different structural arrangements (captive, outsourced, both) result in different obstacles and outcomes. Captive offshoring faces fewer obstacles (Table 9), and results in better perofrmance than outsourcing only (Table 12). This makes sense, as a completely outsourced arrangement is not likely to be aas useful in developing new markets as actually setting up one's own operations in those markets.

From a country perspective, the offshoring of software development is a complex issue. Over 60% of the firms in our full survey are already offshore.[3] Recent studies of new product development in various industry sectors show that offshoring of R&D is continuing apace internationally (Lewin et al., 2009). And most observers feel that it is unlikely that the movement offshore will be reversed. Yet, a new study indicates that only 15% of total R&D spending by software firms is currently offshore, indicating that this is "a huge opportunity untapped[4]".

However, the benefits and costs of offshoring are mixed. While market and dual strategies may drive growth through greater international sales and lower costs to U.S. firms, even an operations strategy can help some firms remain competitive in the face of lower cost competitors from other countries. While offshoring results in some job loss in the U.S, it can also result in job retention efforts in the U.S. if it makes U.S. companies more competitive. Offshore development also can be paired with onshore client service, requirements analysis, and implementation, which provide high quality jobs in the U.S. For example, most of the firms' management policies indicate concern for retention of their U.S. staffs.

The long-term competitive advantage for a country like the U.S. depends on continuing to develop new or improved products that can be sold in international markets as well as at home. Offshore software development can help support that effort by tapping talented people who have insights into their home markets and can develop technologies that are likely to be successful in those markets. In some cases, offshore development helps win favor with policymakers and regulators who can influence market access. Our field interviews with large U.S. firms doing software development in China indicate that the current offshoring impetus is cost oriented, but the

---

[3] The offshoring sample, on which this study is based, represents 60% of the total survey sample of 231 firms; 40% of the sample had not yet gone offshore for software development.

[4] The study by an Indian firm, Zinnov Management Consulting, was reported by Global Services Media, Friday, October 23, 2009, under the heading of "Very little being spent on emerging geographies: report" at `http://www.globalservicesmedia.com/Content/general200910237592.asp`

hope is that in exchange for doing development in China, the firms will be given access to the market for sales—especially to the large government agencies and State-Owned Enterprises. This may or may not pan out, but is a potential benefit for the U.S. software industry

Limitations

As with all surveys, there are potential concerns about response bias—namely that firms identified as following one or another strategy would respond in line with their beliefs about the strategy. However, there are several features of the survey that mitigate this concern. First, respondents were never asked directly about their offshoring strategy. In fact, the phrase never appeared in the questionnaire. Instead, they were asked about the importance of a number of factors in the company's business rationale for conducting software development outside the U.S. We derived the strategies analytically as explained in the methods section. Second, the quantitative measures of performance and the qualitative measures are consistent with one another. Third, the respondents were mostly high level executives in a position to know the facts about their firm's offshoring experience. Together, these three considerations suggest that the responses are valid indicators of the firm's actual experience.[5]

The survey is a cross-sectional one and, therefore, we cannot say anything about the dynamics of offshoring. Nevertheless, the findings suggest that there might be an evolutionary pattern to offshoring, which is complementary to that identified by Carmel and Agarwal (2002). They proposed a deterministic 4-stage offshoring model in which the key third stage, beyond experimentation, is an operations-based strategy. Separately, operations and market firms might go offshore initially for one or the other strategy and never change, or they might expand their strategic scope and come to look like dual firms. Similarly, unfocused firms might focus more clearly on cost—the strategy they are closest to on a number of dimensions—and move up to having a strategy.

Acknowledgements. This research is supported by a grant from the U.S. National Science Foundation (SES-0527180).

References

Bardhan, A.: Managing Globalization of R&D: Organizing for Offshoring Innovation. Human Systems Management 25(2), 103–114 (2006)

Bartlett, C.A., Ghoshal, S.: Managing across borders: new strategic requirements. Sloan Management Review 28(4), 7–17 (1987a)

[5] Beyond these considerations related to our specific survey, perceptual measures are widely accepted in organizational research (Lawrence and Lorsch, 1986) as valid measures, and have begun to appear in leading IS journals since the mid-nineties (e.g., Tallon et al., 2000). Moreover, various studies indicate that qualitative survey responses by knowledgeable professionals are good surrogates for objective measures on topics ranging from IT strategy (Venkatraman and Ramanujam, 1987), to performance (Delone and McLean, 1992); to IT business value (Tallon et al., 2000), to IT productivity (Grover et al., 1998), to business and IT strategic alignment (Broadbent and Weil, 1993).

Bartlett, C.A., Ghoshal, S.: Managing across borders: new organizational responses. Sloan Management Review 29(1), 43–53 (1987b)

Berry, J.: Offshoring Opportunities: Strategies and Tactics for Global Competitiveness. John Wiley and Sons, Hoboken (2006)

Broadbent, M., Weill, P.: Improving business and information strategy alignment learning from the banking industry. IBM Systems Journal 32, 162–179 (1993)

Carmel, E., Agarwal, R.: The maturation of offshore sourcing of information technology work. Management Information Systems Quarterly Executive 1(2), 65–75 (2002)

Carmel, E., Dedrick, J., Kraemer, K.L.: Routinizing the offshore choice: applying diffusion of innovation to the case of EDS. Strategic Outsourcing: An International Journal 2(3), 223–239 (2009)

Carmel, E., Tija, P.: Offshoring Information Technology: Sourcing and Outsourcing to a Global Workforce. Cambridge University Press, New York (2005)

Dedrick, J., Carmel, E., Kraemer, K.L.: A dynamic model of offshore software development. Journal of Information Technology (forthcoming, 2010)

DeLone, W., McLean, E.R.: Information systems success: the quest for the dependent variable. Information Systems Research 1(3), 60–95 (1992)

Dibbern, J., Goles, T., Hirschheim, R., Bandula, J.: Information systems outsourcing: a survey and analysis of the literature. Database for Advances in Information Systems 34(4), 6–102 (2004)

Dibbern, J., Winkler, J., Heinzl, A.: Explaining variations in client extra costs between software projects offshored to India. Management Information Systems Quarterly 32(2), 333–366 (2008)

DiRomualdo, A., Gurbaxani, V.: Strategic Intent for IT Outsourcing. Sloan Management Review 39(4), 67–80 (1998)

Grover, V., Teng, J., Segars, A.H., Fiedler, K.: The influence of information technology diffusion and business process change on perceived productivity: the IS executive's perspective. Information and Management 34(3), 141–159 (1998)

Gurbaxani, V., Whang, S.: The impact of information systems on organizations and markets. Commununications of the ACM 34(1), 59–73 (1991)

Lacity, M.C., Rottman, J.W.: Offshore Outsourcing of IT Work. Palgrave Macmillan, England (2008)

Lawrence, P.R., Lorsch, J.W.: Organization and Environment: Managing Differentiation and Integration. Harvard Business School Press, Boston (1986)

Lewin, A.Y., Couto, V.: Next Generation Offshoring: The Globalization of Innovation. Duke CIBER/Booz Allen Hamilton, Durham (2007)

Lewin, A.Y., Massini, S., Peeters, C.: Why are companies offshoring innovation? The emerging global race for talent. Journal of International Business Studies 40(6), 901–925 (2009)

Metters, R.: A typology of offshoring and outsourcing in electronically transmitted services. Journal of Operations Management 26(2), 198–211 (2008)

National Research Council: Software, Growth, and the Future of the U.S. Economy. National Academies Press, Washington (2006)

Oza, N., Hall, T.: Difficulties in Managing Offshore Software Outsourcing Relationships: An empirical Analysis of 18 High Maturity Indian Software Companies. Journal of Information Technology Case and Application Research 7(3), 25–41 (2005)

Porter, M.: Competition in Global Industries. Harvard Business School Press, Boston (1986)

Porter, M.: What is strategy? Harvard Business Review 74(6), 61–77 (1996)

Rouse, A.C.: Is there an 'information technology outsourcing paradox?'. In: Hirschheim, R., Heinzl, A., Dibbern, J. (eds.) Information Systems Outsourcing: Enduring themes, new perspectives and global changes, pp. 129–146. Springer, Heidelberg (2009)

Sahay, S., Nicholson, B., Krishna, S.: Global IT Outsourcing: Software Development Across Borders. Cambridge University Press, Cambridge (2003)

Tallon, P., Kraemer, K.L., Gurbaxani, V.: Executives perspectives on the business value of information technology. Journal of Management Information Systems 16(4), 145–173 (2000)

Tanriverdi, H., Konana, P., Ge, L.: The choice of sourcing mechanisms for business processes. Information Systems Research 18(3), 280–299 (2007)

Venkatraman, N., Ramanujam, V.: Measurement of business economic performance: An examination of method convergence. Journal of Management 13(1), 109–122 (1987)

Williamson, O.E.: Markets and Hierarchies: Analysis and Antitrust Implications. Free Press, New York (1975)

Willcocks, L.P., Lacity, M.C.: Information systems outsourcing in theory and practice. Journal of Information Technology 10(4), 203–207 (1995)

Willcocks, L.P., Lacity, M.C.: Global Sourcing of Business and IT Services. Palgrave Macmillan, England (2006)

Appendix A. Illustrative Unfocused Firms

Name	Description	Market	History
#286 -25 software staff -60% enterprise sales -Private firm -No international sales -50-100 total employees	Scheduling applications that let consumers schedule services over the Internet and enable service companies to deal with such variables as customer preferences, human resources and driving routes.	The company counts utility companies, telecom and broadband service providers and technology manufacturers among its clients. Software is embedded in some other vendor's systems as well.	Established in 1996. A former MIT aerospace engineer, applied artificial intelligence designed to increase satellite performance to the more earthly problem of scheduling services.
#418 -50 software staff -90% enterprise sales -Private firm -25% international sales -500-1000 total employees	ERP applications for manufacturing and distribution in small to medium size companies.	Manufacturers and distributors in the U.S., Europe and Asia-Pacific. 2,000 customers.	Previously an independent firm, but merged with another and now known by a new name. Company has grown by acquisitions since1986. Offices in the U.S., Europe and Asia-Pacific.
#235 -6 software staff -40% enterprise sales -Private firm -15% international sales -Less than 50 total employees	The company provides applications for DVD and CD recording, addressing tasks such as data storage, archiving, duplication, mastering and publishing.	The company's customers include consumers, corporation, and hardware and software companies that embed GEAR's technology in their own products.	Established in 1987. Maintains a development office in the Netherlands.
#131 -40 software staff -40% enterprise sales -Private firm -10% international sales -205 total employees	Applications for corporate tax compliance in the U.S. and abroad.	1,200 customers, including some Fortune 500 companies in the U.S. No overseas offices; international sales come from overseas subsidiaries of U.S. based firms.	Founded in 1986, acquired by a big four accounting firm in 1996, and acquired by private equity firm in 2006 and then merged with another tax software firm.

Apppendix B. Survey Questionnaire Items

Note: The "Table x" notations below refer to the exact wording of the questionnaire and the possible responses.

Drivers of offshoring (Table 2)
On a scale of 1 to 5 where "1" means "unimportant" and "5" means "important", please rate how important in the past two years the following have been in your company's/business unit's business rationale for conducting software development outside the U.S.

Gain access to local markets	1	Unimportant
Need to be close to our customers	2	
Need for labor flexibility	3	
Reduce labor cost	4	
	5	Important
	8	Don't know
	9	Refused

Firm characteristics (Table 4)
Out of a total of 100%, what percent of your company's total revenues are from sales outside the U.S.?

How many full-time equivalent (FTE) employees work for your company/business unit worldwide?

How many full-time equivalent (FTE) software developers do you have in all of your company's/business unit's in-house locations?

If you outsource software development , please give your best estimate of how many full-time equivalent software developers are employed by your outsourcing providers on your behalf?

Level of offshoring (Table 5)

Out of a total of 100%, what percent of your in-house software developers (including contractors) are located outside the U.S.?	0-100%, don't know, refused
And, again, out of a total of 100%, what percent of your outsourced software developers are located outside the U.S.?	0-100%, don't know, refused

Activities being offshored (Table 6)
What proportion of the following software development activities does your company/business unit do onshore or offshore?

Analysis	1	All onshore
Design	2	Mostly onshore
Coding	3	Half and half
Testing	4	Mostly offshore
Implementation	5	All offshore
Maintenance/support	8	Don't know
Project management	9	Refused
R&D		

Structural arrangements (Table 7)

How many full-time equivalent (FTE) software developers do you have in all of your company's/business unit's in-house locations? Include both employees and contract workers. By software developers we mean anyone involved in analysis, design, coding, testing, implementation or maintenance.	Number of software developers, don't know, refused
Out of a total of 100%, what percent of your in-house software developers (including contractors) are located outside the U.S.?	Percent use in-house, don't know, refused
If you outsource software development, please give your best estimate of how many full-time equivalent software developers are employed by your outsourcing providers on your behalf?	Number of outsourced developers, don't know, refused
And, again, out of a total of 100%, what percent of your outsourced software developers are located outside the U.S.?	Percent use outsourcers, don't know, refused

Obstacles to offshoring (Tables 8 &9)
On a scale of 1 to 5 where "1" means "unimportant" and "5" means "important", please rate how important in the past two years the following have been in your company's/business unit's business rationale for conducting software development outside the U.S.

Offshore workers lack necessary skills	1	Unimportant
Offshore workers lack practical experience	2	
Breaking work up across teams	3	
Inadequate documentation of applications and processes	4	
Intellectual property protection	5	Important
Cross-border culture and communication problems	8	Don't know
Difficulty transferring knowledge to offshore teams	9	Refused
Data security		

Management practices (Table 10)
On a scale of 1 to 5 where "1" means "never used" and "5" means "extensively used", please indicate the extent to which your company/business unit uses each of the following software development management practices.

Locate home office managers, that is, expats, at the offshore location	1	Never used
Rotate offshore managers to home office	2	
Employ formal training programs	3	
Link U.S. managers' compensation to performance of offshore operations	4	
Develop career paths outside the U.S. to attract and retain staff	5	Extensively used
Maintain career paths in the U.S. to retain staff	8	Don't know
Evaluate new projects for suitability for offshoring	9	Refused
Have U.S. and offshore project team members meet face-to-face		

Offshore performance (Table 11)

To what extent have the following increased or decreased as a result of locating development outside the U.S.?

Access to needed skills	1	Decreased a lot
Labor force flexibility	2	Decreased a little
Revenue from non-U.S. markets	3	Stayed the same
Revenue gained from new products	4	Increased a little
Speed of product development	5	Increased a lot
Software quality	8	Don't know
Customer service levels	9	Refused

What percent cost savings has your company/business unit achieved from conducting software development outside the U.S.?	0-100%
Out of a total of 100%, what percent of your company's/business unit's total revenue are from sales outside the U.S.?	0-100%

Strategic Sourcing of R&D: The Determinants of Success

Jacques W. Brook[1] and Albert Plugge[2]

[1] Faculty of Strategy, Marketing and International Business,
Maastricht School of Management, The Netherlands
[2] Faculty of Technology, Policy and Management, Delft University of Technology,
The Netherlands

Abstract. The outsourcing of the R&D function is an emerging practice of corporate firms. In their attempt to reduce the increasing cost of research and technology development, firms are strategically outsourcing the R&D function or repositioning their internal R&D organisation. By doing so, they are able to benefit from other technology sources around the world. So far, there is only limited research on how firms develop their R&D sourcing strategies and how these strategies are implemented. This study aims to identify which determinants contribute to the success of R&D sourcing strategies. The results of our empirical research indicate that a clear vision of how to manage innovation strategically on a corporate level is a determinant of an effective R&D strategy. Moreover, our findings revealed that the R&D sourcing strategy influences a firm's sourcing capabilities. These sourcing capabilities need to be developed to manage the demand as well as the supply of R&D services. The alignment between the demand capabilities and the supply capabilities contributes to the success of R&D sourcing.

Classification: full research article.

Keywords: Sourcing strategies, R&D, outsourcing, capabilities.

1 Introduction

Industrial R&D can be defined as a variety of activities based on scientific and engineering disciplines, with the aim of creating new knowledge or exploiting existing knowledge cleverly (Roussel et al., 1991, Chiesa, 2001). For decades many companies considered industrial R&D to be a core competence that should be part of in-house capabilities. However, fierce competition, increasing cost of technology development, and the globalisation of innovation activities through contract research organisations around the world yielded new perspectives. These perspectives refer to how companies apply R&D for service and product innovation purposes. In the article on the rebirth of European Telecoms, Godell et al (2001) commented that the vertical integration grinds innovation to a halt. He suggested that by outsourcing part of innovation activities, telecom service providers will more easily tap into the vast creative potential of the outside World. Following that logic, Chesbrough (2003) has conceptualized open innovation, stating that a firm does not have to originate the research to profit from it. He argued that external R&D can create significant value and internal R&D is needed to

I. Oshri and J. Kotlarsky (Eds.): Global Sourcing 2010, LNBIP 55, pp. 26–42, 2010.

claim some portion of that value. But, the literature reveals that firms' rationales to contract out their R&D function are based on their need to focus on core competences (Zhao and Calantone, 2003), reduce costs (Piachaud, 2002, Kumar and Snavely, 2004), create resource flexibility (Ernst, 2000, Narula, 2001) and obtain access to suppliers' technology capabilities (Ernst, 2000, Piachaud, 2002, Zhao and Calantone, 2003). Previous research revealed that different types of sourcing strategies have different impact on firm performance. Moreover, the execution of a firm's R&D sourcing strategy depends on its capabilities that are considered to be a critical success factor (DiRomualdo and Gurbaxaini, 1998, McFarlan and Nolan, 1995). When properly planned, the execution of a R&D sourcing strategy can enhance innovation practices and improve the overall company performance significantly (Caudy, 2001, Watanabe and Hur, 2004). Other studies have found that a R&D sourcing strategy that is aimed at contracting out R&D activities may not have a positive impact on the firm's performance (Coombs, 1996, Bounfour, 1999, Gilley and Rasheed, 2000, Kessler et al., 2000). Following their strategic review of R&D outsourcing in the pharmaceutical and biotech industry, research (Bailey and Bhagwat, 2009) suggest that many companies are not fully prepared to address the challenge of managing R&D outsourcing effectively. Executives of firm outsourcing R&D face the following dilemma: How to take advantage of outsourcing R&D activities without hampering the ability of the firm's innovating efficiently?

This study focuses on the understanding of the determinants that influence the success of strategic R&D sourcing. It is based on a theory building approach as prior research found that conceptual framework to assist in understanding how corporate firms develop and nurture capabilities to support a successful execution of their R&D sourcing strategies was lacking (Brook, 2006, Brook, 2007). Based on two case studies in the telecommunication service industry in Europe, we examine the current practice of R&D sourcing strategies that corporate firms pursue by analysing the associated organisation capabilities. Inferences from the analysis of the case studies were used to define a conceptual framework for the strategic sourcing of R&D, aimed at assisting corporate firms in implementing R&D sourcing strategies successfully. We also draw on experiences in the field of IT outsourcing which has been researched extensively. However, attention was paid to the nature of R&D, which is associated with uncertainty of the outcome of the research and the difficulty to measure the results. In this context, it is acknowledged in this study that, while lessons can be learned from the field of IT, the outsourcing of R&D reveals new challenges.

This article is organized as follows. Section 2 addresses literature review of R&D sourcing strategies and sourcing capabilities. Section 3 addresses the applied research methodology while the findings of the case studies are described in section 4. We discuss the findings in section 5. The proposed strategic R&D sourcing management model is presented in section 6. Subsequently, the conclusions are presented in section 7.

2 R&D Sourcing Management

2.1 R&D Sourcing Strategies

R&D strategic sourcing decision-making deals with the approach of a firm to develop R&D expertise in highly specialized knowledge areas, either through in-house activities or through outsourcing. Prior research (Huang et al., 2009) suggest that R&D sourcing strategies can be examined from three perspectives: a core competence perspective (Prahalad and Hamel, 1990), a transaction cost analysis perspective (Tidd and Trewhella, 1997, Howell, 1999b, Brusoni et al., 2001, Narula, 2001, Yasuda, 2005) or a cost advantage perspective (Quinn, 1992, Quinn, 1999, Piachaud, 2002, Kumar and Snavely, 2004, Chesbrough, 2003). The core competence approach is based on the traditional idea that firms with high levels of in-house R&D are likely to enhance their technological competencies that are needed for competitive advantage. This means that a core competence view of R&D will tend to favour a strong in-house R&D organisation as outsourcing R&D is perceived as undermining technology competencies that are vital for the firm. Conversely, other researchers have argued that outsourcing R&D enables a firm to benefit from complementary resources and technology capabilities from external parties (Nohria and Garcia-Pont, 1991, Teece, 1986, Yasuda, 2005, Godell et al., 2001, Chesbrough, 2003). According to the transaction cost viewpoint of R&D, outsourcing is difficult to be implemented because of a high degree of complexity and uncertainty associated with the nature of R&D (Howell, 1999b). It is suggested that the more technology can be codified (described in terms of formulae, blueprint and rules) the easier it is to be contracted out. Considering the parallel fields of IT outsourcing, IT activities and software development activities can easily be outsourced as they can be codified (Oshri et al., 2008). In the context of R&D activities, technologies that cannot be codified tend to be viewed as a candidate for in-house research and development activities (Tidd and Trewhella, 1997, Narula, 2001).

The third perspective involves the notion of cost advantage as researchers have argued that R&D outsourcing will have a positive effect on reducing the costs of new product development (Quinn, 1992, Quinn, 1999, Piachaud, 2002, Chesbrough, 2003). The cost advantage tends to be derived from efficiency improvement of R&D suppliers. Quinn (1991) suggests that firms undertaking R&D outsourcing are not able to prevent the accumulation of internal bureaucracies and inefficiencies. Chesbrough (2003) argue that using external technologies for internal product development is an efficient way of offsetting the rising cost of technology development. However, Kessler et.al (2000) found that R&D outsourcing can create hidden cost which occurs in coordination activities when a firm attempts to integrate external knowledge into its internal knowledge base. This refers to the need for a capability that a firm should have to be able to efficiently absorb the external knowledge from R&D suppliers. The elements that relate to a R&D sourcing strategy also involve scoping issues: the type of knowledge a firm should retain, which activities should be outsourced, and governance processes. The latter is needed in order to manage a complex system of relationships with potentially many external R&D suppliers. Therefore we pose our first proposition as follows:

Proposition 1: A leadership that sets a clear vision on how to manage innovation strategically on a corporate level determines the R&D sourcing strategy.

Studies reveal that corporate firms have engaged R&D outsourcing with little visibility as to the number of outsourcing supplier relationships. It is suggested that firms should learn to assess R&D suppliers and undertake a systematic selection of partners in order to manage the complexity that arises from supplier proliferation. Generic

R&D sourcing strategies involve two types of sourcing arrangements in relation to the number of suppliers. First, a single sourcing approach can be pursued that prefers to focus on a single R&D supplier. This approach provides the advantage of low relationship complexity with external parties, and to foster customer intimacy. However, a single sourcing strategy decreases the flexibility of a firm as to the accessibility of external knowledge. It potentially leads to a lock-in by the R&D supplier that will become less responsive to the firm's R&D needs. Furthermore it may weaken the bargaining power of the firm. Secondly, a multi-sourcing approach is based on a group of preferred R&D suppliers. This approach increases the flexibility of a firm to access external knowledge, mitigating the risk of a lock-in and increasing the bargaining power. On the other side, a multi-sourcing strategy contributes to increasing complexity of the supplier relationships. A study of a strategic reorientation of industrial R&D towards commercial objectives suggests that the strategic side of R&D outsourcing is poorly addressed by corporate firms (Brook, 2006). Based on this gap in previous studies, there is a need for more empirical studies on R&D sourcing strategies. Moreover, the current literature does not address the need to match a selected R&D sourcing strategy with an appropriate set of organisation's sourcing capabilities. This study analyzes the R&D sourcing strategies and their implication for the organisation sourcing capability development. Based on this assumption we pose the following proposition:

Proposition 2: R&D sourcing strategy influences a firm's sourcing capabilities.

2.2 Organisation's Sourcing Capabilities

An organisation capability is defined as an organisation's ability to perform a coordinated task, utilizing organisation resources for the purpose of achieving a particular end result (Helfat, 2003). Previous research has established that the ability of a firm to gain and maintain competitive advantage depends on its organisation capabilities. In this context, firms that outsource R&D to gain a competitive advantage needs to develop and retain certain capabilities to manage the execution of the R&D sourcing strategy successfully. For example, firms that insourced knowledge from external R&D suppliers should be able to absorb this knowledge. This relates to structural issues of managing the demand and supply of knowledge as part of a firm's capabilities. This means that business units should be able to formulate the demand for specific knowledge, their need for innovation and understand the delivery of this knowledge by the external R&D supplier. In essence, the R&D sourcing strategy should provide direction how to develop an operating model that deals with an effective orchestration of the demand and the supply of knowledge within the firm. Discussed sourcing capabilities in more detail, literature revealed a lack of souring capabilities that a firm should possess to support the execution of R&D sourcing strategies. Previous research in the field of IT outsourcing has studied the use of sourcing capabilities (Feeny and Willcocks, 1998). Ample attention has been paid to how firms use sourcing capabilities to manage the demand on the one hand and the supply on the other hand. In this study we recognize the demand management function and the supply management function as distinctive part of the R&D sourcing management that are also interrelated. The separation of these two aspects of the R&D sourcing management is based on the assumption that a strong demand management function will lead to better understanding of the business needs. Furthermore, a strong supply management function will lead to an effective delivery of R&D knowledge. The lack of this clear separation of concern between the demand function and the supply function leads to a tension about how the R&D outsourcing relationship is managed taken boundaries and responsibilities into account. In this study, the sourcing capabilities identified in the field of IT outsourcing, see table 1, are used as a starting point of our analysis to determine which capabilities need to be retained by firms that consider outsourcing their R&D function. For example, sourcing capabilities related to the leadership role, contract management are expected to supportive of the execution of an R&D sourcing strategy. Inferences are made as to what capabilities are used to manage the demand and the supply, respectively. This will lead to the following proposition:

Proposition 3: The alignment between demand capabilities and supply capabilities influences R&D sourcing success positively.

Table 1. Overview nine core IS capabilities (Feeny and Willcocks, 1998)

Sourcing capabilities	Description
Leadership	The Leadership capability addresses the integration of business goals and IT. The main task is to guide organizational arrangements managing the interdependencies between the various capabilities.
Business Systems Thinking	Business Systems Thinking ensures that business processes are envisioned by IT capabilities. Employees who adopt an attitude as business system thinkers contribute to the firm by transforming business processes by means of process reengineering.
Relationship Building	The Relationship Building capability focuses on strengthening the relationship between the business departments and the IT function. Topics like mutual understanding, cooperation and trust contribute to a business-IT alignment.
Architecture Planning	Designing Technical Architecture aims at achieving a coherent structure related to IT infrastructure and applications. This capability ensures that the firm is able to operate effectively.
Making Technology Work	The capability Making Technology Work identifies how business needs can be addressed that cannot be facilitated by technical standards. This capability focuses on strengthening the IT chain by solving problems of IT activities.
Informed Buying	Informed Buying specifically addresses an analysis of the external market. These activities include developing a sourcing strategy, manage the tender process and contract and service management processes.
Contract Facilitation	The Contract Facilitation capability focuses on discussing and recording the services in a sound contract to ensure success. The capability needs to prevent contractual issues and problems that could arise during the arrangement.
Contract Monitoring	Contract Monitoring aims at managing the contracts and services with suppliers as agreed. Moreover, performance measurement forms a part of this capability.
Vendor Development	The Vendor Development capability identifies the added value of suppliers that are involved in outsourcing arrangements. This capability focuses on increasing the business revenues of a firm by analyzing long term supplier goals while creating mutual benefits.

3 Research Methodology

To conduct this study, a qualitative research methodology was applied (McDonough III and Leifer, 1986, Brown and Eisenhardt, 1997). The unit of analysis in this research is the organisational department that is responsible for the R&D sourcing strategy within a corporation. The research design consists of two case studies that permit a replication of logic about the variables and the relationships between those variables (Yin, 1994). Due to the limited number of references available in the literature and the explorative nature of the study, a case study approach appeared to be appropriate as its focuses on "what" and "how" questions (Yin, 1994). The cases were treated as series of independent experiments that confirm of disconfirm the emerging conceptual insights (Brown and Eisenhardt, 1997). These conceptual insights are used to refine the application of the theory of sourcing capabilities in managing the demand and supply of R&D services in the context of a strategic sourcing of the R&D function.

The main procedure used for collecting the primary data for this study was semi-structured interviews. This is an effective means of investigating research questions and conducting explorative research because its allows for flexible questioning, the explanation of questions that are unclear, and probing to help respondents to provide complete information (McDonough III and Leifer, 1986). A total of 25 interviews were conducted that included executives on a corporate level, middle management and consultants on a division level and a business unit level. Follow-up discussions were organised with some interviewees to clarify the points raised during the interviews. Based on a grounded theory approach, each interview was conducted using a set of open-ended questions (Brown and Eisenhardt, 1997, Neman, 2000). The sources of secondary data consist of documents describing the strategic direction, the repositioning of the internal R&D organisation and the evaluation of the implementation of the R&D sourcing strategy.

The transcribed interviews and the secondary data were content analysed (Neuendorf, 2002) to identify general patterns in the data using an iterative process consisting of multiple readings of the interview documents. The goal of this process was to achieve convergence around the set of themes that emerged from the data (McDonough, 2004). Following the data analysis, preliminary individual case studies were drafted. A final cross-case analysis was conducted. This involved matching the evidence that confirm or reject the theoretical model of the strategic R&D sourcing management presented in this study (Neman, 2000). Using our proposed model of strategic R&D sourcing management, a theory building structure was used to analyse the two cases investigated. In this approach the sequence of the sections in the cross-case study report followed the theory building logic (Yin, 1994).

4 Case Studies

Two case studies of firms that have outsourced R&D activities are presented below. The analysis is structured in three parts. The first part is concerns the R&D sourcing strategy pursued by these firms. The second and third parts address the identified demand capabilities and supply capabilities, respectively.

4.1 Case Study 1: Telecom Service Provider in the Netherlands

A Dutch telecom service provider decided to outsource its entire R&D function as part of its corporate strategy to achieve cost-effectiveness in innovation activities. The rationale for the outsourcing decision was that the internal R&D function, which consisted of approximately 500 employees, was no longer regarded as a strategic asset. Originally, internal R&D activities were applied to develop new technologies that contribute to the production of industry standard technology solutions through participation in international research projects. The company shifted its focus to innovation using state-of-the-art technologies that could be provided by any supplier. The firm had no past experience in managing R&D outsourcing.

R&D Sourcing Strategy

The firm decided to adopt a total outsourcing of its R&D function. Executives went beyond the open innovation concept that holds that the internal R&D is complemented with external knowledge. Discussion about what part of R&D should be kept in-house and what part should be outsourced was irrelevant. The entire R&D function was outsourced to a specialized industrial R&D supplier. This decision was motivated by the idea that the R&D function was too small to play a key role, leading innovation in a global market. The corporate innovation strategy shifted entirely from make to buy. The R&D sourcing strategy had two key objectives. First, the fixed costs for R&D needed to be changed into variable costs gradually over a period of 5 years. This implied that the guaranteed workload at the start of the outsourcing arrangement was limited to allow the outsourced R&D function to manage the transition towards a self-sustained organisation. Secondly, the organisation required increasing flexibility to tap into external technology sources to support the development of new services and the enhancement of existing services. This implied that the telecom provider aimed at a multi-sourcing approach for R&D services.

Demand Capabilities

A governance framework was developed to coordinate the demand of R&D services. The main purpose of this governance framework was to build a long-term partnership between the telecom service provider and its external R&D supplier. An executive board was established on a corporate level to this end. The executive board met once a year to discuss the annual strategic agenda. In additional meetings urgent matters were addressed or any disputes resolved on a division level. With regard to the structure of the governance framework, the Leadership on the demand management of R&D services was assigned on business unit level or on division level. The business units operated as direct customers of the external R&D supplier and an annual package of contracted research projects across the business units was agreed with each division. In the adopted structure, the executive management mainly focused on budget allocation and monitoring the R&D projects. It was found that there was lack of strong *Leadership* capability to manage the interdependencies between the contracted research projects across the divisions. This resulted in confusion how to apply the knowledge generated from R&D activities to the business activities of the corporation. In essence, R&D was usually perceived as futuristic and disconnected from the short-term business objectives, stated by the divisions. Only a few strategy advisors were involved to develop a sourcing strategy for R&D services. There were also only few supporting decision makers on a corporate level with sufficient understanding of relevant knowledge areas for the firm. There was a need for an *Informed Buying* capability to support an effective communication with the R&D supplier. However the process was generally fragmented. There was a lack of *Business System Thinking* approach in achieving a consistent view on the type of knowledge needed on a corporate level and the way in which knowledge is shared and applied across the divisions. While the organisation was aware of the need for demand capabilities, only little was done to develop those capabilities and to institutionalise them within the organisation.

Supply Capabilities

To Make Technology Work, external R&D experts were involved in implementing innovative projects on a business unit level within the divisions. Their knowledge of standard technology concepts and frameworks were utilized to design a customized architecture of new telecommunications infrastructure and service platforms. The Leadership involvement was generally operational, and focused on procedures of managing innovative projects throughout the stage gates of go or no go decisions. Managers on a tactical and operational level found the contributions of the R&D experts highly valuable. However, on a strategic level the executive management was still questioning the value of R&D for the corporation. Executive management persistently had the impression that contracted research projects delivered less value. The R&D governance framework that was agreed with the external supplier did not clearly specify the services that captured the value for the business units. We observed that the Contract Facilitation capability was not sufficiently developed. We also found a lack of common process on a corporate level to ensure performance measurement according to the governance framework agreement. The findings revealed that the mobile network division applied a structured process of quarterly review of contracted research projects. In contrast, the fixed network division had an ad hoc process that did not reveal much with regard to expected performance and contribution to the business. In this case it was found difficult to effectively monitor the execution of research projects. The lack of an effective Contract Monitoring process led to ineffective execution of the R&D outsourcing arrangement in the first year. An evaluation revealed that while the external R&D supplier was supposed to conduct long-term oriented contracted research projects based on strategic objectives, in practice almost all projects conducted in the first year were operational projects. The contracted research projects were unbalanced as the business units were pressuring for the implementation of innovation in short-term oriented projects. The short-term orientation was not in aligned with the long-term objective in the contract with the supplier. The Vendor Management capability in the organisation was not used effectively to identify the added value. In essence, the developed vendor management policy did not apply to R&D projects when identifying the added value of R&D related to increased business revenues or enhancing service quality and customer experience.

4.2 Case Study 2: Telecom Service Provider in the UK

A UK telecom service provider decided to transform its R&D function of more than 3000 employees into a business-oriented division with profit-and-loss responsibility. The corporate strategy was inspired by the idea that an R&D function can be managed as a business in its own right. Throughout decades of research, the R&D organisation had accumulated a portfolio of almost 14000 patents based on almost 2000 inventions. The executive management believed that the R&D function could contribute to both cost reduction and revenue generation objectives. In this context the company shifted its R&D function business model from a cost centre to a revenue generating model driven by innovation rather knowledge production only. The R&D function was considered as a driver for innovation with the potential to contribute to the core business of the corporation. The firm had no past experience in managing R&D outsourcing.

R&D Sourcing Strategy

The company adopted a selective R&D sourcing strategy. This was motivated by a corporate innovation strategy inspired by the open innovation concept that builds from the assumption that a dedicated internal R&D function should be complemented with external knowledge by specialized contract research organisations. Long-term research projects were partially outsourced to academic institutions and to specialised R&D suppliers. The latter were perceived as better positioned to achieve a world-class performance in specific knowledge areas. To improve the effectiveness and efficiency of research projects, a sourcing strategy was developed based on three key objectives. First, radical cost reduction of the operation of service platforms should be achieved based on proven and standardized technologies that can be delivered from offshore locations. Secondly, the risk of investments in long-term research projects should be reduced through partnerships with the academic world. Third, the corporation should pursue access to world class technology expertise through joint venture initiatives with specialised technology suppliers around the world. The senior management of the R&D organisation was fully responsible for the development and the implementation of the R&D sourcing strategy. The R&D organisation was operating as an independent business unit alongside other business units within the corporation. The R&D organisation was pursuing a selective sourcing strategy related to specific knowledge areas. Part of the corporate innovation strategy was to retain an in-house R&D function capable to support the absorptive capacity of the external knowledge and accelerate innovation within the firm. The firm also pursued a multi-sourcing strategy of R&D based on a list of preferred suppliers.

Demand Capabilities

An executive leadership council of the R&D function initiated a so-called joint innovation venture in collaboration with business units to align business innovation objectives and R&D objectives. This initiative resulted in a better understanding among senior management on the business units about how R&D activities contribute to the business goals of the corporation. *Building Relationships* with counter parts within the business units was a crucial objective to channel and manage the demand for R&D services. It was found that the R&D function improved its ability to present convincing business cases for the funding of the contracted research projects. The *Informed Buying* capability was recognized by senior management as a determinant for developing a successful sourcing strategy with their suppliers. Applying the *Informed Buying* capability to assess the value of long-term research projects was regarded as very challenging. Business unit managers tend to view long-term research projects as too abstract as in their opinion these projects provide only limited business relevance for their short-term profit-and-loss responsibilities. The senior management of the R&D organisation was responsible for coordinating the identification of new research themes. Furthermore, they developed a collaboration process with the business units based on a *Business System Thinking* approach.

Supply Capabilities

Our empirical research indicated that the *Leadership* capability focused on the vision, the strategic direction and project selection for the development of intellectual properties, derived from the corporate innovation strategy. The main task of the leadership council was to provide governance agreements to assist the middle management of business units in conducting technology foresight as well as the development of a world class research capability. The latter relates to absorbing the external knowledge that is generated from outsourced research projects. The performance management department within the R&D function developed a performance dashboard to monitor both the progress of research projects and commercial exploitation activities. This is related to the use of intellectual property rights. The results of the performance as provided by suppliers were presented to the senior management of the business units. We find that the *Making Technology Work* capability was part of the performance management process. This process describes how technology solutions are translated into innovations in business projects of lines of business. The *Vendor Management* capability was identified that focused specifically on the management of a limited number of preferred R&D suppliers. The added value of suppliers was associated to their ability to deliver world-class performance in either basic research or in emerging technologies. Few academic institutions were selected to conduct basic research activities with a high risk profile and few specialised industrial R&D suppliers were selected to conduct parts of research activities in selective areas of emerging technologies.

5 Discussion

This study has examined how two large European telecom service providers have strategically transformed their R&D function during the last five years. The findings from a cross-case analysis of the two case studies are used to discuss the propositions as stated earlier.

Proposition 1: A leadership that sets a clear vision on how to manage innovation strategically on a corporate level determines the R&D sourcing strategy.

After the liberalisation of the telecom service markets in the late nineties, increased competition forced the incumbent telecom service providers to focus on their core competences. A renewed vision on how to strategically manage innovation started to emerge as executive management were discussing how to radically reduce operational cost and refocus on profitable businesses. Innovation was no longer perceived as an activity that should be driven entirely from an internal R&D organisation. The change in the R&D sourcing strategy followed the decision to reposition the internal R&D organisation. The R&D market has become more mature since specialised R&D suppliers are able to provide R&D services on specific technology areas. Executive management started to view the cost of R&D as a variable as parts of their R&D activities can be contracted out at lower cost. Moreover, outsourcing provides the possibility to upscale or downscale the workload of R&D activities based on a more flexible R&D approach. However, the findings reveal that firms differ in the amount of R&D activities that are outsourced. The Dutch telecom service provider decided to outsource its entire R&D function while the other telecom service provider applied a selective outsourcing approach. Our findings revealed a lack of vision at corporate level of how innovation needs of the firm should lead to an effective R&D sourcing strategy. We found that the R&D sourcing strategy was perceived as ineffective as the rationale for outsourcing was only driven by cost reduction. During the first year of the outsourcing contract many incremental R&D projects were conducted without a major strategic impact. The evaluation of the first year resulted in an adaptation of the R&D sourcing strategy as new investments were directly related to long-term R&D research based on predefined innovation themes. The UK telecom service provider developed a clear vision on innovation on a corporate level, aimed to developing next generation service platform. It provided the context for defining the R&D sourcing strategy that delineated which R&D activities should be conducted internally and which should be outsourced to third parties. This selective approach to R&D outsourcing involves three aspects: 1) a joint venture for specialised knowledge with a high degree of uncertainty where the objective is to reduce the risk; 2) manufacturing-driven development to reduce the cost of technology and achieve a shorter time to market; and 3) strategic partnering to access external intellectual properties and collaborate with academic institutions on basic research. Selective outsourcing combines knowledge from both internal and external R&D sources to innovate. In this particular case, the R&D sourcing strategy appeared to be effective as it provided insight and direction to the senior management of the R&D organisation about the strategic areas of technology. Recent research in the field of IT outsourcing (Lacity et al., 2009) demonstrated that executive leadership's vision is a key determinant in achieving a successful outsourcing arrangement. This is consistent with the findings in this study. We found that such executive leadership vision is also grounded in the corporate innovation strategy of the firm.

Proposition 2: R&D sourcing strategy influences a firm's sourcing capabilities.

The findings from both case studies indicated that prior to the decision to outsource R&D activities, the internal R&D organisations operated almost in isolation from other business units within the corporation. The R&D budget was allocated at the beginning of each year, while a portfolio of research projects was selected later. As one of the senior managers within a R&D organisation under study put it, "money was spent on good research but not in an informal way". After the renewed vision on how to manage innovation strategically, the senior management in the R&D organisation realised that they needed to develop new capabilities. The results of the case study analysis suggest that the adopted R&D sourcing strategy significantly influence the adoption of new capabilities within the R&D organisations. The studied capabilities, as applied in the field of IT outsourcing, can be divided into demand capabilities and supply capabilities. As the business units started to behave as true customers, the senior management within the R&D organisation demonstrated leadership in aligning the demand for R&D projects with the supply of knowledge by external suppliers. The capability *Relationship Building* was recognized to develop a mutual vision on innovation with executive management. The *Informed Buying* approach was identified to manage the demand of R&D services effectively. Furthermore we found that a *Business System Thinking* approach was developed to deliver effective technology solutions that fit into the needs of the lines of business.

Our findings indicated that the pre-selected supply capabilities based on the literature were found that include *Leadership, Making Technology Work, Contract Monitoring* and *Vendor Management*. However, these capabilities were poorly developed and less attention was paid to adapt these capabilities. Recent literature (Plugge and Janssen, 2009) suggests that capabilities must be adapted regularly to meet customer demand. We find that the *Leadership* capability related to the supply of R&D services was exercised on an operational level. Attention tends to be focused on managing the demand side and less on managing the supply side. The *Contract Facilitation* and *Contract Monitoring* capabilities did not enforce the focus on long-term research projects and their values for the business. The perceived value of R&D by the middle management within the business units was limited to *Making Technology Work* in operational projects. In the case of total R&D outsourcing, it appeared that the corporation rushed into a single supplier arrangement without a well-defined vendor management policy for R&D services. Particularly, we find a lack to the presence of a retained organisation that is capable of managing the supply side of R&D. However, in the case of selective R&D outsourcing, a technology foresight team was assigned to manage the supply side of R&D with respect to long-term research projects. Consequently, the *Leadership* and *Vendor Management* capabilities were the focus points of managing the supply side as the firms also pursued a multi-sourcing approach of R&D based on a list of preferred suppliers.

Besides the sourcing capabilities as described in literature (Feeny and Willcocks, 1998), we also found two more important capabilities, *Knowledge Management* and *Intellectual Property Right*. The *Knowledge Management* capability is inherent to the nature of R&D. When a firm decides to outsource R&D activities, knowledge management becomes an essential capability. On the one hand, knowledge management determines which knowledge areas should be retained when activities are outsourced. On the other hand, the knowledge management capability is a prerequisite to develop and maintain the absorptive capacity of external knowledge. The importance of developing a knowledge management strategies enables the creation and exploitation of intellectual capital (Willcocks et al., 2004). The *Intellectual Property Right* capability that we identified is used to protect and commercialise highly valuable knowledge that results from research activities. While in the past intellectual property rights were used only to protect the knowledge by producing patents, attention has shifted to address the commercialisation potential of the intellectual property as research is progressing. In the situation where R&D activities are outsourced, the ownership of intellectual property that may result from the research work needs to be addressed. To retain control over intellectual property rights, knowledge transfer can be applied adequately. Hence, to share and understand common goals and strengthen network ties, the strategic client-supplier relationship needs to be managed from a structural, cognitive, relational, and absorptive dimension (Rottman, 2008). The additional capabilities that were identified are complementary to the sourcing capabilities that we have studied. This is consistent with prior research (Levina and Ross, 2003) arguing that complementary capabilities contribute to strengthening internal or external relationships.

Proposition 3: The alignment between demand capabilities and supply capabilities influences R&D sourcing success positively.

Analyzing these sourcing capabilities, we recognized that some capabilities clearly focus on either the demand side or the supply side while other capabilities relate to both sides. Demand capabilities are directly related to canalise the needs of business units and departments. These business needs must be identified, specified and described to address what needs are required. When taking R&D into account, the process to specify the business needs is essential to determine what type of knowledge is required. Insufficient attention to this process provides unclear requirements that result in a solution that differs from the actual business demand. On the other hand, there are capabilities that focus on the delivery of agreed knowledge. These capabilities are supply-oriented. They are applied to manage external suppliers. In other words, supply capabilities focus on how the solution of a supplier is designed and delivered in an effective way. At the start of a new R&D project the business demands are not always clear. Therefore, a close cooperation with the demand side is required. Since business needs may change over time, sourcing capabilities are applied to deal with the aspect of demand and supply. This means that aligning demand and supply capabilities contribute to the coherence and integration of demand and supply tasks. Table 2 depicts the sourcing capabilities divided as to their nature.

Table 2. Sourcing capabilities related to the demand side and the supply side

Demand-oriented capabilities	Supply-oriented capabilities
Leadership	Leadership
Informed Buying	Informed Buying
Making Technology Work	Making Technology Work
Business Systems Thinking	Contract Facilitation
Relationship Building	Contract Monitoring
Knowledge Management	Knowledge Management
Intellectual Property Rights	Intellectual Property Rights
Architecture Planning	Vendor Development

In the first case study of the Dutch telecom service provider, which outsourced its entire R&D organisation, attention was only paid to the demand side during the operational phase of the contract. The objectives and agreements in the contract with respect to the long-term research projects were neglected. Without appropriate capabilities on the supply side, such as *Contract Monitoring* and *Vendor Management*, the management of the demand side is out of control as the attention of the middle management is shifted to incremental projects. The second case study revealed that specific attention was paid to establish a R&D organisation that is responsible for managing the demand and supply side. The executive leadership of the R&D organisation established regular meetings with senior business managers as well as supplier representatives. The findings demonstrated that a sound alignment between parties involved contribute to the success of the outsourcing arrangement. In particular, the *Leadership* capability can be indicated as key to manage this alignment process between demand and supply. Furthermore, the *Relationship Building* capability was found on the demand side as being an enabler in building relationships between internal and external stakeholders. The findings of both case studies suggest that in order to execute an effective R&D sourcing strategy, demand capabilities and supply capabilities cannot be developed and managed in isolation. They need to be aligned and they should be embedded into a firm's R&D value chain that supports the innovation process within the corporation. For example a knowledge management capability on the demand side within the business units should be aligned with a knowledge management on the supply side from the supplier perspective, to ensure an effective absorptive capacity of the outsourcing firm.

6 Proposed Strategic R&D Sourcing Management Model

In an investigation of the determinants that contribute to the success of strategic sourcing of R&D, this study addressed the question how to take advantage of outsourcing R&D activities without hampering the ability of the firm to innovate efficiently. The objective was to examine the R&D sourcing strategy as well as the associated demand and supply capabilities. Based on the analysis of the case studies we developed a R&D sourcing management model as illustrated in figure 1. The development of the R&D sourcing strategy is derived from the corporate innovation strategy. Moreover, the R&D sourcing strategy should be consistent with the strategy pursued by the R&D supplier. However, this relationship has been kept out of the scope of this study.

The alignment between the demand capabilities and the supply capabilities is a determinant of a successful implementation of the R&D sourcing strategy. Conversely, the R&D sourcing strategy provides guidance the sourcing capabilities that the firm needs to retain or develop. This interactive strategic R&D sourcing management model suggests the imperative for coherence between the variables.

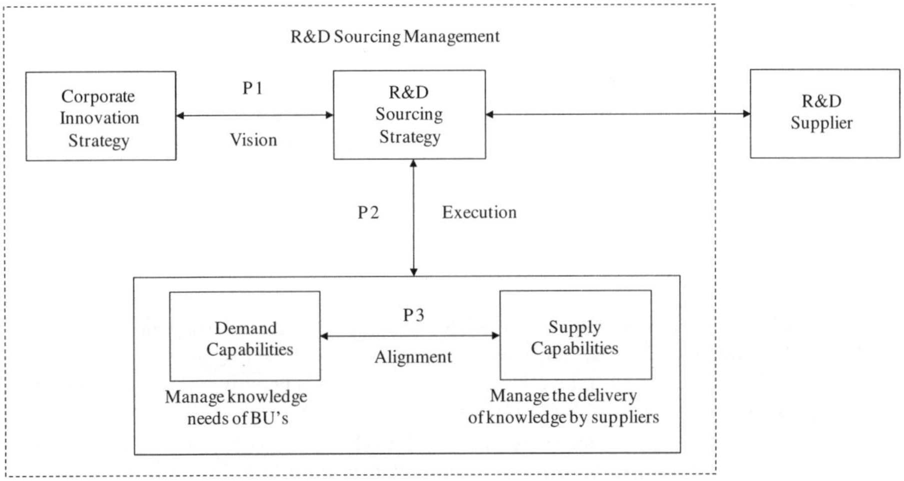

Fig. 1. Strategic R&D Sourcing Management Model

7 Conclusion

Strategic sourcing of R&D by corporate firms is an under-researched topic in sourcing literature. The aim of our research was to create a deeper understanding which determinants influence the success of R&D sourcing. Our case studies show that the presence of a clear vision on a corporate level on how R&D can contribute to the core business of the firm is key to determine an effective sourcing strategy. Our findings provide evidence that the ability of executive management to translate the corporate innovation strategy into a sourcing strategy is a prerequisite. This positively affected the implementation of a R&D organisation that is responsible for the execution of the sourcing strategy. Shifting towards a more commercialised role of R&D within firms, we indicated that existing sourcing capabilities need to be adapted while new capabilities need to be developed. As such, sourcing capabilities can be viewed as strategic as they contribute to the success of an R&D outsourcing arrangement. Moreover, firms need to focus on both demand capabilities and supply capabilities since business needs need to be aligned with supplier solutions. We argue that firms' attention for knowledge management and intellectual property rights are conditional for implementing and applying an R&D sourcing strategy.

This discussion has sought to support both researchers and practitioners involved in strategic sourcing of the R&D function of corporate firms. The case studies shed some light on the under-researched R&D function of corporate firms. Since the determinants that influence the success of an R&D sourcing strategy have been under-researched, our research aims to provide a contribution. Our research also aims to contribute to corporate firms considering outsourcing their R&D function. Most fundamentally, our research demonstrates that corporate firms need to develop a vision to align their corporate strategy with their sourcing strategy. We also identified that firms need to develop or even acquire capabilities that support the demand side and supply side of the sourcing relationship.

The case studies identify multiple issues that require further research.The proposed framework in this study will need to be replicated to gain more insight into how firms developed and implemented demand and supply capabilities in order to execute their R&D sourcing strategies. In particular, study will need to focus on how the additional capabilities as identified in this study are developed by corporate firms. Further study will also cover the R&D supplier side. We would encourage other researchers to explore the topic of strategic sourcing of R&D and enlarge the understanding.

References

Baily, W., Bhagwat, A.: Strategic Review of R&D Outsourcing: An Essential Step Towards R&D Transformation (2009), ATKearny, `http://www.atkearny.com`

Bounfour, A.: Is Outsourcing of Intangibles a Real Source of Competitive Advantage? Intern. J. of Applied Qual. Manag. 2, 127–151 (1999)

Brook, J.W.: Strategic Reorientation of Industrial R&D Towards Commercial Objectives: Investigation of a Paradigm Shift for Managing Industrial R&D Value Creation in the Liberalized Telecommunications Service Industry in Europe. Maastricht School of Management (2006)

Brook, J.W.: Strategic Reorientation of Industrial R&D Towards Commercial Objectives: Organisation Implication for Dynamic Management of Technology Transfer and Innovation Transfer in Global Competitive Business Environments. In: Conf. Proceed. – Beyond Borders: New Global Management Development Challenges and Opportunities, Maastricht, The Netherlands (2007)

Brown, S.L., Eisenhardt, K.M.: The Art of Continuous Change: Linking Complexity Theory and Time-paced Evolution in Relentlessly Shifting Organisations. Adm. Science Quart. 42, 1–34 (1997)

Brusoni, S., Prencipe, A., Pavitt, K.: Knowledge Specialization and the Boundaries of the Firm: Why Do Firms Know More Than They Do? Adm. Science Quart. 46, 597–621 (2001)

Caudy, D.W.: Using R&D Outsourcing as a Competitive Tool. Med. Dev.and Diag. Ind. Magazine (2001)

Chesbrough, H.: Open Innovation: The New Imperative for Creating and Profiting From Technology. Harvard Business School Press, Boston (2003)

Chiesa, V.: R&D Strategy and Organization: Managing Technical Change in Dynamic Contexts. Imperial College Press, London (2001)

Coombs, R.: Core Competences and the Strategic Management of R&D. R&D Manag. 26, 345–355 (1996)

DiRomualdo, A., Gurbaxaini, V.: Strategic Intent For IT Outsourcing. Sloan Manag. Rev. 39, 67–80 (1998)

Ernst, D.: Inter-Organizational Knowledge Outsourcing: What Permit Small Taiwanese Firms to Compete in the Computer Industry? Asia Pac. J. of Manag. 17, 223–255 (2000)

Feeny, D.F., Willcocks, L.P.: Core IS Capabilities for Exploiting Information Technology. Sloan Manag. Rev. 39, 9–21 (1998)

Gilley, K.M., Rasheed, A.: Making More By Doing Less: An Analysis of Outsourcing and Its Effects on Firm Performance. J. of Manag. 26, 763–790 (2000)

Godell, L., Mines, C., Nordan, M.M., Saleem, A., Smit, M.K.: The Rebirth of the European Telecoms, Forrester report (2001)

Howell, J.: Research and Technology Outsourcing and Innovation Systems: An Exploratory Analysis. Ind. and Innov. 6, 111–129 (1999)

Huang, Y.-A., Chung, H.-J., Lin, C.: R&D Sourcing Strategies: Determinants and Consequences. Technov. 29, 155–179 (2009)

Kessler, E.H., Bierly, P.E., Gopalakrishnan, S.: Internal vs. External Learning In New Product Development: Effects on Speed, Costs And Competitive Advantage. R&D Manag. 30, 213–223 (2000)

Kumar, S., Snavely, T.: Outsourcing and Strategic Alliances For Product Development: A Case of Banta Digital Group. Technov. 24, 1001–1010 (2004)

Lacity, M., Khan, S.A., Willcocks, L.P.: A Review of the IT Outsourcing Literature: Insights for Practice. J. of Strat. Inform. Syst. 18, 130–146 (2009)

Levina, N., Ross, J.: From The Vendors Perspective: Exploring The Value Proposition In Information Technology Outsourcing. MIS Quart. 27, 331–364 (2003)

McDonough III, E.F., Leifer, R.P.: Effective Control of New product Projects: The Interaction of Organizational Culture and Product Leadership. Journal of Product Innovation Management 3, 149–157 (1986)

McDonough, W.: Principles, Practices, and Sustainable Design: Toward a New Context for Building Codes (2004), `http://www.mcdonough.com`

McFarlan, F.W., Nolan, R.L.: How to Manage an IT Outsourcing Alliance. Sloan Manag. Rev. 36, 9–23 (1995)

Narula, R.: Choosing Between Internal and Non-Internal R&D Activities: Some Technological and Economic Factors. Techn. Anal. and Strateg. Manag. 13, 365–387 (2001)
Neman, W.L.: Social Research Methods: Quantitative and Quantitative Approach. Allyn and Bacon, Boston (2000)
Neuendorf, K.A.: The Content Analysis Guidebook. Sage, Thousand Oaks (2002)
Nohria, N., Garcia-Pont, C.: Global Strategic Linkages and Industry Structure. Strateg. Manag. J. 12, 105–124 (1991)
Oshri, I., Kotlarski, J., Liew, C.M.: Four Strategies for Offshore 'Captive' Centers. Wall Street Journal (May 12, 2008)
Piachaud, B.S.: Outsourcing in the Pharmaceutical Manufacturing Process: An Examination of the CRO Experience. Technov. 22, 81–90 (2002)
Plugge, A.G., Janssen, M.F.W.H.A.: Managing Change in IT Outsourcing Arrangements: An Offshore Service Provider Perspective on Adaptability. Strateg. Outsourc: An Intern. J. 2, 257–274 (2009)
Prahalad, C.K., Hamel, G.: The Core Competence of the Corporation. Harv. Bus. Rev. 68, 79–93 (1990)
Quinn, J.B.: Intelligent Enterprise: A Knowledge and Service Based Paradigm for Industry. Free Press, New York (1992)
Quinn, J.B.: Strategic Outsourcing: Leveraging Knowledge Capabilities. Sloan Manag. Rev. 40, 9–21 (1999)
Rottman, J.W.: Successful Knowledge Transfer Within Offshore Supplier Networks: A Case Study Exploring Social Capital in Strategic Alliances. J. of Inform. Techn. 23, 31–43 (2008)
Roussel, P.A., Saad, K.N., Tamama, J.E.: Managing the Link To Corporate Strategy: Third Generation R&D. In: Arthur, D., Little, I. (eds.) Harvard Business School Press, Boston (1991)
Teece, D.J.: Profiting from technological innovation: implications for integration, collaboration, licensing and public policy. Research Policy 15, 285–305 (1986)
Tidd, J., Trewhella, M.: Organizational and Technological Antecedents for Knowledge Creation and Learning. R&D Manag. 27, 359–375 (1997)
Watanabe, C., Hur, J.Y.: Resonant R&D Structure for Effective Technology Development Amidst Megacompetition: An Empirical Analysis of Smart Cooperative R&D Structure in Japan's Transport Machinery Industry. Technov. 24, 955–969 (2004)
Willcocks, L.P., Hindle, J., Feeny, D., Lacity, M.C.: IT and Business Process Outsourcing: The Knowledge Potential. Inform. Syst. Manag. 21, 7–15 (2004)
Yasuda, H.: Formation of Strategic Alliances in High-Technology Industries: Comparative Study of the Resource-Based Theory and the Transaction-Cost Theory. Technov. 25, 763–770 (2005)
Yin, R.K.: Case study research. Design and Methods. Sage, Thousand Oaks (1994)
Zhao, Y., Calantone, R.J.: The Trend Toward Outsourcing in New Product Development: Case Studies in Six Firms. Intern. J. of Innov. Manag. 7, 51–66 (2003)

Exploring the Media Mix during IT-Offshore Project

Erik Wende, Gerhard Schwabe, and Tom Philip

Information Management Research Group, Department of Informatics, University of Zurich, Binzmühlestrasse 14, CH-8050 Zurich, Switzerland
{wende,schwabe,philip}@ifi.uzh.ch

Abstract. Offshore outsourced IT projects continue to gain relevance in the globalized world scenario. The temporal, geographical and cultural distances involved during the development of software between distributed team members result in communication challenges. As software development involves the coding of knowledge, the management of knowledge and its transfer remain critical for the success of the project. For effective knowledge transfer between geographically dispersed teams the ongoing selection of communication medium or the media channel mix becomes highly significant. Although there is an abundance of theory dealing with knowledge transfer and media channel selection during offshore outsourcing projects, the specific role of cultural differences in the media mix is often overlooked. As a first step to rectify this, this paper presents an explorative outsourcing case study with emphasis on the chosen media channels and the problems that arose from differences in culture. The case study is analyzed in light of several theoretical models. Finally the paper presents the idea of extending the Media Synchonicity theory with cultural factors.

Keywords: Case study, offshore, outsourcing, software, communication, media selection, culture.

1 Introduction

Increased globalization and the consequent dispersion of business across the world have driven the growth of global IT outsourcing. The trend of relocating software development projects will remain in the years to come, with Asia, primarily China and India, as the preferred locations. Software development has been described as a collaborative problem-solving activity where success is dependent upon knowledge acquisition, information sharing and integration, and the minimization of communication breakdowns [1]. The differences in cultural background make the communication processes even more challenging.

As offshore software development increases, clients must establish new methods and models to handle the enormous amount of knowledge [2]. Knowledge management and knowledge transfer are critical success factors in this scenario.

Knowledge management has many definitions, e.g. the process of continuously creating new knowledge, disseminating it widely through the organization and embodying it

I. Oshri and J. Kotlarsky (Eds.): Global Sourcing 2010, LNBIP 55, pp. 43–54, 2010.

quickly in new products/services, technologies and systems [3]. Knowledge transfer is basically giving background information on software projects to people who do not have it [4].

For geographically dispersed teams the ongoing selection of communication medium (media channel mix) becomes very important for effective task performance (e.g. knowledge transfer).

This paper explores the communication and media channel mix for an offshore outsourced IT project, along with analysis of the data in several applicable frameworks and theoretical models from the current literature. We find that the existing research does not place enough emphasis either on media selection during offshore projects or on the specific cultural challenges of knowledge transfer.

2 Research Methodology

In order to gain a deeper understanding of communication, media selection and cross-cultural issues, the use of an in-depth single-case study design was chosen [5]. It was the most appropriate methodology for our research to obtain rich data in unexplored areas.

Selecting the case was important, because we needed to get full access to a project on-site and off-site with the possibility of collecting as much data as necessary up to the level of "theoretical saturation" [6]. The case we selected offered an exclusive insight into the knowledge transfer tasks and the selections of communication media in a cross-cultural (German - Indian) environment.

The research was exploratory in nature and relied on an interpretive in-depth case study [7, 8]. The collection of data included interviews as primary sources and secondary information from email and instant messenger (IM) log files, which included documents and questionnaires regarding software development which we correlated [7].

The interviews lasted 45 to 90 minutes and involved both the client (4 interviewees) and the vendor (7 interviewees). In total we interviewed 11 people. The interviews were semi-structured to allow flexibility and to ensure that the researchers captured any interesting phenomena [8]. Questions were formulated according to perceived performance of the knowledge transfer, cultural differences, quality of the relationship, trust between the partners, the project communication, the standards and details of the development process, and the appearance of context-relevant information. The interviews were conducted with senior management, project managers, and developers of each company together with a review of project documentation, emails, IM logs and formal presentation material.

In the tradition of explorative and interpretive research, our goal was not to test theoretical propositions, but to develop a theoretical contribution [6, 9].

We employed the grounded theory approach to help us define the boundaries and scope of our research and guided the search for relevant concepts and categories in the empirical data. This allowed us to link the theory and the data step by step [6], while we went back and forth between the collected data and possible theoretical conceptualizations [10]. The exploratory single-case study approach fits well with the grounded theory method because it allows for an in-depth understanding and detailed insight of the phenomena at study [11]. The theory served alongside the qualitative data for the purposes of conceptualization, guiding and enabling the theory-building process [10].

In the first step of analysis we sorted the interviews, personal notes, and secondary data from the first round of interviews to write contact summary sheets and a chronology of the project. With the help of the summary sheets we classified and coded interviews and the secondary material (e.g. documents, emails and IM logs). After coding the material we analyzed the codes and tried to build themes and categories upon it. After completion of the first round of analysis, we entered a sequence of analysis cycles where we analyzed the data (field notes, coding, displaying data, conclusions) and searched for extended literature from related fields for relevant concepts and categories. While studying the data it was important to cross check the interpretations with the theoretical definitions [12]. We reviewed the extending theoretical models and frameworks in IS research pertaining to communication, media and culture. Further, we reconciled our findings with the extending literature (see section 3) to help us explain the media mix in offshore IT projects. The second round of analysis with the data showed that several phenomena were grounded in the extending models, which will be discussed in the following sections.

3 Theoretical Background

In order to understand the data we looked at the current literature to find categories, models and theories which help explain our results.

The following table presents the identified concepts, categories and theories:

Table 1. Identified Concepts and Theories

Concepts/Theories	Short Description	Source
Culture relations		
National Culture Approach	defines fifth basic dimension to characterize national cultural values	[13]
Situated Culture Approach	describes culture as jointly negotiated by actors within specific contexts and resulting in situated learning	[14]
Media selection		
Time, Interaction, and Performance	defines three basic categories of functions of group processes	[15]
Media Richness Theory	focuses on single tasks and argues that task performance will be improved when task needs are matched to a medium's richness	[16]
Media Synchronicity Theory	is not limited on a single task, it describes media capabilities rather then specific media tools and it define tasks as a set of communication processes to generate shared understanding, which may need different media capabilities	[17]

3.1 Cultural Approach

Communication processes in the focus of Information Systems (IS) are influenced by cross-cultural aspects as businesses collaborate, or expand to foreign markets. In recent years, companies have therefore increasingly recognized the importance of incorporating culture into global processes such as positioning in external markets or satisfying international customers. Yet culture still seems to be a feared aspect of communication due to its immense impact on the outcome of cross-cultural business co-operations.

Literature research have shown that the understanding of culture has a decisive influence on the outcome of communication processes; or even that disregarding culture often results in failure [18]. In interpersonal communication processes, for instance, negotiations may fail due to cultural misunderstandings between business partners [19]. However, in most IS literature, culture is understood at a macro level, neglecting the individual or group, but focusing on nations and universal values [20]. These universal values refer to relationships among abstract categories that are characterized by strong affective components and imply a preference for a certain type of action [14]. Values are acquired through lifestyle-altering experience, such as childhood and education. They provide a society with fundamental assumptions about how things are. Once a value is learned, it becomes integrated into an organized system of values where each value has a relative priority. This value system seems stable but can change over time reflecting changes in culture as well as personal experience. However, culture does not refer to values solely. Culture refers to practices as well [14], which are learned later through socialization at the workplace after an individual's values are firmly in place. They provide a society with learned ways of doing things, such as facts about the world, how it works, and cause-effect relationships. Whereas values are fairly hard to change, practices can be altered [14].

A key issue that emerges is the relationship between values and practices. Values are affected by practices during the formative years in which values are starting to form. Later on in life, practices do not influence values. On the other hand, practices are always evolving. Therefore, we believe that practices should be taken into account as well for cultural research in IS.

The national culture approach is primarily composed of differences in values on a national (countries) level [13]. Most of cultural research in the IS field has tended to rely almost solely on Hofstede's cultural model.

The limitation of Hofstede's model is the focus on cultural dimensions on a national level and the lack of reflexivity and change in the model [21]. Thus, we propose taking a different approach, the situated culture approach. This suggests that cultural understanding is locally situated, mainly behavioral and embedded in everyday and evolving practices, jointly negotiated by actors within specific contexts and constituting situated learning [22, 23]. According to this theory, culture does not refer to stable, generalized dimensions assumed to be held in common by members of a particular group. Rather, it is fluid, contextually dependent, and created by actors within a group who may hold conflicting assumptions.

For this case study, the situated cultural approach shows a way to understand and integrate the national culture model with the dynamics of building their own workgroup culture (sub-culture). Most importantly the analysis shows a way to describe the cultural change inside a workgroup. In other words, it provided us a way to analyze the process of building a professional sub-culture in which members agreed on practices. Further research will show how long it took to build a sub-culture and how the process was affected/influenced.

3.2 Time, Interaction, and Performance (TIP)

Offshore software development (OSD) projects are characterized by group work and the appropriate communication channels are indispensable for the collaboration between team members. The TIP theory explains what functions the communication between the onsite and offshore teams has to fulfill during OSD projects.

The TIP theory suggests that project teams engage in both task-oriented activities and socio-emotional activities. McGrath (1990) noted that communication media could have both positive and negative effects on a work group's production, group well-being, and member support functions [24].

In addition to impacting task production, this study suggests that a communication medium's ability to reduce task uncertainty and ambiguousness may also affect a work group's ability to build their own professional culture and carry out its group well-being and member support functions.

According to McGrath's (1990) TIP theory, work groups engage in three concurrent functions: production, group well-being, and member support [15, 24]. The production function refers to the focused activity performed by the group. Work groups are typically assigned to a project that can be split up into work packages. During implementation of the work packages, a project team must: identify goals and select a strategy for project implementation; select techniques, procedures or algorithms to carry out the project; resolve conflicts, values, and interests within the group; and engage in task performance.

Group well-being refers to activities aimed at maintaining an intact and continuing social structure. Activities associated with the well-being function include: use of appropriate communication channels; acquisition of role clarity; conflict resolution; and conducting interpersonal interactions needed for task performance.

The member support function refers to inclusion of and cooperation with project team members. In the maintenance of member support, project team members will: display acceptance and support of another team member's contribution; allow participation and status attainment of others; and conduct conflict resolution through negotiation.

3.3 Media Richness Theory (MRT)

The media channels differ in terms of symbol sets conveyed between team members and thus affect the communication through the distance in varying degrees. The MRT was applied to our data in the first attempt to explain the media mix in OSD projects.

Daft and Lengel (1986) state that people engage in communication activities in order to reduce uncertainty and ambiguousness associated with the information requirements of their assigned tasks [16]. Uncertainty reduction refers to the elimination of the lack of information needed to complete tasks. Kydd and Ferry (1994) identified a continuum on which a communication medium can be placed based on the richness of information it was capable of transmitting [25]. Information richness content was rated on the availability of immediate feedback, the number of verbal and nonverbal cues, back-channeling cues, socio-emotional communication, and interpersonal interaction associated with a communication medium. Uncertainty reduction is handled most efficiently utilizing "lean" (e.g. e-mail and computer-mediated communication) media where there are minimal socio-emotional cues present thereby limiting the transmission to factual information. Equivocality reduction is best-addressed using rich media (e.g. face-to-face, videoconferencing) where there can be the immediate exchange of information and supporting nonverbal and back-channeling cues. Media differ in media richness and consequently differ in the extent to which they could adequately support team collaborative problem solving and decision-making. The lack of ability of lean media (e.g. IM), to convey socio-emotional content in messages was found to cause lower satisfaction and productivity with the problem-solving process, when compared to face-to-face communication [17, 26].

3.4 Media-Synchronicity Theory (MST)

The OSD project communication involves varying levels of synchronicity, which affects the project outcome. The open questions that resulted from the analysis of the MRT theory in the offshore project context were analyzed further using the MST theory.

Dennis, Fueller and Valacich (2008) argue that the fit between the information transmission and information processing needs of the communication processes and the information transmission and information processing capabilities of media will influence the misuse or use of the media and in the end communication performance. They contend that convergence processes have a greater need for rapid information transmission and a lesser need for information processing, while the reverse is true for conveyance processes. Convergence processes benefit from synchronicity while conveyance processes do not. They contend that certain media capabilities influence the way individuals can transmit and process information and the degree they can work – their level of synchronicity. Thus there is a fit between communication processes and media capabilities that facilitates better appropriation, leading to better outcomes. It is not solely the media or their capabilities that directly influence communication performance, but also the way in which they are appropriated and used [17].

The MST describes six main differences from prior media theories. First, tasks are set of communication processes to generate shared understanding, which are basically composed of two processes, conveyance of information and convergence on meaning. Two, these communication processes (conveyance and convergence) have both interpersonal aspects and cognitive aspects. In order to perform conveyance or convergence, an individual must engage in two individual processes: information transmission (preparing information, transmitting, and receiving) and information processing (understanding the meaning of information). Third, the theory identifies physical media capabilities that impact how individuals can transmit and process a message. Forth, the theory refers to a set of media features rather than to specific media tools. For example, IM used be described as a text medium, yet many new IM tools now provide audio, video, image sharing, and even application sharing. Fifth, the manner in which individuals use media influences their communication performance (the development of shared understanding). Lastly, one medium is not better than another. Most tasks are composed of a series of communication processes that need different media capabilities. Additionally, as the familiarity with the task, individuals, and communication media increases, needed synchronicity is reduced.

4 Case Description

This case study refers to a web development project from a German client, offshore outsourced to an Indian vendor.

In this case, the particular interest was in presenting a detailed description and analysis using a case study research setting and providing the findings on what effect the use of different media channels offers to improve the knowledge transfer process, bridge cultural differences and build trust relationships in OSD projects.

This particular project was chosen as a case study because it contained the traditional problems associated with knowledge transfer, e.g. the conveyance of the software requirements, background information, cross-cultural communication, trust building, etc. Additionally, this project provided the perfect opportunity to observe the entire range of media channels, as the participants communicated via a complex mixture of media. Because our research focuses on the process, the actual content of the project is not important to this case study.

Before the project started the client manager had expected a duration of three months, which was also the estimation of the vendor. The project started in November 2007 and actually lasted seven months. The project was broken up into four phases: analysis and conception; implementation; quality assurance; and rollout and documentation.

During the analysis and conception phase the teams had time to familiarize themselves with the other team members and, unusual for such a project, there was no kick-off meeting. Instead, they were given time to gather information about the project and other team members on an intranet platform. During the other phases the communication was also self-directed.

The two teams were divided into typical software development team roles: manager, project manager, and software engineer. Although the project was for web development, it was based on modifying an existing system; therefore the client team provided a software engineer to support the vendor team.

Table 2. Roles in the Project

	Manager	Project Manager	Software Engineers	$\sum$
Vendor Team	2	1	4	7
Client Team	1	1	2	4

The two teams communicated with a wide range of media channels. The project management provided a set of channels and allowed the team members to decide among themselves which one to use when. Due to the geographic separation the only face-to-face (F2F) meetings were once between client and vendor management and once between client project management and vendor management. The provided media channels were: video conferencing, phone, IM, email and paper documents. All team members had access to all media channels.

The data collection was mainly in the form of IM log-files, phone and meeting minutes and interviews of key project members. Secondary information was drawn from relevant project documents and the contract for triangulation purposes. IM was the main communication media between client and vendor. Chat logs were also an important source for data analysis.

A total of 16 hours of qualitative, semi-structured interviews were conducted with key participants including both project managers and software engineers. An extensive interview with the client project manager provided a well-rounded perspective on the case. Interviewees were questioned closely about the impact of cultural issues on task performance.

5 Results

All interviews were transcribed and then, along with the chat logs, were coded for communication, cultural and knowledge transfer topics. In total we collected approximately 7,000 lines of coded communication.

The following table shows the distribution of media channels during the project phases. In total we counted 67 communication sessions; it is important to note that we counted chat sessions per day. Normally these chat sessions were opened once and kept online the whole day. So, one chat session consist of several communication sessions with different topics.

Table 3. Chosen media channels during the project

	Face-to-Face	Video Chat	Phone	Chat	Mail
Analysis and conception	2	1	2	4	8
Implementation	-	-	2	23	4
Quality assurance	-	1	2	6	3
Rollout and Documentation	-	-	1	4	4

While analyzing the 67 communication sessions we attempted to identify the various common topics between sessions. With the background of the TIP Theory we build a coding schema and we coded each transcript and came up with a "codebook" that contained more than 50 codes, each describing a particular topic. In the second step, we grouped the single codes into more generic terms. As a result, we were able to identify the following repeated communication topics:

- Clarification: attempts to explain or comment on questions (questions like: "how does this work…", "what is that for…")
- Escalation: the participants escalated the decision to the management
- Negotiation: the participants held different viewpoints and had to come to a compromise

- Planning: the participants agreed upon schedules and/or timelines
- Training: communication for explaining the functionality of the system
- Scope definition: framing the work packages (e.g. what was in the packages and what was not)
- Goal definition: determining project targets, etc
- Socializing: personal, non-project-related information shared between the team members
- Reporting: the project members agreed on regular project reporting
- Status info: giving the status of the current work package

Table 4 compares the frequency of the coded communication tasks with the chosen communication medium. We categorized the media selection by the capability to hold a synchronous communication. Channels with a "high" synchronicity are face-to-face meetings, video-chat sessions and phone-calls. Instant messaging (chat) was categorized as "medium" in terms of synchronicity and the other channels such as mail and documents had no synchronous communication, therefore were categorized as "low". Beside the differentiation between high and low synchronicity we categorized the media channels regarding their symbol set. Media channels like F2F or video chat provide a "rich" symbol set and media like email have a "lean" symbol set.

Table 4. Frequency of coded tasks and chosen media

	high/rich (F2F, video, phone)	medium/rich (instant messaging)	low/lean (email, documents)
Clarification	2	67	7
Escalation	6	0	0
Negotiation	6	3	2
Planning	3	2	4
Training	3	0	0
Scope definition	3	8	4
Goal definition	2	6	2
Socializing	5	29	0
Reporting	0	3	8
Status info.	0	23	4
$\sum$	30	141	31

Representative anecdotes

In order to illustrate some of the communication and cultural issues during the project, we have selected a few anecdotes that are representative of these issues. These are listed here for reference and aided the identification of relevant frameworks and theoretical models to explain the media mix during OSD projects. A) Because the project was a modification to an existing system the client team had large amount of domain knowledge that first had to be transferred to the vendor team. This led to

many repeated questions from the vendor team, which caused frustration on the client team. On the other hand the vendor team appeared to enjoy the openness of communication directly between engineers.
B) The client project manager told us in an interview, "I didn't want to socialize, I just wanted (the vendor team) to do the job."
C) During another interview a vendor software engineer told us " (the client project manager) came across as so intelligent that we didn't want to ask silly questions."
D) One of the vendor software engineers expressed during an interview that he was very interested in learning more about the personal life his counterpart.
E) All of the vendor engineers expressed their enjoyment of the open communication channels throughout the project, especially the instant messaging.

Cultural Approach
The anecdotes above illustrate the range of cultural issues during the project. Most of the problems were related to the difference in power-distance, for instance the project manager from the client side told us that the vendor team was too autocratic for the client team. Another example was from a vendor project manager: he told us that his project members were surprised/shocked by the independence of the client team, which illustrates the difference between individualism and collectivism between the teams.

Overall we found evidence for the following cultural dimensions, which effected communication between the teams: power-distance, uncertainty avoidance, individualism, long-term orientation and harmony vs. mastery.

Analyses showed the range of cultural influence during the communication. Interviewees noted that synchronous media channels were more affected by cultural issues. On the other hand, interviewees told us that IM was the preferred media channel for collaboration and was less affected by cultural issues.

Time, interaction and performance
The TIP theory helped us to understand and categorize the group processes during the project. Furthermore, with the help of the theory we were able to analyze the team communication and we found evidence for all three functions (production, group well-being, and member support).

However, the TIP theory could not explain effect of the media selection on the performance and the influence of cultural issues during the project execution.

Media Richness Theory
The MRT provides some insight for media selection (e.g. the client team chose rich media for the purpose of negotiation and escalation; see Table 4). But on the other hand the MRT does not explain why the vendor team chose lean media over rich media for problem solving and clarification. Most importantly the MRT does not explain the influence of culture during the communication.

Media-synchronicity Theory
The MST provided us a way to understand the media selection over the project duration. Table 4 shows the relation between communication task and chosen media to fulfill the task, with each communication task counted for each channel.

Of note is the fact that lean media was used more in the beginning instead of rich media. In the first project phase the tasks were more characterized by conveyance and the teams used less synchronous media. Later on, during the convergence processes the team used more synchronous media channels (IM).

However, the MST does not explain the cultural influence on communication for distributed groups or give advice which media mix should be used for certain communication-tasks.

6 Conclusion and Future Work

We believe that a major weakness in the current literature is that very few researchers link culture influence, communication and media channels selection with optimization of task performance. Furthermore, we believe that media selection and cultural influence plays a significant role in the knowledge transfer process, a role that is almost completely overlooked in the current research.

Our case study was a first step in exploring the communication and media selection during an offshore software development project. So far, the findings of the study show the influence of culture on communication and ability of media selection to bridge cultural differences between the parties and members involved. We also found evidence that media selection and cultural influence plays a significant role in the knowledge transfer process.

We found media-synchronicity theory (MST) to be much powerful than previous theories in explaining the media selection for knowledge transfer in offshore outsourced IT projects. However, it could not explain all phenomena that we observed. Therefore, we propose extending the MST with the situated cultural approach in order to better understand the influence of culture. Additionally it would be valuable if further research could identify categories of tasks with an appropriated media mix.

References

1. Walz, D.B., Elam, J.J., Curtis, B.: Inside a software design team: Knowledge acquisition, sharing and integration. Communications of the ACM 36(10), 63–77 (1993)
2. Desouza, K.C., Awazu, Y., Baloh, P.: Managing Knowledge in Global Software Development Efforts: Issues and Practices. IEEE Software 23(5), 30–37 (2006)
3. Takeuchi, H., Nonaka, I.: Hitotsubashi on Knowledge Management, p. 250. Wiley, Hoboken (2004)
4. Stellman, A., Greene, J.: Applied Software Project Management. O'Reilly Media, Sebastopol (2005)
5. Stebbins, R.: Exploratory Research in the Social Sciences. Sage Publications, Thousand Oaks (2001)
6. Eisenhardt, K.M.: Building theories from case study research. Academy of Management Review 14(4), 532–550 (1989)
7. Yin, R.K.: Case Study Research: Design and Methods, 3rd edn. Applied Social Research Methods Series, vol. 5, p. 200. Sage Publications, Inc., Thousand Oaks (2002)
8. Saunders, M., Thornhill, A., Lewis, P.: Research Methods for Business Students, 4th edn., p. 656. Prentice Hall, Upper Saddle River (2006)

9. Miles, M.B., Huberman, M.: Qualitative Data Analysis: An Expanded Sourcebook, 2nd edn., p. 352. Sage Publications, Inc., Thousend Oaks (1994)
10. Glaser, B.G.: Doing Grounded Theory: Issues and Discussions. Sociology Press, Mill Valley (1998)
11. Levina, N., Ross, J.: From the vendor's perspective: Exploring the value proposition in information technology outsourcing. MIS Quarterly (2003)
12. Eisenhardt, K.M., Graebner, M.: Theory building from cases: Opportunities and challenges. Academy of Management Journal 50(1), 25–32 (2007)
13. Hofstede, G.: Cultures Consequences: International Differences in Work-Related Values. In: Cross Cultural Research and Methodology, vol. 5. Sage Publications, London (1984)
14. Karahanna, E., Evaristo, J.R., Srite, M.: Levels of Culture and Individual Behavior: An Integrative Perspective. Journal of Global Information Management 13(2), 1–20 (2005)
15. McGrath, J.E.: Time, Interaction, and Performance (TIP) A Theory of Groups. Small Group Research 22(2), 147–174 (1991)
16. Daft, R.L., Lengel, R.H.: Organizational Information Requirements, Media Richness and Structural Design. Management Science 32(5), 554–571 (1986)
17. Dennis, A.R., Fuller, R.M., Valacich, J.S.: Media, tasks, and communication processes: A theory of media synchronicity. MIS Quarterly 32(3), 575–600 (2008)
18. Damian, D., Zowghi, D.: An insight into the interplay between culture, conflict and distance in globally distributed requirements negotiations. In: HICSS 2003 (2003)
19. Carmel, E., Tija, P.: Offshoring information technology: sourcing and outsourcing to a global workforce. Cambridge University Press, Cambridge (2005)
20. Rogers, P., Tan, J.-S.: Fifty Years of Intercultural Study: A Continuum of Perspectives for Research and Teaching. SSRN eLibrary (2008)
21. Ali, M., Brooks, L.: Culture and IS: A Criticism of Predefined Cultural Archetypes Studies. In: AMCIS 2008, pp. 1–12 (2008)
22. Ali, M., Brooks, L.: A situated cultural approach for cross-cultural studies in IS. In: EMCIS 2008, pp. 1–14 (2008)
23. Weisinger, J.Y., Trauth, E.M.: The importance of situating culture in cross-cultural IT management. Information Technology & People 15(4), 306–320 (2003)
24. McGrath, J.E.: Time matters in groups, in Intellectual Teamwork: Social and Technological Foundations of Cooperative Work. In: Galegher, J., Kraut, R., Egido, C. (eds.), pp. 23–61. Lawrence Erlbaum, Hillsdale (1990)
25. Kydd, C.T., Ferry, D.L.: Managerial Use of Video Conferencing. Information & Management 27(6), 369–375 (1994)
26. Straus, S.G., McGrath, J.E.: Does the Medium Matter? The Interaction of Task Type and Technology on Group Performance and Member Perceptions. Journal of Applied Psychology 79(1), 87–97 (1994)

Parallel Transitions in IT Outsourcing: Making It Happen

Erik Beulen[1] and Vinay Tiwari[2]

[1] Tilburg University, P.O. Box 90153, 5000 LE Tilburg, The Netherlands // Accenture, The Netherlands
[2] Rotterdam School of Management, Erasmus University, P.O. Box 1738, 3000 DR Rotterdam, The Netherlands

Abstract. Global sourcing of IT services is growing consistently over the last decades. Along with this rapid growth, instances of failures, sore relationships or unsatisfactory performances during IT outsourcing engagements are prevalent and require management attention. Over two-thirds of the problems in these unsuccessful engagements arise due to failed or poor transition. Transition is immediately followed by contract signing and precedes service delivery phase. It sets the tone for the entire relationship and involves handover of outsourced services from either the client's internal IT department or the incumbent service provider. Recently second and third generation outsourcing engagements are coming into existence, with offshoring and multi-sourcing as an integral component of these engagements. Multi-sourcing deals, involving several service providers are emerging and require transition to be implemented in parallel. These developments exacerbate the complexity of transitions due to the presence of multiple service providers and several distributed or offshore locations, thereby further enhancing its bearing on the success of an engagement. What are the Critical Success Factors for parallel transitions? We conducted an initial Delphi study to explore success factors for parallel transitions. The findings highlight the importance of understanding the contractual agreement including transition exit criteria. Also the implementation of a joint steering committee contributes to transition success. All the stakeholders, including representatives of the incumbent service provider(s), should be represented in the steering committee to act responsive. Finally, the findings emphasis the need to manage dependencies between the transitions not limited to time lines and availability of critical resources for knowledge transfer and balancing between business continuity and timely and effective knowledge transfer.

Keywords: Accenture, Delphi study, IT outsourcing, offshore outsourcing, parallel transition, transition.

1 Introduction

Information technology (IT) has become increasingly important over the last decades (Carmel and Tjia, 2005; Cohen and Young, 2005; Willcocks and Lacity, 2008; Lacity and Rottman, 2008). The total IT spend also grow over the last decades, predominantly the external spend: outsourcing. This growth was not limited to domestic IT

I. Oshri and J. Kotlarsky (Eds.): Global Sourcing 2010, LNBIP 55, pp. 55–68, 2010.

spend. Especially the IT spend is growing in low cost countries, such as Brazil, Russia, India, China (the BRIC countries) and the Philippines. Global sourcing of IT services is growing consistently and currently represents a $108.8 billion market in 2008 (IDC, 2009). The current economic climate has had an impact on the growth of the outsourcing market. As illustrated by the analyst companies IDC and Gartner this is only temporary. In the years to come the growth of the outsourcing market will continue (Harris et al., 2009; IDC, 2009) . Along with this rapid growth, instances of failures, sore relationships or unsatisfactory performances during IT outsourcing engagements are prevalent and require management attention. Over two-thirds of the problems in these unsuccessful engagements arise due to failed or poor transition due to a lack of focus and training of the staff of the retained organization, the absence of acceptance criteria and an immature economic model for the transition (CIO Magazine, 2007). Despite its importance for carrying out successful outsourcing initiatives, transition has received limited academic attention.

Transition is immediately followed by contract signing and precedes service delivery phase (Gottschalk and Solli-Saether, 2006). It sets the tone for the entire relationship and involves handover of outsourced services from either the client's internal IT department or the incumbent service provider. Transitions include critical stages such as conducting knowledge transfer, determining and implementing new governance structures, and applying the processes of the service provider. On average a transition takes two to three months (Hirschheim et al., 2006). Prior to contract signing there are contract negotiations including responding to a Request for Information and Request for Proposal followed by a Due Diligence and a Best and Final Offer (BAFO). In the contract the responsibilities including service levels and transition plan are embedded. Transition is a pre-requisite to implementing an outsourcing contract successfully (Ross et al., 2005). According to Lacity and Willcocks (Lacity and Willcocks, 2000: 23), the objective of transition phase is to achieve operational performance and it includes activities such as validate service scope, costs, levels, and responsibilities for baseline services; and foster realistic expectations of service provider performance. In addition check points are important in transitions. A transition is a project, with a clear set of objectives, deliverables, milestones and a strict timeline. Transition is defined by Cullen and Willcocks as "implementing the new way of operating" (Cullen and Willcocks, 2003: 151).

The cost of transition is substantial and ranges from 2 to 15% of the total cost of the first year of the outsourcing deal (Ambrose and Matlus, 2005). The transition costs depend on the type of to be transferred IT services. The transition cost will be lower if the underlying IT services are commodity services such as desktop management, as the knowledge transfer is limited. The costs for the transfer of knowledge related to customized IT services, such as application management, are much higher. Critical transition issues are, sometimes, overlooked during contract negotiations resulting in too short time lines and an insufficient transition budget (Beulen et al., 2006).

Building on the foundations of outsourcing, knowledge management and organizational learning literature, we conceptualize transition as a combination of three significant and inter-related organizational processes – transfer, learning and adaptation because it possesses key elements of each of these processes (Tiwari, 2009). For instance, after an outsourcing contract is signed, client personnel need to transfer knowledge, experiences and routines to service provider personnel (Carmel and Tjia, 2005), who need to absorb these and learn to replicate outsourced activities. Learning, during transition, takes places on two dimensions: learning to perform outsourced tasks such as client-specific application development activities (Chua and Pan, 2008) etc. and learning to adapt organizational setting, for example, restructuring retained organization (at client organization) (Feeny and Willcocks, 1998) or mirroring client's structure (at service provider) (Oshri et al., 2007). Adaptation, which manifests from learning and involves "modifying or combining practices", plays a significant role to integrate the knowledge transferred and learning acquired during transition (Williams, 2007). Furthermore, transition involves smoothly performing these processes till a pre-defined operational performance (as agreed in the contract) is achieved (Lacity and Willcocks, 2000) but each of these processes involves significant challenges that need to be overcome, for a successful transition. Transition involves not only transfer of broader organizational knowledge related to outsourced activities, for instance, best practices (Szulanski, 1996) but also and more importantly, specific routines related to performing these activities. Transferring these operational routines, in an inter-organizational setting, such as transition, is difficult mainly because they are highly contextualized, have an emergent quality (such as, accumulated experience) and partial inarticulacy (difficult to articulate, such as, tacit knowledge) (Cohen and Bacdayan, 1994; Cyert and March, 1963). Furthermore, service provider personnel face difficulties with learning as client personnel, who possess much of the knowledge that needs to be transferred lack motivation (for instance, due to job insecurity) (Cullen and Willcocks 2003). Finally, with limited transfer and insufficient learning, adaptation – in the form of modified structures or processes at either organization is - challenging to perform, increases risks and can lead to costly mistakes (Williams, 2007).

In a longitudinal study on transition, Tiwari et al. (2009) found that four factors significantly influence its performance – Transition Planning, Knowledge Transfer, Retained Organization and Transition Governance. Within these, factors Knowledge Transfer and Transition Governance have a stronger influence on transition performance in offshore outsourcing relationships as compared to the other transition factors Transition Planning and Retained Organization. This was explained by two arguments. First, the factors Knowledge Transfer and Transition Governance have a higher potential to disrupt transition. Secondly these factors require in increased level of coordination, which is more challenging than in the other two factors (Tiwari et al., 2009).

2 Parallel Transitions

Recently second and third generation outsourcing engagements are coming into existence, with offshoring and multi-sourcing as an integral component of these engagements. Multi-sourcing deals, involving several service providers are emerging and require transition to be implemented in parallel. The multi sourcing is linked to portfolio management of Ward and Peppard (2002), Jeffery, and Leliveld (2004) and Harries and Harrison (2009). Levina and Su address this phenomenon for information technology and offshoring as global multi sourcing strategy (2008). This type of outsourcing is in the analyses of Currie and Willcocks labeled as "multiple sourcing" versus "single sourcing" for outsourcing to only one service provider (1998). By implementing multi sourcing major cost saving and risk reductions can be achieved (Cohen and Young, 2005; Sharma, 2009). However, prior to achieving these benefits a transition is required. Multi sourcing outsourcing engagements require higher transition costs (Matlus, 2009). Managing multi sourcing engagements also requires a mature retained organization (Ridder et al., 2009), as intellectual property rights, compliancy and security require additional attention (Sharma, 2009).

Multi sourcing transforms the requirements for transitions. Instead of transferring the responsibility for the service provision to a single service provider, the responsibility for the service provisioning is in parallel transferred to two or more service providers. For example the responsibility for desktop management is transferred to service provider A, for server management and network management to service provider B, for ERP application management to service provider C and for all non-ERP application management to service provider D: see Figure 1 for as illustration of a parallel transition from an internal IT department to two service providers. The implication is that in parallel the relevant knowledge has to be transferred to the different service providers: Transition Project 1 and Transition Project 2. This requires a lot of coordination to manage the dependencies and ensuring a proper service provisioning.

The dependencies related to availability and capabilities of the knowledge givers, the knowledge takers, the transition managers, who are responsible for managing the transition and the information managers of the retained organization. Chua and Pan investigated the five IS body of knowledge areas namely, technology, application domain, IS application, organizational and IS development process knowledge (2008). As in parallel transitions the number of involved organizations is larger, the knowledge transfer will be more difficult, lengthier and complex especially in the body of knowledge area "organizational" knowledge. In addition to the content dimension of knowledge transfer, Blumenberg et al. (2009) report in an IT outsourcing context on the send-receiver dimension of the transfer processes as described by Lin et al. (2005). The later dimension of the transfer processes describes explicit, documented interaction structures between parties (Blumenberg et al., 2009). Especially in parallel transitions the complexity of the sender-receiver dimension will increase significantly as the number of stakeholders is increased.

So far service providers have not been very successful in addressing offshoring and multi-sourcing in the IT outsourcing landscape. Only five percent of the enterprises from around the world see their approach to outsourcing as expert with well-developed and deployed multi sourcing competencies (Ridder, 2009). These recent developments exacerbate the complexity of transitions due to the presence of multiple service providers and several distributed or offshore locations, thereby further enhancing its bearing on the success of an engagement. In this paper, we aim to provide a deeper understanding of parallel transition from the service provider's perspective to manage novel IT outsourcing engagements successfully. We specifically aim to answer the question: what are the Critical Success Factors for parallel transitions?

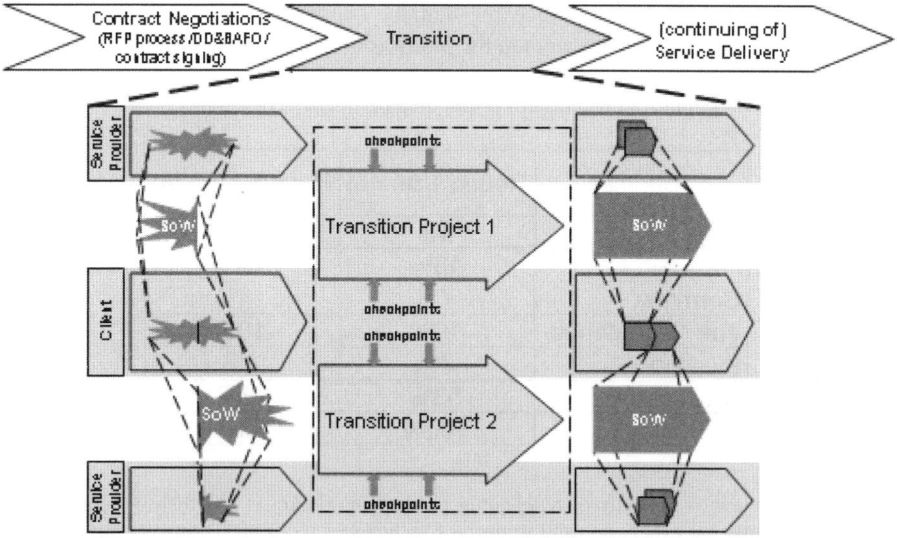

Fig. 1. Transitioning multiple Statements of Work (SoWs) in parallel in IT outsourcing engagements

3 Methodology

Delphi method

The Delphi method is an experienced-based methodology (Dalkey, 1969; Linstone and Turoff, 1975), which is appropriate to identify success factors for parallel transitions as this is organizing and prioritizing the collective judgment of a group of experts. The experts receive feedback in the form of their own previous responses. This technique results in consensus on major points, but also uncovers minority opinions (Dalkey and Helmer, 1963; Schmidt, 1997). The Delphi method is helpful in decision making (Landeta, 2006), such as transition management in parallel transitions. The Delphi method is also a popular method in information research (Okoli and Pawlowski, 2004).

Selection of the participants

Accenture[1] provided a mailing list of 146 European certified transition managers located in Belgium, France, Germany, the Netherlands, UK and Sweden. Table 1 provides an overview of the percentage of responding participants by country. UK has by far the most transition managers, as the UK is in terms of IT outsourcing the most mature country and size of the Accenture company by far the largest compared to the other in scope countries. Table 2 provides an overview of the seniority of the

[1] Accenture is a global management consulting, technology services and outsourcing company, with more than 176,000 people serving clients in more than 120 countries. The company generated net revenues of US$21.58 billion for the fiscal year ended Aug. 31, 2009 (www.accenture.com).

responding participants. It is noticeable that the senior transition managers have a high participation in this research than the junior transition managers.

Table 1. Percentage of responding participants by country

Countries	Round 1 (n=45)	Round 2 (n=28)
Belgium	4%	4%
France	13%	18%
Germany	7%	14%
The Netherlands	16%	18%
Sweden	7%	4%
UK	53%	43%
	100%	100%

Table 2. Overview of seniority of responding participants (junior is less than five years of IT outsourcing transition experience and senior is five years or more of IT outsourcing transition experience)

Countries	Round 1 (n=45)		Round 2 (n=28)	
	junior (n=19)	senior (n=26)	junior (n=7)	senior (n=21)
Belgium	5%	4%	0%	5%
France	11%	15%	14%	19%
Germany	5%	8%	14%	14%
The Netherlands	11%	19%	14%	19%
Sweden	11%	4%	0%	5%
UK	58%	50%	57%	38%
	100%	100%	100%	100%

Surveying

The language in the survey was English. No particular translation problems were encountered, as English is the company language of Accenture. This study started in December 2008 by mailing the first-round questionnaire to the Accenture certified transition managers in Belgium, France, Germany, the Netherlands, UK and Sweden. The transition managers were requested to list up to ten success factors for parallel transitions. Forty five transition managers provide 363 parallel transition success factors. The achieved response rate of 31% was considered as good. We analyzed the response from the first round. We also grouped these 363 parallel transition success factors into sixteen success factors. There were fourteen success factors for parallel transitions which we clustered in a seventeenth bucket: miscellaneous success factors for parallel transitions. In the next round of our research we continued with the sixteen success factors for parallel transitions. This grouping resulted in an initial ranking of success factors for parallel transitions. The number of certified transition managers who listed a single success factor determined the initial ranking. In the second round we submitted the list of sixteen success factors for parallel transitions to the forty eight transition managers for responded to the first round of our research, including three respondents who input for the first round was not taken into account due to ambiguity of their input. The participants who didn't respond to the first round were dropped from our research. This second round resulted in a response of twenty eight, yielding a response rate of 58%. The participants were asked to list the ten most important parallel transition success factors in the order of importance, using a rating scale from 1 to 10 (10=most important).

Findings

The top ten success factors for parallel transitions in IT outsourcing is detailed in the Table 3. The top ten success factors didn't change in the second round except for the success factors "Implement Change Management Initiatives at Client Organization (incl. communication to impacted staff.)" and "Utilize Standard Transition Tools and Processes." These success factors were in the second round no longer part of the top ten.

The absence in the top ten of the for the success factors "Implement Change Management Initiatives at Client Organization (incl. communication to impacted staff.)" in the second round can possibly be explained by the increasing number of second and third generation IT outsourcing engagements. In these engagements the transfer of staff from one service provider to another service provider is possible, but not as usual as in first generation engagements. In first generation engagements the responsibility is transferred to a service provider, where in second or third generation engagements the responsibility is transferred from the incumbent service provider to another service provider, often located in a low cost country. Therefore the changes required in the client organization are more limited and also the communication to the impacted staff is much less. The drop out of the top ten of "Utilize Standard Transition Tools and Processes." in the second round might be explained by the inability to standardize transition tools and processes across service providers. Each service provider has their own standardize transition tools and processes. Instead of standardizing across service providers should the interfaces between the different toolsets and processes be managed and monitored closely. Participants might have realized this in preparing a response in the second round.

These two success factors are replaced by the success factors "Conduct a Comprehensive Due Diligence" and "Manage Expectations of Stakeholders Involved". In preparing for a successful parallel transition verifying the AS-IS situation is a prerequisite for preparing a transition plan and for transition success. The not all the participants of this research have experience in preparing for and planning a transition. This might be an explanation for the higher ranking in the second round for the success factor "Conduct a Comprehensive Due Diligence". As senior management attention in parallel transition is very high, stakeholder management is key. The absence of this success factor might be explained by the difference in seniority of the participants in the first and the second round. As stakeholder management in parallel transitions is mostly the responsibility of the more senior transition managers.

Table 3. Success factors for parallel transitions in IT outsourcing

Success factors for *Parallel Transitions*	
1	Understand the Contractual Agreements including Understanding of Scope of the Service Provisioning and Transition Exit Criteria
2	Implement a Joint Steering Committee, include Representatives of Client and Service Providers
3	Manage Dependencies between the Transitions
4	Ensure a Clear and Regular Communication between Client and Service Provider Team During Transition, including a Proper Collaboration between Onsite and Offshore Team
5/6	Ensure Commitment of Senior Client and Service Provider Management
5/6	Implement Transition Governance, Monitoring & Reporting
7	Conduct a Comprehensive Due Diligence
8/9	Approve Transition Planning, Deliverables and Budget
8/9	Ensure Capability & Availability of Client and Service Provider Transition Team Resources
10	Manage Expectations of Stakeholders Involved

Success factor 1 - Understand the Contractual Agreements
Important in multi sourcing engagements is to ensure a good understanding of the contractual agreements including the scope of the service provisioning. As there are multiple service providers also the responsibilities between the services providers have to be clearly demarcated. This requires in addition to service level agreements with the client company also operating level agreements between the involved service providers (Heiden and Maurer, 2009; Pultz et al., 2009). The operating level agreements detail the responsibilities and governance between the involved service providers towards the client company.

Outsourcing contracts can also not be exhaustive. Wareham et al. (1998) and Beulen and Ribbers (2003) applied the incomplete contract theory of Tirole (1989) on outsourcing. In the transition, by implementing the governance, also agreements on how to deal with situation where there is no or sufficient contract guidance have to be addressed. As there are multiple service providers implementing this element of governance requires substantial management attention to address the dependencies adequately.

Finally the transition exit criteria have to be understood prior to the start of the transition by all involved organizations (Beulen et al., 2006). Understanding the exit criteria in advance ensures the right focus of all participants in transitions.

Success factor 2 - Implement a Joint Steering Committee
Parallel transitions are very dynamic and there are a lot of dependencies between the client company and the (incumbent) service providers. To ensure governance in outsourcing a steering committee is required (Weill and Ross, 2004; Hirschheim et al. 2006). In order to manage the transition adequately a joint steering committee is a pre-requisite. All the stakeholders should be represented in the joint steering

committee. The transition managers can address their issues and concerns in these meetings. As all the stakeholders are represented in a joint steering committee decisions can be taken and delays and / or unclarity can be avoided. Acting fast and decisive contributes to the success in (parallel) transitions.

Success factor 3 - Manage Dependencies between the Transitions

A parallel transition is a program of multiple transition projects run in parallel. This requires multi-project planning as described by Payne (1995) and by Levy and Globerson (1997). In parallel transitions the dependencies are predominantly around the availability of the knowledge givers and the knowledge receivers. The knowledge givers have to balance between continuing to ensuring the business continuity of the information technology and transferring knowledge to the IT professionals of the new service providers, where the knowledge takers have to be made available for receiving the knowledge. The knowledge takers have to be freed up from other projects and / or have to be recruited. Delays in the transition projects might impact the scheduled activities in the parallel transitions.

Success factor 4 - Ensure a Clear and Regular Communication

In addition to the joint steering committee also communication on the operational level is essential for parallel transition success. Especially communication between the onsite teams and the offshore teams is important. In offshore outsourcing time zone difference, language barriers and cultural difference have to be bridged (Carmel, 1999; Fenema, 2002). Technology, such as teleconferences, video conferences and collaborative tools can support the communication. Important in parallel transitions is also to determine which stakeholders of which participants are present at what meetings. Sensibility for differences in organizational level of participants of the different organizations in the meetings is contributing to success in (parallel) transitions.

Success factor 5 - Ensure Commitment

From project management literature we learned that management sponsorship is a pre-requisite for success. Lucier and Torsiliera (1997) and Ruggles (1998) linked the management sponsorship to knowledge management. In parallel transitions senior management from both the client and the service providers have to support the transition projects in addition to the implementation of a joint steering committee. Senior management can show commitment by for example attending meetings, such as the kick off meeting or communicating periodically internally on the importance of transition success. On senior management levels it is also essential that there is a clear consensus between the senior management of all the involved organizations.

Success factor 6 - Implement Transition Governance, Monitoring and Reporting

In order to successfully manage transition, both client and service providers need to develop and implement an appropriate governance model for efficiently conducting day-to-day activities and for monitoring it at a higher level. This model includes clarity in the roles and responsibilities of both organizations along with defining communication, control and reporting structure (Carmel, 1999; Lacity and Willcocks,

2000; Mahring, 2002; Choudhary and Sabherwal, 2003). The implementation of joint steering committee is contributing to this success factor.

Success factor 7 - Conduct Comprehensive Due Diligence
Before the service providers make a final offer during contractual negotiations, a thorough due diligence activity is required to closely understand the actual outsourced work and its related dependencies within the client organization, along with possible challenges and risks associated with it. This represents a crucial activity to determine any missing information gaps that could potentially impact or disrupt the outsourcing relationship (Kern and Willcocks, 2001; Cullen and Willcocks, 2003; Sparrow, 2003). The due diligence provides starting points for transitions. A due diligence also potentially defines actions to be executed in the transitions, such as baselining and an implementing compliancy.

Success factor 8 - Approve Transition Planning, Deliverables and Budget
As transition represents a critical and complex stage during outsourcing, its planning and preparation serves as an important factor in achieving a successful outsourcing relationship (Cullen and Willcocks, 2003; Sparrow, 2003; Carmel and Beulen, 2005). This involves jointly (by both client and service providers) defining an appropriate overall methodology for transition i.e. big bang or staged approach, followed by detailed planning related to knowledge transfer (covering elements such as, who transfers what to whom), pilot projects (determining the simple tasks that are operationally transferred to the service provider followed by more complex ones) and tracking budget (including costs of service providers personnel visiting client sites for knowledge transfer activity).

Success factor 9 - Ensure Capability and Availability of Resources
Extensive planning and thorough due diligence, along with other previously mentioned factors are not enough to ensure a successful transition if both organizations cannot devote a team of highly capable personnel to conduct transition (Cullen and Willcocks, 2003; Sparrow, 2003). Transition involves several challenges as a client organization and multiple service providers begin to align their operations and work closely with each other to generate a combined output; this presents a dynamic activity with continuous changes and the need for quick solutions. Availability of personnel represents another issue, particularly for client organizations, as they need to carry out their routine operational activity besides helping to transition.

Success factor 10 - Managing Expectations of Stakeholders
Transition during an outsourcing relationship involves several stakeholders, from client's senior IT management to their IT personnel working on the actual activities being outsourced. Since outsourcing represents a phenomenon that involves movement of jobs, all stakeholders closely observe it, particularly the ones whose job might potentially be moved. The importance on employment will decrease as a result of second generation and beyond outsourcing engagements. As the transfer from the incumbent service provider to the new service providers of choice is not often materialized.

While senior management is closely involved during contractual negotiations, it is important to periodically and cautiously communicate about the approach, updates and issues. The focus of senior management is not so much on the transition itself but is more on ensuring business continuity and the realization of the business case for outsourcing. This requires a careful management of expectations of all the stakeholders involved (Lacity and Rottman, 2008; Carmel and Tjia, 2005; Cullen and Willcocks, 2003).

4 Conclusions

Most second and third generation outsourcing engagements include multi sourcing and offshoring. Also in the coming decades outsourcing is expected to continue to grow. This will result in an increase of the number of parallel transitions. In this research project has resulted in an initial overview of success factors for parallel transitions including detailing the different aspects of dependencies in parallel transitions.

Limitations of our research project are the origin of the participants of the survey and the limited number of rounds leading to consensus. The participants are all European Accenture participants. Although Accenture is a tier one global service provider the limited diversity of the participants might have impacted the identified success factors and the ranking of identified success factors for parallel transitions. Expanding the group of participants and expanding the number of rounds might result in achieving increased consensus.

Understanding the success factors helps in setting priorities, swift decision making, discussing alternatives, having escalation paths in place and most important contributes to business continuity. In addition to a cost effective transition and a proper hand over of the responsibility for the execution of the services, ensuring business continuity should be the primary focus in parallel transitions.

Overview survey data by survey round.

Success factor for parallel transition	Round one original rank	number of times mentioned		round two original rank	mean rating
Understand the Contractual Agreements including Understanding of Scope of the Service Provisioning and Transition Exit Criteria	1/2	38		1	5.64
Implement a Joint Steering Committee, include Representatives of Client and Service Providers	1/2	38		2	5.29
Manage Dependencies between the Transitions	3/4	33		3	4.86
Ensure a Clear and Regular Communication between Client and Service Provider Team During Transition, including a Proper Collaboration between Onsite and Offshore Team	3/4	33		4	4.75
Ensure Commitment of Senior Client and Service Provider Management	7	24		5/6	4.54
Implement Transition Governance, Monitoring & Reporting	8	23		5/6	4.54
Conduct a Comprehensive Due Diligence	11/12	15		7	4.21
Approve Transition Planning, Deliverables and Budget	6	26		8/9	3.82
Ensure Capability & Availability of Client and Service Provider Transition Team Resources	5	27		8/9	3.82
Manage Expectations of Stakeholders Involved	13	14		10	3.70
Prepare and Execute Knowledge Transfer Planning	14	13		11	2.54
Implement an Integrated Operating Model including Operating Level Agreements (OLAs)	11/12	15		12	2.43
Implement Change Management Initiatives at Client Organization (incl. communication to impacted staff.)	9	20		13	2.09
Address Differences in Organizational Culture between Client and Service Provider adequately	15	10		14	0.98
Ensure the Capability of Retained Organization are at Level	16	4		15	0.96
Utilize Standard Transition Tools & Processes	10	16		16	0.84

References

Ambrose, C., Matlus, R.: Following Best Practices to Manage Transitions in Outsourcing relationships. Gartner research report, G00124899 (January 4, 2005)

Beulen, E., Ribbers, P.: IT outsourcing contacts: practical implications of the incomplete contract theory. Paper presented at Hawaii International Conference on Systems Sciences 2003, US (January 2003)

Beulen, E., Ribbers, P., Roos, J.: Managing IT Outsourcing, governance in global partnership. Routledge, Oxon (2006)

Blumenberg, S., Wagner, H., Beimborn, D.: Knowledge transfer processes in IT outsourcing relationships and their impact on shared knowledge and outsourcing performance. International Journal of Information Management 29(5, 10), 342–352 (2009)

Carmel, E.: Global Software Teams: Collaborating Across Borders and Time Zones. Prentice Hall, New Jersey (1999)

Carmel, E., Beulen, E.: Managing the offshore transition. In: Carmel, E., Tjia, P. (eds.) Offshoring Information Technology Sourcing and Outsourcing to a Global Workforce, pp. 130–148. Cambridge University Press, Cambridge (2005)

Carmel, E., Tjia, P.: Offshoring Information Technology Sourcing and Outsourcing to a Global Workforce. Cambridge University Press, Cambridge (2005)

Choudhury, V., Sabherwal, R.: Portfolio of Control in Outsourced Software Development Projects. Information Systems Research 14(3), 291–314 (2003)

Chua, A., Pan, S.: Knowledge transfer and organizational learning in IS offshore sourcing. Omega 36(2, 4), 267–281 (2008)

Robinson, M., Iannone, P.: 9 Ways to Avoid Outsourcing Failure, a three-part approach to maximizing the value of an IT outsourcing deal. CIO Magazine (July 5, 2007), `http://www.cio.com.au/index.php/id;28653977;pp;1;fp;4;fpid;15` (accessed August 8, 2009)

Cohen, M.D., Bacdayan, P.: Organizational Routines Are Stored as Procedural Memory: Evidence from a Laboratory Study. Organizational Science 5(4), 554–568 (1994)

Cohen, L., Young, A.: Multisourcing: Moving beyond outsourcing to achieve growth and agility. Harvard Business School Press, Boston (2005)

Cullen, S., Willcocks, L.: Intelligent IT outsourcing: eight building blocks to success. Butterworth-Heinemann, Oxford (2003)

Currie, W., Willcocks, L.: Analysing four types of IT sourcing decisions in the context of scale, client/supplier interdependency and risk mitigation. Information Systems Journal 8(2, 04), 119–143 (1998)

Cyert, R., March, J.: A Behavioral Theory of the Firm. Englewood Cliffs, New Jersey (1963)

Dalkey, N.: The Delphi method: an experimental study of group opinion, RM-5888-PR, Rand Corporation, Santa Monica CA (1969)

Dalkey, N., Helmer, O.: An experimental application of the Delphi method to use of experts. Management Science 9(3), 458–467 (1963)

van Fenema, P.: Coordination and Control of Globally Distributed Software Projects. PhD. Thesis, Erasmus University Rotterdam, The Netherlands, Erasmus Institute of Management Ph.D. Series Research in Management 19 (2002), `http://hdl.handle.net/1765/360`

Feeny, D., Willcocks, L.: Core IS Capabilities For Exploiting Information Technology. Sloan Management Review 39(9), 9–21 (1998)

Gottschalk, P., Solli-Saether, H.: Managing Successful IT Outsourcing Relationships. IRM Press, Hershey (2006)

Harries, S., Harrison, P.: IT Value: The Challenges of Implementing Portfolio Management. Information Systems Control Journal 1, 22–25 (2009)

Harris, J., Hale, K., Brown, R., Young, A., Morikawa, C.: Outsourcing Worldwide: Forecast Database, ID:ITST-WW-DB-DA03. Gartner (July 2, 2009)

van der Heiden, G., Maurer, W.: Defining operating-level agreements to enhance performance when outsourcing. Gartner research report, G00163282, August 10 (2009)

Hirschheim, R., Heinzl, A., Dibbern, J.: Information Systems Outsourcing, enduring themes, new perspectives and global challenges, 2nd edn. Springer, Berlin (2006)

IDC: Worldwide and U.S. IS Outsourcing Services 2009-2013 Forecast, Terrance Strom, IDC, Market Analysis #217341 (March 2009)

Jeffery, M., Leliveld, I.: Best Practices in IT Portfolio Management. MIT Sloan Management Review 45(3), 41–49 (2004)

Lacity, M., Willcocks, L.: IT Outsourcing Relationships: A Stakeholder Perspective. In: Zmud, R. (ed.) Framing the Domains of IT Management Research. Glimpsing The Future Through The Past. Jossey Bass, New York (2000)

Lacity, M., Rottman, J.: Offshore Outsourcing of IT Work: Client and Supplier Perspectives. Palgrave Macmillan, New York (2008)

Landeta, J.: Current validity of the Delphi method in social sciences. Technology Forecasting and Social Change 73, 467–482 (2006)

Levina, N., Su, N.: Global multisourcing strategy: the emergence of a supplier portfolio in service offshoring. Decision Sciences 39(3), 541–570 (2008)

Levy, N., Globerson, S.: Improving multi-project management by using a queuing theory approach. Project Management Journal, 40–46 (December 1997)

Lin, L., Geng, X., Whinston, A.: A Sender-Receiver Framework for Knowledge Transfer. Management Information Systems Quarterly 29(2), 197–220 (2005)

Linstone, H., Turoff, K.: The Delphi method: technique and applications. Addison-Wesley, New York (1975)

Lucier, C., Torsiliera, J.: Why knowledge programs fail. Strategy and Business 4, 14–28 (1997)

Mähring, M.: IT Project Governance: A Process Oriented Study of Organizational Control and Executive Involvement. SSE/EFI Working Paper Series in Business Administration, No 2002:15, Stockholm, Sweden, http://swoba.hhs.se/hastba/abs/hastba2002_015.htm (assessed January 23, 2010)

Maltus, R.: Understanding outsourcing evaluation, selection and transition costs to lower risk. Gartner research note, G00167572 (May 11, 2009)

Okoli, C., Pawlowski, S.: The Delphi method as a research tool: an example, design considerations and applications. Information Management 42(1), 15–29 (2004)

Oshri, I., Kotlarsky, J., Willcocks, L.: Managing Dispersed Expertise in IT Offshore Outsourcing. Management Information Systems Quarterly Executive 16(2), 53–65 (2007)

Payne, J.: Managing of multiple simultaneous projects: a state of the art review. International Journal of Project Management 13(3), 163–168 (1995)

Pultz, J., Scott, D., Cappuccio, D., Coyle, D., Adams, P.: Recommendations from IT I&O leaders workshop. Gartner publication, G00166045 (April 16, 2009)

Ridder, F.: How to achieve efficient and effective multisourcing. Gartner research note, G00168520 (June 23, 2009)

Ridder, F., van der Heiden, G., Maurer, W.: Optimizing your investments in people, processes and technology for more-mature multi sourcing capabilities. Gartner research note, G00169420 (August 3, 2009)

Ross, C., Pohlmann, T., Ester, O.: Confronting Outsourcing Myths, Forrester research report, December 13 (2005)

Ruggles, R.: The state of the notion: knowledge management in practice. California Management Review 40(3), 80–89 (1998)

Schmidt, R.: Managing Delphi survey using nonparametric statistical techniques. Decision Sciences 28(3), 763–774 (Summer, 1997)

Sharma, A.: Challenges with multi sourcing, IDC report, # AU22120RQ (January 2009)

Tiwari, V., Beulen, E., van Heck, E.: Understanding Transition During Offshore Outsourcing: Factor Model of Transition Performance. In: Proceedings of Global Sourcing conference 2009, US (2009)

Sparrow, E.: Successful IT Outsourcing: From Choosing a Provider to Managing the Project. Springer, London (2003)

Szulanski, G.: Exploring internal stickiness: Impediments to the transfer of best practice within the firm. Strategic Management Journal 17, 27–43 (1996)

Tirole, J.: The industry of organizations. MIT Press, Cambridge (1989)

Tiwari, V.: Transition During Offshore Outsourcing: A Process Model. In: Proceedings of the ICIS 2009, Phoenix, Arizona (2009)

Ward, J., Peppard, J.: Strategic Planning for Information Systems, 3rd edn. John Wiley & Sons, Chichester (2002)

Wareham, J., Bjoern-Andersen, N., Neergaard, P.: Reinterpreting the demise of hierarchy: a case study in information technology, empowerment and incomplete contracts. Information Systems Journal 8(4, 10), 257–272 (1998)

Willcocks, L., Lacity, M.: Information Systems and Outsourcing: Studies in Theory and Practice. Palgrave Macmillan, New York (2008)

Williams, C.: Transfer in context: Replication and adaptation in knowledge transfer. Strategic Management Journal 28(9), 867–889 (2007)

Management of Globally Distributed Software Development Projects in Multiple-Vendor Constellations

Katharina Schott, Roman Beck, and Robert Wayne Gregory

E-Finance Lab & Institute of Information Systems, Johann Wolfgang Goethe University
Frankfurt am Main, Germany

Abstract. Global information systems development outsourcing is an apparent trend that is expected to continue in the foreseeable future. Thereby, IS-related services are not only increasingly provided from different geographical sites simultaneously but beyond that from multiple service providers based in different countries. The purpose of this paper is to understand how the involvement of multiple service providers affects the management of the globally distributed information systems development projects. As research on this topic is scarce, we applied an exploratory in-depth single-case study design as research approach. The case we analyzed comprises a global software development outsourcing project initiated by a German bank together with several globally distributed vendors. For data collection and data analysis we have adopted techniques suggested by the grounded theory method. Whereas the extant literature points out the increased management overhead associated with multi-sourcing, the analysis of our case suggests that the required effort for managing global outsourcing projects with multiple vendors depends among other things on the maturation level of the cooperation within the vendor portfolio. Furthermore, our data indicate that this interplay maturity is positively impacted through knowledge about the client that has been derived based on already existing client-vendor relationships. The paper concludes by offering theoretical and practical implications.

Keywords: Globally distributed software development projects, nearshoring, offshoring, global outsourcing, multi-sourcing, interpretive research.

1 Introduction

The increasing amount of information systems (IS) development offshoring is an apparent trend that is expected to continue in the foreseeable future (King and Torkzadeh 2008). Both, established offshore outsourcing markets as well as emerging nearshore locations that are closer to the client's home country from a geographical and cultural perspective are continuously accumulating professional know-how, including both technical and industry-specific functional knowledge (Carmel and Abbott 2007). Thereby, IS-related services are increasingly provided from different geographical sites simultaneously, i.e. offshore, nearshore, and onshore delivery locations come into

I. Oshri and J. Kotlarsky (Eds.): Global Sourcing 2010, LNBIP 55, pp. 69–81, 2010.

operation within one global sourcing model (Willcocks, Lacity and Cullen 2007). Beyond that, firms enhance their sourcing strategies through making use of multiple service providers based in different countries (Levina and Su 2008).

While previous research in IS has already deepened our understanding of the management of global software development outsourcing projects (Heeks, Krishna, Nicholson and Sahay 2001; Rao 2004; Oshri, Kotlarsky and Willcocks 2007; Gregory, Prifling and Beck 2008; Rottman and Lacity 2008), we still have little knowledge on the effect of the involvement of multiple service providers within globally distributed software development projects (Martens & Teuteberg 2009). Thus, we aim at answering the following exploratory research question: *How does the involvement of multiple service providers influence the management of global software development outsourcing projects?*

This question is explored by interpreting the results of 21 qualitative interviews from a single-case study comprising a global software development outsourcing project initiated by a large financial services institute in Germany. The project's objective was the migration of the bank's online banking system to a new underlying technology. Whereas the previous system has been developed and maintained by a single long-time service provider, the bank now decided to increase flexibility and thus to pursue a multi-vendor sourcing strategy. Following a best-fit-for task approach, four vendors have been contracted being responsible for the work packages architectural framework, functional and technical design including software development, software test and front-end design. Furthermore, the bank also attached importance to including near- and offshore outsourcing concepts into the overall delivery model in order to be able to reengineer the online banking system as cost efficient as possible. In summary, roughly 100 people from five organizations (one client and four vendors) have been working geographically distributed across nine locations in four countries (Germany, Spain, Brazil, and India) in order to technically reengineer a critical business system with high visibility to the end customer.

This paper is structured as follows. The following section gives an overview over the extant literature on the management of global IS outsourcing projects. In the subsequent methodology section, we explain the reasons for conducting a qualitative and exploratory case study and provide information on how we employed principles of the grounded theory method to build, rather than test theory. After a short case description, we then focus on the analysis of the data where we present the core categories and their relationships that emerged in this exploratory and theory-building study. The final section presents the key findings and the implications for research and practice.

2 Literature Review

With the development towards a knowledge-based economy and the disappearance of global work boundaries, offshore and nearshore IS projects are growing in numbers and importance (Apte and Mason 1995; King and Torkzadeh 2008). This is not surprising, considering the expected benefits and cost advantages that client firms can achieve due to significant differences in labor costs between Western countries and offshore locations in Middle and Eastern Europe or Asia (Rottman and Lacity 2004; Schaaf 2004). However, these cost advantages do not materialize easily since "inter-country outsourcing" is accompanied by unique challenges that can offset the expected benefits (King and Torkzadeh 2008). Accordingly, researchers have put forth numerous studies addressing various aspects of the management of global IS outsourcing projects. In doing so, a large part of studies has been focusing on management aspects that are directly related with the offshore-specific distance between client and vendor, comprising the geographic distance between client and vendor (Carmel and Agarwal 2002; Rao 2004; Espinosa, DeLone and Lee 2006), language barriers (Carmel and Agarwal 2002; Rao 2004; Zatolyuk and Allgood 2004), and cross-cultural differences (Heeks, Krishna et al. 2001; Nicholson and Sahay 2001; Carmel and Agarwal 2002; Krishna, Sahay and Walsham 2004; Rao 2004). Other studies have looked at management tasks such as communication (Gupta and Raval 1999; Heeks, Krishna et al. 2001; Kotlarsky and Oshri 2005; Rottman 2006; Kotlarsky, van Fenema and Willcocks 2008) and the management of expectations and trust (Gupta and Raval 1999; Heeks, Krishna et al. 2001; Levina and Vaast 2008). However, the larger part of these studies addresses dyadic relationships, whereas the impact of multi-vendor constellations on the management of global IS outsourcing projects has been scarcely addressed.

Multiple-vendor sourcing is primarily defined through the involvement of a single client and multiple vendors (Dibbern, Goles, Hirschheim and Jayatilaka 2004). Extant literature in IS has analyzed the multi-sourcing phenomenon mainly regarding the number of suppliers. On the one hand, firms engage in relationships with multiple service providers in order to mitigate the risks of dependency and vendor opportunism resulting from dyadic relationships (Cross 1995). On the other hand, researchers have emphasized the importance of restricting the number of suppliers in favor of a few preferred suppliers providing services in long-term relationships (Lacity and Willcocks 1998; Aron, Clemons and Reddi 2005). Furthermore, the tradeoffs resulting from using one or many suppliers are being discussed: while single-sourcing increases the vendor's commitment but comes with the risk of dependency, multi-sourcing provides the ability to choose the supplier with the best fit but in return increases cost in terms of additional management overhead (Levina and Su 2008).

As the involvement of multiple service providers into one project turns more and more into a defining characteristic of global outsourcing (Levina and Su 2008) we intend to close this gap with our research.

3 Research Methodology

Our epistemological position for this research is interpretive, i.e. among other issues we particularly acknowledge the subjective nature of the world and aim at interpreting the reality from the viewpoints of our interview partners (Walsham 1993). Hence, we did not predefine any hypothesis in a deductive manner from existing theories. Rather, we adopted a qualitative research approach and conducted an interpretive in-depth exploratory single-case study focusing on theory-building as opposed to theory-testing (Stebbins 2001; Yin 2003). Due to the lack of understanding regarding the management of nearshore and offshore relationships in multiple vendor constellations (King and Torkzadeh 2008), we consider an exploratory research approach as most appropriate. The primary unit of analysis is a globally distributed software development outsourcing project undertaken by a German bank and several vendors. With regards to data collection and data analysis, we adopt techniques suggested by the grounded theory method, including constant comparisons and theoretical sampling (Glaser 1978; Glaser 1998). The ultimate goal is to enhance our understanding of how the involvement of multiple service providers influences the management of global software development outsourcing projects.

Due to the project's time schedule, the data collection took place in two phases. We started the interviews in July and August 2009 and continued with a second round of interviews in November and early December 2009. The interview partners were selected from multiple organizational levels of the client as well as from the four vendor companies and comprise interviewees from strategic management, project management, subproject management, as well as selected project team members. Thereby, the overall number of interviews has been determined based on the criterion of "theoretical saturation", i.e. we continued the data collection until further interviews did not contribute additional insights any more (Glaser and Strauss 1967). In total, we conducted 21 interviews with 19 individuals for our primary data collection, resulting in over 28 hours of interviews and 110 pages of interview transcriptions. The interviews lasted between one and two hours while on average interviews were around 1.3 hours. Except of one phone interview with an interviewee located in Brazil, we conducted all interviews face-to-face, in which 11 interviews have taken place in Germany and 10 interviews in Spain. The interview languages were German and English depending on the respective country background of the interviewee. All interviews were conversational in nature and have been conducted using an interview guideline consisting of semi-structured interview questions, whereas we individualized the questions according to a respondent's role and previously collected data. In parallel to the interviews, we have collected secondary data such as status reports, lessons learned documents, and a motivation survey conducted within vendor 2 by request of the bank in order to supplement the primary data as well as for data triangulation purposes.

Due to the banks corporate policy we were not permitted to tape-record the interviews. As a consequence, we organized our research team in such way that one researcher conducted the interview while the second researcher concentrated on extensive note taking and complemented the interview questions where applicable (Eisenhardt and Bourgeois 1988). As according to the grounded theory method data collection and data analysis are interwoven with each other, we transcribed the field notes immediately after each interview session and used the generated insights to identify appropriate interviewees and questions for the forthcoming interviews (principle of theoretical sampling). We coded the interview transcriptions by identifying, naming, and categorizing phenomena related to our research question. Thereby, we first compared the interviews among each other as well as with the secondary data (principle of constant comparison). After we discovered the main conceptual themes in the data due to their high frequency of mentioning (principle of emergence) we started comparing the interview data with the conceptual themes. As the study developed the identified themes became more elaborated in terms of developing more general categories as well as structuring these emerging categories. In order to facilitate the overall coding and conceptualization process we used the software product ATLAS.ti.

4 Case Analysis and Description

Detailed Case Description

The case upon which our analysis is based comprises a global multi-vendor ISD outsourcing project. The overall project goal is the reengineering of a bank's online banking system. With more than one million users per day the online banking system is a critical business system with high importance and visibility. Even if the old system is still able to meet the bank's requirements and to serve the increasing number of customers, its underlying technology requires a high degree of costly expertise and will not be maintained anymore in the future. As a consequence, the bank has decided to migrate to a sustainable but well-established (as opposed to latest technologies) technology allowing for reusability through a modular architecture and being supported by a much broader supplier base. In order to reach the project goal the bank has decided to involve multiple, partly internationally operating, service providers into the reengineering of the system. All vendors have been selected on a best-fit basis and have been directly contracted by the bank. Thus, the project's multi-vendor constellation including global sourcing elements fits perfectly to the bank's sourcing strategy aiming especially at continuity, flexible vendor selection (based on a pool of certified strategic vendors) and cost efficiency.

The subsequent section briefly describes each vendor and his area of responsibility. Table 1 below provides a summary of the project's vendor portfolio. Vendor 1 is a German boutique consulting firm focusing on IT transformation. In the context of the project at hand vendor 1 was responsible for designing the architectural framework of the new online banking system. Furthermore, vendor 1 has been explicitly assigned to support vendor 2 with the technical design documents (knowledge transfer and coaching) and to control whether the implementation activities of vendor 2 are compliant with the principles of the defined architectural framework. Vendor 2 is a leading international IT service providers for the financial services sector, providing IT solutions and services in three business areas (services, resourcing and software) and is one of the bank's preferred service providers since many years (e.g. vendor 2 was operating and maintaining the old online banking system). In the course of the reengineering project the responsibility of vendor 2 comprises the following areas: (1) creation of functional design documents based on the experience with the old system, (2) creation of technical design documents in close cooperation with vendor 1, and (3) implementation of the new online banking system (based on vendor 1's architectural framework). Vendor 2 utilizes his global delivery model involving four locations in Spain and a captive center in Brazil. Vendor 3 is an Internet agency also based in Germany. In the project, vendor 3 is responsible for the frontend screen design. Vendor 4 is a large IT service provider with international operations. Within the project vendor 4 is responsible for the software testing being conducted in a newly established test factory in India. Thus, with regards to its geographical footprint the project includes both near- (Spain) and offshore (Brazil and India) outsourcing destinations.

Table 1. Overview on the multi-vendor portfolio

Party	Areas of responsibility	Locations involved in the project
Vendor 1	- Definition architectural framework - Implementation controlling of vendor 2	2 locations in Germany
Vendor 2	- Functional design - Technical design - Implementation	4 locations in Spain 1 location in Brazil
Vendor 3	- End-user front-end design (look & feel)	1 location in Germany
Vendor 4	- Software test	1 location in India (test factory)

The project started in October 2008 and has been completed in December 2009. Its complexity was high with regards to several dimensions. The major driver of complexity was the number of involved parties. Further complexity is added through the project's geographical footprint including both near- and offshore outsourcing destinations and last but not least, complexity is again elevated due to the project's very short timeframe.

Case Analysis and Discussion

Multi-vendor projects are characterized by the fact that the responsibility for service delivery is distributed across several vendors. Thus, the interplay between the involved vendors needs to be setup in such a way that the individual service delivery parts resulting from the different areas of responsibility intertwine smoothly in order to ensure a successful overall service delivery. Prior research has shown that the orchestration of multiple vendors burdens global outsourcing projects with higher coordination and control cost compared to single-vendor projects, i.e. multi-sourcing strategies are generally associated with an increased management overhead especially on the client side (Levina and Su 2008; Sia, Koh and Tan 2008). However, our research indicates that the required effort for managing global outsourcing projects with multiple vendors, i.e. the degree of client-driven governance, depends among other things on the maturation level of the cooperation within the vendor portfolio (interplay maturity). Furthermore, our data suggest that this interplay maturity is positively impacted through knowledge about the client that has been derived based on already existing client-vendor relationships (relational knowledge). The following paragraphs elaborate upon the key dimensions of the model as well as on the cause-effect-relationships, as depicted in figure 1.

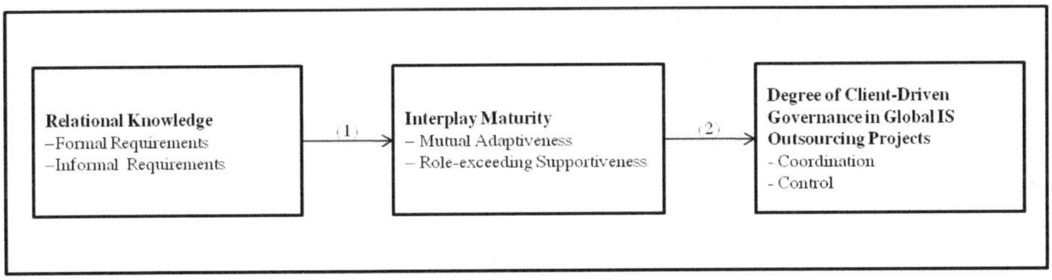

Fig. 1. The relationship between Relational Knowledge, Interplay Maturity and Degree of Client-Driven Governance in global IS outsourcing projects with multiple vendors

Relational Knowledge

In the case at hand, all vendors have been involved in prior projects with the bank, i.e. there was already an existing client-vendor relationship between the bank and each of the vendors before the project started. However, the vendors themselves have never interacted with each other in a multi-vendor setting before. Accordingly, as the project started, there was no significant need for to transfer business respectively process knowledge from the client to the vendors, as this knowledge has already been built up over years. During this time the vendors were able to also gather valuable knowledge regarding the bank's work practices and as a consequence to direct their work mode towards the resulting requirements. As a vendor project manager explained, this alignment did not only concern well documented, formal requirements such the project management methodology but also informal requirements respectively expectations that are implicitly contained in the bank's behavior and work practices only: *[...] we have adapted our policies, methods, and infrastructure that way that it is pretty easy for us to work with the bank. As we already have maintained the old system for many years we also have a lot of social experience with the customer himself. We can estimate the customer's expectations and behaviors very well, this helps.*

Thus, based on the pre-existing client-vendor relationships, the vendors had the opportunity to already acquire considerable client-specific as well as relational knowledge about their customer which allowed them to enter into the specific client-vendor-relationship of the project at hand without too much effort for further alignment with the client.

Another important factor was that the project had to deal with considerable top level management attention as the online banking system is of great importance and high visibility to the end customers of the bank. As one of the bank's vendor manager outlines, this lead to a continuous information exchange also on management level: *We frequently meet with the senior management of the vendors in order to discuss the project's progress on a high level, but also to share more general information on how the respective business develops. Therewith, we want to increase our knowledge about each other and to understand about the current status and future developments.*

That is to say that relational knowledge was not only being created and maintained on working level, but was also being fostered and reinforced on senior management level in order to ensure a stable relationship between client and vendor. According to the involved vendors, this stability facilitated that the vendor companies were able to pro-actively approach the cooperation amongst the vendors. A vendor project manager illustrates: *We know that the other vendors have also been working for the bank before [...]. But we have a different focus and we do not lose a big part through this setting, even one vendor would be easier to manage. Our relationship with the bank is established, so we do not compete but work on the joint objective.*

In summary, by strengthening the client-vendor-relationship between each vendor and the bank, the existing relational knowledge also supported a smooth start into the multi-vendor constellation. Thus, we finally argue that relational knowledge was an important prerequisite stimulating the evolution of interplay maturity within the vendor portfolio, as reflected in the following proposition:

Proposition 1. Relational knowledge about formal and informal requirements has a positive impact on the level of interplay maturity within the vendor portfolio of a global multi-sourcing software development project.

Interplay Maturity

Another key concept, that emerged inductively from the analysis of our interview data was the concept of interplay maturity referring to the maturation respectively quality level of the cooperation within the vendor portfolio. As described above, the allocation of the service delivery responsibility to multiple vendors results in a higher coordination and control effort on the client side. However, this constellation also brings a significant need for alignment on the vendor side with it, i.e. a smooth overall service delivery depends amongst others things on the quality of the cooperation amongst the participating vendors. In case the cooperation within the vendor portfolio is being hampered this needs to be compensated through client-driven governance. Thus, client-driven governance can only be reduced if the cooperation amongst the vendors is characterized by a sufficient level of interplay maturity. In our case study, interplay maturity has particularly taken shape in form of the following two dimensions, on which we elaborate in detail in the subsequent section: mutual adaptiveness and role-exceeding supportiveness.

Mutual adaptiveness refers to the willingness of the involved vendors to not only take the client's requirements and expectations into account, but also to respond to the particular needs and features within the vendor portfolio in order to ensure a smooth collaboration. In our case, this willingness appeared, e.g., in the context of a vendor-to-vendor knowledge transfer. Due to the project-specific allocation of tasks a significant amount of knowledge needed to be transferred from a small team of experienced experts (vendor 1) to a large geographically distributed implementation team with various competence and practice levels (vendor 2). When engaging in the knowledge transfer process, it became apparent to vendor 1 that his usual knowledge transfer approach, which had worked well in other situations, was not successful this time, as a project manager from vendor 1 explained: *After a while, we realized that the knowledge transfer was too theoretical and the practical elements have been missing. Many things that have been written down on paper make no sense until one begins doing it.*

The main reason for the obstacles was that vendor 2's global service delivery concept involved several near- as well as one offshore destination. Due to this global setup, not all developers could participate personally in the knowledge transfer so that the knowledge had to be internally multiplied across several locations and countries. Even though this was rather an organization-internal challenge, vendor 1 has pro-actively changed his prior learning-by-being-told approach to a more practitioner-oriented, learning-by-doing approach. This significantly increased the learning curve and in this way also facilitated the multiplication of knowledge. As vendor 1's project lead observed: *[...] Therefore, we have conducted frequent workshops, in the course of which we concentrated on misunderstandings and errors. We have discussed a lot with the developers, trying to establish a joint discussion towards a shared learning. This means a lot more examples; the party the knowledge is transferred to needs to be involved intensively and especially as early as possible.*

Beyond that, mutual adaptiveness has not only been shown in the context of adapted behavior, but also with regards to the mindset. When the project started, vendor 2 seemed to have another self-concept than the rest of the vendors based on his prior very intense cooperation with the bank. He was accustomed to a large autonomy with regards to his implementation activities which came along with sparse control through the client. In this project however, due to the multi-vendor-constellation tasks such as the architectural framework and software test that have been performed by vendor 2 in prior projects are now with other vendors. Furthermore, his design and implementation activities were being controlled not by their client but by another vendor (vendor 1). Thus, in the course of this project, a change of mind of vendor 2's employees was required not only regarding the content, i.e. learning the new software architecture, but also regarding his role and responsibilities. The project manager illustrated this mind change as follows: *For sure, we would prefer to also have the responsibility for the framework, as it is part of our portfolio. But the client has decided differently [...], so now we are jointly responsible for this project. As a consequence, we have to prioritize the project goals higher than our goals as a service delivery company in order to create a win-win-situation. Even this is not easy, as you do not have a guarantee that you get back what you invest.*

In summary, mutual adaptiveness has helped the participating vendors to cope with the obstacles introduced through different work processes, setups, and styles without any active involvement of the client and thus reducing especially the coordination effort on client side.

While the vendors' mutual adaptiveness was concerned with overcoming any kind of disparities within the vendor portfolio, role-exceeding supportiveness relates to the readiness of the involved vendor companies to render assistance for one another also beyond their roles and areas of responsibility. As a vendor project manager explained, it's in the nature of software development that the requirements cannot be completely specified respectively requirements change or even newly occur in the course of the development process. This has been shown, e.g., when it came to the system's technical design. Although the responsibility of writing the design documents was with vendor 2, vendor 1 has strongly supported this process due to his familiarity with the software architecture. Thus, vendor 1 has exceeded his role as a controlling instance and has actively participated in the writing process.

In summary, our data suggests that mutual adaptiveness and role-exceeding supportiveness manifest a certain level of maturation concerning the interplay amongst the involved vendors. Whereas at the beginning of the project the bank has strongly acted upon the cooperation between the vendors in order to reinforce the concept of roles and responsibilities and to foster the evolution of a stable working mode, the coordination and control effort has been gradually decreased in favor of the self-organizing mechanism mutual adaptiveness and role-exceeding supportiveness among the vendor companies. A vendor project manager describes this development: *At the beginning they arranged formal meetings, managed by the bank, but later there was more and more direct interaction between the vendor companies. [...] The bank was not the driver of communication, but was always informed to sustain transparency.*

Thus, the reduction of client-driven governance is being stimulated by the increasing maturity regarding the interplay amongst the vendors. Interplay maturity is expected to have a positive impact on the degree of client-driven governance, as reflected in the following proposition:

Proposition 2. Interplay maturity with its dimensions mutual adaptiveness and role-exceeding supportiveness reduces the required degree of client-driven governance of a global multi-sourcing software development project.

Degree of Client-driven Governance

At the beginning of the project, the client decided to start the project with a dedicated initialization period in order to ensure that the involved parties first understand and accept their own roles and responsibilities as well as those of the other parties, and second implement this understanding in their daily business activities and interactions. In the so-called ramp-up phase the interplay between the involved vendors has been practiced and mutual expectations and needs have been adjusted. A member of the client project team summarized the importance of this phase as follows: *From my point of view, the ramp-up phase at the beginning of the project was very important and reasonable. In the course of this phase, we practiced and evaluated based on selected business transactions how the overall service delivery has been setup and how the performance was with regards to process and outcome quality. Finally, the ramp-up phase has been concluded with a workshop, where the lessons learnt have been discussed and the further proceeding has been decided.*

Through practicing and reinforcing the allocation of task and the required patterns of interaction out of it over a fixed period, the client created the basic prerequisite to keep the coordination effort in his multiple vendor-setting within a reasonable limit. Furthermore, in order to ensure transparency and an equal level of information for all parties, the client established a weekly meeting with representatives from all involved vendors in the course of which the project status as well as any problems or obstacles that had emerged in day-to-day project work have been discussed. Third, the client has setup the project planning as well as the according status tracking jointly with the involved vendors. Beyond that, there was no active governance towards the cooperation between the vendors, as the client project manager explained: *Instead of employing one of the vendors as main contractor, we have kept hold of the overall project management responsibility comprising the typical associated tasks such as project planning, status reporting, and progress control, i.e. we pull the strings. But beyond that, we do not coordinate respectively control the cooperation between the involved vendors. For instance, there is frequent direct communication between the vendors without our involvement.*

In summary, our analysis indicates that an increased client-driven coordination and control is required at the beginning of the project only (e.g. setting the project objectives, determining roles and responsibilities, setup of project structures, initializing of cooperation processes between client and the involved vendors as well as amongst the vendors). However, when the vendor portfolio is characterized through interplay maturity, the client can gradually reduce his control and coordination efforts in favor of the emerging mechanisms mutual adaptiveness and role-exceeding supportiveness.

5 Conclusions

This paper is a first step towards a better understanding of the impact of multiple-vendor constellations on the management of globally distributed software development projects. While many researchers have studied various aspects of the management of global IS outsourcing projects up to now few have considered the impact of the phenomenon multi-sourcing with regards to the required management effort. Thus, our research aimed at filling this gap. Having analyzed the revelatory case at hand, the paper has two main theoretical contributions: first, by applying a grounded theory approach we were able to inductively generate a model that describes how the required degree of client-driven governance is being influenced by the quality of cooperation within the vendor portfolio. In particular, the results of our analysis indicate that mutual adaptiveness and role-exceeding supportiveness amongst the vendors are able to reduce the client's effort for coordination and control concerning the cooperation within the vendor portfolio. As the concept of interplay maturity represents a novel approach to decrease the management effort associated with the involvement of multiple vendors in one project, the results of our analysis have enhanced the discussion of multi-sourcing with the aspect of the quality of the vendor interplay. The second theoretical contribution refers to the concept of relational knowledge: while the importance of existing client-vendor-relationships is already being discussed in the extant literature in the dyadic context of client and vendor, the interpretation of the case study has revealed the stimulating leverage of this kind of knowledge for the interplay maturity amongst the vendor companies. Thus, we contribute to this literature stream by emphasizing the value of relational knowledge for the cooperation quality within a multi-vendor constellation.

Beyond that, the paper also offers practical contributions. Our main suggestion for practitioners is to take the results of this study into account in the course of the vendor selection process: instead of applying a best-fit-for-task strategy only, aspects such as existing relationships need to be considered. Furthermore, the findings may help client project managers to identify starting-points such as fostering mutual adaptiveness tendencies within the vendor portfolio in order to improve the cooperation within a multi-vendor constellation finally leading to less management effort on client-side.

However, as this is still research in progress, there are several limitations to be taken into account: first, at the time of completion of this paper, we did not have the opportunity to interview representatives from all vendors that have been participating in the project due to the projects tight timeline. However, our long-term engagement with the industry partner provides us with the opportunity to collect and analyze additional data as long as required independently from the project's lifetime. Hence, we will continue with our interviews within the next months. Nevertheless we are aware of the potential inaccuracies that result from the missing vendor perspectives. Second, the results of this study are particular to large IT reengineering projects in the German financial services industry. Thus, further research is needed to study the posed research question in other contexts and settings. In addition, the analysis of this paper which focuses on maturation level of the vendor cooperation to decrease the client's management effort in multiple-vendor constellations could be extended to indentify further dimensions of the concept interplay maturity.

References

1. Apte, U.M., Mason, R.O.: Global Disaggregation of Information-Intensive Services. Management Science 41, 1250–1262 (1995)
2. Aron, R., Clemons, E.K., Reddi, S.: Just Right Outsourcing: Understanding and Managing Risk. Journal of Management Information Systems 22, 37–55 (2005)
3. Carmel, E., Abbott, P.: Why nearshore means that distance matters. Communications of the ACM 50, 40–46 (2007)
4. Carmel, E., Agarwal, R.: The Maturation of Offshore Sourcing of Information Technology Work. MIS Quarterly Executive 1, 65–78 (2002)
5. Cross, J.: IT Outsourcing: British Petroleum's Competitive Approach. Harvard Business Review 73, 94–102 (1995)
6. Dibbern, J., Goles, T., Hirschheim, R., Jayatilaka, B.: Information Systems Outsourcing: A Survey and Analysis of the Literature. The DATA BASE for Advances in Information Systems 35, 6–102 (2004)
7. Eisenhardt, K.M., Bourgeois, L.J.: Politics of Strategic Decision Making in High-Velocity Environments: Toward a Midrange Theory. Academy of Management Journal 31, 737–770 (1988)
8. Espinosa, J.A., DeLone, W., Lee, G.: Global Boundaries, Task Processes and IS Project Success: A Field Study. Information Technology & People 19, 345–370 (2006)
9. Glaser, B., Strauss, A.: The Discovery of Grounded Theory: Strategies for Qualitative Research. Aldine Publishing Company, Chicago (1967)
10. Glaser, B.G.: Theoretical Sensitivity. The Sociology Press, Mill Valley (1978)
11. Glaser, B.G.: Doing Grounded Theory: Issues and Discussions. Sociology Press, Mill Valley (1998)
12. Gregory, R., Prifling, M., Beck, R.: Managing Cross-Cultural Dynamics in IT Offshore Outsourcing Relationships: The Role of Cultural Intelligence Second Global Sourcing Workshop. Val d'Isere, France (2008)
13. Gupta, U., Raval, V.: Critical Success Factors for Anchoring Offshore Projects. Information Strategy 15, 21–27 (1999)
14. Gupta, U.G., Raval, V.: Critical Success Factors for Anchoring Offshore Projects. Information Strategy 15, 21–27 (1999)
15. Heeks, R., Krishna, S., Nicholson, B., Sahay, S.: Synching or Sinking: Global Software Outsourcing Relationships. IEEE Software 18, 54–60 (2001)
16. King, W.R., Torkzadeh, G.: Information Systems Offshoring: Research Status and Issues. MIS Quarterly 32, 205–225 (2008)
17. Kotlarsky, J., Oshri, I.: Social ties, knowledge sharing and successful collaboration in globally distributed system development projects. European Journal of Information Systems 14, 37–48 (2005)

18. Kotlarsky, J., van Fenema, P.C., Willcocks, L.P.: Developing a knowledge-based perspective on coordination: The case of global software projects. Information & Management 45, 96–108 (2008)
19. Krishna, S., Sahay, S., Walsham, G.: Managing Cross-Cultural Issues in Global Software Development. Communications of the ACM 47, 62–66 (2004)
20. Lacity, M., Willcocks, L.: An Empirical Investigation of Information Technology Sourcing Practices: Lessons From Experience. MIS Quarterly 22, 363–408 (1998)
21. Levina, N., Su, N.: Global Multisourcing Strategy: The Emergence of a Supplier Portfolio in Services Offshoring. Decision Sciences 39, 541–570 (2008)
22. Levina, N., Vaast, E.: Innovating or Doing as Told? Status Differences and Overlapping Boundaries in Offshore Collaboration. MIS Quarterly 32, 307–332 (2008)
23. Nicholson, B., Sahay, S.: Some Political and Cultural Issues in the Globalisation of Software Development: Case Experience from Britain and India. Information and Organization 11, 25–43 (2001)
24. Oshri, I., Kotlarsky, J., Willcocks, L.P.: Global Software Development: Exploring Socialization and Face-to-Face Meetings in Distributed Strategic Projects. The Journal of Strategic Information Systems 16, 25–49 (2007)
25. Rao, M.T.: Key Issues for Global IT Sourcing: Country and Individual Factors. Information Systems Management 21, 16–21 (2004)
26. Rottman, J., Lacity, M.: A US Client's learning from outsourcing IT work offshore. Information Systems Frontiers 10, 259–275 (2008)
27. Rottman, J.W.: Successfully Outsourcing Embedded Software Development. IEEE Software 39, 55–61 (2006)
28. Rottman, J.W., Lacity, M.C.: Twenty Practices for Offshore Sourcing. MISQ Executive 3, 117–130 (2004)
29. Schaaf, J.: Offshoring: Globalisation Wave Reaches Services Sector. Deutsche Bank Research Economics 45, 2–15 (2004), `http://www.dbresearch.com/`
30. Sia, S.K., Koh, C., Tan, C.X.: Strategic Maneuvers for Outsourcing Flexibility: An Empirical Assessment. Decision Sciences 39, 407–443 (2008)
31. Stebbins, R.A.: Exploratory Research in the Social Sciences. Sage Publications, Thousand Oaks (2001)
32. Walsham, G.: Interpreting Information Systems in Organizations. John Wiley & Sons, Inc., Chichester (1993)
33. Willcocks, L.P., Lacity, M.C., Cullen, S.: Information Technology Sourcing Research: Critique, Lessons and Prospects. In: 13th Americas Conference on Information Systems, Keystone, Colorado, USA (2007)
34. Yin, R.: Case Study Research - Design and Methods. Sage Publications, Thousand Oaks (2003)
35. Zatolyuk, S., Allgood, B.: Evaluating a Country for Offshore Outsourcing: Software Development Providers in the Ukraine. Information Systems Management 21, 28–33 (2004)

Knowledge Integration in Global R&D Networks

Rose Erkelens*, Bart van den Hooff, Paul Vlaar, and Marleen Huysman

KIN research, VU University Amsterdam
De Boelelaan 1105, 1081 HV Amsterdam,
The Netherlands
R.Erkelens@feweb.vu.nl

Abstract. This paper reports a qualitative study conducted at multinational organizations' R&D departments about their process of knowledge integration. Taking into account the knowledge based view (KBV) of the firm and the practice-based view of knowledge, and building on the literatures concerning specialization and integration of knowledge in organizations, we explore which factors may have a significant influence on the integration process of knowledge between R&D units. The findings indicated (1) the contribution of relevant factors influencing knowledge integration processes and (2) a thoughtful balance between engineering and emergent approaches to be helpful in understanding and overcoming knowledge integration issues.

Keywords: Specialization-Integration; Knowledge management; Engineering-Emergent approaches; Global R&D networks.

1 Introduction

In recent years, multinational corporations have increasingly adopted a global approach to research and development (R&D) activities. Partly relocating the R&D function in response to push factors such as a lack of talent and mounting cost pressure in their home country (Pro Inno Europe, 2007), and pull factors in overseas countries such as highly skilled science and engineering talent, and increased proximity to their customer bases (Lewin, Massini and Peeters, 2009; Trefler, 2005; Von Zedwitz and Gassmann, 2002). According to the 2009 World Investment Prospects Survey (UNCTAD), this trend of relocating R&D will continue in the years to come, with Asia and primarily China and India as preferred locations.

By 'offshoring' various R&D units overseas companies create dispersed knowledge centers, or centers of excellence, with each unit having its own specializations (Moore and Birkinshaw, 1998). In order to reap the benefits of specialization, organizations try to integrate knowledge of different R&D units in their "R&D network", i.e. combining specific knowledge of individuals in order to exploit and generate new

* Corresponding author.

I. Oshri and J. Kotlarsky (Eds.): Global Sourcing 2010, LNBIP 55, pp. 82–102, 2010.

combinations of existing knowledge (Kogut and Zander, 1992). Development of new products in particular involves wide-ranging integration between specialist knowledge bases of a number of individuals (Clark and Fujimoto, 1991; Grant, 1996b: 377). Corresponding to this view on new product development, Singh (2008) argues that while the geographical distribution of R&D does not necessarily increase the quality of a company's innovative output in itself; the integration of knowledge of multiple locations can make specialization valuable. Hence, though specialization can be seen as the motive for global R&D, it is the integration between specializations that makes global R&D successful in practice. This agrees with the Knowledge-Based View of the firm (e.g. Grant, 1996a), which argues that effective knowledge creation relies on *specialization* by individuals or units (leading to a collection of heterogeneous knowledge assets), with the firm as being to establish *integration* of these knowledge assets.

Scholars have observed the need for both knowledge specialization and integration. Postrel, for example, argues that 'mutual ignorance across specialties is usually optimal' for the alignment of specialization, but that development of knowledge benefits from certain key interactions between these specialties (Postrel, 2002: 304). In other words, managing knowledge involves a tension between specialization on the one hand (in order for specialized knowledge creation to occur) and integration on the other (in order for the organization to be able to benefit from the combination of the various pockets of specialized knowledge) (Grant, 1996a). The process of integrating knowledge itself, often realized by setting up cross-functional multisite projects, is challenging (Clark and Fujimoto, 1991). Integrating specialist knowledge means bringing individuals together and making them understand each other, with the aim of combining specialist knowledge, allowing cross-functional learning, and bringing forward and applying new knowledge. In the context of geographically (and culturally) dispersed R&D units, integration processes are likely to be influenced by, for instance, differences in knowledge bases, communication, ways of working, culture, and lack in time overlap between onsite and organizational units. In this paper, we explore which factors have a significant influence on the integration process of knowledge between R&D units, and how these factors are dealt with in practice.

To structure our analysis, we use an inductive exploratory approach. Since we aim to build theory on the relatively new subject of integration of dispersed R&D activities, we rely on semi-structured, in-depth interviews with managers and key informants directly involved with global R&D (see also Kumar et al., 1993), aim to establish at which factors considerably influence the integration of knowledge between distinct units in global R&D networks. We have therefore conducted twelve interviews with representatives of four multinational organizations possessing and developing global R&D networks.

Our findings illustrate the tension between specialization of different units in the R&D network, and the need to integrate the knowledge of different units to fully capture the benefits of specialization in practice. Specialization across units can be achieved by for example defining strategy and scope, differentiation, formulating boundaries, and concentration in one unit, while integration of knowledge amongst units requires a more emergent approach to the management of global R&D networks. More specifically, our findings indicate that integration of knowledge amongst units relies on factors related to the *units* involved in these processes, factors related to the *knowledge* being created and shared, and factors associated with the *relationships* between these units. First, on the level of the units involved in knowledge integration processes, findings reveal interrelated factors of dominant logics and cultural awareness to influence the integration process. Second, in terms of the knowledge being created and shared, knowledge integration is largely dependent on similarity of knowledge bases and the embeddedness of knowledge. As a consequence of specialization, specialist knowledge becomes more embedded in the people, tools, routines and sub networks of one unit, while in order to understand the value of knowledge of other units, knowledge should be partly embedded in the relation between units (e.g. Nielsen, 2005). Third, with regard to the relationship between R&D units we found structural and relational embeddedness to be important factors in facilitating knowledge integration.

Building on this, the main contribution of this paper is to identify a number of factors influencing the knowledge integration process between R&D units, and illustrating that this integration process relies on a combination of a more engineering approach based on the knowledge based view of the firm, and a more emergent approach towards knowledge. Where previous research has mainly approached the tension between specialization and integration from a purely engineering perspective, our findings show that the emergent nature of knowledge processes should also be taken into account in order to achieve a balance between specialization and integration in globally dispersed R&D.

2 Background Literature

The shift towards a more transnational view of R&D, as described above, is characterized by intense market and technology interaction, cross-functional learning, interactive technology transfer between geographical locations and units, and multiple centers of excellence which are geographically dispersed (Gerybadze and Reger, 1999). A center of excellence can be defined as an 'organizational unit that embodies a set of capabilities that has been explicitly recognized by the firm as an important source of value creation, with the intention that these capabilities be leveraged by and/or disseminated to other parts of the firm' (Frost, Birkinshaw and Ensign, 2002:1000). Within such centers of excellence, specialized knowledge is developed: scientific and technical knowledge concerning product or process innovation as well as knowledge about customers and competitors, and knowledge underpinning several organizational capabilities (Collinson, 2001).

Specialization is the main underlying principle for the firm (Williamson, 1985), but according to Birkinshaw (2002), the ability to integrate knowledge of different units is crucial to R&D networks, referring to the bringing together and combining of different knowledge sources of an organization, with the aim of generating new capabilities. Determinants of knowledge integration are for example the relatedness of technological competencies (Ramanujam and Varadarajan, 1989), spatial distance, cultural distance, and whether interactions take place across national borders, formal organizational structure, and informal cross-subsidiary relations between specialists (Foss and Pedersen, 2003; Granovetter, 1985; Hansen and Løvas, 2004), but also characteristics of the knowledge involved, such as knowledge categorized as information or know-how based (Kogut and Zander, 1992).

Where R&D benefits from specialization and integration at the same time, a tension can be found between dispersing and assimilating specialist knowledge. As Collinson (2001) argues, 'there is a difficult balance between specialization and the 'fragmentation' of knowledge (its distribution into specialist functional divisions) and the need to integrate specialist knowledge for particular tasks. Correspondingly, Postrel (2002) argues that specialties should be separated for an optimal concentration in that specialty, but that certain specialist knowledge can develop when it interacts with other specialist knowledge. This balance between specialization and integration is central to the Knowledge Based View (KBV) of the firm, which states that knowledge creation relies on specialization: An organization consists of a collection of heterogeneous knowledge assets, and the goal of the firm is the integration of these heterogeneous assets (Grant, 1996b).

Previous research in the area of specialization and integration has identified various ways of coping with the tension between the two. For example, Puranam et al. (2009) have studied post merger integration of technological capabilities and found that structural integration can negatively influence the innovative capabilities of the firm because of disruption of a unit's autonomy which inhibits innovative capabilities of that unit. They furthermore suggest that realizing common ground between units can facilitate coordination and can work as an alternative way to benefit from the combination of different specialist knowledge. Hansen and Birkinshaw (2007) suggest from a network perspective that cross-unit networks can stimulate conversion of ideas in the organization because new connections between different specializations can be established. Song and Shin (2008) argue that when host unit's technological capabilities are superior to that of the head quarter's unit, knowledge integration is more likely to occur because of the potential value this new knowledge can bring to the organization. Another example can be found in Singh's (2008) study on informal integration mechanisms, in which he suggests having incentives and processes in place to motivate employees to share knowledge and to organize more employees to develop cross-functional knowledge. However, these studies have analyzed either formal or informal mechanisms to integrate knowledge, and previous literature has strongly focused on a managerial (engineering) perspective and has given insufficient attention to the practice-based (emergent) nature of knowledge (Blackler, 1995; Brown & Duguid, 2001; Van den Hooff and Huysman, 2009). Due to the nature of knowledge involved in integration processes between R&D units, which is merely know-how based and situated in people, tools and practice (Argote et al. 2003), we question if literature has given sufficient attention to the practice nature of knowledge. The aim of our study is to explore from a neutral stance what factors influence knowledge integration processes.

3 Methods

3.1 Research Design

Since we aim to develop theory and since research on integration processes with regard to dispersed R&D activities is relatively new, we rely on semi-structured, in-depth interviews. To investigate which factors have a significant impact on the integration of knowledge between distinct units in global R&D networks, the interviews allowed the collection of differing perspectives on the topic assessed exploration of the 'how' question of knowledge integration processes, something which cannot be achieved through quantitative studies (Eisenhardt and Graebner, 2007; Shah and Corley, 2006; Yin, 2008).

3.2 Data Collection

Data was collected from multinational corporations with several offshore R&D affiliates. Most of the organizations were headquartered in the Netherlands and had R&D affiliates in Europe, USA and Asia. Twelve semi-structured interviews were conducted with managers and key informants directly involved with Global R&D (see also Kumar et al., 1993) in four organizations. The interviews were semi-structured and conducted with the help of an interview protocol (appendix A). Hitherto, we have conducted twelve interviews with representatives of three organizations possessing and developing global R&D networks. Table 1 presents an overview of the characteristics of the interviewees and their organizations.

Table 1. Overview of organizations and interviewees

	Company profile	Interviews
Company A	> 20.000 employees R&D Units in e.g.: The Netherlands (HQ)*, Canada Romania	R&D Director Integration Manager Information Manager
Company B	>100.000 employees R&D units in e.g.: The Netherlands (HQ) China USA England	R&D Director Vice president Senior Vice President Scientist Department Manager
Company C	> 10.000 employees R&D units in e.g.: The Netherlands (HQ) India USA Poland Australia	R&D Director Researcher Department Manager Department Manager
Company D	> 100.000 employees R&D units in e.g.: The Netherlands (HQ) China USA India Argentina	Knowledge Manager

*R&D headquarters.

The semi-structured interview protocol evolved during the data collection period, starting with a general interview protocol for the first interviews and being refined with more focused questions. The general interview protocol contained only questions regarding the position, history in the company, a typical working day, relationships between units and learning moments in working with geographically distributed R&D units. Once a general overview of the situations of the interviewees was understood, the protocol became more focused with questions regarding for example specialization and integration, and collaboration and communication between units.

The interviews, which took seventy-five minutes on average, were fully transcribed and coded in Atlas.ti. Interpretations made by the researcher of the meanings and stories told by the interviewee were discussed during the interviews, leading to a notion of mutual understanding which enhanced the quality of further levels of interpretation (Kvale, 1989).

3.3 Data Analysis

Transcription was undertaken soon after each interview, and each interview was separately reiterated during the transcription process, offering understanding of the interviewees' thoughts as well as a grasp of the organization's characteristics. During this process, concepts and constructs were identified and discussed by the researchers involved in this study. Possible constructs and concepts on factors influencing knowledge specialization and integration were proposed, however, separated from subsequent interviews in order to prevent premature or false conclusions.

After transcription, the interviews were segmented and coded with Atlas.ti. The coding process was done in five stages. The first stage concerned open coding of each interview, i.e. each part of text in an interview was labeled with the name(s) of a subject or issue discussed in that part. For example, if an interviewee mentioned face-to-face importance, the label 'face-to-face importance' was assigned to that part of text. In the first stage, about 35 different codes that occurred in at least more than one interview and on average in 4 interviews were generated. These codes represented categories that were partly connected to the questions (such as if and how to collaborate with other units), and that were partly raised by the interviewees themselves (such as 'us vs. them' issues within the firm).

The second stage consisted of a text search function of Atlas.ti, where several different names for the same category were checked for a code. An example of this search is 'specialist knowledge', for which the words 'know-how' or 'experience' were also used to describe the same kind of concept. The word 'understanding' in particular resulted in many hits that eventually counted for a broad description and valuation of mutual understanding, which at a later stage appeared to be very valuable.

The third stage consisted of subcategorizing the categories formed in stage 1, making them more concrete. For example, the category 'different ways of working' was subcategorized into different concepts such as 'formal structure' or 'communication behavior', different opinions about these concepts, and different perceived consequences of these concepts. In the fourth stage, a network view of the different codes and their linkages was made. The relations created in this stage came directly from relations and links explicitly discussed in the interviews. For example, in many interviews the label 'us vs. them' and the label 'building relationships' were explicitly mentioned as being related.

In the fifth stage, the concepts of dominant logics, cultural awareness, similarity in knowledge base, knowledge embeddedness, structural embeddedness and relational embeddedness were introduced in a side network since they covered a variety of labels and sub labels. Concepts were also categorized on a unit, knowledge or relation level (Argote et al. 2003). These different codes were displayed in their context as explained by the respondents, without drawing conclusions from a priori theory.

4 Findings

We identified several factors that influence knowledge integration between R&D units and their underlying mechanisms, which in accordance with the framework for analyzing knowledge management research of Argote et al. (2003) can be distinguished by three variables: a unit level, a knowledge level, and a relationship level. Table 2 provides an overview at the end of the findings section. Besides providing factors and coping strategies to deal with these factors, the findings illustrate the tension between knowledge specialization and integration processes.

4.1 The Emergence of Specialized Centers of Excellence vs. Integration of Specialist Knowledge

From a specialization perspective, interviewees explain that especially during the startup, a new R&D unit is likely to require sufficient guidance and time to develop specific knowledge about the organization's products and processes. In time, the new R&D unit develops understanding to contribute as part of the larger intraorganizational R&D network. Its knowledge base in this particular field starts to exceed the knowledge from other units, i.e. it develops into a center of excellence. Compared to how R&D structures in the organizations studied were originally centralized in the organization's home country (before internationalization), R&D units face more complex relationships when new decentralized structures are introduced, as is illustrated by the following statement:

> 'Before the internationalization of our R&D we could say: "We are on top of the world". That was our attitude. But now you can see that part of our R&D work is done elsewhere. Here people still believe other units should work according to how we work. Many do not see that we can learn from them and use their input.' (Information manager in the Netherlands, company A)

When differentiated centers of excellence start collaborating in multisite projects, they face difficulties in this collaboration. The findings reveal a tension emerging between, on the one hand, the need for specialization in different units and, on the other, the need for linking knowledge of different specializations in order to benefit from the organization's own resources. In other words, this means that part of the development process of an R&D unit is done elsewhere and centers of excellence of an organization are now scattered over distant areas, while at the same time, for integration to take place, the organization tries to link these different excellences.

Knowledge integration in the R&D network is commonly realized in projects with specialists of different R&D units. Interviewees point to how their organization stimulates knowledge integration in projects, and at the same time, specialization in units. Differences between units increase when R&D is dispersed, compared with how R&D was originally organized more centrally to the corporate organization. Integrating knowledge of different units therefore becomes more challenging, and requires more management attention. Consider the following quotes that illustrate the need for knowledge integration between R&D units:

> 'I think 80 percent of our projects involve people of different locations. This means that the project manager can be located here, the R&D guy can be located in Bangalore, and the marketing manager can be located in the United States. That is quite usual.' (R&D director in the Netherlands, company B).
>
> 'Our program management has overview of all projects within our R&D. From this view we discuss and request developed competences or technologies from other locations that we would like to apply in our project.' (R&D Department head in China, Company C).

By exploring the process of knowledge integration between R&D units, we identified several influencing factors consistent with prior work. First, at a unit level, interviewees were very aware of the influence of a unit's dominant logic and culture on the

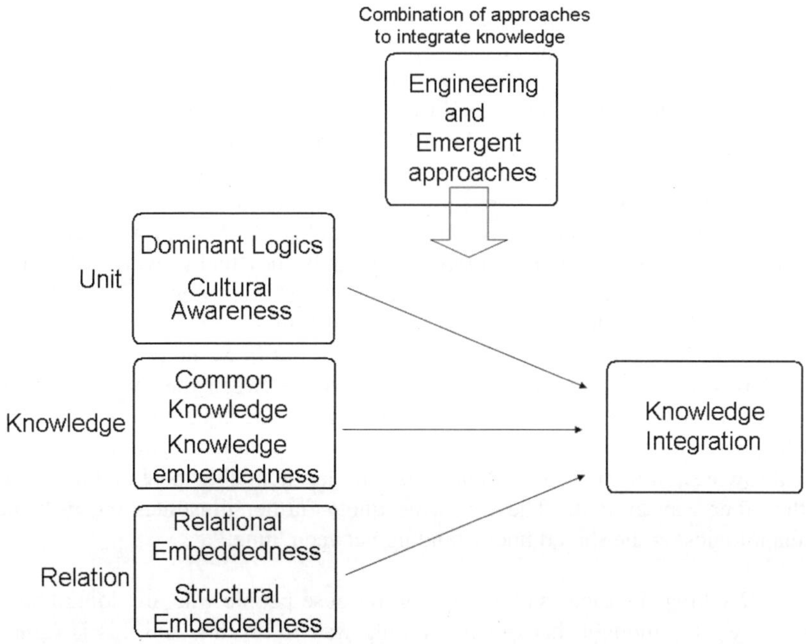

Fig. 1. Factors influencing knowledge integration

knowledge integration process between different R&D units. Second, at a knowledge level, similarity in knowledge base positively influences the ability of knowledge integration. Furthermore, knowledge embedded in a common context facilitates the ease of understanding knowledge from other specialists. Third, at a relationship level, an adequate intensity of relational embeddedness (mutual trust, identification) is likely to provide shared understanding between units. This is facilitated by structural embeddedness of this relationship (see figure 1).

4.2 Specialized Units

Dominant logics

Particularly in the startup of collaboration between units but definitely also in more mature relationships, more than half of the interviews indicate that each unit supposes its own *dominant logic* to be the starting point of how collaboration should take place. Dominant logic refers to belief structures and frames of reference (Bettis and Prahalad, 1995) a unit is supposed to function according to, and the interpretation of how work should be done. Consider the following illustrative example: an R&D unit of a large multinational organization has thus far always been located in one country, which was near the headquarters. All 54 specialists and engineers of the unit worked together in one building, and all of them knew each other for years. They worked in the same organizational structure for years, which was informal, but familiar and most comfortable for all. The way they worked, the daily routines were supposed to be the right way to do the job. One day the organization decided to expand the R&D function, and with the help of two expats it started up a new unit in India. There, ten Indian specialists were hired to virtually collaborate in projects with the team in the organization's home country. The new unit developed its own structure, rules, and compensation policies, which emerged from more Indian standards. The organization decided to develop some concepts in multisite projects, so insights could be shared and concepts could be developed from the best of both worlds. Both teams were instructed, communication lines were set up, and collaboration could commence. However, this is not what happened. Instead, many employees of the original unit failed to understand the value of the collaboration. Suddenly they had to work with strangers who knew nothing about the company or how things were done, who had different ways of working and who spoke a strange kind of English. Employees of the original unit did not believe that the extra effort they had to put in would benefit them in their work. This situation caused boundaries to emerge between the two groups, which made it difficult for both parties to see the benefits of the collaboration and inhibited knowledge sharing. One specialist recalled: 'This has a bit to do with our culture. We are real rowdies, you know. We often think: Oh, let them anticipate on how we work, not the other way around.' The following quote further illustrates the influence of dominant logics on the shared understanding between units:

> 'Nothing right and nothing wrong, because people who are doing one activity, they thought that this is the only way to do this, and this is right. And they were working for a number of years. Now, a person of that status of knowledge will really have a hard time if another person comes and then tells 'he, what you are doing is not right in the present scenario'. Sometimes

it is very difficult to believe that because we believe that what we do is the only thing that is right. It's human nature.' (R&D Manager in India, company C).

Besides a unit's own dominant logic, awareness of dominant logics of other units is found to support shared understanding. If units get more involved with each other's dominant logic, they are more likely able to interact with each other:

> 'Success of multisite projects depends on how well we do this together. We do have the technical expertise. Results will come if involvement is there, not the other way around.' (R&D Department head in China, company B).
>
> '... and it will demand a huge change in our mentality, because we have to learn to be aware that specialists in that unit know more from some concepts than we do.' (Information manager in the Netherlands, Company A).

Interviewees explain how a significant sub concept of dominant logics, *differences in ways of working,* can negatively influence the knowledge integration process. Interviewees recall compensation policies, time-to-market and hierarchical structure as factors that contribute to differences in the way R&D units function. When collaboration between units takes place, these differences need attention.

> 'In the European unit people make a plan for a year and then stick to the plan, more traditional. It is relatively stable and when you have good ideas you can experiment on it. But in Shanghai you don't have such kind of free time. Our time to market differs. We define a project with high pressure, deliverables, manage changes, you even see changes every day. Then you have to adapt and adjust your plan. So you see the communication can have problems because of different situations.'(Technical specialist, Company B).

Interviewees explain how their former R&D network (one location) in the past did not demand a higher level of formalization because informal structures were satisfactory. After starting up foreign R&D labs, informal structures are of less function, and much of the misunderstanding between R&D units in time can be avoided by a higher level of *formalization* of ways of working and responsibilities.

> 'A certain transparency in our project management was something we lacked. That's something we were confronted with when we started working with the Asians. That is how they work, very structured focused on progress. We've experienced all kinds of conflicts, actually because our way of working was not structured. That was 5 years ago. In the meantime we made up for lost ground.'(R&D Integration manager, Company A).

Cultural awareness
Interviewees pointed to the importance of *cultural awareness*, or the ability to recognize how the behavior of others can be influenced by culture. According to the interviewees, differences in culture have caused several situations of miscommunication and misunderstanding between units:

> 'In order to collaborate, it is important to be able to understand each other. This is not just about understanding technical knowledge, after that, or before, it is all about awareness of each other's culture.' (R&D Department head in China, company B).

Differences in culture can also become evident for example in hierarchical structures, ways of working, and communication patterns:

> 'The people there always say: yes, yes, yes, while they actually mean no, no, no. Their feelings for hierarchy and compensation policies are different from what we are used to. Now we know, but before this brought along a lot of miscommunication, and with that irritation.' (R&D Director, Company C).

In addition, interviewees explain how they learn to become better aware of differences in culture. Cultural awareness is stimulated by management through for example meetings and courses on culture. However, most awareness develops during daily practices.

4.3 A Knowledge Perspective

Knowledge Embeddedness

Knowledge embeddedness refers to how knowledge is situated, e.g. in people, technologies and specific contexts (practice) and it assumes that knowledge integration is more likely to benefit from embedded knowledge when it is embedded on both the unit and the relationship level. This means knowledge should be embedded in a specific unit, but at the same time relevant knowledge should be embedded in a shared context so units can collaborate in a common context. The concept can be illustrated by an anecdote that was provided by a manager of an R&D unit in China. He explained that for a Dutch specialist who has worked for the company for more than 25 years, half a page of requirements is usually perceived as sufficient information to design a new concept. The remaining requirements, which could fill as much as three books, were all in his head. He just knew what was being asked and what to do. This way of working was routine for everyone, and whenever there were requirements that needed clarity, specialists just stepped by at each others' offices. This all changed when multisite projects with the Chinese were introduced. The Chinese specialists had formal technical knowledge and often experience in the same industry. However, they did not have the specifics of three books of requirements needed to deliver the same concepts in their head, something which was implicitly assumed by the Dutch specialists. A complete set of requirements should have been communicated, but in practice this was not the case. The result: the Chinese received a list of requirements and started to work on it, without asking questions. After a few weeks they proudly presented their developed concept, which contained the communicated requirements but had hardly anything in common with what the Dutch had expected them to deliver. The manager reported: 'Their ideas were criticized mercilessly, and so was their specialist knowledge'.

Embeddedness of knowledge in a shared context facilitates common ground between units, while the more locally embedded knowledge is, the more difficult this becomes. Research and development work in particular, where knowledge can be highly tacit and is often embedded in peoples' experience, knowledge integration can be problematic.

> 'We base our work on what we experience in this field, in our country. If our colleagues overseas do not understand us, this (specific circumstances) is sometimes difficult to be aware of and explain.' (Technical specialist, Company B).

Similarity in Knowledge Base

Units can only recognize and value the knowledge of other units if both units have some kind of overlap in their basic knowledge, here referred to as *similarity in knowledge base*. Our analysis indicates that in most cases, scientific, technical and academic knowledge of specialists is relatively overlapping. This means that specialists of different units can understand each other at the basic level of technical requirements. This agrees with other studies investigating offshoring R&D, in which one of the main motives is access to skilled labor (e.g. Lewin et al. 2009).

> 'It is different (knowledge base of units). But purely the technical view I don't see the big difference.' (R&D Director in the Netherlands, Company A).

For knowledge integration to take place, for example to situate part of an R&D unit overseas where the unit has better opportunities to develop highly specialized knowledge, the common way to 'transfer' specialist knowledge is to station experienced specialists in the new unit and to station specialists of the new unit in the experienced units for an extended period. This allows close collaboration, and can the opportunity to build a shared context.

> 'We have two Dutch specialists stationed there and two Chinese specialists here, and they will stay for at least 6 months. This is the only way we are able to transfer our expertise.' (R&D Director in the Netherlands, Company C).

However, if knowledge is too embedded in a shared context, parties are not able to learn from each other because knowledge is too related and not new. Some interviewees emphasize the importance of having a shared knowledge base, but also argue that it is important to do work separately. They note that a certain amount of competition in these separate projects is vital for the R&D function in general.

> 'Some things you have to do at two, sometimes at three places. And then you discover, wow, the other guys actually developed an incredibly good lamp (LED). This triggers everyone to understand how they developed it and how you can learn from them.' (R&D Director in China, Company B).

4.4 Relations in the R&D Network

Relational Embeddedness

The factor found to significantly influence knowledge integration between units on a relational level is *relational embeddedness*, which refers to the quality and depth of relationships between units. From the interviews, it became clear that direct cohesive ties between units work as a mechanism for gaining valuable information and knowledge, and that they facilitate integrating knowledge from other units. A manager working in Singapore told us about a situation when ten specialists from two different units started working together in a project on a print color device. A formal communication structure was set up and tasks were divided, but that was not enough to make the team collaborate. People from one unit did not know the specialists from the other unit, and did not feel they could trust the others with their work. The specialists were organized as one team, but most of the times they worked as two separate groups. Whenever the two groups came together to discuss progress, which now was only once in two months, problems emerged because the results of the work of both units were too deviant to fit together. Management acknowledged the problem and forced formal agreements and contact hours, but an 'us vs. them' feeling in the team left tensions between specialists of the two locations. Only after some of the project specialists visited the other unit and met other project members face to face, the specialists started to build mutual trust and valued each others' work. This slowly triggered more emergent and spontaneous collaboration in the project, which was necessary to successfully conclude the project. One manager recalled: 'You should put specialists together and keep the communication lines short. They get to know and understand each other. Sometimes it is the best if they can be put together in one room. If this is not possible because the project is dispersed over different locations, at least place these specialists in one team with direct contact between them.'

Almost all interviewees referred to the importance of getting familiar with 'the other side', in order to understand each other. Building such relationships facilitates mutual trust, identification and cohesion between units, which is necessary to reach an adequate level of shared understanding. If there is a lack of strong relationships, which can especially be the case in an R&D unit's startup, units are less likely to develop a shared understanding and, in turn, find it difficult to learn from each other.

> 'What is unknown is unloved. I myself had this same feeling. Before my first visits I did not understand many of their actions and thought they were doing things that didn't make sense.' (R&D Director in the Netherlands, company A)

> 'One of our Dutch specialists we intentionally posted in Singapore for a period to improve collaboration, because he had difficulty coping with the distant relationship. This measure has helped enormously.' (Integration manager in China, company A).

Structural Embeddedness

Getting to know each other and building a relationship can be accomplished by visiting the other R&D site and meeting the other team members, joining in multisite projects and events. We refer to the process of the organization structuring and coordinating

Table 2. Summary of concepts

Level and concepts	Sub concepts	Definition	Exemplary quotes
Unit level			
Dominant logics		Belief structures and frames of reference (Bettis and Prahalad, 1995)	'We have to understand how our actions can trigger certain behavior of our colleagues overseas, how they think, and overseas they should be able to do the same with us.'
	Ways of working	Ways of working in terms of hierarchy, policies, compensation structure, and communication patterns	'…they are also expecting that those things should be done in the same way by the other people in different parts of the world. And in different parts of the world, we have some different way to do those things.'
Cultural awareness		Cultural norms and beliefs a unit or group espouses	'The unit and local cultures are different there, which is something we should pay attention to. It is all about understanding each other.'
Knowledge level			
Similarity in knowledge base		Knowledge possessed by employees	'At the headquarter we have decades of experience and learning in our technologies. In India we have enough new scientists, but no experience. This excellence is difficult to transfer.'
Knowledge embeddedness	Common knowledge	Knowledge that is embedded in a shared context which is understandable for both units	'Formal technical knowhow is comparable.'
	Local knowledge	Knowledge embedded in one unit which is difficult to integrate because of differing contexts	'We use our market knowledge to develop many concepts, which can be difficult to understand for nonlocals.' 'What we know here is a collection of years and years of work.' 'Local policies influence how and what we communicate around here.'
Relationship level			
Structural embeddedness	Cohesion	Bonding between units	'One thing we did, we deliberately chose to structure different hierarchical lines forth and back between units.'
Relational embeddedness	Trust	To believe employees in another unit can be entrusted with their work in a project	'…and you should have some trust, sharing your documents, others will look into it.'
	Identity	The extent to which units in a relation form a shared identity	'Especially the us-them thoughts we try to nip in the bud.'
	Face to face contact	The ability to communicate and work face to face	'Well, maybe not even that you actually have to meet face to face with everybody separately, I think it is important that you've been there at their work place for more than one day.'

relationships between units as *structural embeddedness,* and assume that structural embeddedness in turn facilitates the development of relational embeddedness by providing foundation for relationships between units. Creating relational embeddedness by facilitating structural embeddedness becomes more difficult if units are dispersed over different continents, but is nevertheless seen as a prerequisite for collaboration in multisite projects. The following statement is illustrative in this respect:

> 'You need to sit around the table with each other. This doesn't work by phone. It all becomes more and more global. This means traveling budgets. If you save on these budgets, you burn your own fingers.' (R&D director in China, company B).

In addition to creating strong relationships, units should also enhance their weak ties with other units, because such ties are vital for the development of different knowledge sets and require less trust, identification and cohesion. Findings reveal that units are likely to benefit from each other's knowledge by creating a kind of optimal strength in the embeddedness of their relation. Taking structural and relational embeddedness to its extremes can cause either a lack of understanding because the units' knowledge bases are too diverse, or a lack of new knowledge contribution because knowledge of the units is too related.

> 'For me once in a while face to face contact is always good, but when people who are interesting to work with have already met face to face once or twice, then I think it is not necessary to meet again and again in order to get certain things done.' (R&D Manager in India, Company C).

5 Discussion

In this paper, we have explored which factors have a significant influence on the integration process of knowledge between R&D units in a global R&D context. Drawing on the findings, and taking into account literature on knowledge integration processes, our analysis complements existing literature, which is primarily focused on a managerial perspective, by emphasizing the importance of taking both managerial perspectives and practice-based perspectives into account when dealing knowledge integration processes. Much research on integration of knowledge and capabilities issues is characterized by a focus on the managerial perspective (e.g. Puranam, 2009; Hansen and Birkinshaw, 2007; Song and Shin, 2008) in which it is assumed that knowledge integration can be achieved by management interventions in the form of appropriate organizational and technical infrastructures (Van den Hooff and Huysman, 2009). However, this view ignores the complementarity that praxis and practices can have on coping with knowledge integration, which is suggested by the practice-based (emergent) perspective. This view, which presumes knowledge as being embedded in practice and as something people do instead of have, observes knowledge integration as a process which is socially constructed between sender and receiver and which is difficult to manage top-down (Blackler, 1995; Hislop 2009). In this study, a combination of insights from both a managerial perspective and a practice-based perspective is found to be effective in coping with the delicate balance between knowledge integration and specialization. The combination of a managerial view with a practice-based view is related to work on strategy as practice in which strategy, in contract to most strategy research, is seen as a social practice and facilitated by factors such as strong relationships, revealing and addressing social problems, and recognizing embeddedness at different levels (Whittington, 2007). Consequently, we argue that the knowledge integration processes should not only be studied from a managerial perspective, as the practice-based nature of knowledge processes must be given more attention in research.

First, at the level of the *units* involved, we found that interrelated factors of dominant logics and cultural awareness influence the integration process. Dominant logics are a fundamental aspect of organizational intelligence (Bettis and Prahalad, 1995), and our analysis shows that differences negatively influence knowledge integration between units, thus constraining the ability to learn from other R&D units. We reveal that coping mechanisms are found in managerial perspective interventions such as formalization and bridging diverse ways of working. Taking into account literature on dominant logics (e.g. Grant, 1988; Ramanujam and Varadarajan, 1989; Prahalad and Bettis, 1986), not much is known about what actions an organization can undertake to effectively manage dominant logics of units or organizations. In order for a unit to be receptive towards dominant logics of other units or new knowledge in general it has to "unlearn" (some of) its own dominant logics. Bettis and Prahalad (1995) suggest that since changes in structure and systems are strongly related to dominant logics, they are likely to facilitate this process of unlearning. Alternatively, overcoming cultural differences and creating cultural awareness, established in actual immersion in shared practices, helps develop understanding of others' tacit assumptions (Hislop, 2009). Thus, coping with this factor relies more on a practice-based approach towards knowledge than on any managerial intervention. Awareness of other unit's culture creates understanding of the behavior and actions of members that unit.

Second, at the level of the *knowledge* being created and shared, we found similarities in knowledge bases and the embeddedness of knowledge in both the units' local context and the shared context between units to influence the knowledge integration process. The purpose of dispersed R&D, knowledge specialization, is likely to negatively influence the emergence of a shared knowledge base because most of the experience of specialists is developed in separate contexts. Consistent with Simonin (1997), our findings suggest that if know-how is developed in a shared context, in this study the context of multisite projects, R&D units develop the ability to understand and adopt proper procedures and mechanisms for knowledge integration. This is supported by literature on a knowledge-based view of the firm (e.g. Grant, 1996a) in which the value of joint know-how has long been recognized as essential for knowledge integration of both tacit and explicit knowledge. Interestingly, while similarity in knowledge bases is first of all reached by more managerial approaches such as relocation of specialists, the embeddedness of knowledge in a local or shared context is more likely to be developed by specialization and daily practices in multisite projects. From a practice-based perspective, a characteristic of knowledge embedded in a local context is that this knowledge is more difficult to appropriate for specialists outside this local context. Moreover, because knowledge is embedded, and in its local context gradually taken for granted, specialists often cannot value and articulate it to specialists of other units (Sole and Edmondson, 2002). Literature on knowledge embeddedness (e.g. Sole and Edmondson, 2002; Brown and Duguid, 2001; Cummings and Teng, 2003) suggests practice-based approaches such as mutual engagement in activities and forms of communities of practice to create a shared repertoire, so that knowledge can be created and embedded in a shared context. Our findings reveal that working together in practice in the context of multisite projects provides the basis for building common context in which knowledge can reside which, in turn, can be recognized by specialists regardless of their local context.

Third, at the level of the *relationship* between the units involved, the data indicates that structural and relational embeddedness of units significantly influence knowledge integration. Again, from a managerial and practice based perspective, there is a distinction between coping mechanisms. The development of structural embeddedness between units, which can be organized by for example cross-unit responsibilities and direct communication lines, is primarily reached by a top-down managerial approach. Creating relational embeddedness however, requires a more practice based approach in which specialists become familiar with each other and each other's practices through work visits and face to face contact. Considering the relatively tacit nature of specialist knowledge and the dispersedness of R&D units, distribution of R&D is found to negatively influence actual collaboration in multisite projects. Knowledge integration is a process of knowledge sharing and learning, facilitated by immersion in shared practices and intensive information exchange, and more likely in highly embedded relationships (Uzzi, 1996; Hansen, 1999; Hislop, 2009). Establishing such relationships takes time but is nevertheless necessary to create trust, a shared identity and cohesion between units. These findings are consistent with other research on global R&D networks. For example, Dhanaraj et al. (2004) in their study of dynamics in tacit and explicit learning in an international context found that relational embeddedness has a positive impact on the transfer of tacit knowledge.

Our findings illustrate work on knowledge integration and the tension with specialization in several ways. For example, results illustrate the notion that specialization of units itself is likely to inhibit knowledge integration, because for specialization to take place, a unit requires a certain degree of autonomy to develop its own knowledge, which is likely to cause more differences between units. This, as described above, limits a unit's ability access knowledge of other units, to recognize, link and create new knowledge from combining its own specialism with that of other (internal) R&D units (see for example Singh, 2008). Accordingly, the integration of knowledge between dispersed R&D units is only possible if a sufficient level of *relative absorptive capacity* exists on both sides. Our findings show that all factors identified strongly influence the ability of one R&D unit to value and absorb (useful) knowledge of other units. This is in line with, and extends, Lane and Lubatkin (1998)'s work on relative absorptive capacity, in which they found that 'the ability of a unit to learn from another unit is jointly determined by the relative characteristics of the two units, denoting similarities in 'know-what' (knowledge), 'know-how' (knowledge processing systems), and 'know-why' (dominant logics) (Lane and Lubatkin, 1998:473). It furthermore extends the concepts of 'absolute absorptive capacity', which is conceptualized as the ability of a unit to value, assimilate, and apply new external knowledge (Cohen and Levinthal, 1989), but does not take into consideration the fact that units differ in their capacity to learn from other units. Our findings suggest that overlap between characteristics of different units probably encourages shared understanding and, in turn, knowledge integration between these units, which is in line with Lane and Lubatkin (1998). Our work extends literature on relative absorptive capacity by suggesting that the ability to integrate knowledge between R&D units can benefit from both managerial and practice-based perspectives, and it provides insight in coping strategies that are used to deal with relative characteristics of different units.

Elaborating on the above, practical implications can first of all be found in the different factors and their interrelatedness identified that influence collaboration and integration between geographically dispersed R&D units. Second, knowledge integration processes benefit from the complementary view of using engineering and more emergent approaches which indicates a combination of the two to be favorable. Specifically, when managing the relation between different R&D units with the aim of combining knowledge of these units, managers should be aware not only of their manageable courses of action, but also of complementary self-organizing processes that emerge and exist in the social context of practice for which they can provide a fruitful context but cannot influence directly (Van den Hooff & Huysman, 2009).

Finally, while our findings provide deep and useful insight into knowledge integration processes, it is limited in the amount of data available, twelve in-depth interviews. Since this work is "research in progress", it will in the future be extended by more interview data, and the framework presented in this study will be elaborated on in in-depth case studies.

In conclusion, we emphasize that earlier work on knowledge integration in the context of global R&D networks has underappreciated the essential effect practice-based approaches can have on knowledge integration processes, and how a thoughtful balance between engineering and emergent approaches can help understand and overcome integration problems.

References

Argote, L., McEvily, B., Reagans, R.: Managing Knowledge in Organizations: An Integrative Framework and Review of Emerging Themes. Management Science 49(4), 571–582 (2003)

Bardhan, A.D.: Managing globalization of R&D: Organizing for Offshoring Innovation. Human Systems Management 25, 103–114 (2006)

Bettis, R.A., Prahalad, C.K.: The Dominant Logic: Retrospective and Extension. Strategic Management Journal 16(1), 5–14 (1995)

Birkinshaw, J.: Managing Internal R&D Networks in Global Firms: What Sort of Knowledge is Involved? Long Range Planning 35(3), 245–267 (2002)

Blackler, F.: Knowledge, Knowledge Work and Organizations: An Overview and Interpretation. Organization Studies 16(6), 1021–1046 (1995)

Brown, J.S., Duguid, P.: Knowledge and Organization: A Social-Practice Perspective. Organization Science 12(2), 198–213 (2001)

Clark, K.B., Fujimoto, T.: Product development performance. Harvard Business School Press, Boston (1991)

Cohen, W.M., Levinthal, D.A.: Innovation and Learning: The Two Faces of R & D. The Economic Journal 99(397), 569–596 (1989)

Collinson, S.: Knowledge management capabilities in R&D: a UK-Japan company comparison. R&D Management 31(3), 335–347 (2001)

Cummings, J.L., Teng, B.S.: Transferring R&D knowledge: The key factors affecting knowledge transfer success. Journal of Engineering and Technology Management 20(1-2), 39–68 (2003)

Demsetz, H.: The theory of the firm revisited. In: The nature of the firm, pp. 159–178. Oxford University Press, New York (1991)

Dhanaraj, C., Lyles, M.A., Steensma, H.K., Tihanyi, L.: Managing Tacit and Explicit Knowledge Transfer in IJVs: The Role of Relational Embeddedness and the Impact on Performance. Journal of International Business Studies 35(5), 428–442 (2004)

Eisenhardt, K.M., Graebner, M.E.: Theory Building from cases: Opportunities and challenges. The Academy of Management Journal 50(1), 25–32 (2007)

Foss, N.J., Pedersen, T.: Transferring knowledge in MNCs: The role of sources of subsidiary knowledge and organizational context. Journal of International Management 8(1), 49–67 (2002)

Frost, T.S., Birkinshaw, J.M., Ensign, P.C.: Centers of Excellence in Multinational Corporations. Strategic Management Journal 23(11), 997–1018 (2002)
Gerybadze, A., Reger, G.: Globalization of R&D: recent changes in the management of innovation in transnational corporations. Research Policy 28(2-3), 251–274 (1999)
Granovetter, M.: Economic Action and Social Structure: The Problem of Embeddedness. The American Journal of Sociology 91(3), 481–510 (1985)
Grant, R.M.: On dominant logic', relatedness and the link between diversity and performance. Strategic Management Journal 9(6), 639–642 (1988)
Grant, R.M.: Toward a Knowledge-Based Theory of the Firm. Strategic Management Journal 17, 109–122 (1996a)
Grant, R.M.: Prospering in Dynamically-Competitive Environments: Organizational Capability as Knowledge Integration. Organization Science 7(4), 375–387 (1996b)
Gupta, A.K., Govindarajan, V.: Knowledge Flows within Multinational Corporations. Strategic Management Journal 21(4), 473–496 (2000)
Hansen, M.T.: The Search-Transfer Problem: The Role of Weak Ties in Sharing Knowledge across Organization Subunits. Administrative Science Quarterly 44(1), 82–111 (1999)
Hansen, M.T., Birkinshaw, J.: The Innovative Value Chain. Harvard Business Review, 121–130 (June 2007)
Hansen, M.T., Løvas, B.: How do multinational companies leverage technological competencies? Moving from single to interdependent explanations. Strategic Management Journal 25(8-9), 801–822 (2004)
Hislop, D.: Mission impossible? Communicating and sharing knowledge via information technology. Journal of Information Technology 17, 165–177 (2002)
Hislop, D.: Knowledge Management in Organizations. Oxford University Press, Oxford (2009)
Kogut, B., Zander, U.: Knowledge of the Firm, Combinative Capabilities, and the Replication of Technology. Organization Science 3(3), 383–397 (1992)
Kumar, N., Stern, L.W., Anderson, J.C.: Conducting Interorganizational Research Using Key Informants. The Academy of Management Journal 36(6), 1633–1651 (1993)
Kvale, S.: The qualitative research interview. Journal of Phenomenological Psychology 14(1), 171–196 (1983)
Lane, P.J., Lubatkin, M.: Relative Absorptive Capacity and Interorganizational Learning. Strategic Management Journal 19(5), 461–477 (1998)
Lewin, A.Y., Massini, S., Peeters, C.: Why are companies offshoring innovation? The emerging global race for talent. Journal of International Business Studies 40, 901–925 (2009)
Moore, K., Birkinshaw, J.: Managing knowledge in global service firms: Centers of Excellence. The Academy of Management Executive 12, 81–92 (1998)
Nielsen, B.B.: The role of knowledge embeddedness in the creation of synergies in strategic alliances. Journal of Business Research 58(9), 1194–1204 (2005)
Postrel, S.: Islands of Shared Knowledge: Specialization and Mutual Understanding in Problem- Solving Teams. Organization Science 13(3), 303–320 (2002)
Puranam, P., Singh, H., Chaudhuri, S.: Integrating Acquired Capabilities: When Structural Integration Is (Un)necessary. Organization Science 20(2), 313–328 (2009)
Prahalad, C.K., Bettis, R.A.: The Dominant Logic: A New Linkage between Diversity and Performance. Strategic Management Journal 7(6), 485–501 (1986)
Pro Inno Europe: The implications of R&D off-shoring on the innovation capacity of firms. Helsinki School of Economics (2007)
Ramanujam, V., Varadarajan, P.: Research on Corporate Diversification: A Synthesis. Strategic Management Journal 10(6), 523–551 (1989)

Roth, J.: Enabling knowledge creation: learning from an R&D organization. Journal of Knowledge Management 7, 32–48 (2003)

Singh, J.: Distributed R&D, cross-regional knowledge integration and quality of innovative output. Research Policy 37(1), 77–96 (2008)

Shah, S.K., Corley, K.G.: Building Better Theory by Bridging the Quantitative-Qualitative Divide. Journal of Management Studies 43(8), 1821–1835 (2006)

Sole, D., Edmondson, A.: Situated Knowledge and Learning in Dispersed Teams. British Journal of Management 13, S17–S34 (2002)

Song, J., Shin, J.: The paradox of technological capabilities: a study of knowledge sourcing from host countries of overseas R&D operations. Journal of International Business Studies 39, 291–303 (2008)

Simonin, B.L.: The Importance of Collaborative Know-How: An Empirical Test of the Learning Organization. The Academy of Management Journal 40(5), 1150–1174 (1997)

Trefler, D.: Services Offshoring: Threats and Opportunities. Brookings trade forum (2005)

Tsai, W., Ghoshal, S.: Social Capital and Value Creation: The Role of Intrafirm Networks. The Academy of Management Journal 41(4), 464–476 (1998)

Uzzi, B.: The Sources and Consequences of Embeddedness for the Economic Performance of Organizations: The Network Effect. American Sociological Review 61(4), 674–698 (1996)

Van den Hooff, B., Huysman, M.: Managing knowledge sharing: Emergent and engineering approaches. Information & Management 46(1), 1–8 (2009)

Von Zedtwitz, M., Gassmann, O.: Market versus technology drive in R&D internationalization: Four different patterns of managing research and development. Research Policy 31(4), 569–588 (2002)

Whittington, R.: Strategy Practice and Strategy Process: Family Differences and the Sociological Eye. Organization Studies 28(10), 1575–1586 (2007)

Williamson, O.E.: The economic institutions of capitalism. Free Press, New York (1985)

Yin, R.K.: Case study research: Design and methods. Sage Publications, Thousand Oaks (2008)

Appendix A: Interview Protocol Semi-structured Interviews

1. Can you describe your position and work activities? *Can you describe the history of your career in short?* *How long do you work for this organization?* *How long do you have this position?* *What responsibilities does your position entail? /What does an ordinary day look like?*
2. How is R&D organized at … in general? *How is the organization structured?* *How is R&D located?* *Why is R&D located there?* *Is R&D captive or outsourced? (distribution intern/extern)* *Does the organization collaborate with other organizations on R&D?*
3. How is R&D organized at your specific division? *What technologies and products is your R&D division involved in?* *What is the background of employees working in this division?*

Is R&D in this division held captive or is it outsourced? *Does this division collaborate with other divisions or organizations?* *How is performance of R&D measured in this division?*
4. Can you explain how onshore and offshore units collaborate? *Are there formal agreements on how to work together between onshore and offshore units?* *Who (or what) carries responsibility for the well-being of this collaboration?* *How does this collaboration work out in practice? In other words, do you see differences between formal agreements and practice?* *What differences do you experience between onshore and offshore units?*
5. How does knowledge sharing/transfer take place between onshore and offshore R&D units?(process/practice) *How do onshore and offshore units communicate with each other?* *What tools/systems are used to communicate with each other?* *How important is personal contact in knowledge sharing and transfer?* *How frequent do onshore and offshore employees share knowledge? (e.g. constantly, daily, weekly, monthly)* *What persons/functions have to share/transfer knowledge with each other?* *Can you explain if and how agreements on this knowledge sharing/transfer are established?* *Do onshore and offshore units exchange employees?*
6. What are properties of the kinds of knowledge that is transferred or shared between onshore and offshore R&D units? *Can you give examples of the kind of knowledge shared between R&D onshore and offshore units?* *Can you describe the level of embeddedness of knowledge and expertise in people, systems and routines?* *Can you elaborate some more on the complexity of the knowledge shared?*
7. What factors influence knowledge transfer between onshore and offshore R&D units? *Can you name similarities and differences between the knowledge base of employees of onshore and offshore units?* *To what extent does the onshore unit understands knowledge of the offshore unit? What factors influence this extent?* *To what extent does the offshore unit understands knowledge of the onshore unit? What factors influence this extent?*
8. How do these factors influence the process of knowledge sharing?

Portfolios of Control: Researching Discourses in IT Outsourcing

Eleni Lioliou and Leslie Willcocks

London School of Economics and Political Science
Houghton Street, WC2A2AE
London, UK

Abstract. This research aims to enhance our understanding of IT outsourcing governance and the influence of its formal and relational mechanisms in executing IT outsourcing. More specifically, our study will demonstrate the role of wider "outsourcing discourses" in disciplining the behavior of the outsourcing partners but also how they permit the creation of avenues to escape discipline and responsibility. The study will introduce a Foucauldian view in the examination of how these "outsourcing discourses" are enacted and will encompass the perspectives both from the client and the supplier organizations.

Keywords: IT Outsourcing Governance, Foucault, Control.

1 Introduction

With the advent of globalization and enhanced levels of competition, many organizations have acknowledged the difficulties of developing and maintaining the range of expertise and skills necessary to compete successfully. In such an era of turbulent marketplaces and volatile technology, firms are relying more and more on information technology (IT) to remain competitive. One consequence of this pervasive dependence on IT has been an important upsurge of IT outsourcing.

IT outsourcing has been regarded as a promising avenue for cost-reduction and the creation of distinctive competencies. However, while the multi-billion dollar industry of IT outsourcing is growing, a number of IT outsourcing agreements have been terminated or have been under-performing. A recent survey from the International Association of Outsourcing Professionals (IAOP) showed that outsourcing governance and control is the top challenge that outsourcing professionals are facing today (IAOP, 2008). Furthermore, recent statistics from Deloitte have indicated that a number of outsourcing arrangements have been terminated early or have been underperforming as a result of poor governance (Deloitte, 2008). On this basis, governance in outsourcing ventures has a very high profile, and prior research has indicated a significant business performance difference depending on the effectiveness of governance arrangements.

While both academic and commercial publications point out the significance of governance in outsourcing ventures, our understanding of how governance operates as a result of the conjunction between formal and informal governing mechanisms

I. Oshri and J. Kotlarsky (Eds.): Global Sourcing 2010, LNBIP 55, pp. 103–118, 2010.

remains relatively fragmented. This research aims to enhance our understanding of outsourcing governance by analyzing the disciplinary effects of wider "outsourcing discourses" on the partnership.

2 Literature Review

Current research on the IT outsourcing relationship has been mostly concerned with the key factors that influence the outcome of the venture. From an economic perspective a number of researchers concentrated on the contractual agreement as a key determinant for the desirable outcome in inter-organizational partnerships. For example, Parkhe (1993) concentrated on the completeness of the contract and argued that the more complete the contract, the smaller the exposure to the potential opportunism of the vendor and the smaller the probability that costly renegotiations will be needed. Aubert et al (2003) on the other hand, argued that in cases of activities that are not easy to predict or difficult to measure, more incomplete forms of contracts are required. Gietzmann (1996) as well as Beulen and Ribbers (2003) appeared to be more concerned with the importance of flexibility at the contractual level, and argued that adjustments and changes may be needed at any point of the outsourcing relationship, especially in its early stages. Andersen and Christensen (2002) further underlined the value of flexibility by pointing out that "when making adjustments is costless the problem is trivial, but if adjustment entails costs in an uncertain environment, then the problem becomes much bigger". Saunders et al (1997) on the other hand, highlighted precision as an important attribute of a good contract. The authors explained that ill-defined contracts generally result in high IT costs and poor IT service levels. Allery (2004) further asserted that without clarity there is an element of uncertainty that, apart from legal problems, it can also cause operational problems and result in the creation of "hidden costs". Bennedsen and Schultz (2005) went a step further and indicated that an adaptive, "trial and error" approach when preparing the contract, may be a good way to prevent errors.

Still, a significant a number of authors argued that there are no "one-size-fits all" clauses and thus that partnership quality goes to a large extent beyond the contents in the contracts to rely on more social factors. Researchers from this social stream of enquiry moved beyond the contractual arrangement to investigate upon other, "soft" and "more human" aspects of the relationship (i.e. Kern & Willcocks, 2002; Barthelemy, 2003; Lee & Kim, 2003; Tompkins et al, 2006). Trust was widely acknowledged as a key indicator of the quality of the outsourcing relationship (i.e. Sabherwal, 1999; Barthelemy, 2001; Barthelemy, 2003). The importance of trust was widely acknowledged as a key indicator of the quality of the outsourcing relationship (i.e. Lohtia et al, 2009; Mao et al, 2008; Barthelemy, 2003). Pruitt (1981) emphasized that trust is highly related to firms' desire to collaborate while Zand (1972) highlighted the fact that its absence diminishes the effectiveness of problem solving. Anderson and Narus (1990) went a step further and noted that once trust is established "firms learn that joint efforts will lead to outcomes that exceed what the firm would achieve if it acted solely in its own best interests". Sahay et al (2003) emphasized on the dialectical relationship between trust and control and supported that the need for control can be minimized in a trusting environment.

Relationships based on mutual trust provide grounds for the development of stronger bonds between the two parties (Lee & Kim, 2003). Trust has been found to enhance co-ordination and generate loyalty among trading partners (Lohtia et al, 2009; Krishnan et al, 2006). Barthelemy (2001) highlighted even more the importance of trust in outsourcing relationships by suggesting that in essence, it constitutes the antidote to opportunism. Once a party develops trust in the other, a pattern of commonality arises and both parties become increasingly ready to work cooperatively towards established goals and objectives (Brunard & Kleiner, 1994).

Trust is also of fundamental importance to an outsourcing relationship because it is interdependent with commitment (Mohr & Spekman, 1996). Greater commitment leads to greater trust and vice versa. Either party's commitment to the outsourcing relationship is a clear indication that the party is willing to exert effort on behalf of the relationship and is motivated to make it a success (Mohr & Spekman, 1996). Furthermore, trust and relational ties were found to be particularly important in the management of uncertainty as well as the generation of co-operative norms and joint expectations of the behavior of each outsourcing partner (Zhou et al, 2008). Lohtia et al (2009) suggested that the demonstration of the supplier's capabilities and benevolent intentions to contribute to the venture are critical in breeding relations of trust.

Several authors also highlighted the importance of communication in breeding relationships based on trust and commitment (Kern & Willcocks, 2002; Sahay et al, 2003). Only through honest and ongoing exchanges of information the outsourcing relationship can be effectively monitored (Tompkins et al, 2006). The study by Kotlarsky et al (2008) on global sourcing ventures emphasized on the importance of social mechanisms of co-ordination in the generation of social capital. Knowledge sharing has also been found to be important in breeding relationships of trust (Ghosh & Scott, 2009; Kotlarsky et al, 2008; Kotlarsky & Oshri, 2005). Furthermore, communication was recognized to be key for the settlement of conflicts and misconceptions, facilitation of solutions, reduction of uncertainty and generation of flexibility (Kern & Willcocks, 2002). The quality of communication, information sharing and inter-firm adaptation were found to be important generators of trust (Mao et al, 2008). Sahay et al (2003) studied offshore software outsourcing relationships and emphasized that IS development is "communication-intensive" even in conditions of co-location and physical proximity.

Another stream of researchers though, considered the power-play between the client and the vendor to be more important in determining the outsourcing relationship. The power-play in outsourcing ventures is mainly a result of dependency and tends to cause a power-control dilemma (Easton, 1992). According to Fitzgerald and Willcocks (1994), it is difficult to maintain partnerships in the field of outsourcing due to an asymmetry of resources and in the power relationship that favors the service provider. Service receivers initially have greater influence than service providers in their relationships. As the nature of the relationship between the service receiver and the provider changes from one that is relatively independent to one that is tightly coupled, service providers are likely to gain more power since service receivers will be facing important switching costs (Lacity & Hirschheim, 1993; Fitzgerald & Willcocks, 1994). Kern & Willcocks (2002) also pointed out that in total outsourcing deals, the supplier will dominate the relationship from the start, as the client is totally dependent on the vendor's services, whereas in selective outsourcing the situation may be more balanced. More recently Heiskanen et al (2008) identified the evolving power relations between the outsourcing parties as an important determinant of their possibilities for action and behavior.

Other authors on the other hand, stressed the pursuit of mutual benefits as a factor that can generate mutual dependency. When the interests of the client and the vendor are tightly coupled, the bonds in the outsourcing relationship are enhanced. The notion is that the closeness and achievement of mutual goals, the allocation of risks and the shared responsibility, generate a strong feeling of "chemistry" that strengthens the relationship between the client and the vendor (Mohr & Spekman, 1994; Kumar & Van Dissel, 1996).

Another stream of research tried to investigate when tight contracts is more preferable as a mode of governance than softer elements such as trust. For example, Barthelemy (2003) used a high-level approach and found that a mix of contractual and relational governance was more associated with outsourcing success, rather than distinct uses of contracts of relationships as modes of governance. Beaumont and Costa (2002) focused on the type of activities outsourced and found that tight governance structures are more efficient in the case of commodity type services, while for more innovative types of service outsourcing, relational elements in the governance become more important.

From the literature review it turns out that previous research tended to treat the contractual and the relational aspects of outsourcing governance as distinct dimensions in the execution of the venture. More recently, there has been an effort towards developing a more thorough understanding on the interrelationship and interaction between the contract and the relational aspects in outsourcing. On this issue, Sullivan and Ngqenyama (2005) suggested that the use of penalties and incentives can be useful in the alignment of interests between the outsourcing parties, yielding thus relational benefits for the venture. Lee et al (2008) investigated the role of SLAs in the development of relational attributes such as trust and commitment in outsourcing. According to their findings, well-structured SLAs can breed relational attributes which are important for the success and the sustainability of the venture. The authors also suggested the importance of knowledge-sharing processes in enhancing social interaction and communication between the outsourcing partners. Mellewight et al (2007) emphasized for a need to expand "our view of contracts beyond the predominant control function". While they highlighted the role of contracts in the coordination of activities (which to a good extent constitutes a continuation of a focus on the technical or process-oriented function of contracts), they went a step further to illustrate a more relational function of contracts and more specifically their role in preventing opportunistic behavior.

Rocco (2005) found that the codification of rules and processes can become an indirect source of trust. His views are in accordance with the notion of "institutionally based trust", according to which process formalization can generate a sense of trust. Following Bijlsma-Frankema and Costa (2005), Vlaar et al (2007) elaborated on the role of formalization in the "codification and enforcement of inputs, outcomes and inter-organizational activities and tried to illustrate how it interferes with collaborative endeavors between the outsourcing partners. Regarding the role of institutional arrangements in the generation of trust, they highlighted the role of social norms around institutional arrangements which can actually generate varying degrees of embedded trust.

Zheng et al (2008) suggested that although there appears to be enough evidence to support for an integrated approach between the contractual and relational elements in outsourcing governance, there is still a lot to be learnt in relation to "how, why and when contracts and relational mechanisms complement and/or substitute for each other" (Klein Woolthuis et al., 2005 R. Klein Woolthuis, B. Hillebrand and B.Zheng, et al, 2008; Woolthuis et al, 2005).

In our research we will predominantly aim towards addressing the question of "how contracts and relational mechanisms complement and/or substitute for each other". In that respect, we will try to extend the study by Vlaar et al (2007) on the role of social norms around institutional arrangements in the generation of varying degrees of embedded trust among the outsourcing partners. In order to achieve this, we will examine the disciplinary effects of wider "outsourcing discourses" on the execution outsourcing arrangements. More specifically we will analyze the ways that the outsourcing partners are trying to exploit these "outsourcing discourses", but also escape their disciplinary effects. In our study we will not focus on the effect of these wider "outsourcing discourses" on the development of trust between the outsourcing partners, but we will try to assess their impact on different relational aspects of the venture.

3 Theory

In our study we are going to distinguish between modes of control that are established within an organization and those that come from outside. Regarding control mechanisms that are established within an organization we are going to use the notion of *systemic control* that was developed by Pennings and Woiceshyn (1987). *Systemic* control constitutes a shift from personal and direct forms of control to more impersonal and indirect forms of control. These are emerged in three structural properties of organizations, namely *technology, social structure* and *culture.* In our analysis we will focus on the systemic forms of control through *social structure* and *culture.* Control through *social structure* is embedded in to a firm's policies, processes, procedures, rules and so on. Control through *culture* operates through shared norms and values that shape behavior and influence individual activity. As far as control mechanisms outside an organization are concerned we will analyze *professional modes* of control. These refer to commonly accepted practices within a professional body or an industry.

Our research will adopt a Foucauldian view on power relations. For Foucault, the "sovereign" view of power that refers to situations of absolute domination constitutes a very constraint view on how power operates. For him, power relations is rather a dynamic set of relationships that is constantly changing from one point in time to the next. He suggested that such power relations do not need to be experienced negatively and highlighted that apart from its constraining character, power can have productive results. Regarding its constraining character, Foucault suggested that in addition to "sovereign" forms of power where power is exercised directly from those with authority, there is a form of "disciplinary" power which is exercised indirectly through a range of mechanisms and institutions and not directly or physically from individuals. Contrary to the "sovereign" form of power, "disciplinary" power is less visible and operates through the neutrality and objectivity of apparatuses of knowledge or ethics. Along these lines, we will analyze how systemic and professional forms of control (i.e. indirect forms of control that are not exercised directly from an authorized individual to the other) are enmeshing and influencing the evolution of the outsourcing venture.

Regarding the productive character of power, we will refer to the Foucauldian notion of a "discourse". Foucault has attributed a variety of meanings to the notion of "discourse" and similarly to Knights and Morgan (1991) we are not going to attempt a detailed discussion of these meanings or establish a "correct" definition of discourse. Similarly to Knights and Morgan (1991) in our study we will conceive discourse as "a set of ideas and practices which condition our ways of relating to, and acting upon, particular phenomena". On this basis a "discourse" constitutes a way of seeing which is embedded in social practices and is reproduced by them (Knights & Morgan, 1991).

"Discourse can be both an instrument and an effect of power, but also a hindrance, a block, a point of resistance and a starting point for an opposing strategy" (Foucault, 1980). In other words, power works through discourse to shape popular attitudes towards phenomena. In such a way, discourses can be used as a powerful tool to shape behavior. However, expert discourses are very often opposed by competing discourses that create ways for escaping discipline. On this basis, in our study we will illustrate how "outsourcing discourses" shape and discipline behavior for outsourcing partners, but also how possibilities to escape discipline are being generated.

4 Methodology

Against this theoretical background we produced a case study of a European insurance company that will be named DUTCH. The case is anonymized for the purposes of publication at the request of the insurance company and its suppliers. We studied the outsourcing experiences of DUTCH from 2004 to 2009. In particular we focused on three outsourcing arrangements operational from January 2008, the contracts, governance structures and processes, and how these were utilized and with what outcomes over the first two years of five year contracts.

Our data collection methods included documents and a total of twenty four interviews. More specifically, we examined the outsourcing contracts in order to get an in-depth understanding of the formal processes through which governance was enacted. The interviews helped us to investigate how governance worked in action. We included the perspectives both from the client and the suppliers' organizations, which is relatively rare in the outsourcing literature. The roles of our research participants included:

- Three client contract managers (one for each of the outsourcing arrangements under investigation)
- Four client IT managers
- Two client sector managers (responsible for outsourcing arrangements)
- One client senior IT manager
- One client business manager
- One client lawyer
- One client process analyst

- One contract manager from Supplier A
- One contract manager from Supplier B
- One client director from Supplier B
- One senior business manager from Supplier C

We also conducted follow-up interviews with seven of our research participants (namely with the client senior IT manager, the three client contract managers, the client sector manager, the contract manager form Supplier A and the client director from Supplier B).

Interestingly, we found that similar governance structures and control processes existed among the client and its three suppliers, nevertheless these produced different experiences. To the best of our knowledge, this is the first study that has attempted such a comparison. The next section will provide a thorough presentation of our data related to the outsourcing governance between the insurance company and its three suppliers. Initially we will provide a background to our study in order to illustrate the outsourcing experience and governance challenges of the client organization. We will proceed with organizing our data along the dimensions of the emergent systemic and professional modes of control and we will include a brief section on specific issues with the suppliers that the client faced. Our analysis will draw on these results and depict how wider "outsourcing discourses" shape and discipline the behavior of outsourcing partners, but also how possibilities to escape discipline are being created.

5 Case Study

Background
DUTCH engaged for the first time on an outsourcing arrangement in 2004. Its first outsourcing contract was on the mainframe environment with Supplier A. During the first year of the outsourcing arrangement the performance of the supplier was not reaching the desirable levels but it did stabilize latter on. After this initial get-to-know period, the venture appeared to work effectively, the value of the outsourcing contract grew from about 20 million in 2004 to 80 million in 2009 and Supplier A became from number ten, the number one vendor of DUTCH. While the governance seemed to work and the performance of Supplier A was good, about late November 2007, DUTCH decided to outsource on three contracts including the one that they had with Supplier A. The two additional suppliers were Supplier B for office supplies and Supplier C for networks. At some stage, Supplier B were taken over by Supplier C but operated as an independent organization.

While DUTCH has been satisfied with Supplier A it faced a lot of issues in bringing the outsourcing arrangements with Supplier B and Supplier C to a desirable level of performance. Around January 2008 DUTCH was in chaos internally. And although there was a strong governance process put in place, this was not completely enacted. So far as the governance in place was not enacted, it was not particularly effective in terms of motivating either the performance of Supplier B or of Supplier C. Gradually DUTCH realized the importance of keeping a tight control over its outsourcing arrangements. The company built up their own internal management capability which however still does not seem to be strong enough. While DUTCH activated much more of the governance procedures, it also realized that the formal governance itself was not actually going to solve all of its issues. Thus, the company started to focus on other more relational aspects of the venture, including the cultural attitude of Supplier B and Supplier C.

Although performance issues with Supplier C appeared to be resolved to some extent, things never really improved with Supplier B. The performance of Supplier B was consistently unsatisfactory, to the point where the exit clause could be triggered in fact if they wanted, even though they are still in transition. Interestingly, there appear to be some ironies about governance. Firstly, it does not appear that there were many weaknesses in their governance procedures and processes, although the DUTCH representatives did admit to a couple of improvements that could be made. As an example of such improvements, some of the metrics were probably not disaggregated enough to actually challenge the supplier on exactly where they were failing. Furthermore, these metrics were averaged too much so that supplier performance looked quite good at a general level and was actually teasing out why there was such a level of disappointment about some parts of the supplier's performance.

An explanation for the consistently bad performance of supplier B was that there was an important internal struggle within the organization. It appeared that the energy and the resources of the company were being used up internally. Consequently, when it got to Supplier B facing the customer, the people did what they could but they were getting no support and no empowerment to get resources or to solve problems from the rest of the Supplier B factory. And where the tension should have been between the customer facing manager and the operations manager of Supplier B, the tension actually ended up between customer facing manager and the Supplier B factory. To make matters worse, the person in charge (it is worthwhile noting on this issue that three people undertook this role subsequently within two years) did not have enough power to actually influence getting the resources or getting solutions to the problems he was having to face. The only way that DUTCH really brought the attention to the issues was by going straight to the vice president of Supplier B and say: "look, you actually need to do something about this because no one else is doing anything about it". And that was the only time the DUTCH actually got his attention. So that was an event outside the governance structure and there was an attempt to go straight to the top of Supplier B.

Interestingly the financial aspects of motivation were not that critical for Supplier B according to our DUTCH interviewees. They seemed to think that DUTCH put the incentives in the contract to motivate innovation and encourage the anticipation of problems. Along these lines, they did not seem to think that it was the financial aspects that were explaining poor performance. They regarded that the problem was Supplier B itself being in chaos. It seemed to be related to the way that Supplier B was organized in terms of silos and not being really customer focused but being mainly product focused.

DUTCH interviewees also pointed out that although they transferred all the DUTCH staff to Supplier B by mid-January 2008, by July 2008 those people that had initially formed a customer focused group back to DUTCH, all of them were latter moved into the Supplier B factory. As a result, the knowledge, the motivation, the incentive and the relationship they had with DUTCH had gone completely.

Thus, while new people were coming in DUTCH from the suppliers' companies, DUTCH was not operating a governance structure which was exactly the point in time where it really needed to have some level of stability in its processes. However, it is actually when new people are coming in a project that stronger and tighter governance processes need to be followed.

No one really explained why that happened, why those people went off the contract, relatively soon after they went into Supplier B. This could be attributed to different reasons for example, some reorganizing inside Supplier B, the redistribution of workforces and probably some people that were particularly good were used for other contracts. While it is difficult to explain why these people left the contract, their movement clearly impinged upon the relationship. Having the same people would stabilize the relationship, establish the commitment of the workforce and would have enabled them to build knowledge on their client. This knowledge was lost during transition because of the change of people in these roles.

For a long time (approximately 18 months) the governance structures although they appeared sound and reasonable, they were not really operationalized. DUTCH was facing many problems in the mean time but they were dealing with them reactively. In time DUTCH realized that a reactive relationship-based approach was not effective enough and realized that they had to reinitiate their governance structures and hierarchies. This happened under the new IT director.

Regarding the formal governance in place, the four major challenges that DUTCH is focusing upon include:

1. Improved governance and communication
2. Information accuracy that is coming out of report meetings (i.e. how factual information is, clarity of information, what decisions were made, what was wanted, what was unwanted etc).
3. Need for more detailed metrics and measurement.
4. Different interpretations of the contract which were mainly around the annexes.

Although a number of our research participants within DUTCH recognized the importance of dealing with these governance challenges, they also appeared to be very much concerned about the general attitude and culture of Supplier B and Supplier C. These misfits were reported as major reasons why the outsourcing arrangements with Supplier B and Supplier C have not successful and will be further discussed latter on.

Systemic Control Through Rules and Procedures

At present, DUTCH is getting more and more interested in fulfilling their governance structure and introducing much more detailed metrics as a way of gaining further control over their outsourcing arrangements. Their current governance structure includes three levels: the operational level (issues of discussion involve day to day business and service levels), the tactical level (this level deals with a more general overview of management of processes and their impact) and the strategic level (discussions between directors regarding the vision and strategic direction of their organizations).

Apart from the formal KPIs and SLAs that each of the vendors is expected to achieve, there are some softer criteria upon which the suppliers are being assessed.

Within DUTCH these softer criteria appear to be more important at the moment. These soft KPIs which are called "Strategic Performance Indicators" (SPIs) are also contracted and they are concerned with issues such as on-time delivery, on budget and so on. DUTCH has credits on the KPIs and bonuses on the SPIs. According to the DUTCH lawyer the SPIs are not really used the way they were meant to, and they are not focusing on issues such as innovation.

The customer satisfaction survey is another formal procedure aimed at controlling the outcomes of vendor performance. However, according to a number of our DUTCH interviewees the customer satisfaction survey was constructed in such a way that it did not reflect the real performance of Supplier B and Supplier C. In other words, while the customer satisfaction survey produced a relatively satisfactory image it did not reflect the real situation with Supplier B and Supplier C, just because of its content and structure.

Furthermore, in June 2009, DUTCH introduced two new key performance indicators on service requests and incident management that were not there before. This is an indication that there was a luck of detail in the governance in terms of metrics in the original contract.

Another tool for governing and stirring the behavior of suppliers is the "innovation tool". More specifically, there is an innovation budget both on DUTCH and on the vendor side. Inside DUTCH there is also a mechanism to decide what part of its budget will be used for innovation projects and what part will be used for other kind of projects. The innovation board at DUTCH decides how this budget is going to be spent. If the vendor performs well, then they get a bigger share of the DUTCH part of the innovation and contribute less themselves. More specifically, the SPIs are attached to the outsourcing goals and based on the scores on these indicators the budget is split between DUTCH and its suppliers. In other words, DUTCH has a reservation for money and the vendors have some kind of pre-sales money in the contract. This mechanism was meant to incentivize suppliers as DUTCH would spend more on the innovation projects with the vendor that is performing well. At the moment however this mechanism has not been implemented completely because of problems of getting reports on KPIs and SPIs. It also appears that the suppliers of DUTCH are not particularly triggered to achieve innovation.

Additionally, during the period of transition, the existence of an inadequate retained function with inadequate benchmarks and measurements gave the chance to suppliers to take advantage of the situation. On this basis, both Supplier B and Supplier C have been doing bad (Supplier C to a lesser extent) and have been taking every opportunity to have excuses so as to why their performance was poor. In essence, they were trying to escape responsibility for their poor performance.

Systemic Control Through Culture

A major issue appears to be that the DUTCH culture did not really support a disciplinary form of outsourcing. This might be partly because they have some DUTCH people to the suppliers and thus these people continued working on the basis of personal relationships with their former colleagues and not contracts. It might also be partly because DUTCH appears to be more in favor of an informal culture and way of doing business. Thus, although the company adopted formal aspects in sourcing their IT, they did not necessarily change the way that they managed or treated people.

This might be an important reason that the relationship with Supplier B and Supplier C run into problems. In other words, the DUTCH culture was moved into the suppliers as well in their service delivery units through the people transfer, running an extension of the belief that this was not really outsourcing culturally. In this way, DUTCH did not take the advantages of being more formalized and more disciplined. Thus, it appears that DUTCH was running into problems because they were in a different situation from the one where the culture would have worked – i.e. having totally internal delivery of the management.

Furthermore, a number of our respondents within DUTCH appeared to be concerned about cultural misfits between their company and Supplier B and with Supplier C as well. As an example, one senior IT manager from DUTCH very vividly emphasized: "*Supplier C is the largest network provider in the Netherlands.... Sometimes they behave as if DUTCH should be thankful for the time they spend*". With the same spirit, a number of interviewees characterized the culture within Supplier B and Supplier C as arrogant. In particular, the DUTCH contract managers for Supplier B and Supplier C were repeatedly mentioning their frustration with the culture and attitude of the vendors they were managing. To make matters worse, neither Supplier B nor Supplier C were indicating any proactive signs of behavior. This caused a big frustration among our DUTCH research participants as a proactive attitude constituted a major expectation for them. They also supported that a major reason that their organizations could not serve DUTCH well enough was that DUTCH had a culture of not being open enough about its operations and business. The climate between DUTCH, Supplier B and Supplier C was under a lot of tension. This atmosphere in conjunction with the on-going operational problems of the outsourcing arrangements did not leave space to consider issues such as the accomplishment of innovation, which led to further frustration the managers from the DUTCH.

Another major issue had been the culture of competition between the three suppliers. Although it has been more than two years that the three suppliers of DUTCH have been trying to work together, they are still competing. According to the DUTCH vendor manager of the Supplier A, this competition among the three suppliers instead of settling down it has actually gotten worse. What is even more intriguing is that competition appeared to exist even among Supplier B and Supplier C that have become one company.

Professional Modes of Control

Regarding professional modes of control in outsourcing, it could be suggested that so far there have not been any firmly established standards. While organizations like the National Outsourcing Institute in the UK or the International Association for Outsourcing Professionals are trying to set out some points of reference for "outsourcing professionals", it appears that we are relatively far from establishing a framework of professional codes for outsourcing practitioners.

In our study "professional modes" of control will be referring to some more general professional principles, codes and attitudes in conducting business. For example, industry regulations imposed on DUTCH the responsibility to use KPMG as an independent institute to audit the management competency for IT within DUTCH and also of the suppliers in terms of processes they followed. It appears however that one of the weaknesses of that governance required by regulation, is that it did not audit performance, it only audited the framework in which good performance should occur. For this reason, these audits and controls were not helping much in the cases of Supplier B and Supplier C where performance was below the desirable levels.

There was also a customer contact group that appeared to exercise to a good extent some indirect control over the perception of Supplier B. This was a discussion group which some of the DUTCH employees belong to. In this way DUTCH realized that their problems were not unique and that there were other customers of Supplier B that were similarly dissatisfied.

Additionally, there was a national survey in the Netherlands which included information on the largest Dutch suppliers, including Supplier B. According to this survey, the performance of Supplier B had been very low and a very high percentage of Dutch managers had responded that they would not recommend this company to their colleagues.

6 Analysis

Partnering discourse

One of the biggest discourses in outsourcing is partnering. Both clients and suppliers talk about it and it appears they do recognize it as an important facilitator for their relationship. This outsourcing discourse in essence conditions their expectations right at the front and it constitutes a philosophy whose significance for doing business can hardly be questioned. Partnering signals a special business relationship and managers across sectors would agree that it is a very desirable element in their inter-organizational arrangements. Partnering as a business philosophy creates specific expectations, attitudes, cultures and belief systems that are relatively common, widely accepted and constitutes a way of stirring and disciplining behavior. This kind of disciplining can be seen as an instance of Foucault's disciplinary power (1980) in that power operates in an indirect way through the ethics and good principles of conducting business. However, while this outsourcing discourse probably constitutes a means to bring organizations and people closer, its main value and contribution may or may not come depending on how partnering is actually enacted. On this basis, what is particularly important is what alternative or competing discourses and rationalities around ethics and good principles of conducting business come into play.

The client organization and Supplier A appeared to have a partnership approach into outsourcing that worked for both. However, we found that the cultural misfits between the client organization and Suppliers B and C did not allow for the enactment of a partnership behavior that complies with the commonly accepted standards of partnerships. Although our respondents from these organizations tended to have a compatible view on what partnership is, the cultures within their organizations had important misfits that did not allow for the enactment of a partnership as they defined it. For example, a number of our respondents from DUTCH tended to view the culture of Suppliers B and Supplier C as arrogant. They felt that although Supplier B and Supplier C should give some relative priority and importance to the needs of DUTCH, this was never happening. On the other hand, our representatives from Supplier B and Supplier C tended to complain about messy requirements on behalf of the customer and for the unwillingness of the customer to be open with their business.

Another discourse around outsourcing is that in essence the outsourcing arrangement constitutes a commercial business relationship. Thus, management has to be very focused into measurement, explicit control, KPIs, SPIs, customer satisfaction surveys and benchmarking as well as make performance more concrete and more transparent. These processes appeared to work well with Supplier A. In particular, the contract manager from Supplier A had actually commented on the importance of some of these mechanisms in getting the outsourcing venture on track.

The case was not the same however with Supplier B and Supplier C. For example, the customer satisfaction survey constituted a tool for DUTCH to evaluate the performance of its suppliers. Nevertheless, it appeared that this tool was not properly constructed to reflect the real performance of the suppliers. What finally tended to happen was that managers within Supplier B and Supplier C were trying to partially mask and justify their underperformance. In other words, they were trying to identify all sorts of loopholes in order to try to make themselves look better and escape their responsibilities. Interestingly, although there was evidence for Supplier B that its organization is underperforming across its clients in the Netherlands, its managers would still try to present a better picture of how things really were.

The same issues were coming up with Supplier B and Supplier C due to the poor KPIs, SPIs and measurements. It appears that because the contractual agreement was not precise enough, Supplier B and Supplier C were trying to find ways of escaping. Outsourcing is heavily dependent upon measurement and probably some measurements (i.e. hours between service failure and recovery, network availability and so on) can be very objective. But the integration of these data can be tricky and outsourcing partners are going to use the data in the way that enhances their power status over the relationship. Following Foucault's notion on disciplinary power (1980), discipline is enacted through the objectivity and neutrality of knowledge generated by scientific processes. However, when the results of these scientific processes come into question, not because the measurements have not necessarily been correct, but because the data have presumably not been integrated in a correct manner, the possibility to escape discipline is being created. Thus, Supplier B and Supplier C found excuses to escape discipline and justify their actions even though it was manifestly obvious that they were not actually meeting the performance they had agreed. They were empowering themselves to get away from the disciplinary process of what the service level agreements and other measurements represented.

Discourses on core competencies

One of the main drivers for outsourcing has been the need for a company to focus on its core competencies. In other words, the idea was that it is in the benefit of a company to specialize on what is doing best, exploit its key capabilities and competencies and create expertise that it will be very difficult for other organizations to outperform. The notion of the "core competencies" has been grounded on the seminal work of Prahalad and Hamel (1990) who supported the focus on a company's core business and the outsourcing of its secondary (or non-core) activities.

One of the reasons that DUTCH engaged into outsourcing in the first place back in 2004 was the fact that it wanted to focus on its core competencies. The DUTCH vendor manager of the Supplier A contract mentioned: "*A basic reason we decided to outsource was... almost every company says that "it is not our core competency*".

However, a common mistake that clients do is that they do not retain enough of the IT function. While IT plays a supporting function in many industries, including the insurance industry that we have studied, its significance for the execution of the front-office services is vital. From our case it appears that DUTCH did not have a good understanding of the processes it outsourced. The DUTCH contract manager of Supplier B referred to the outsourced activities as “garbage”. Outsourcing a set of processes over the client it-self has not managed to have an adequate understanding very often leads to messier situations. Along these lines, not only the underperformance of Supplier B could have been partially anticipated but also the fact that Supplier B will be empowered to escape responsibility for underperforming.

The second element in this discourse is related to a firm taking advantage and exploiting the core competencies and expertise of its supplying organizations. Very often customers want a reduction in cost together with innovation which to some extent are exclusive of one another. On this basis, customers want cost together with innovation and while there is a trade-off there, they are not very often willing to take it. The managers of DUTCH would very often refer to cost savings they wanted to achieve through outsourcing but also on the fact that they contracted for innovation that they never received. It appears that the managers of DUTCH had a mindset that their suppliers should be responsible for bringing new and innovative ideas for the business of DUTCH. This is what the DUTCH managers were referring to, when they were complaining that their suppliers do not show any signs of proactive behavior.

7 Conclusions

From our research it appears that there are wider discourses around outsourcing that shape the behavior of clients and suppliers. One discourse encompasses expectations around trust, commitment, collaboration and investments in the relationship that affects the conduct of outsourcing clients and suppliers. An alternative discourse views outsourcing as a transactional business relationship and thus focuses onto measurements, benchmarking and other formal controls. However, the way that these discourses are enacted and compete with alternative discourses held to be rational create avenues that very often are being used by the outsourcing partners to escape discipline and accountability.

Further discourses on outsourcing are related to core-competencies and the reduction of cost. The discourse around core-competencies involves the idea that a firm should concentrate on what it does best and outsource its secondary activities. However, in this case the management of the retained function is key for the client for two reasons: first, the client is enabled to keep a better control of the outsourcing service they receive and secondly, the supplier is disempowered from escaping responsibility when performing poorly. The discourse around the reduction of cost encompasses the wide-spread idea that outsourcing will lead to major cost savings. While this appears to be accepted as a legitimate idea among our respondents both in the client and the suppliers’ organizations, issues appear to be arising in relation to the innovative efforts from the suppliers.

We also found that the relational dimensions of governance are of vital importance for the management of the outsourcing relationship. The hardcore governance framework by itself can not really substitute for these mechanisms. While it is an enabling framework in terms of governing it does not go beyond the very formal way of operating. This finding adds to the literature that supports the complementarily between formal and relational governance.

Regarding the information of management and practice, according to our findings, it appears that when the outsourcing venture runs into turbulence, it is the relational governance where the outsourcing partners have to do most of the work. From our research it turned out that the formal governance process can be relatively constrained to fix relationship problems. They establish a framework for action but if performance is very low or the relationship is very poor, the formal governance mechanisms can not do much to bring the outsourcing venture on track. This is a finding that should alert practitioners about the importance of on-going relational governance as the essence of keeping and retaining personnel with the relevant skills to such posts.

References

Allery, P.: Effective Outsourcing: Practice and Procedures. Pagination, UK (2004)

Andersen, T., Christensen, M.: Contract Renewal Under Uncertainty. Journal of Economic Dynamics and Control 26(4), 637–652 (2002)

Anderson, J.C., Narus, J.A.: A Model of Distributor Firm and Manufacturer Firm Working Partnerships. Journal of Marketing 54(1), 42–68 (1990)

Aubert, B., Houde, J.F., Patry, M., Rivard, S.: Characteristics of IT Outsourcing Contracts. In: Proceedings of the 36th HICSS (2003)

Barthelemy, J.: The Hidden Costs of IT Outsourcing. Sloan Management Review 42(3), 60–69 (2001)

Barthelemy, J.: The Hard and Soft Sides of IT Outsourcing Management. European Management Journal 2(5), 539–548 (2003)

Beaumont, N., Costa, C.: Information technology outsourcing in Australia. Information Resources Management Journal 15(3), 14–31 (2002)

Bennedsen, M., Schultz, C.: Adaptive Contracting: The Trial and Error Approach to Outsourcing. Economic Theory 25(1), 35–50 (2005)

Beulen, E., Ribbers, P.: IT Outsourcing Contracts: Practical Implications of the Incomplete Contract Theory. In: Proceedings of the 36th HICSS (2003)

Deloitte: Why Settle For Less?: Deloitte Consulting 2008 Outsourcing Report (2008), `http://www.deloitte.com/assets/DcomSweden/Local%20Assets/Documents/se_survey_why_settle_for_less_050208.pdf`

Foucault, M.: Power/Knowledge: Selected Interviews and Other Writings 1972-1977. Harvester, London (1980)

Fitzgerald, G., Willcocks, L.: Contract and Partnerships in the Outsourcing of IT. In: Proceedings of the Fifteenth ICIS, Vancouver, British Columbia (1994)

Gietzmann, M.B.: Incomplete Contracts and the Make or Buy Decision: Governance Design and Attainable Flexibility. Accounting, Organizations and Society 21(6), 611–626 (1996)

IAOP: The, IAOP Governance Forum (2008), `http://www.outsourcingprofessional.org/content/23/154/1607/`

Kern, T., Willcocks, L.: Exploring Information Technology Outsourcing Relationships: Theory and Practice. Strategic Information Systems 9, 321–350 (2000)

Kern, T., Willcocks, L.: Exploring Relationships In Information Technology Outsourcing: The Interaction Approach. European Journal of Information Systems 11(1), 3–19 (2002)

Kumar, K., Van Dissel, H.G.: Sustainable Collaboration: Managing Conflict and Cooperation in Interorganizational Systems. MIS Quarterly 20(3), 279–300 (1996)
Lee, J.N., Kim, Y.G.: Effect of Partnership Quality on IS Outsourcing Success: Conceptual Framework and Empirical Validation. Journal of Management Information Systems 15(4), 29–61 (1999)
Lee, J.N., Kim, Y.G.: Exploring a Causal Model for the Understanding of Outsourcing Partnership. In: Proceedings of the 36th HICSS (2003)
Lee, J.N., Minh, H.M., Hirschheim, R.: An Integrative Model of Trust on IT Outsourcing: Examining a Bilateral Perspective. Information Systems Frontiers 10, 145–163 (2008)
McFarlan, W., Nolan, R.: How to Manage an IT Outsourcing Alliance. Sloan Management Review 36(2), 9–23 (1995)
Mohr, J.J., Spekman, R.E.: Characteristics of Partnership Success: Partnership Attributes, Communication Behavior, and Conflict Resolution Techniques. Strategic Management Journal 15(2), 135–152 (1994)
Mohr, J.J., Spekman, R.E.: Perfecting Partnerships. Marketing Management 4(4), 34–43 (1996)
Parkhe, A.: Strategic Alliances Structuring: a Game-theoretic and Transaction Cost Examination of Interfirm Cooperation. Academy of Management Journal 36(4), 794–829 (1993)
Pennings, J.M., Woiceshyn, J.: A Typology of Organizational Control and its Metaphors in Bacharach, S.B., Mitchell, S.M.: Research in the Sociology of Organizations, Greenwich, pp. 73–104 (1987)
Pruitt, D.: Negotiation Behavior. Academic Press, New York (1981)
Rocco, E.: Trust, Distance and Common Ground. In: Bijlsma- Frankema, K.M., Klein Woolthuis, R.J.A. (eds.) Trust under Pressure: Empirical Investigations of the Functioning of Trust and Trust Building in Uncertain Circumstances, pp. 186–205. Edward Elgar (2005)
Sahay, S., Nicholson, B., Krishna, S.: Global IT Outsourcing – Software Development Across Borders. Cambridge University Press, UK (2003)
Sabherwal, R.: The Role of Trust in Outsourced IS Development Projects. Communications of the ACM 42(2), 80–86 (1999)
Saunders, C., Gebelt, M., Hu, Q.: Achieving Success in Information Systems Outsourcing. California Management Review 39(2), 63–79 (1997)
Tompkins, J., Simonson, S., Tompkins, W., Upchurch, B.: Creating and Outsourcing Relationship. Supply Chain Management Review 10(2), 52–58 (2006)
Zand, D.: Trust and Managerial Problem Solving. Administrative Science Quarterly 17(2), 229–239 (1972)

Governance of Offshore IT Outsourcing at Shell Global Functions IT-BAM Development and Application of a Governance Framework to Improve Outsourcing Relationships

Floor de Jong[1], Jos van Hillegersberg[2], Pascal van Eck[2], Feiko van der Kolk[1], and Rene Jorissen[1]

[1] Shell International B.V., PO Box 162, 2501 AN The Hague, The Netherlands
floor.dejong@shell.com
[2] Center of Telematics and IT, University of Twente, PO box 217, 7500 EA, Enschede, The Netherlands

Abstract. The lack of effective IT governance is widely recognized as a key inhibitor to successful global IT outsourcing relationships. In this study we present the development and application of a governance framework to improve outsourcing relationships. The approach used to developing an IT governance framework includes a meta model and a customization process to fit the framework to the target organization. The IT governance framework consists of four different elements (1) organisational structures, (2) joint processes between in- and outsourcer, (3) responsibilities that link roles to processes and (4) a diverse set of control indicators to measure the success of the relationship. The IT governance framework is put in practice in Shell GFIT BAM, a part of Shell that concluded to have a lack of management control over at least one of their outsourcing relationships. In a workshop the governance framework was used to perform a gap analysis between the current and desired governance. Several gaps were identified in the way roles and responsibilities are assigned and joint processes are set-up. Moreover, this workshop also showed the usefulness and usability of the IT governance framework in structuring, providing input and managing stakeholders in the discussions around IT governance.

1 Introduction

Gartner (2005) observed that organisations generally do not have the proper governance in place, especially when the organisation is involved in outsourcing. “Through 2008, poor sourcing decisions will diminish the achievable value of services in 80 percent of service deals (0.7 probability)”. As a result, organizations involved in outsourcing face lost opportunities, higher costs and many risks.

Shell Global Functions IT Business Application Management (BAM) is no exception. This part of Shell concluded recently that management control over at least one of their outsourcing relationships needed to be improved and required comprehensive governance of the outsourcing relationship. In this study we report on the effort by Shell BAM to assess and improve current outsourcing governance practices.

I. Oshri and J. Kotlarsky (Eds.): Global Sourcing 2010, LNBIP 55, pp. 119–150, 2010.

To better understand the need for outsourcing governance we start by reviewing outsourcing risks. These risks can occur during the contracting phase and after an outsourcing relationship is set up. We focus on the latter, as many organisations, including BAM, face the largest challenges after contracts have been signed. Furthermore we focus on a body shop relation, in contrast with for example a Managed Service relationship. In a body shop relation the outsourcer hires a specific amount of FTEs from an insourcer, while in a Managed Service relation they outsource a complete set of services and the amount of FTEs is not relevant. Beulen et al. (2006) provides a comprehensive overview of outsourcing risks categories (see Table 1).

Table 1. Partnership management risk categories (Beulen et al. 2006)

Risk category	Aspects requiring attention
Cost control	IT service delivery costs must be controlled.
Management control	The service recipient must clearly define the role of the service provider and manage the details and specifics of their service delivery.
Demand management	Service recipients need service delivery interfaces, both for their company's divisions and the provider.
Priority	The service provider must assign sufficient priority to the recipient's needs.
Confidentiality	No confidential information may be divulged to outsiders or unauthorized persons.
Information requirements definition	Service recipients must be able to define which IT services their providers must supply.
Business knowledge	Service providers must have sufficient knowledge of their client's business to ensure continuity in the delivery of the services needed.
Business dynamics	Service providers and the contracts made with them must never hinder the recipient adapting the delivery requirements as a consequence of business management changes.
Innovation	Service providers must regularly introduce new technologies in order to make possible and stimulate the recipient's innovation processes.
Vendor lock-in	Service recipient must always be able to change providers, and must not become dependent on any one supplier.

Furthermore, Beulen mentions five possible disadvantages of outsourcing that directly link to these risks. These disadvantages are (1) the increased dependence on suppliers, which is related to the risk category 'vendor lock-in' mentioned above, (2) a loss of knowledge and know-how, which is linked to 'business knowledge', (3) higher costs that is linked to 'cost control', (4) confidentiality risks that have clear overlap with 'confidentiality' and finally (5) difficulty in selecting the right service provider, which is a contracting risk instead of a managing risk.

Cross-checking this framework with risks that other authors define learn that Beulen's framework covers all risks. According to Yang "the most prominent risks in outsourcing are information security concerns and loss of management control" (Yang et al. 2007), which belong to respectively the second and the fifth category

Beulen mentions. King states that firms have higher risks in general when they have a higher dependence on the offshore vendor, which lands in the category 'vendor lock-in' (King et al. 2008).

Also Aron (2005) mentions that vendor lock-in is likely to happen, because "as outsourcing contracts mature, the power in relationships shifts from the buyers to the sellers", which means that "they cannot bring those processes back into the organization on short notice". This is what Aron calls a structural risk, because it appears on the long term. Another structural risk is that "rivals may steal their intellectual property and proprietary processes if they transfer processes offshore, especially to emerging markets", part of Beulen's risk category 'confidentiality'. As opposed to structural risks Aron identifies operational risks that are more critical in the initial stages of offshoring and outsourcing. One of the reasons for operational risks is the lack of effective, complete metrics because then the outsourcer has no idea of how the insourcer executed the work compared to how they did it themselves. This risk belongs to the category 'management control'. The second reason for operational risks is that knowledge and tasks are not codified or codifiable. This means that "service providers won't be able to execute business processes as well as their employees perform them in-house" and that there has to be room for a learning curve of the insourcer's employees. This falls under Beulen's category 'business knowledge'. Structural risks are caused by the extent to which you can measure the process quality (as with operational risks) and the ability to monitor work (Aron et al. 2005).

Research by Lacity confirms this. She states that "in the offshore outsourcing market, knowledge transfer has been one of the biggest impediments to success", which falls in the category 'business knowledge'. Furthermore, she also mentions high turnover as a risk, whereby interesting work is the key to prevent it (Lacity et al. 2008). Also Mirani (2007) recognises the problem of turnover, stating that rival vendors recruit staff away with 15-20% higher salaries, causing staff attrition rates to be as high as 45% (Mirani 2007).

Shell BAM's assessment of one of their outsourcing relationships revealed that some of the outsourcing risks were clearly present. There was a need to improve outsourcing governance to be able to prevent these risks to decrease the benefits of outsourcing and to mitigate these risks whenever they would occur. The research project we report on in this paper aims at identifying a framework that could guide Shell BAM in improving the governance of the service provision relationship with the insourcer.

Many authors stress the importance of good IT governance in outsourcing relationships. According to King "the offshoring of information systems and services has been one of the most discussed phenomena in IS [(Information Systems)] in recent years; it has significantly influenced the thinking of both academics and practitioners" (King et al. 2008). First, day-to-day outsourcing relations will be improved because an insourcer's activities can be closely monitored and coordinated (Gopal et al. 2003). Secondly, good governance will improve the chance on success of (offshore) outsourcing; several authors report that the fate of offshoring strategies is decided by the governance choices (Aron et al. 2005; Kern et al. 2001). Thirdly and finally, it has been argued that good outsourcing governance will help organisations to prevent poor management of interfirm relationships, which result in lower market value on the long term (Holcomb et al. 2007).

While much has been published on outsourcing benefits, contracting and risks, the topic of governing the outsourcing relationship has received less attention. As will be shown in section 3, governance literature mainly provides generic management frameworks and high-level best practices. In the Shell BAM project it became apparent that the current body of knowledge on governance of IT outsourcing did not provide enough guidance to design and implement governance structures. Shell BAM expressed the need for a generic but customizable framework that could be easily applied to improve the governance of the service provision relationship with the insourcer. Such a framework should help in setting up governance especially in areas were risks are likely to occur or would have a large impact. As no such method or framework could be found, it was decided to develop such a framework in this research.

The following research question was devised: *How can a generic but customizable framework be developed to aid an organisation in improving the governance of the service provision relationship with the insourcer?*

The remainder of this paper describes the research approach (section 2), research on IT governance (section 3), the development of the framework (section 3 and 4) and the application of the framework to Shell BAM (Section 5).The final section presents conclusion and future research.

2 Research Approach

We follow a design science research approach as described by Hevner et al. (2004). Design research aims to achieve both rigor and relevance. "Design Science creates and evaluates IT artifacts intended to solve identified organizational problems" (Hevner et al. 2004). The artefact created in this research is the IT governance framework. Following the design science tradition, the requirements for the artifact are set by business needs, which are elicited by interviewing experts both inside and outside Shell. Also according to design science principles, we apply theories from the IT governance and outsourcing knowledge base to design the artefact. The artefact is assessed by applying it to the Shell BAM situation and by running a workshop with stakeholders to test its usability and understandability. Finally, as suggested by the design science approach, steps to implement the framework in BAM are suggested and contributions to the current literature are presented. Table 2 describes how the research approach adheres to the design guidelines expressed by Hevner et al (2004).

Figure 1 shows the steps in the research approach sequentially over time. The arrows show the outcomes needed in order to reach the goal, according to the technique as described by Verschuren and Doorewaard (1999).

Figure 1 shows that *(a)* a literature exploration about IT outsourcing will enable us to define our IT governance meta model. *(b)* The combination of this meta model with information from theory, the market and within Shell will enable us to define a generic IT governance framework. *(c)* Application of this framework on the current situation of Shell will test and demonstrate that *(d)* the framework is useful for workshops, being both generic and customizable.

Table 2. How the research approach follows design science guidelines

Design Science Guideline	**How the guideline is applied in this research**
Design as an Artifact	A customizable IT governance framework is created
Problem Relevance	The main problem of this research is both important and relevant to Shell GFIT BAM and comparable businesses that aim to improve their outsourcing governance. Experts internal to Shell and external experts on outsourcing were interviewed
Design Evaluation	In this research we performed a workshop with various stakeholders in Shell GFIT BAM to use and evaluate the IT governance framework
Research Contributions	The main contribution of the research is the Design Artefact itself, being the IT governance model. A customizable governance framework that is tested in and documented is currently lacking in literature
Design as a Search Process	Because researches have a certain scope and assumptions about the problem space, existing artifacts may not directly solve a problem in practice. The practical requirements guided us towards striving for a customizable framework. Multiple stakeholders with varying backgrounds may have different requirements. Therefore the assessment using a workshop helps in guiding the search process. Ideally, the artifact needs continuous development through similar workshops in Shell and other organizations
Communication of Research	The framework is described using visual and textual representations. In addition RASC charts are used to describe roles for certain process areas. To serve both Technology-oriented audiences and Management-oriented audiences formal and complex process notations are avoided. The goal was to find a balance between understandability and expressive power of the framework

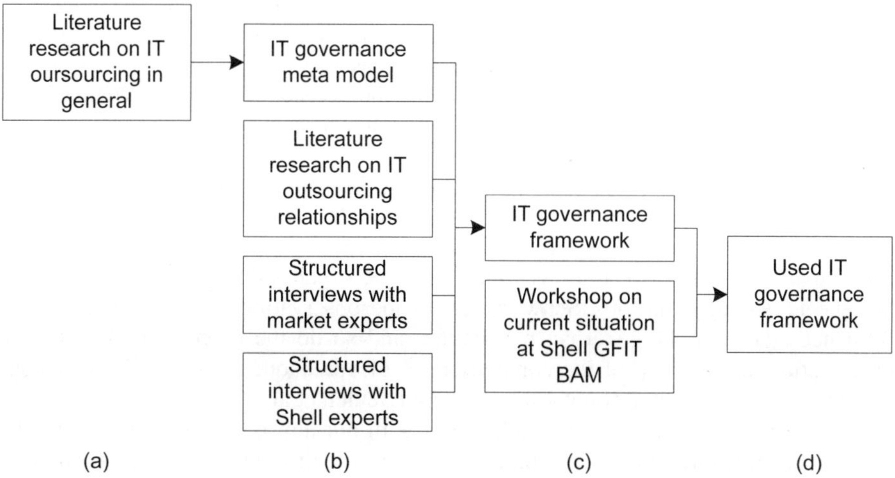

Fig. 1. Research approach

3 Developing an IT Governance Metamodel

This research focuses on IT Governance of the relationship between the insourcer and Shell GFIT BAM. IT governance has been defined in different ways. Beulen (2006) gives an overview of the most important IT governance definitions (Table 3).

Table 3. Definitions of IT governance (Beulen et al. 2006)

Researchers	IT governance definition
(Brown et al. 1994)	IT governance describes the locus of responsibility for IT functions.
(Luftman 1996)	IT governance is the degree to which the authority for making IT decisions is defined and shared among management, and the processes managers in both IT and business organizations apply in setting IT priorities and the allocation of IT resources.
(Sambamurthy et al. 1999)	IT governance refers to the patterns of authority for key IT activities.
(van Grembergen 2002)	IT governance is the organizational capacity by the board, executive management and IT management to control the formulation and implementation of IT strategy and in this way ensure the fusion of business and IT.
(Weill et al. 2002)	IT governance describes a firm's overall process for sharing decision rights about IT and monitoring the performance of IT investments.
(Schwartz et al. 2003)	IT governance consists of IT-related structures or architectures (and associated authority patterns), implemented to successfully accomplish (IT-imperative) activities in response to an enterprise's environment and strategic imperatives.
(IT Governance Institute 2004)	IT governance is the responsibility of board directors and executive management. It is an integral part of enterprise governance and consists of the leadership and organizational structures and processes that ensure that the organization's IT sustains and extends the organization's strategies and objectives.
(Weill et al. 2004)	IT governance is specifying the decision rights and accountability framework to encourage desirable behaviour in using IT.

(Brown et al. 1994) discuss mainly the locus (place) of IT decision-making. (Luftman 1996; Sambamurthy et al. 1999) focus on the decision-making processes. Weill (2002) added return on investment, and in the same period van Grembergen (2002) stated that organisations should as well ensure the organisational *capacity* to formulate the IT strategy. In 2003 Schwartz added the observations that the environment influences the right IT governance structure, and so do the perceptions that the IT organisation and the rest of the company have of one another. Finally, Weill recognized the importance of accountability in 2004 (Beulen et al. 2006).

However, the definition that matches best with our aim is the definition of the IT Governance Institute (2004). Several other authors use this definition (e.g. (Gewald et al. 2006; van Grembergen et al. 2005)) and the advantage in the context of this research is that the distinction between organisational structures and processes is concrete enough to relate to the business (Brown et al. 1994).

Based on the definition of a governance model as described below by Gewald (2006) and our definition of IT governance as described above, we define a governance framework for managing an offshore outsourcing relationship as follows:

A governance framework of an offshore outsourcing relationship is a structure that describes the joint processes and organisational structures, whereby also control indicators and responsibilities are defined.

A governance framework should address the questions "what to do", "how to do it", "who should do it" and "how it should be measured"" (Gewald et al. 2006). The joint process fields describe the "what to do", "how to do it" is described by the combination of those processes with the organisational structures into roles and responsibilities, the organisational structures define "who should do it". How it should be measured" is the topic of the control indicators (CIs).

As described before, we are looking for a generic and customizable 'IT governance framework'. We therefore start by presenting a Meta-Governance model. This model is defined at a higher level (the meta level) and can be instantiated based on the organizational requirements to create a governance framework for a specific outsourcing relationship. The meta governance framework is depicted in Figure 2:

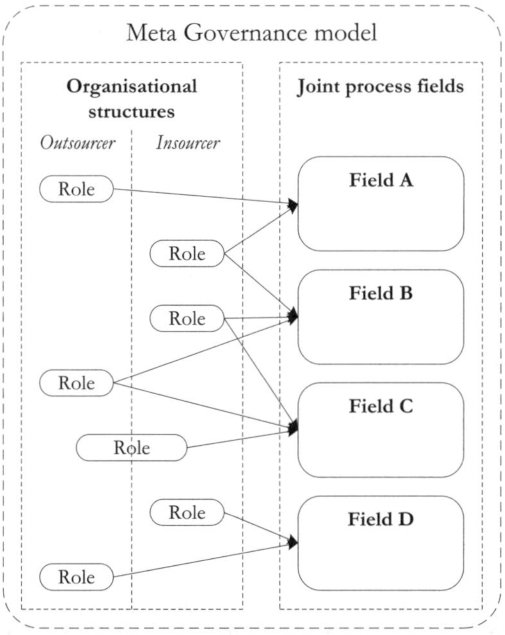

Fig. 2. Meta Governance Model

The meta governance model in Figure 2 can be specified on three hierarchical levels of an organisation; the strategic, tactical and operational level. This paper focuses on the tactical level. The tactical level defines the framework wherein the strategy will be executed, giving the defined direction to the organisation. Tactical roles translate the strategy in executable actions and divide the resources over the organisation. The tactical level focuses on middle term (in IT around 1 to 3 years).

3.1 Organisational Structures

The first element, the organisational structure, comes straight from our definition of IT governance and is also an element of Gewald's governance model. Gewald states that "the organizational structure comprises roles, functions and the necessary reporting and decision structure in the new organization". He further notes that responsibilities between organisational levels and partners are part of the organisational structures. Some responsibilities lay within the outsourcer's or insourcer's organisation and some are joint (Gewald et al. 2006).

Responsibilities are indeed part of our governance framework, but unlike Gewald, we argue that responsibilities are defined by the combination of organisational structures and processes and not within organisational structures only (also see 3.3 Responsibilities).

The 'who' from "who should do it" is defined by the roles in an organisation. For proper IT governance it is important that certain roles are fulfilled. Therefore we focus on roles and the "necessary reporting and decision structure" between them.

3.2 Joint Process Fields

The second element of an IT governance framework, the combination of the joint process fields, is also derived from the definition of IT governance and is the 'what' from "what to do" (Gewald et al. 2006). Gewald (2006) sees processes as a part of a governance model, whereby he specifically looks at *joint* processes. Joint processes are the processes that the in- and outsourcer share, so where roles from both in- and outsourcer are involved. This is also reasonable for this research regarding the focus on the connection between the outsourcing and the insourcing company.

We do not describe all joint processes in detail, as that would not have much sense because organisations have different detailed processes. Nevertheless, on a high level it is possible to describe fields of processes that are related to each other.

3.3 Responsibilities

The third element in the meta model is the linkage between roles and joint process fields. These arrows together describe the responsibilities of the organisation as a whole and relate to Gewald's question "how to do it" (Gewald et al. 2006).

A common way to define the responsibilities on a high level is to define a RASC-chart, or one of it variants. A RASC chart is a matrix with roles on a vertical axe and the joint process fields on a horizontal axe. The chart defines per intersection if the role is responsible (R), has to approve or accept (A, also called accountable), supports the person in the R role (S), or is a consultant for the other roles (C) for the concerning process field. It is possible to have a combination of responsibilities for one intersection and the combination A/R is not uncommon. There is a certain kind of hierarchy in the responsibilities, in the order A, R and S, where C should be consulted but stays outside this hierarchy.

A common alternative is RACI, were the I stands for a role that should be informed. We have followed Beulen (2006) in adapting the RASC chart because in our view it is common that stakeholders should be informed, and the S is relevant to agree on who executes the processes in the end.

3.4 Control Indicators

By defining control indicators (CIs) it is possible to answer the question "how it should be measured" (Gewald et al. 2006). CIs are linked to each other in a hierarchy, and together answer the question "are we in control?".

It is impossible to prescribe the entire hierarchy of CIs in a governance framework. The CIs should be defined in close cooperation with the business, should reflect their needs and therefore should be flexible by nature. Therefore we do not include specific CI's in the generic governance model.

4 A Governance Framework for Managing IT Outsourcing Relationships

In this section we instantiate the IT governance meta model into a specific IT governance framework based on a review of the literature and interviews with experts within and outside Shell. This instance of the meta model (the IT governance framework) is specific for a body shop relation.

As described before in Figure 1 - Research approach, there are four building blocks for this framework. The meta model defines the elements of the framework. First, a theoretical version of the framework was composed based on literature research on IT outsourcing relationships. Beulen's (2006) research on roles and their hierarchies has been used as the basis for the organisational structures. Gewald's (2006) research on joint processes was used as the basis for the joint process fields. Our research differs from Beulen's and Gewald's researches because we first define a meta model, which we then customize to an IT Governance Framework, which then again can be customized in a workshop to fit a specific organization's views, context and needs. The results of this second step are not described in this paper, but as it was the basis for the interviews in the third and fourth blocks, it is incorporated in the final framework as described below.

The second and third blocks were composed by structured interviews, with four external outsourcing experts and three experts within Shell. The external experts were selected independently from their relation to Shell, they are recognized outsourcing experts. Mr. Vriends works at Getronics Consulting, Mr. Beulen is from Accenture and Mr Lachniet & Prins work for Logica. Mr. Hussey, Mr. Overbeeke and Mr. Brink work for Shell outside BAM and have experience with a major outsourcing programme in infrastructure. All experts agreed that their opinions could be quoted and used for the construction of the governance framework. The interviews took place between the 30th of September and the 15th of October 2008 and the following main questions were discussed:

1. What is your role and what is your experience with governance?
2. What roles would/did you define? And why?
3. What joint process fields would/did you define? And why?

4.1 Organisational Structures

The first of the three parts of the IT governance framework is the organisational structure. This paragraph describes the roles that should exist in an outsourcing relationship, according to the literature and interviewees.

Figure 3 shows the organisational structure that should be in place to enable a manageable outsourcing relationship. It is generic because it describes roles that are known to all organisations in this situation, with descriptions mainly based on literature.

The following two sub paragraphs describe the roles for respectively the out- and the insourcer, including the reporting lines. A third sub paragraph discusses the communication lines between all roles. Together these descriptions add up to Figure 3 below.

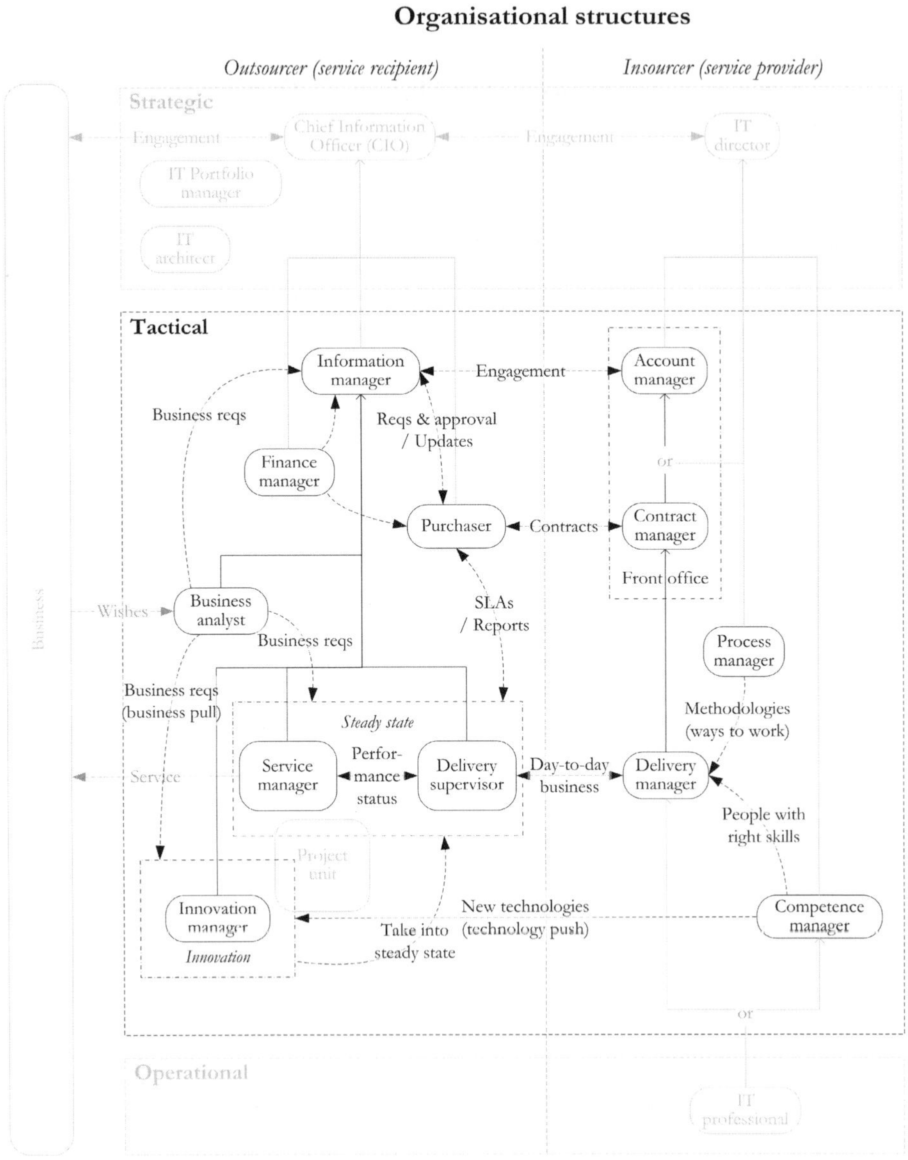

Fig. 3. Overview of all roles, reporting lines and communication from practice

The figure clearly shows that there are two different parts within the organisational structures; the outsourcer and the insourcer. In literature these are also referred to as the service recipient and service provider or supplier respectively (Beulen et al. 2006). We do not use these terms because often the service recipient is also an internal service provider and we are primarily interested in the relation between the two companies. Therefore we need to make a distinction based on organisational instead of functional boundaries. Another term for the outsourcer that can be found in literature is 'the retained organisation' (Gewald et al. 2006). However, for the sake of clarity we consequently use the term outsourcer throughout this entire paper.

4.1.1 Outsourcer

The roles at the outsourcer's side and the reporting lines between them are depicted in Figure 4. Just as in other figures, the grey areas are out of scope.

The overall role of the outsourcer is to receive and check the service provided by the insourcer. The outsourcer's department that takes up this role can be, and often is, a service provider within the outsourcer's organisation. The roles described below are the roles within the outsourcer's organisation on the interface with the insourcer, regardless of the relation to other roles within the outsourcer's organisation.

Information Manager

Beulen (2006) defines this role as follows: "Information managers are responsible for the IT services and the implementation of their company's IS [(Information Systems)] and IT strategies. They serve as contact persons for the company's divisions who must define their information needs. In large companies there may be several Information managers, each with responsibility for part of the company. Information managers report to the Chief information officer (CIO)" (Beulen et al. 2006).

There are no other authors who mention this kind of role, but because it clearly maps to some of the joint processes (as we will show in paragraph 4.2) we consider it necessary.

On the role of Information manager was little discussion in the interviews. On the tactical level Information managers have the most accountabilities and responsibilities as they are responsible for the IT services and the implementation of their company's IS and IT strategies (Beulen et al. 2006).

Service Manager and Delivery Supervisor

These roles are derived from what Beulen calls the Service delivery supervisor (Beulen et al. 2006). He defines this role as follows: "Service delivery supervisors manage external IT providers and, if applicable, the internal IT department. They report to their Information manager" (Beulen et al. 2006). From the RASC chart that Beulen sketches it becomes clear that the Service delivery supervisor should also manage the contracts and makes sure they are aligned with the business's requirements.

Gewald et al. (2006) describe two roles within the retained (i.e. the outsourcer's) organisation that together form a similar role as the service delivery supervisor; the contract manager and the service level manager. The contract manager maps to the Service delivery supervisor with respect to the contract responsibilities, as he "ensures that the service provider (i.e. the insourcer) delivers according to the contract". The

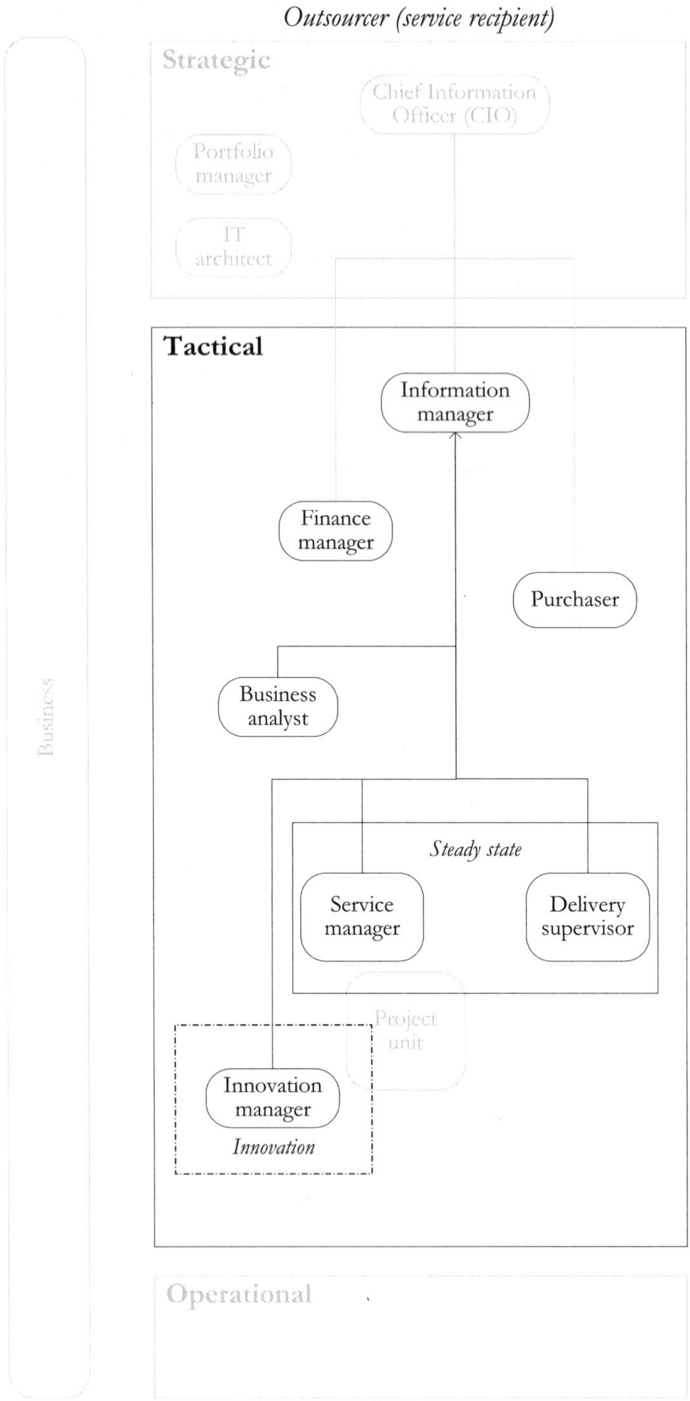

Fig. 4. Roles at the outsourcer

service level manager is more concerned with the content part of the Service delivery supervisor's responsibilities as he is "responsible for the quality of the services delivered in accordance with the SLAs" (Gewald et al. 2006).

As a result of the interviews with Mr. Brink, Overbeeke and Vriends, we have split this role in two: the Service manager and the Delivery supervisor. They are responsible for two different axes within the IT organisation; the service for the business and the functionality or applications delivered by the insourcer. The service delivered by a Service manager is a combination of functionalities delivered by different Delivery supervisors, and the functionalities (the applications) that a Delivery supervisor delivers is input to several services of several Service managers. This is depicted in Figure 5 and implies that the Service manager focuses on the business and the Delivery supervisor on the insourcer.

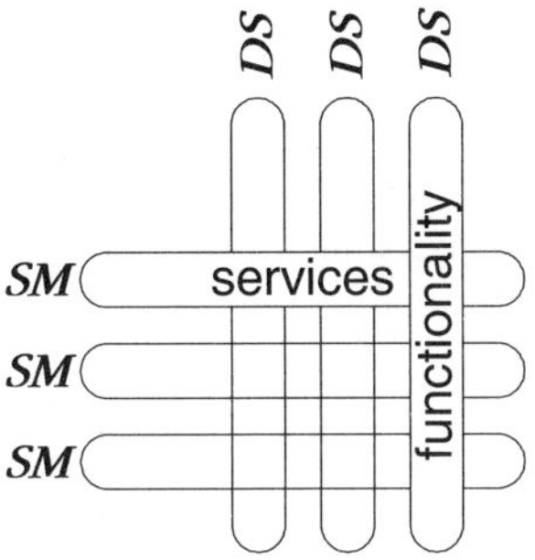

Fig. 5. Service managers vs. Delivery managers

How many Service managers and Delivery supervisors an organisation has depends for example on the size of the organisation, the amount and complexity required services and the size and complexity of the outsourced functionality. Both the Service manager and the Delivery supervisor report to the Information manager, where the two lines of functionality and services are combined. Apart from that they both give input to the Portfolio manager, who has to align the services and functional landscape.

There is a clear relation between the Service manager and Delivery supervisor and the description of the Service delivery supervisor from Beulen (2006). As discussed before, Beulen states that "Service delivery supervisors manage external IT providers and, if applicable, the internal IT department", but it also becomes clear that the Service delivery supervisor also manages the contracts and makes sure they are aligned with the business's requirements (Beulen et al. 2006). Here we see actually two roles within the description of a Service delivery supervisor; the Delivery supervisor who manages the external IT providers and the internal IT department, and the Service manager who makes sure that the delivered services are aligned with the business's requirements. As we described earlier, also Gewald defines a Service level manager, who is "responsible for the quality of the services delivered in accordance with the SLAs" (Gewald et al. 2006).

Purchaser

Beulen defines this role as follows: "Purchasers support their Information managers and the service provider's contract manager in selecting and managing external IT providers and, if applicable, managing the internal IT department. They represent both the IS function's interests and those of the company's divisions. They do not report to any official within the IS function" (Beulen et al. 2006).

Having a mainly supportive role, the purchaser is probably not the most critical role. Furthermore we found no other authors that identified this role. Nevertheless, the purchaser is involved in many of the tactical processes (as will be explained in paragraph 4.2).

From the interviews with Mr Brink, Hussey and Overbeeke it can be concluded that another name used for the Purchaser is the Contracting & Procurement role. The Purchaser is responsible for everything that concerns the contractual part of agreements and contracts.

Business Analyst

Beulen defines this role as follows: "Business analysts implement the IS and IT strategies. They serve as contact persons for the company's divisions who must define their information needs. In large companies there are several business analysts, each with responsibility for part of the company. They report to their respective Information managers" (Beulen et al. 2006). As business analysts form the link to the business, this role corresponds with what Gewald (2006) calls the Business Unit Manager.

The Business analyst is the linking pin to the business and helps them to transform their wishes into requirements. Interviewees agreed with the theoretical view on Business analysts. The Business analyst reports to the Information manager, but he is consulted throughout the outsourcer's organisation for his expertise and knowledge about the business.

Finance Manager

The Finance and/or Administration manager is mentioned by Gewald as one of the roles at the retained organisation. Beulen (2006) does not include this role. According to Gewald "financial and administrative functions are necessary to validate the service provider invoices ensuring adherence to the contract and the agreed prices as well as inter-company invoicing to the business units" (Gewald et al. 2006).

In the IT governance framework, the Finance/Administration manager is renamed to Finance manager because this role did not have specific administration tasks with respect to the joint processes that we defined. Interviewees agreed on the importance of this role with respect to its financial responsibilities. The Finance manager reports to the CIO.

IT Architect and Innovation Manager

Gewald (2006) identifies an architect or innovation role. According to Gewald the IT architect "ensures that the technical ability stays within the retained organization in order to maintain and to control architectural design. The architect has to ensure that the IT architecture reflects the business requirements" (Gewald et al. 2006).

However, most authors consider the IT architect as a strategic role, and so do our interviewees. But with the positioning of the IT architect on a strategic level, there remains a gap on tactical level with respect to Innovation Management, as also described in paragraph 4.2 (Vriends 2008). Therefore the Innovation manager role is included and is responsible for the exploration and implementation of innovations on both business as technology areas, as long as they remain within the strategy as formulated on strategic level by amongst others the IT architect and Portfolio manager. The Innovation manager reports to the Information manager and has a functional line towards the IT architect and Portfolio manager.

4.1.2 Insourcer

The roles at the insourcer and their reporting lines are depicted in Figure 6. The grey areas are out of scope. The following paragraphs explain the roles defined at the insourcer's side.

The insourcer is mainly concerned with providing the agreed services. Nevertheless, as their customer's needs often change over time, they should be flexible in adapting their agreements as well. So their goal may not be to deliver the *agreed* services, but to deliver the *needed* services.

In order to do so, the insourcer needs to fill in the following roles (Beulen et al. 2006). Unfortunately, we have found no other authors in the field of IT governance and outsourcing that define the insourcer's roles.

IT Director

Beulen defines this role as follows: "IT directors carry final responsibility for the delivery of IT services as well as for the continuity of service delivery by external and, if applicable, internal IT providers. They are the IS function's strategic-level contact persons. If the IT services are outsourced, this role is played by the supplier's general manager" (Beulen et al. 2006).

Although Beulen defines the IT director as a tactical role, interviewees stated that he belongs to the strategic level. Hussey stated that because he is the highest in hierarchy at the insourcer he is the counterpart of the CIO. Of course this also depends on the importance of the insourcer to the outsourcer; if the insourcer is not very important the IT director will be the counterpart of the Information manager and thus on tactical level in the relationship.

Account Manager

Beulen defines this role as follows: "Account managers maintain relationships with the IS function (and the managers of the recipient company's divisions). Their contacts partly focus on widening the scope and increasing the scale of their contracts. They are held accountable for the scale of the services delivered and for customer satisfaction. Account managers serve as tactical-level contact persons for the IS function; together with the contract managers they are the provider's front office" (Beulen et al. 2006).

The interviewees mostly agreed with this definition of Account manager. Hussey mentioned that his work may to a certain extent be strategic as the Account manager is responsible for fulfilling all the outsourcer's needs. Nevertheless, as his main counterpart is the Information manager, he remains on a tactical level, as Beulen also explicitly stated (Beulen et al. 2006). He reports to the IT director.

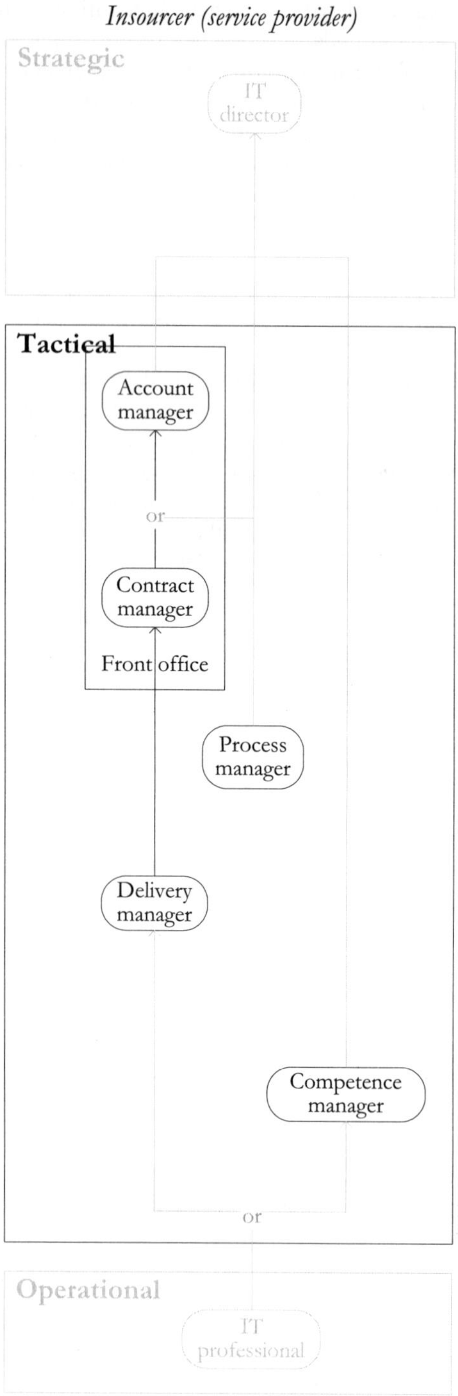

Fig. 6. Roles at the insourcer

Contract Manager
Beulen defines this role as follows: "Contract managers are responsible for delivering the IT services contracted and for reporting and invoicing. For these aspects contract managers serve as contact persons for the IS function; together with the account managers they are the provider's front office" (Beulen et al. 2006).

The interviewees agreed on this role of the Contract manager. In his interview Beulen stated that he reports to either the Account manager or the IT director.

Delivery Manager
The Delivery manager is deducted from Beulen's Service Delivery Manager. "Service delivery managers (SDMs) manage the IT professionals who deliver the IT services. They report to the contract managers" (Beulen et al. 2006).

The Delivery manager is purely responsible for delivering the products as specified in the contract and therefore manages one or more IT professionals. Brink, Hussey, Overbeeke and Vriends all stressed that in a body shop relation it is unimportant to the insourcer how these products map to services, as this is the responsibility of the outsourcer (the Service manager and Delivery supervisor). The Delivery manager reports to the Contract manager.

Process Manager
Beulen defines this role as follows: "Process managers set up and maintain the processes and certification of the IT services delivered. This responsibility does not pertain to any specific contract but to the IT services delivered for all the supplier's contracts. Process managers report to their IT director" (Beulen et al. 2006).

The insourcer's Process manager makes sure that IT professionals use the right methodologies and processes, such as for example ITIL, the ISO standards or specific tools for testing (Hussey 2008). In that way they ensure certification, which does, as Beulen (2006) mentions, not pertain to any specific contract but to all the supplier's contracts.

Competence Manager
Beulen defines this role as follows: "Competence managers investigate the potential of new technologies. This responsibility does not pertain to any specific contract but to the IT services delivered for all the supplier's contracts. The intention is to ascertain delivery continuity. Competence managers report to their IT director" (Beulen et al. 2006).

Hussey and Overbeeke indicated that the Competence manager is responsible for delivering the right people with the right skills to the Delivery manager. Furthermore, Vriends agreed with the definition that the Competence manager investigates the potential of new technologies. These two responsibilities fit together because training the right people with the right skills highly depends on the skills in technologies that outsourcers ask for.

IT Professional
Beulen defines this role as follows: "IT professionals deliver the IT services and investigate the potential of new technologies. They report to either the service delivery manager or to the competence manager" (Beulen et al. 2006).

As a result of the interviews, the IT professional is on an operational instead of a tactical level as Beulen (2006) indicates. All interviewees stated that the reason is that he is the professional who in the end delivers the products as described in the contract. Even though he may have a supportive role to the tactical level, his responsibilities remain on an operational level.

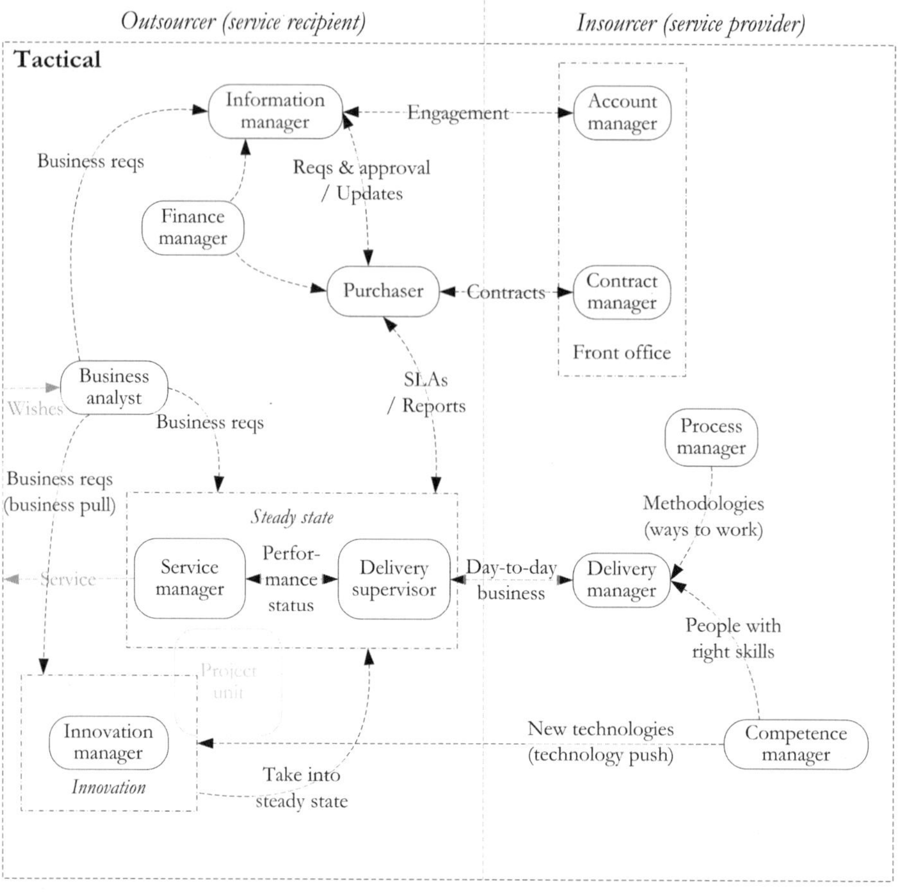

Fig. 7. Communication between roles

4.1.3 Communication

The communication lines between roles and out- and insourcer are depicted in Figure 7 below. This figure focuses only on tactical level and neglects communication already implied by the reporting lines.

Most of the internal communication within the outsourcer or the insourcer is already described above. What this figure clearly shows is that on a tactical level, there are four different levels on which out- and insourcer communicate together. First, there is interaction with respect to engagement on the highest level. The Account manager and Information manager focus on relational aspects and evaluate issues concerning the engagement.

Secondly, the Purchaser and Contract manager discuss contractual matters, including the negotiation in the setup phase of the relation. When a contract is in place, the relation between the Steady state and the Contract manager is stronger than between the Purchaser and the Contract manager. The reason is that the Service manager and Delivery supervisor are using the contract on an ongoing basis, although the contract owner will still be the Purchaser. Therefore the Purchaser gets involved if there are contract issues that require changes to the actual contract.

Nevertheless, for the Service manager and the Delivery supervisor the third interaction is most important, which is the relation with the Delivery manager and concerns the daily business.

The fourth important interaction on tactical level concerns new technologies. Both the Competence manager and the Innovation manager are responsible for innovation within their own organisation so they have to align which technologies are emerging and in which areas it is wise to invest.

4.2 Joint Process Fields

The second of the three parts of the IT governance framework are the joint process fields. This paragraph describes the joint processes that are desired to exist in an outsourcing relationship, based on literature and interviews.

Figure 8 shows the joint process fields of the IT governance framework, which we based on theory and the interviews. The theoretical basis for all processes except Performance Management comes from Gewald (2006).

As displayed in Figure 8 there are two different kinds of processes; horizontal and vertical processes. Vertical processes exist on multiple levels, while the horizontal processes only take place on tactical level (Gewald et al. 2006).

The following paragraphs describe each of these process fields, followed by a subparagraph that discusses alternative views of the cited authors and why we did not choose to incorporate these views.

4.2.1 Contract Management

The goal of Contract Management is *to facilitate contracts throughout all phases of the outsourcing lifecycle* and has a slightly administrative character (Beulen 2008). The financial maintenance of the contract, such as paying penalties or bonuses, is part of Financial Management (see the respective paragraph). Contract Management includes for example the set-up of a contract, but also the maintenance; adjusting the contract when business needs have changed. Also evaluation of the contract is part of contract management.

Other authors than Gewald that prescribe Contract Management as an important governance process field are Beulen (2006) and Van Bon (2007). Beulen states that ‘contract facilitation’ is one of the tactical processes concerning the governance of offshore outsourcing relationships and Van Bon states that “the services, service scope and contract reviews in comparison with original business requirements” should be monitored closely within the process supplier management in order to minimize risks (Beulen et al. 2006; van Bon et al. 2007).

Interviewees agreed with the positioning and definition of Contract Management in the framework (Brink 2008; Hussey 2008; Vriends 2008).

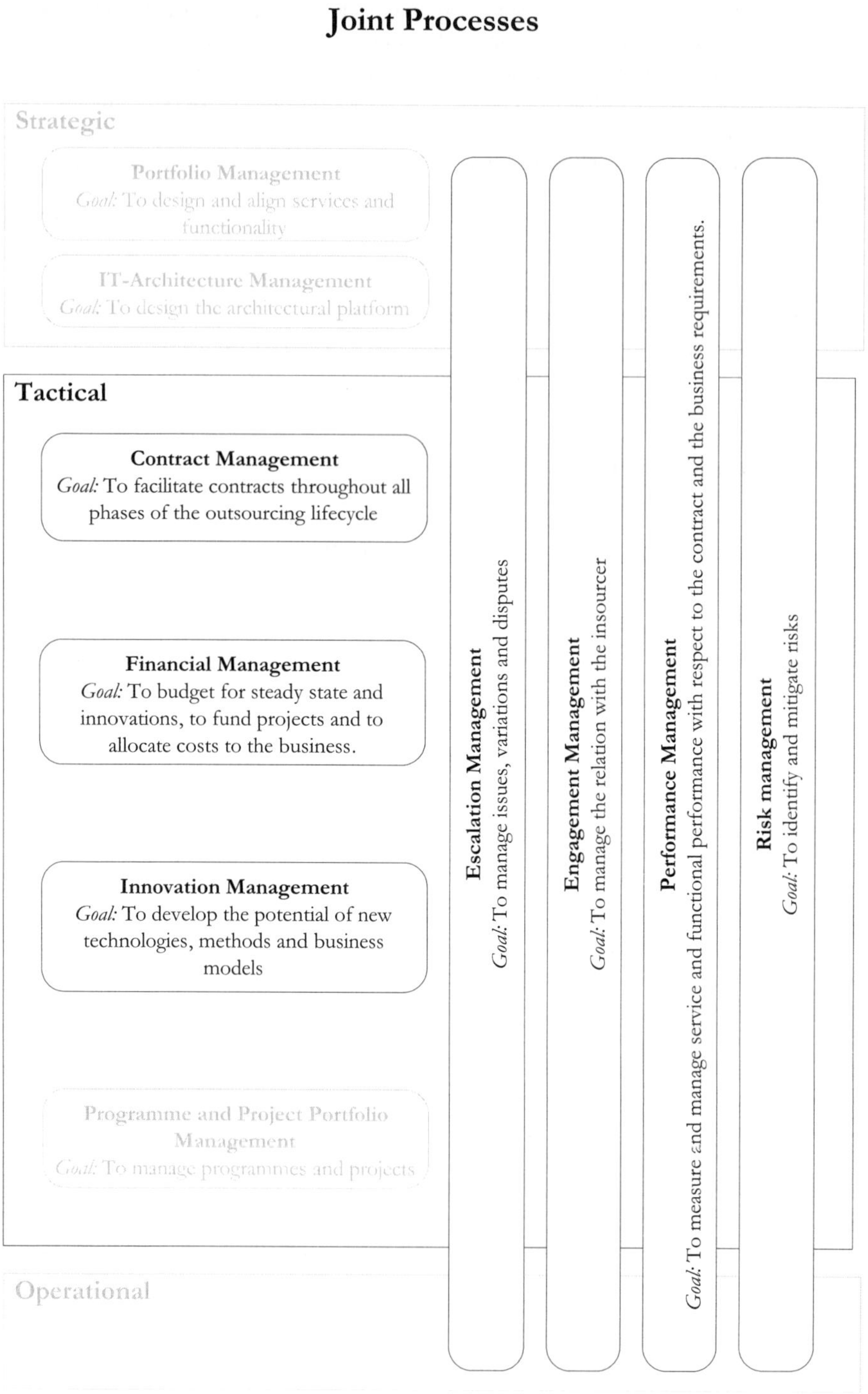
Joint Processes
Strategic
Portfolio Management
Goal: To design and align services and functionality
IT-Architecture Management
Goal: To design the architectural platform
Tactical
Contract Management
Goal: To facilitate contracts throughout all phases of the outsourcing lifecycle
Financial Management
Goal: To budget for steady state and innovations, to fund projects and to allocate costs to the business.
Innovation Management
Goal: To develop the potential of new technologies, methods and business models
Programme and Project Portfolio Management
Goal: To manage programmes and projects
Operational
Escalation Management
Goal: To manage issues, variations and disputes
Engagement Management
Goal: To manage the relation with the insourcer
Performance Management
Goal: To measure and manage service and functional performance with respect to the contract and the business requirements.
Risk management
Goal: To identify and mitigate risks

Fig. 8. Joint processes

4.2.2 Financial Management

Three interviewees added Financial Management to the framework, being Brink, Lachniet and Prins, and Vriends. The goal of Financial Management is *to budget for steady state and innovations, to fund projects and to allocate costs to the business*, and is mainly unrelated to the contract. It includes supply and demand forecasting, as budgets are based on those forecasts (Vriends 2008). Also reporting to the strategic processes that decide whether to invest or disinvest is a part of Financial Management. This joint process area is not specified in theory.

4.2.3 IT-Architecture and Innovation Management

Gewald (2006) mentions IT-Architecture and Innovation Management as one process field. Beulen (2006) states that 'architecture planning' is a strategic instead of a tactic process and 'investigating and developing the potential of new technologies' is tactical. On the basis of our interviews the IT governance framework also states that IT-Architecture Management is a strategic process, and Innovation Management is not. In his interview Beulen also stated that IT-Architecture Management has as goal *to design the architectural platform* and is therefore mainly technology focused, in contrary to IT Portfolio Management.

The goal of Innovation Management is *to develop the potential of new technologies, methods and business models.* Innovation Management focuses on two kinds of innovations:

- Technical innovations; innovation of IT related methods and techniques such as SOA, ESB etc.
- Business innovations; e.g. new business models such as offshoring or e-business.

Furthermore, Innovation Management has two main tasks:

- Translating the IT strategies in concrete plans that can be implemented on operational level (business pull),
- Providing innovative developments and opportunities on the market / in-sourcer to Functional Planning and IT-Architecture Management (technology push).

4.2.4 Escalation Management

The goal of Escalation Management is well described by Cullen (2005) and is *to manage issues, variations and disputes*. Gewald (2006) considers this process field as a vertical field that overlaps all organisational levels. In fact Escalation Management is vertical in its very nature, because issues, variations and disputes are escalated up the hierarchical tree. Only the most severe issues will reach the strategic level.

Brink, Hussey, Lachniet and Prins, and Vriends agreed upon the focus and place of Escalation Management. Nevertheless, both Overbeeke and Beulen mentioned the relation to Incident Management (an operational process). Where Overbeeke saw Escalation Management as a part of Incident Management, Beulen stated that it is closely related, as Incident Management is the delivery process and Escalation Management is the relational process.

We decided to include Escalation Management in two flavours; horizontal escalations and vertical escalations. Horizontal escalations are escalations on the same level for e.g. additional knowledge or advise from a related team or colleague. Vertical escalations run up the hierarchy and may concern disputes, but also for example the need for extra resources. Vertical escalations may run parallel to incidents as Beulen suggested in his interview, but Escalation Management comprises of more than incidents, such as general performance issues or contractual issues.

4.2.5 Engagement Management

Engagement and Project Management is one of the three vertical processes of Gewald (2006), because it takes place on all levels of the organisation. Other authors mention 'vendor development' (Beulen et al. 2006) and 'invest in the relation' (Cullen et al. 2005). The term 'project' in Engagement and Project Management means something different from the same term in Programme and Project Portfolio Management as mentioned below. Insourcers use the term 'project' to refer to a contract with one of their outsourcers, which is the meaning in this context. We find it confusing to have two processes that address two different meanings of projects, so we renamed Engagement and Project Management to Engagement Management. The goal of this joint process is *to manage the relation with the insourcer*.

Three of our interviewees (Beulen, Hussey and Vriends) indicated that Engagement Management is not a process but should be a general norm or value, built in roles and functions. However Brink argued that Shell's Common Process Model explicitly describes a similar process; Supplier Relationship Management. Furthermore both Vriends and Beulen specified specific KPIs for this process, which implies that certain activities should take place to measure them and influence them if they are not satisfactory. Therefore Engagement Management is one of the processes of the IT governance framework.

4.2.6 Performance Management

Gewald does not mention Performance Management, although he already says in his paper that his processes are only examples of joint processes. Almost all other authors do address Performance Management as a distinct process field and therefore we have added it (Beulen et al. 2006; Cullen et al. 2005; de Looff 1997; van Bon et al. 2007). The goal of Performance Management is *to evaluate the performed work compared to the agreements in the contract and to measure the compliance to the business requirements*. Reporting is one of the main activities within this process field and Performance Management is a vertical process field.

All interviewees confirm the importance of Performance Management. Beulen and Lachniet and Prins see it as a part of Contract Management, but Brink and Vriends do not agree. Where Contract Management focuses on the contracts and is more administrative, Performance Management focuses on services and functionality and measures its performance. Performance Management also compares this to both the contracts and the business requirements, and triggers Contract Management if they are not aligned anymore and the contract should be revised. Performance Management has much to do with the day-to-day business.

4.2.7 Risk Management

The goal of Risk Management is *to identify and mitigate risks*. A part of Risk Management is to plan contingencies (Cullen et al. 2005). Also the IT Governance Institute considers Risk Management as one of the five most important process fields (IT Governance Institute 2004).

Risk Management is a vertical process with responsibilities on every level, as confirmed by Beulen, Hussey and Vriends. Risks in for example supply and demand forecasting should be aligned with the supplier to be able to mitigate them. Risk Management is a broad process, which includes:

- Capacity & availability management
- Information security, or privacy & compliancy
- Continuity management.

4.2.8 Portfolio Management

Portfolio Management is derived from what Gewald calls Functional Planning (Gewald et al. 2006). Because Gewald did not give a definition of this process, we initially defined the goal of Functional Planning as: *to design a functional roadmap for IT assets*. However, Hussey and Vriends indicated that they saw Functional Planning as a strategic process. According to Vriends, Functional Planning is comparable to the more common term Application Portfolio Planning, as a functional roadmap should also be a part of an application landscape. Furthermore, also Shell's Common Process Model does not specify Functional Planning but does specify Portfolio Management & Standards as a process on strategic level. Brink states that this process is comparable to what we mean with Functional Planning. In short, Functional Planning has several characteristics of processes at a strategic level; it designs the functional roadmap, which is setting the direction. Defining the desired functionalities is also intertwined with the core and identity of the organisation, which is a strategic characteristic.

For all these reasons we decided to move Functional Planning to a strategic level and rename it to IT Portfolio Management. IT Portfolio Management in this context does not only include Application Portfolio Management, but also Service Portfolio Management. The goal is *to design and align services and functionality*. Concretely, this means that this process has as output the strategy for the service catalogue ('which services do we want to deliver and how?') and the application landscape ('which functionalities/ applications do we want to deliver and how?'). The process is focused on the business and translates business needs into the IT strategy.

4.2.9 Programme and Project Portfolio Management

Gewald is the only author that mentions Programme and Project Portfolio Management (in this context). We define the goal as *to manage programmes and projects in order to improve business and IT alignment* and consider that as a process that adds value to the framework. Beulen, Brink, Hussey, Lachniet and Prins as well as Vriends agreed on the importance and focus of Programme and Project Portfolio Management. However, as projects are out of scope the process is greyed out.

4.2.10 Other Process Fields from Cited Authors

Of course, the authors cited above also mention other processes than the ones mapped to our framework. This subparagraph shortly lists the reasons why these process fields were not incorporated in the framework.

'Maintain internal capacity', as proposed by De Looff, is not a joint process. On the contrary, both 'Measure compliance to requirements' and 'Enforce compliance' are relevant. As we do not see fit with one of Gewald's processes, both can be linked to a 'new' relevant process field; Performance Management (de Looff 1997).

Van Bon says that the performance of suppliers should be monitored, which is done by Performance Management. Secondly, he states that the services, service scope and contract reviews in comparison with original business requirements should be monitored. We consider this part of Contract Management as it is related to the insourcer-outsourcer contract and its linkage with the business (van Bon et al. 2007).

Finally, Cullen mentions nine activities that are relevant for existing outsourcing relationships. We consider the first, 'Invest in the relationship (plan, assess and improve)', part of Engagement Management. The second is 'Meaningful reporting and analyses', which we see as a general value that is important for each and every process field. It is therefore not included in Figure 8. The same holds for the third and fourth processes; 'Regular communication and meetings' and 'Diligent documentation and administration'. Activity five is 'Manage risks and plan contingencies' and part of Risk Management. We see the sixth activity, 'Manage issues, variations and disputes', as part of the vertical Escalation Management process field. For the seventh activity, 'Effect continuous improvement and streamlining', the same holds as for the second to fourth activities; it is a general activity that should be implemented throughout all process fields. Finally, the eight and ninth both are part of Performance Management as they are 'Evaluate and audit supplier (controls, performance, compliance)' and 'Evaluate organization both as a customer and contract manager' (Cullen et al. 2005).

4.3 Responsibilities

The third and final part of the IT governance framework is the responsibilities of the defined roles in the defined joint processes.

When combining the organisational structures with the joint process fields, it is possible to describe responsibilities by defining a RASC chart (see subparagraph 3.3). Table 4 shows the accountable, responsible, supportive, and consulting roles, which are explained below in Table 5. This chart was initially based on a literature study, where some of the responsibilities are adopted from Beulen (2006). The result of this initial study was discussed in the interviews with experts from inside and outside Shell, which in the end resulted in the RASC chart displayed below.

5 Application of the Governance Framework to Shell BAM

To test the applicability of the IT governance framework in practice, we have again customized the framework in a third layer which is specifically designed for Shell Global Functions IT BAM, a part of Royal Dutch Shell plc which currently is involved in an outsourcing relationship. The third layer for BAM is their specific desired situation.

This section starts with a high level introduction of Shell (GFIT) BAM, then describes the workshop that we did with representatives, and ends with the outcomes of the workshop regarding the usability and usefulness of the framework. For reasons of confidentiality, we cannot report on the details of the Shell BAM outsourcing governance. We do not view this as a very critical constraint as the main objective of the Shell BAM case study is to validate the Governance framework rather than to zoom in on the specifics of the outsourcing relationship.

Table 4. RASC chart from practice

			Outsourcer							Insourcer					
	Process Fields	**Role**	Information manager *a*	Purchaser *b*	Finance manager *c*	Business analyst *d*	Service manager *e*	Delivery supervisor *f*	Innovation manager *g*	Account manager *h*	Contract manager *i*	Delivery manager *j*	Process manager *k*	Competence manager *l*
Horizontal	Contract Management	*1*		A/R	S		S	S			R	S		
	Financial Management	*2*			A/R		S	S				S		
	Innovation Management	*3*	A			C	S	S	R			S		C
Vertical	Escalation Management	*4*	A				R	R		R	R	R		
	Engagement Management	*5*	A							R				
	Performance Management	*6*	A	C		C	R	R	C			R	S	S
	Risk Management	*7*	A/R	S	S	S	S	S	S	R	S	S	S	S

5.1 IT Governance at Shell GFIT BAM

Global Functions IT Business Application Management (GFIT BAM, or simply BAM) is responsible for the applications of the business[1], including support, transition to support and service delivery. A different part of GFIT is responsible for all infrastructure, including the infrastructure for the applications, but BAM has the final responsibility to deliver the services to the business.

BAM is using ‘body shopping’ or ‘staff augmentation’ to hire people at the insourcer, which means that the insourcer reserves a specific number of FTE’s per BAM team, specified per technology group of applications. A technology group is a group of applications that are based on the same technology (e.g. Visual Basic, .Net, etc.).

BAM’s customers for support are the businesses, that provide the complaints and wishes on which the relation with the insourcer is based. The end-users are Shell employees within these businesses that use the applications. This is depicted in Figure 9.

We conducted a stakeholder and problem analysis within BAM, which showed that BAM faces a common problem in outsourcing relations: there is a lack of management control in at least one of their offshore body shop outsourcing relations. As described in the introduction, this is one of the key risks and problems that the outsourcing industry currently faces.

---

[1] For the sake of clarity a different part of GFIT, called the ‘Line of Business’, is not considered in this description. The LoBs are placed in between the BAM and the businesses, but this is not relevant for the remainder of this paper.

Table 5. Description of responsibilities

Cell	Explanation
1b	On a tactical level, the Purchaser is both accountable and responsible for Contract Management. Organisation wide, the accountability of the contracts may lay with a different role on a strategic level.
1c, e, f	The Finance manager, Service manager and Delivery supervisor support the Purchaser in Contract Management. The Finance manager will support the Purchaser in his financial negotiations. As described before, the Service manager and Delivery supervisor will trigger the Purchaser if contracts should be revisited. They are managing the contract on a daily basis, but the ownership of the contract remains with the Purchaser.
1i, j	From an insourcer's perspective, the Contract manager is responsible for Contract Management. He is supported by the Delivery manager for input from performance perspective.
2c	The Finance manager is both accountable and responsible for Financial Management.
2e, f, j	The Service manager, Delivery supervisor and Delivery manager support the Finance manager by providing budget proposals and performance information.
3a, g	The Information manager is accountable for Innovation Management, but delegates the actual investigation and implementations to the Innovation manager.
3d, l	The Information manager consults the Business analyst to get the business requirements and innovation needs (business pull) and the Competence manager for technical innovations (technology push).
3e, f, j	The Service manager and Delivery supervisor support the Innovation manager by taking innovation into the steady state and advising him how to align innovations with the steady state. The Delivery manager will in the end implement the innovations at the insourcer.
4a, e, f	As the highest in the outsourcer's hierarchy, the Information manager is on a tactical level accountable for Escalation Management. The Service manager and Delivery supervisor are responsible because they have other people reporting to them, and are the first point of contact in the escalation path for these people.
4h, i, j	Within the insourcer the Account manager is responsible that escalations are also managed across boundaries towards the outsourcer, and he delegates that to the roles under his reporting line, the Contract manager and Delivery manager.
5a, h	The Information manager is accountable for the engagement with the insourcer, and the Account manager is responsible, as it is his core role.
6a, e, f, j	The Information manager is accountable for good Performance Management towards the strategic level. He delegates the responsibilities towards the Service manager and Delivery supervisor on the outsourcer's side, and to the Delivery manager on the insourcer's side. They manage the day-to-day Performance Management.
6b, d, g	The Purchaser and Business analyst advise the Service manager and Delivery supervisor in Performance Management in the matters of respectively contracts and business requirements. The Innovation manager advises them in upcoming innovations that should be taken into the steady state.
6k, l	The insourcer's Process manager and Competence manager support the Delivery manager in respectively working according to the insourcer's standards, methods and techniques, and making use of the right people with the right skills.
7a, h	The Information manager is accountable and responsible for Risk Management on a tactical level. Part of this responsibility also resides with the Account manager, as he has the responsibility to comply as much as possible with the needs of the outsourcer. He therefore also has to assess risks together with the Information manager
7b, c, d, e, f, g, i, j, k, l	All other roles support the Information manager and Account manager in assessing and mitigating the risks on their own fields, like Financial Management, Innovation Management and Performance Management. They have to report high risks to the Information manager or Account manager.

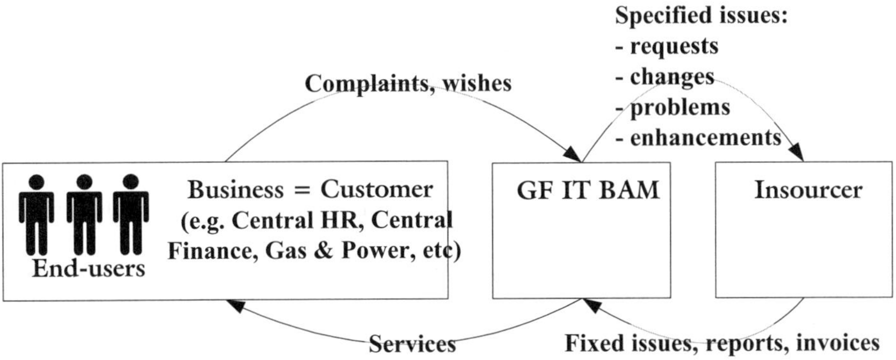

Fig. 9. Relations of BAM Support

5.2 Workshop for Shell BAM

In order to help BAM to increase the management control in their outsourcing relationships we conducted a workshop with representatives of the organisation. The goal of the workshop was twofold: (1) to help BAM increase control, but also (2) to test the usability and usefulness of the framework in a concrete situation.

We selected the participants on the basis of their involvement during the research and their role in the current organisations. We seeked to invite an audience who would cover most roles in our framework.

From the outsourcer (i.e. Shell) participated the following people:

- Service Manager HR, whose dominant role was Service manager.
- Delivery Manager non-SAP EU team, whose dominant role was Delivery supervisor.
- Business Analyst, whose dominant role was obviously Business analyst
- On/off boarding team lead and Contract Resourcing, whose dominant role was Purchaser.

From the insourcer participated one person:

- Engagement manager, whose dominant role was Account manager.

5.2.1 Workshop Methodology

The workshop took three hours, including a 15-minute coffee break. Before the workshop we explained the framework to all participants individually to make them comfortable with it and to enable us to start quickly with the contents during the workshop. They received the programme one week in advance with a 10-page explanation of the framework and the following homework assignment:

"Identify, prior to the workshop, three 'best practices' and three issues that you see from your current role with respect to the current IT governance in your IT outsourcing relation(s). E.g.:

- Best practice: There is one person that manages all my contracts and he/she is reachable for all my questions and issues.

- Issue: My counterpart at the insourcer gets his assignments and information from several persons throughout our organisation. He sometimes knows more than I do and executes work I did not know of, while I am responsible for his actions."

The workshop was led by one person and assisted by another. The assistant did not have specific knowledge of the framework or research but primarily helped with making photos and notes. We did not record or film the workshop, as this could limit the openness of the attendees.

After the workshop we analysed the notes, photos and forms that the participants filled in. We split the workshop in two parts, where the part before the break was about the current situation (IST) and after the break about the desired situation (SOLL).The programme is shown in Table 6. During the first part we started with a few slides to welcome everybody and quickly showed the framework. In round 2 the participants each had to put stickers with their own colour on the roles and processes they identified themselves with. They also had to put an A, R, S or C on the stickers they put in the processes. During round 3 we discussed these roles and processes in a plenary session and combined them into a RASC chart. The first part took an hour longer than planned, but as the discussion in round 3 was very important to come up with a shared RASC chart we catered for this.

After the break we focused on the input from the homework assignment, and participants were divided into pairs. They jointly had to fill in a form where they linked the issues and best practices to the framework and designed their desired situation. In round 5 they presented their views. A lively discussion followed about specific outsourcing items. This shows that stakeholders were engaged in the practical discussion around the subject and practical implications of the framework. The debate was not about the structure or limitations of the framework, but about its contents. Finally, we wrapped up and thanked the participants for attending the workshop.

Table 6. Workshop programme

Time (mins)	**What**	**How**
15	Welcome & introduction to framework	Plenary presentation
30	Match your role, activities & responsibilities	Stickers on poster
45	Combine responsibilities in one RASC chart (IST)	Plenary on flip over
15	*Break*	
30	Map good points/ issues to IST and framework and come up with Shell solution (SOLL).	In two smaller groups on basis of forms
25	Present SOLL	Two presentations
20	Wrap up & thanks	Plenary

5.3 Usability and Usefulness of the IT Governance Framework in the Workshop

The detailed outcomes of the workshop that relate to the current and desired practice at BAM are confidential. Nevertheless, most important for this paper is the question whether we achieved the goals of the workshop: did we help BAM to increase management control, and how useable and useful was the framework?

In general, participants were enthusiastic about the workshop, the use of the framework, as well about the outcomes and recommendations for BAM. The workshop showed that the framework was particularly useful in two areas: the contents of IT governance and the stakeholder management.

Concerning the contents of IT governance, the use of the framework added value for several reasons:

- The framework worked as a tool that enabled to describe the current and desired situation in detail. It made a rather intangible and broad concept IT governance very tangible and provided the level of detail to enable a meaningful discussion. Basically it proved to structure the discussion and analysis.
- Using the framework, the current and desired states could be described in detail. The framework identified clear gaps between the current and desired situation.
- Thirdly, besides the meta model also the IT Governance framework is customisable; it does not prescribe one truth. In the workshop the IT governance Framework was customized into the third layer; the desired situation for BAM specifically. BAM deviated mainly on the RASC chart, details are confidential.

Concerning the stakeholder management, the framework proved also to be very valuable:

- The framework helped participants understand their added value in the bigger picture, and also the value of other roles and hence people in their organisation. This forced them to think broader than just their own 'kingdom' and role, but instead focus on the bigger picture.
- The discussion between people helped them to break through false assumptions. For example participants may assume accountability for a process lies with a certain person, while in practice this is not true (independent from what it should be).
- The proposed situation in the framework can be rather confronting, because it makes participants think about their real value and their core responsibilities. As one of the attendees commented on the conclusions drawn from the workshop: "this shows a very clear understanding of the Shell case, and considerable insight into what is missing and what can be done about it".

6 Conclusions and Discussions

An outsourcing relationship comes with many risks, concerning areas such as confidentiality, business knowledge and management control. Industry and theory have an increasing need to manage the relationship with insourcers. This research has addressed the question 'what practices can be developed to better govern the relationship with offshore vendors?', which is in the top-3 of key outsourcing research issues. Current literature on IT governance has resulted in many definitions and descriptions of IT Governance. Unfortunately, these are generally too vague to practically address in an organisation. Based on a literature survey and expert interviews this study develops a meta model consisting of (a) organisational structures, (b) joint process fields, (c) responsibilities and (d) control indicators, which is then customized into an IT governance framework. The first three elements are addressed in this paper. The presented IT governance framework gives researchers insight in the best practices currently available in the market, as well as an overview of research done on IT governance frameworks for offshore outsourcing relationships so far. Another strength of using a customized meta model is that it can also be customised for e.g. a Managed Services relationship, as we now did for a body shop relation.

To validate the usefulness and usability of the developed framework, this research also applies the Governance framework to the case of Shell GFIT BAM, which gives valuable information about the applicability of the Governance Framework in a real world situation. The workshop organized indicates that the framework can be very useful as well as useable to a company that outsources part of its work and needs to setup, assess or improve governance of the relationship. The framework is particularly valuable because it provides a structure for the discussions and analysis, a founded proposal to arrange the IT governance, as well as a means to involve stakeholders and manage their assumptions, views and (self-)criticism. The second customization into the desired situation gives organisations the flexibility to fit the situation to their own context and needs, which can for example been done in a workshop.

On a high level, another lesson learned about the governance of offshore IT outsourcing relationships is that it is extremely important for an outsourcer to *co-operate*. Many of the risks in outsourcing are mitigated by one or more of the joint processes defined in the IT governance framework. For example, information security and confidentiality is perceived as an issue in practice and a risk within literature. The reason is that information crosses organisational boundaries and the amount of control by the outsourcer decreases. The joint process Risk Management mitigates this risk, because in- and outsourcer are jointly responsible for security and confidentiality. A RASC chart makes these responsibilities clear and shows that although the outsourcer is accountable, the insourcer is also responsible. This ‘softens’ the organisational boundaries and enables the outsourcer to have more control when information crosses this line.

Another example is the lack of innovation, one of the main risks described in literature. The joint process Innovation Management makes sure that innovation is in place, and that the insourcer also has certain responsibilities in this process. In this way outsourcers make sure that also the insourcer innovates.

Nevertheless there is room for improvement and extra research regarding the framework and this research. First of all, further research on maturity models and designing a maturity model suited for the IT governance framework may give more insight in the dynamics of the framework. A maturity model can offer clear guidance on priorities and phases in the implementation trajectory. Furthermore also the relation to capability models like e.g. the eSourcing Capability Model from Carnegie Mellon is interesting to investigate. It is promising to see how this framework influences the capabilities of the insourcer, which will probably also make the value of the framework for the insourcer clearer. Second, it can be very valuable to validate the IT governance framework on the basis of more case studies. Research questions can address issues such as: “what is the typical RASC chart?” and “which variables influence the customization of the governance framework?”. Variables that might cause the framework to change are for example: the size of the company, the size of the outsourcing contract, previous experience of both parties with outsourcing, the amount of trust and formalization in the relationship, the base country of out- and insourcer, ... etcetera. By investigating more cases, best practices will come to light. Third, further research on customising the meta model for a Managed Service relationship instead of the current body shop configuration will add value to many companies, including Shell. Many outsourcers have started their relationships on the basis of body shopping, but are currently looking into outsourcing the complete management of services. The expectation is that in the framework certain roles and responsibilities will move towards the insourcer, but probably it is also necessary to create new roles and/or processes. Fourth, a thorough investigation on the insourcer's vision, risks and concerns related to the framework will eliminate some of the limitations. The current situation at the insourcer will become clear, as well as the gaps that influence the outsourcing relationship. As literature mainly describes outsourcing from an outsourcer's perspective this may also have a positive theoretical impact. Fifth, the impact on the relationship with the business is not taken into account. Still, it is very important to involve the business in developing the governance structure. Often, the business does not trust the IT governance structure when they do not have a say in it, as also Mr. Brink indicated in the interview. Therefore, it will be interesting to investigate the relation between the outsourcer's IT department(s) and the business who in the end has to pay for the services. Finally, through conducting multiple case studies, a library of common and proven Control Indicators (CIs) could be defined. This can make it feasible for organisations to select possible or widely used CI hierarchies from a library and fill in the measurement area of the Governance meta model.

References

Aron, R., Singh, J.V.: Getting offshoring right. Harvard Business Review 83(12), 135–143 (2005)

Beulen, E., Ribbers, P., Roos, J.: Managing IT Outsourcing, Governance in global partnerships. Routledge, Abingdon (2006)

Brown, C., Magill, S.: Alignment of the IS functions with the enterprise: toward a model of antecedents. Management Information Systems Quarterly 18(4), 371–403 (1994)

Cullen, S., Seddon, P., Willcocks, L.: Managing Outsourcing: The Life Cycle Imperative. MIS Quarterly Executive 4(1), 229–246 (2005)

de Looff, L.: Information Systems Outsourcing Decision Making: A Managerial Approach, p. 304. Idea Group Publishing, London (1997)

Gartner: Management Update: Six Steps to a Sourcing Governance Framework (2005)

Gewald, H., Helbig, K.: A Governance Model for Managing Outsourcing Partnerships. In: Proceedings of the 39th Hawaii International Conference on System Sciences, p. 194c (2006)

Gopal, A., Sivaramakrishnan, K., Krishnan, M.S., Mukhopadhyay, T.: Contracts in Offshore Software Development: An Empirical Analysis. Management Science 49(12), 1671–1683 (2003)

Hevner, A.R., March, S.T., Park, J., Ram, S.: Design Science in Information Systems, Research. MIS Quarterly 28(1), 75–105 (2004)

Holcomb, T.R., Hitt, M.A.: Toward a model of strategic outsourcing. Journal of Operations Management 25, 464–481 (2007)

IT Governance Institute Board Briefing on IT Governance, 2nd edn. ISACA, Illinois (2004)

Kern, T., Willcocks, L.: The relationship advantage: Information technologies, sourcing, and management. Oxford University Press, Oxford (2001)
King, W.R., Torkzadeh, G.: Information systems offshoring: Research status and issues. MIS quarterly 32(2), 205–225 (2008)
Lacity, M.C., Willcocks, L.P., Rottman, J.W.: Global outsourcing of back office services: lessons, trends, and enduring challenges. Strategic Outsourcing: An International Journal 1(1), 13–34 (2008)
Luftman, J.: Competing in the Information Age. Oxford University Press, Oxford (1996)
Mirani, R.: Procedural coordination and offshored software tasks: Lessons from two case studies. Information & management 44(2), 216–230 (2007)
Sambamurthy, V., Zmud, R.: Arrangements for information technology governance: a theory of multiple contingencies. Management Information Systems Quarterly 23(2), 261–290 (1999)
Schwartz, A., Hirschheim, R.: An extended platform logic perspective of IT governance: managing perceptions and activities of IT. Journal of Strategic Information Systems 12(2), 129–166 (2003)
van Bon, J., de Jong, A., Kolthof, A., Pieper, M., Tjassing, R., van der Veen, A., Verheijen, T.: Foundations of IT Service Management Based on ITIL V3, 3rd edn. Van Haren Publishing, Zaltbommel (2007)
van Grembergen, W.: Introduction to the minitrack: IT governance and its mechanisms. In: Proceedings of the 35th Hawaii International Conference on System Science (HICSS), Hawaii (2002)
van Grembergen, W., de Haes, S.: Measuring and Improving IT Governance Through the Balanced Scorecard. Information Systems Control Journal 2 (2005)
Verschuren, P., Doorewaard, H.: Designing a Research Project, 2nd edn. LEMMA, Utrecht (1999)
Weill, P., Ross, J.: IT Governance, How Top Performers Manage IT Decision Rights for Superior Results. Harvard Business School Press, Boston (2004)
Weill, P., Vitale, M.: Place to Space, Migrating to eBusiness Models. Harvard Business School Press, Boston (2002)
Yang, D.-H., Kim, S., Nam, C., Min, J.-W.: Developing a decision model for business process outsourcing. Computers & Operations Research 34(12), 3769–3778 (2007)

Software-as-a-Service Vendors: Are They Ready to Successfully Deliver?

Tsipi Heart, Noa Shamir Tsur, and Nava Pliskin

Department of Industrial Engineering and Management
Ben-Gurion University of the Negev
Beer-Sheva, Israel

Abstract. Software as a service (SaaS) is a software sourcing option that allows organizations to remotely access enterprise applications, without having to install the application in-house. In this work we study vendors' readiness to deliver SaaS, a topic scarcely studied before. The innovation classification (evolutionary vs. revolutionary) and a new, Seven Fundamental Organizational Capabilities (FOCs) Model, are used as the theoretical frameworks. The Seven FOCs model suggests generic yet comprehensive set of capabilities that are required for organizational success: 1) sensing the stakeholders, 2) sensing the business environment, 3) sensing the knowledge environment, 4) process control, 5) process improvement, 6) new process development, and 7) appropriate resolution.

The results show that most vendors perceive SaaS as an evolutionary rather than revolutionary innovation hence do not employ radically new business processes. Some lessons were drawn from the past ASP failure, but a deep learning process was scarcely employed. These findings were particularly typical to leading vendors in the software product market who recently added SaaS to their business. In contrast, pure-SaaS vendors thought differently.

Respondents consistently perceived their organizational capabilities higher than the rank calculated from indirect measures of the capabilities. This may well mean that the respondents' organizations were in fact less ready than expected. Furthermore, 'appropriate resolution' and 'new model development' were ranked low by the respondents, while highly correlated with customer satisfaction from SaaS. The readiness of SaaS vendors, therefore, especially those who are accustomed to delivering software products, is questionable.

1 Introduction

In a recent survey conducted by the CIO Magazine in August 2008 among 173 IT and business leaders, 81% of respondents indicated they are using, or are planning to use, cloud computing in the near future (McLaughlin 2008), which means using organizational IT functionality remotely via the Internet. Software-as-a-Service (SaaS) is the most popular service (51% of the respondents) in the 'cloud', whereby organizations remotely access applications via the Internet rather than off their local servers, paying the service providers per-use or per-user (Heart et al. 2007).

I. Oshri and J. Kotlarsky (Eds.): Global Sourcing 2010, LNBIP 55, pp. 151–184, 2010.

Although cloud computing and SaaS are relatively new terms, the concept of accessing organizational applications remotely instead of installing them locally, is not new. In the late 1990s a similar concept termed Application Service Provision (ASP) was forecasted to replace traditional application sourcing to become the dominant global paradigm (Lixin 2001; Kern et al. 2002; Carr 2005; Konary 2005). This, however, did not materialize, and by the beginning of the new millennium most ASP vendors either discontinued this offering or went out of business altogether.

In light of the renewed interest in the remote application sourcing option now termed SaaS or, in a broader view, Cloud Computing (TenWolde 2007; McLaughlin 2008), this study, which focused on mission-critical, enterprise software sourcing, aimed at assessing the readiness of the current SaaS vendors to deliver the service. Vendor readiness was assessed based on three criteria: 1) vendors' interpretation of SaaS as either disruptive or evolving innovation, and implications of this assessment on their business processes, 2) lessons learned from the ASP history, and 3) vendors' capabilities strength based on a new, seven fundamental capabilities framework. This framework defined seven organizational capabilities as fundamental to any organization in all industries for achieving solid performance. These capabilities are: 1) sensing the stakeholders, 2) sensing the business environment, 3) sensing the knowledge environment, 4) process control, 5) process improvement, 6) new process development, and 7) appropriate resolution capabilities (Kashi 2007). Consequently, answers to the following research questions were pursued in this study: 1) What are the vendors' perceptions of SaaS as an innovation? 2) What have SaaS vendors learned from the past ASP experience? and 3) What are the vendors' perceptions of the capabilities required to thrive in the SaaS market? Examination of these questions can shed light on vendors' readiness to successfully deliver SaaS.

The rest of the paper is organized as follows. We next bring a background and literature survey about SaaS, innovations, and the Seven Fundamental Organizational Capabilities Model. The research method is then presented, followed by the results. The paper is concluded with a discussion including implications for research and practice.

2 Background and Literature Survey

2.1 Software as a Service (SaaS)

Enterprise-wide applications such as enterprise resource planning (ERP) and customer relationships management (CRM) are nowadays becoming a standard in medium- and large-sized organizations. While mostly delivered as a product, there are signs that this is perhaps about to change, and software is predicted to become a service rather than a product. The next section describes this transformation (Ross and Westerman 2004).

2.1.1 SaaS Evolution

In the past forty years enterprise computation has evolved from central mainframe to virtual Software as a Service. Waters (2005) described four waves of evolution (Figure 1), measured by *internal administrative burden* and *time between investment of capital and benefit received.*

```
┌─────────────────────────────────────────────────────┐
│                  40 Years of                        │
│              Enterprise Computing                   │
│                                                     │
│  Internal                          Time between    │
│  administrative    ┌──────────────┐  investment of │
│  burden            │  Wave One    │  capital and   │
│                    │ Central Mainframe│ benefit received│
│  Extremely         │              │  Extremely     │
│  heavy             │ The user carries the│  long    │
│    ▲               │ data to the computer│    ▲    │
│    │               │              │      │         │
│    │               │Customer's capital investment: $$$$$$$│
│    │               ├──────────────┤      │         │
│    │               │  Wave Two    │      │         │
│    │               │ Client-Server │      │         │
│    │               │  Computing   │      │         │
│    │               │              │      │         │
│    │               │User requires direct connect│  │
│    │               │terminal with client software│ │
│    │               │Customer's capital investment: $$$$│
│    │               ├──────────────┤      │         │
│    │               │ Wave Three   │      │         │
│    │               │Internet Protocol (IP)│        │
│    │               │  Computing   │      │         │
│    │               │              │      │         │
│    │               │User needs simply a│            │
│    │               │"thin client" browser│          │
│    │               │Customer's capital investment: $$$│
│    │               ├──────────────┤      │         │
│    │               │  Wave Four   │      │         │
│    │               │Software as a Service│          │
│    │               │              │      │         │
│    │               │Bought like on-demand utility│  │
│    │               │Both user and administrator│   │
│    │               │use simple web browser│        │
│    ▼               │              │      ▼         │
│  Extremely         │Customer's capital investment: Zero│ Nearly │
│  light             └──────────────┘  instant       │
└─────────────────────────────────────────────────────┘
```

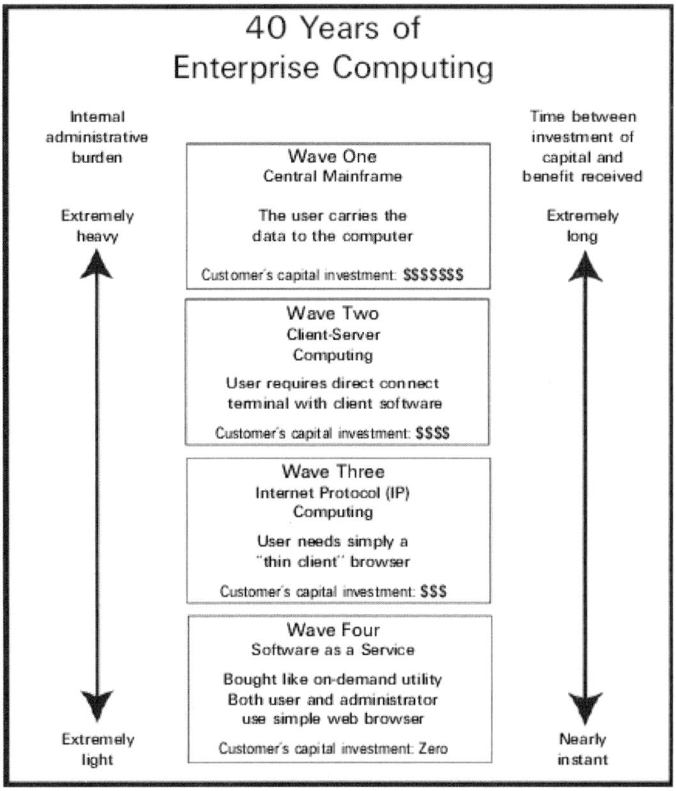

Fig. 1. Evolution of enterprise computing (Waters 2005)

As evident in Figure 1, the current wave of enterprise computing evolution is SaaS, where, according to Waters, administrative burden is extremely light and the time between investment of capital and benefits received is nearly instant. SaaS enables transforming software from a product to a service.

SaaS is a software application delivery model where a software vendor develops a web-native software application and hosts and operates (either independently or through a third-party) the application for use by its customers over the Internet. Customers pay not for owning the software itself but for using it (Turner et al. 2003; Konary 2005; Dym 2007). Although the term SaaS is relatively new, the changing approach from software as a product to software as a service is already under way for quite some time. Research identified three phases of organizational software services, differentiated by the level of dependence on the provider (Currie 2004): IS Outsourcing, Application Service Provision (ASP) and On Demand Computing, and Utility Computing (UC), illustrated in Figure 2 (Kern et al. 2002; Kern et al. 2002). As evident in Figure 2, SaaS is considered the latest manifestation of the current, second phase before a forecasted future transition to Utility Computing.

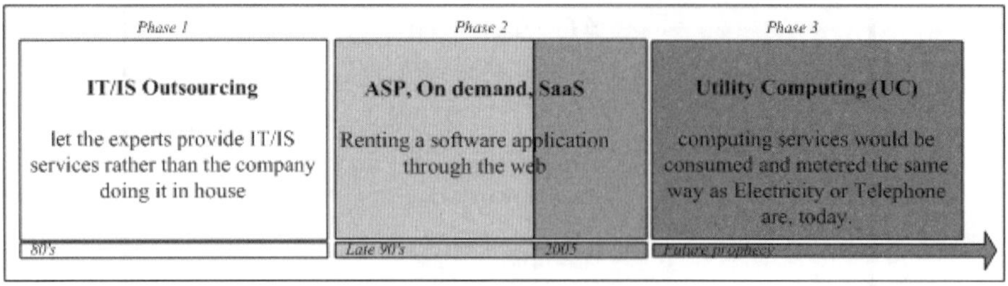

Fig. 2. Software services evolution

According to Gartner's Hype Cycle for emerging Technologies, 2005 (Figure 3), SaaS is past its 'peak of inflated expectations' and 'trough of disillusionment' phases, where it was located during the ASP era until the dot.com collapse in the early 2000s. Hence, it is now positioned, as evident in Figure 3, in the 'slope of enlightenment', where its diffusion gradually grows based on more realistic expectations, until it reaches the 'plateau of productivity', forecasted here to prevail in 2007-2010 (Fenn and Linden 2005).

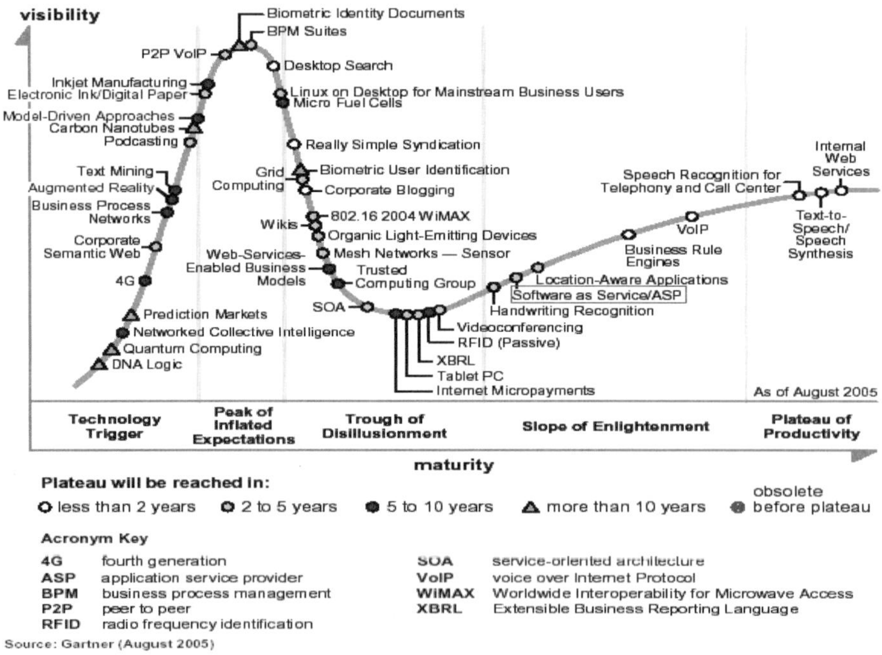

Fig. 3. Hype Cycle for Emerging Technologies (Fenn and Linden 2005)

Based on McKinsey's May 2007 quarterly report, revenues of SaaS vendors rose from $295 million in 2002 to $485 million in 2005, an 18 percent increase (Dubey and Wagle 2007). Moreover, IDC and Saugatuck Technology Inc. predicted that the

SaaS market will gradually upgrade its services to a SaaS2.0 model in the next few years. They explained that SaaS (or SaaS1.0) refers to mainly reduce costs, while SaaS2.0 would enable transforming the way of doing business, and should be more adequately termed Business Services Provisioning (Koenig 2006; MacGregor 2006; McNee 2007; TenWolde 2007).

2.1.2 Diffusion and Adoption of ASP and SaaS

Since SaaS and ASP are similarly defined, we hereafter use the two terms interchangeably, referring to the earlier phenomenon as ASP and to the current service as SaaS.

Being a relatively new concept, most of the following literature review refers to ASP rather than to SaaS, on which literature is still scarce. Most ASP research discussed the customer side as briefly reviewed next. Our focus, however, is the vendor side, elaborated more afterwards.

2.1.3 The Customer's Perspective of Renting SaaS

Several benefits to the customer from opting for SaaS are discussed in the literature, which can be divided to financial and strategic benefits, technical and infrastructural benefits, and technological benefits. From a financial and strategic point of view, renting a software service is assumed to reduce unexpected implementation costs, and facilitate easier upgrades. Price based upon usage rather than a fixed cost enables paying only for used functionality. In addition, it increases time to value as time-consuming processes of installation in the customer's premises are eliminated. In addition it increases strategic focus on core competencies rather than allocating resources to handle hardware and software (Bennett and Timbrell 2000; Lixin 2001; Patnayakuni and Seth 2001; Kern et al. 2002; Currie et al. 2003; Ross and Westerman 2004; Waters 2005). From a technical and infrastructural point of view it is supposed to enable higher reliability (24X7 availability and support), and increase security, data safety, and disaster recovery capabilities (Lixin 2001; Patnayakuni and Seth 2001; Waters 2005; Currie et al. 2007). From a technological aspect, the SaaS customer is able to implement state of the art technology without having to acquire in-house software development and maintenance expertise (Bennett and Timbrell 2000; Lixin 2001; Patnayakuni and Seth 2001; Ross and Westerman 2004). This point can also be considered strategic. On the negative side, several barriers to adoption were counted. A questionable financial model was mentioned as a barrier (Ekanayaka et al. 2002; Ekanayaka et al. 2003), as well as high perceived risk and low level of trust in the vendor's viability and ability to deliver (Patnayakuni and Seth 2001; Heart and Pliskin 2002; Currie 2003; Ratnasingam 2005). Additional barriers are cited next.

2.1.4 The Vendor's Perspective of Providing SaaS

For the vendor, SaaS introduces several benefits above software as a product, among them financial, marketing, and strategic benefits. From a *financial* aspect the vendor enjoys lower development costs and a steady cash flow, a faster time to market (TTM) due to its ability to deliver the same software to many customers ('one to many' model) and to the ease of maintaining one instance of the application (Greschler and Mangan 2002; Walsh 2003; Saeed and Jaffar-Ur-Rehman 2005).

From a marketing and strategic point of view the vendor can increase total available market since the Internet is used as the primary delivery channel which is broadly accessible by customers; it can closely monitor customer use in real-time, and develop and upgrade the software according to current requirement and functionality comprehension which emerges from close understanding of the customer actual use and the market (Saeed and Jaffar-Ur-Rehman 2005). Furthermore, if developed under pure SOA principles and structures, i.e. properly componentized, customers are theoretically able to acquire only the required software features. This elevates the service flexibility and adherence to requirements of a larger customer base (McNee 2007).

In spite of the aforementioned benefits, past attempts to deliver software as a service, for example in the ASP era in the late 1990s, did not fulfill expectations, and diffusion was slower than anticipated (Ma et al. 2005), thus vendors have suffered from insufficient growth of their customer base. Among commonly cited reasons for the ASP failure are concerns about data security and systems availability due to the low reliability of the Internet, the limited range of applications offered in this model and integration problems, concerns about enhanced dependence on vendors and lack of vendor trustworthiness, and apprehension pertaining to the actual long-term cost savings (Greschler and Mangan 2002; Desai and Currie 2003; Ekanayaka et al. 2003; Vassiliadis et al. 2006; Heart et al. 2007).

In spite of the past failure of ASP, leading software vendors have recently either begun to deliver software in SaaS mode in addition to delivering software products, or have shifted to the SaaS business model altogether for some or all markets. For example, from 2007 Microsoft is offering Dynamic CRM, a Customer Relationship Management (CRM) solution in SaaS mode (http://www.microsoft.com/dynamics/crm/live/default.mspx); Oracle is marketing Oracle CRM on demand (Huang and Gutierrez 2006); and starting in 2008, SAP delivers (still in beta mode) its Business ByDesign Enterprise Resource Planning (ERP) software to the mid-sized organization market, in SaaS mode only (http://www.sap.com/sme/solutions/businessmanagement/businessbydesign/index.epx). The entry of the 'big' players in the software arena to the SaaS market, as opposed to their absence from the past ASP environment, perhaps attests to their belief in the viability of this business model. However, while these initiatives are still at their infancy, Salesforce.com which provides SaaS-only CRM solutions since its launch in 1999 (http://www.salesforce.com/company/milestones/), is the only manifestation of a pure-SaaS (provides products which were developed to be delivered as SaaS, and these products only) software provider who succeeded to acquire a large customer base and become profitable and viable.

Since much of the failure of ASP was attributed to customer apprehension about the service to start with, and with disconfirmation afterwards (Currie et al. 2007), it may well be that past disappointment with ASP is related to the fact that a unique value chain is required to appropriately deliver SaaS (Featherman and Wells 2004). This may be the case if indeed SaaS is regarded as a disruptive rather than an evolutionary innovation.

2.2 Innovation

Innovation has long been regarded as one of the keys to economic growth, yet the innovativeness of the services sector has been elusive (Sheehan 2006). Various definitions of innovation exist: "The first or early use of an idea by one of a set of organizations with similar goals" (Becker and Whisler 1967, p. 463); "Adoption of a change new to an organization and to the relevant environment" (Knight 1967, p. 478) ; "An idea, practice, or object that is perceived as new by an individual or another unit of adoption" (Rogers 1983, p. xviii; Lyytinen and Rose 2003). Since SaaS is a new service it can be considered an innovation for both providers and customers. Yet what type of innovation is SaaS?

Various types of innovation classifications have been proposed. Daft (1978) based his classification on their origin in the organization, whether in the technical or administrative core, and Zmud (1982) distinguished between product and process innovation, where product innovation is market-oriented, and process innovation is rather internal. In light of the abundance of Services organizations, Zmud's classification is clearly quite narrow, since a new service offered by an organization to its customers might also be considered a market-oriented innovation. Indeed, a research rooted in the financial services sector (Avlontis et al. 2001) suggested the six types of innovations based on their orientation and the level of internal or external novelty. Although originally developed in the financial services context, these six types may be applicable to any service-oriented industry (Avlontis et al. 2001).

While the previous classification applies to organizational innovations in general, Swanson (1994) was more specific and explicitly related to IT innovation. Swanson defined three types of IT innovations and tagged them as Type I, Type II and Type III. Type I are innovations confined to the IS task, for example – system programming and data administration; Type II are innovations supporting administration of the business, for example – accounting system; and Type III are innovations embedded in the technical foundations of the business, for example - airline reservation system and material requirement planning (Swanson 1994). Based on this classification, mission-critical enterprise applications delivered as SaaS can be classified as Type III innovation, implying that SaaS adoption entails significant organizational effort.

Lyytinen and Rose (2003) have adopted another classification of innovations and discussed disruptive or radical vs. evolutionary or incremental innovations in information systems. Evolutionary innovation pertains to a gradual modification of existing technologies, whereas a disruptive or radical innovation bursts to the market and renders existing technologies obsolete (for example web computing that replaces client-server computing). Dewar and Dutton (1986) have analyzed the differences in the adoption of radical vs. incremental innovation specifically pertaining to adoption of new technologies. One of their major finding was that knowledge resources are more important for a disruptive innovation adoption, than for an incremental innovation. Thus, if SaaS is considered a disruptive innovation it clearly bears significant consequences to SaaS vendors. Therefore it is important to investigate what capabilities are required for a vendor to succeed as a SaaS provider.

2.3 Organizational Fundamental Capabilities

In this chapter we briefly review the concept of organizational fundamental capabilities, and introduce a recently developed new model (Kashi 2007): The Seven Fundamental Organizational Capabilities (FOCs) Model, which later serves as the lens for the analysis of SaaS vendors' readiness.

2.3.1 Background

An organizational capability is defined as "a high-level routine (or collection of routines) that, together with its implementing input flows, confers upon an organization's management a set of decision options for producing significant outputs of a particular type" (Winter 2003, p. 991). Winter's definition pertains to organizational routines required to convert inputs to significant outputs, yet is silent about the ability to consistently achieve the process goals, namely – to maintain a reliable process. Dosi et al.'s (2000, p. 2) definition partially addresses this lacuna: "To be capable of something is to have a generally reliable capacity to bring that thing about as a result of intended action".

Prior research has acknowledged the centrality of organizational capabilities as a means to improve performance (Rulke et al. 2000) and maintain competitive edge, particularly in response to environmental dynamism (Porter 1996). The concept of dynamic capabilities (Teece et al. 1997; Eisenhardt and Martin 2000) or complex adaptive systems (Choi et al. 2001) was indeed the focus of recent research: "Alternative perspectives, developed under the guise of the capabilities, competence or knowledge-based theories of the firm, have gained attention recently" (Mota and de Castro 2004, p. 295). Prior to the notion of dynamism, the resource-based view of the firm (RBV) has identified capabilities as the ability to acquire valuable, rare, inimitable, and immobile resources (Wernerfelt 1984; Barney 1991), for example tacit knowledge (Poppo 1998). Although RBV gained vast popularity it was criticized for the static approach to capabalities acquisition and retention (Eisenhardt and Martin 2000). Researchers also pointed at the paucity of theories in strategic management pertaining to the elements and structure of organizational capabilities (Kusunoki et al. 1998; Mota and de Castro 2004; Wang et al. 2007).

In spite of the general consensus about the centrality of acquiring capabilities, no holistic and generic theory or model pertaining to fundamental organizational capabilities has been developed. Rather, the literature dealt with capabilities required for specific activities such as acquiring and retaining customers (Day 2003), developing new products (Kusunoki et al. 1998), or inventing new processes (Nonaka and Takeuchi 1995). To address this gap, a recent research (Kashi 2007) proposed a generic, holistic model of organizational fundamental capabilities.

2.3.2 The Seven Fundamental Organizational Capabilities Model

The Seven Fundamental Organizational Capabilities (FOCs) model has been developed based on the extant literature, and is aimed at presenting a holistic and generic approach. It includes a parsimonious yet comprehensive set of organizational capabilities that are essential to all organizations regardless of size, industry, type of organization (for example, for-profit or not), and phase in its life cycle (e.g. a start-up or an established organization). Furthermore, all seven capabilities are required for each organizational activity, internal or market-oriented, although their relative strength may change according to the circumstances. For illustration purposes, and in line with the process-oriented definition of an organization adopted in this study (see Table 1), we embedded the capabilities within a generic process control schema (Figure 4).

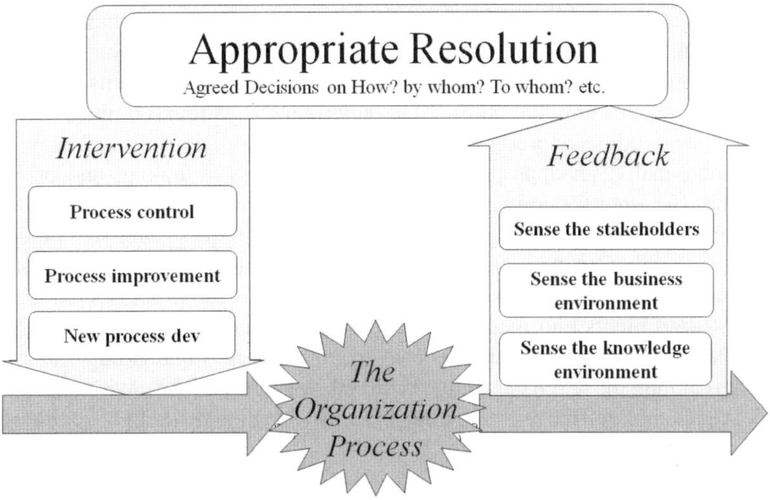

Fig. 4. The Seven Fundamental Organizational Capabilities Model

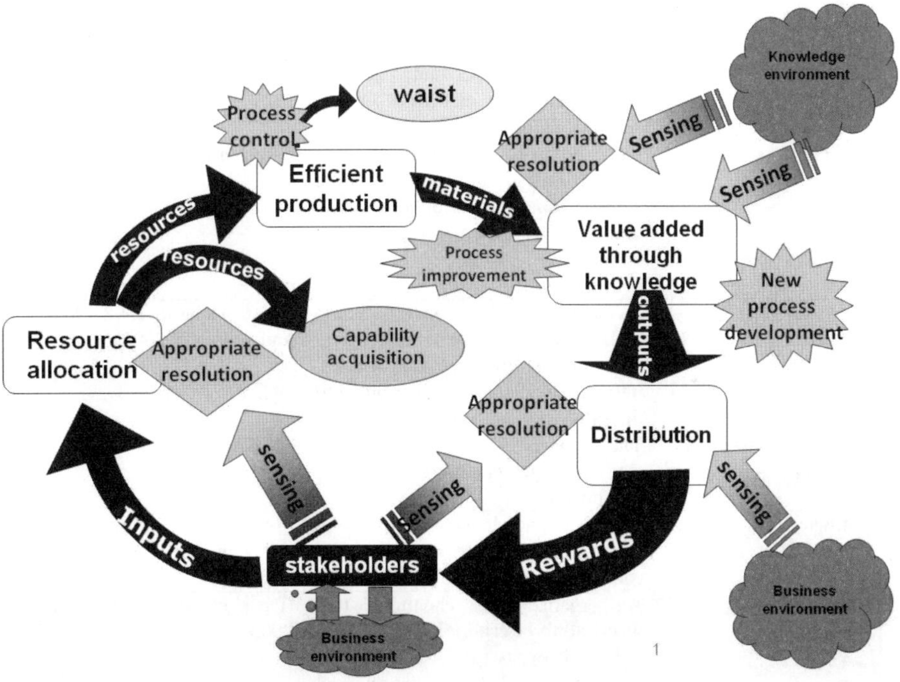

Fig. 5. The seven FOCs within the conversion process

A process control requires examination of the process outputs (feedback), appropriate decision about the implications of the feedback, and implementation of a required intervention in the process. Accordingly, the seven FOCs are grouped into three categories: sensing capabilities required for the feedback phase, intervention capabilities, and a resolution capability.

Three sensing capabilities are proposed: sensing the stakeholders, sensing the business environment, and sensing the knowledge environment. Similarly, three intervention capabilities are outlined: process control, process improvement, and new process development. Finally, an appropriate resolution capability is linking and bridging the sensing and the intervention capabilities. All capabilities are embedded in each organizational process which starts with inputting resources into the process, and culminates in distributing the outputs back to the stakeholders while applying knowledge, interventions, and appropriate resolutions during the various sub-processes required during the conversion of inputs into more valuable significant outputs. To summarize, Figure 5 displays the FOCs embedded in the conversion process, highlighting the roles and relationships among the seven capabilities, the stakeholders, and the environments.

Table 1 presents definitions of the terminology used, and the FOCs are defined in Table 2.

Table 1. Definitions of terminology used in the model

Term	Definition	References
Organization	A temporary agreement among stakeholders to cooperate in conducting a certain process according to some rules under certain conditions	(Adams 1965; Schein 1990; Adams and Neely 2002)
Stakeholders	ìAny group or individual who can affect, or is affected, by the achievement of the organization's objectives" (e.g. stockholders, employees, customers, suppliers, community)	(Freeman 1984, p. 25)
Organizational process	A mechanism that converts assets and capabilities, inputted by a collaborating group of stakeholders, into outputs that are re-distributed to the same stakeholders	(Daft Richard 1998; Marin and Schnitzer 2002)
Business environment	The group of all organizations who can exchange stakeholders with the organization	(Rabinowitz et al. 2008)
Knowledge environment	The total knowledge that exists in the organization's environment, and can be accessed by the organization	(Senge 1990; Nonaka and Takeuchi 1995; Rulke et al. 2000)
Fundamental capability	An organizational capability that meets all three criteria: It exists (to a certain level) in each organization and every organizational process It exists throughout the organization's life cycle All other organizational capabilities are based on it	(Dosi et al. 2000; Winter 2003)

Table 2. Definitions of the seven fundamental organizational capabilities (Kashi 2007)

Capability	Definition
Sensing the stakeholders	The ability to identify the stakeholders, and to understand and map their requirements and expectations from the organization
Sensing the business environment	The ability to identify, understand, and map risks and opportunities that are relevant to the organization
Sensing the knowledge environment	The ability to identify, understand, and map opportunities to acquire relevant organizational knowledge
Appropriate resolution	The ability of the stakeholders to reach an agreed resolution concerning the sources of the inputs, its conversion processes, and the re-distribution of the outputs back to the stakeholders
Process control	The ability to achieve and sustain a desirable standard in the organizational process and in each of its sub-processes
Process improvement	The ability to increase the output to each unit of input in the organizational process and in each of its sub-processes
New process development	The ability to develop new processes as part of the organizational process or its sub-processes, whose output per unit of input is significantly higher than in the existing processes in the organization or its accessible environment

3 Research Methods

Qualitative and quantitative research methods were used in this study. Qualitative methods are useful when researching areas not easily partitioned into discrete entities, or when examining the dynamics of a process rather than its static characteristics at a fixed point in time (Eisenhardt, 1989). The strength of qualitative research lies in its usefulness for rich and insightful understanding of the meaning and context of the studied situation (Benbasat et al. 1987; Myers 1997; Seaman 1999; Kaplan and Maxwell 2005). Use of qualitative methods has accelerated in IS research (Benbasat et al. 1987) due to the complexity of many IS-related phenomena and processes involving multiple factors (Seaman 1999; Kaplan and Maxwell 2005). Semi structured and unstructured interviews are among the most suitable qualitative techniques employed for investigating new research arenas, due to their suitability to understand yet unexplored or young phenomena, as is the case in this study.

Face-to-face semi-structured interviews have been employed as the data collection. The sampling frame for this phase has included decision makers and senior managers in five SaaS vendors, covering all local vendors who deliver enterprise systems in SaaS mode.

The quantitative data was aimed at empirically assessing the research questions. To this end, about 500 SaaS companies around the world have been contacted online or by phone, based on their involvement in the SaaS market as elicited from an online search in various search engines. All companies either deliver SaaS exclusively or alongside software products. Respondents were managers in these companies, who were contacted by e-mail and asked to fill a survey questionnaire.

3.1 Qualitative Data Collection

The qualitative data collection was aimed to sense unique characteristics of the SaaS delivery value chain and the SaaS market in general from the providers' point of view. Particularly, we were interested in the vendors' perceptions about SaaS as an innovation. Data were collected via semi structured interviews.

3.1.1 Semi Structured Interviews

The semi-structured questionnaire used for the interviews was pre-tested prior to the actual interviews by three IT experts. The questions were examined for relevance, clarity, content, and sequence logic. The resulting format is listed in Appendix 1 in four tables, reflecting the four main topics covered in the interview as drawn from the literature: 1) company profile and market positioning, 2) familiarity with, and lessons learned from, past ASP experience, 3) perceptions of SaaS as an innovation, and 4) attitude towards capabilities required to provide SaaS.

Respondents were managers in their organizations. Each interview was conducted in the vendor's office and took up to an hour and a half. Four of the interviews were openly recorded after getting the interviewee's consent, yet notes were taken during the interview by the interviewer for clarity and backup purposes. Table 3 describes the interviewees' organizations. In order to maintain answer anonymity the identifications are hereafter disguised.

Table 3. Interviewees demographics (the semi-structured interviews)

Company Name (foundation date)	Business Domain	SaaS application
Microsoft (1975)	A multinational company. A pioneer developer of operation system for home computers. Today divided to Microsoft Platforms & Services Division, Microsoft Business Division and Microsoft Entertainment & Devices Division	CRM Dynamics
MyBusiness (2003)	An Israeli CRM solutions provider, primarily designed for SMBs looking for a solution that meets the very highest standards, but does not require the investment of many thousands of dollars in servers and licenses	MyBusiness CRM
Oracle (1977)	A multinational firm. Business domains divided to: database management, middleware applications, and business applications	Siebel on demand (CRM)
One1	An Israeli company. Customer focused, End-to-End solutions in various market sectors	SalesForce.com business partner (CRM)
SAP (1972)	global market leader in collaborative, enterprise business solutions as ERP	SAP Business ByDesign (ERP)

3.1.2 Qualitative Data Analysis Method

The semi structured interview analysis was performed using qualitative analysis techniques.

Each recording was first transcribed, assisted by the manual notes taken during the actual interview process, where required. The text was analyzed for concepts and constructs that were elicited from the transcription, without prior identification of concepts or constructs, to maintain openness. Later, the elicited concepts and constructs were collapsed and coded based on conceptual similarity. A matrix of all elicited concepts was then created, where the concepts and constructs were listed in the rows and the interviewees in the columns, enabling analysis of each interview both vertically (as a whole) and horizontally (compared to other answers). Examples of the coding method are presented in Appendix 2.

The interviews were then re-analyzed to elicit the indirect reference of the interviewees' to the seven fundamental capabilities, since we refrained from asking the interviewees direct questions regarding the capabilities to decrease complexity. For each answer in the five interviews, the answer was tagged for a capability if the context of the answer referred to a fundamental capability. After analyzing all answers in all the interviews a count of the number of references to a fundamental capability was performed in three levels: 1) the number of interviewees referring to each fundamental capability in each question; 2) the number of times each fundamental capability was referred to by an interviewee throughout the interview; 3) the number of times a fundamental capability was mentioned in all interviews. A coding example is presented in Appendix 2.

3.2 Quantitative Data Collection

The next step aimed at quantitatively assessing respondents' perceptions of the seven FOCs. Data were collected using a pre-validated survey instrument (Kashi 2007), although the content of the statements has been adapted to the SaaS context (Appendix 3).

3.2.1 Survey Structure and Administration

At the beginning of the questionnaire, the seven capabilities were presented and defined. Respondents were then asked to rate the strength of each capability in the interviewee's organization on a 1 (very low) to 6 (very high) Likert scale. Next, respondents were asked to rate 63 statements indirectly measuring each capability, 7-9 items per capability, listed in a random order, on the same Likert scale. The next section aimed to subjectively assessing the performance of the SaaS organization. In this part, respondents were asked to rate five measures indicating organizational performance on a 1 (very low) to 6 (very high) Likert scale. Subjective evaluations were used because objective indicators were unavailable, yet the literature supports the positive correlation between subjective and objective performance measures when respondents are top managers (Wall et al. 2004). The last part of the survey included seven statements aimed at assessing the subjective importance of each of the seven fundamental capabilities to SaaS delivery success, on a 1 to 3 scale (1- Not Important, 2-neutral, 3- Important). The instrument is presented in Appendix 3.

The questionnaire was administered either in Hebrew or in English according to the respondent's native language. Both English and Hebrew versions were pre-tested and revised by 3 experts fluent in both languages.

Sample organizations were located using different electronic tools as web search, Google alerts, automatic feeds, SaaS-Showplace website, LinkedIn and Facebook, searched by the following criteria: Independent Software Vendors (ISV) which provide self-developed SaaS applications, or Service Providers (SP) which deliver applications developed by third parties in SaaS mode.

This effort generated a global sample of organizations from various countries. The survey instrument was communicated to the respondents in approximately 500 companies using an electronic questionnaire via e-mail or on the phone. 52 top managers and decision makers of SaaS providers responded, yielding response rate of about 10%, yet only 37 were usable questionnaires, reducing the actual response rate to ~7%, which could be expected in such surveys where no incentive is offered to respondents (Deutskens et al. 2004). The survey data were analyzed using SPSS 17.0

4 Results

4.1 Results of the Qualitative Data

Of the five interviewees, four served in large companies (number of employees > 500) and one in a small company (number of employees < 100). Only the small company was a pure SaaS provider and founded as such, whereas the other four delivered SaaS in addition to software products, with the SaaS line of business recently added. Four of the five participants represented vendors delivering CRM solutions (one of which represented a CRM SaaS only developer), and one delivered ERP software.

4.1.1 Lessons Learned from the ASP Era

Three main reasons were commonly noted as drivers of entering the SaaS markets: 1) Market need and readiness, 2) Technological ability, and 3) Avoiding staying behind competition. All interviewees have agreed that the success of Salesforce.com was an indicator of market readiness and a driver of the SaaS market growth.

With respect to Past ASP experience, interviewees were asked whether their organizations addressed the following barriers cited in the literature as hindering ASP adoption: Internet and connectivity risks, trust in the provider, reluctance to be locked in a long-term contract, insufficient range of applications offered, application integration, customization issues, customer expectations disconfirmation, and inadequate financial model. Four of the five interviewees said their organizations have discussed application integration issues and the financial model of the service delivery. Three have confirmed addressing the issues of customization and Internet risks, and two have dealt with the trust concerns. None have dealt with the contract duration, range of applications, and customer disconfirmation issues. In the open part of the interview, however, only one interviewee admitted conducting a deliberate 'lessons learned' session, saying: *"...it has been considered by learning the weaknesses and strengths of ASP "*.

In contrast to the common wisdom in the former ASP era, where marketing efforts were largely aimed at small and medium-sized organizations, three of the four CRM companies have noted that one of the key success factors is being able to market and sell the service to large customer-organizations. They specifically noted that succeeding in this effort required developing integration interfaces with many other applications. For example, one interviewee specifically stated that *"...the design of the software enables high level of integration and interfacing..."* and another interviewee said that integration with other applications was a key success factor, and noted that their product was built as *"... a bridge to other applications providing the simplest interfaces..."*.

4.1.2 SaaS as an Innovation

All interviewees perceived their organizations as innovators. Two have classified SaaS as a revolutionary innovation: the pure SaaS provider delivering its own developed software, and a service provider delivering several SaaS solutions developed by third parties. The other three interviewees representing providers of both software as a product and as a service, perceived SaaS as an evolutionary innovation. All interviewees stated their organizations were aware of the diffusion of innovation theory, particularly the need to rapidly acquire a critical mass of early adopters. Thus, three of the four CRM companies have attracted early adopters by offering lower prices or free trials. The ERP provider had a mechanism for identifying potential innovators as early adopters. All companies attempted to recruit a "champion" contact at the customer organization as a leader or "ambassador", as stated by one of the interviewees: *"We approach each level (business and technological levels [author clarification]) and look for an innovative leader in order to convince..."*

4.1.3 Capabilities Required to Succeed in the SaaS Market

Sensing the customer (within the 'sensing the stakeholders' capability) was cited by all interviewees as very important. There was likewise a consensus among all interviewees that becoming a software service provider required some different business models than those required for providing software product, yet none emphasized major changes their organizations underwent. Three emphasized that becoming a software service provider has forced organizational changes in marketing and sales, and in the revenue model, and three of the CRM providers pointed at having to introduce a strict SLA with their customers, and at having to invest in call centers in order to ensure a 24x7 support. These changes implied the need for 'process improvement' and 'develop a new process' capabilities.

Counting all implicit references to the seven capabilities in the interviews (Figure 6), it is evident that the three sensing capabilities had the highest number of references in the interviews, followed by the process capabilities, while the decision capability was assessed as the least important judged by the number of implicit references in the interviews.

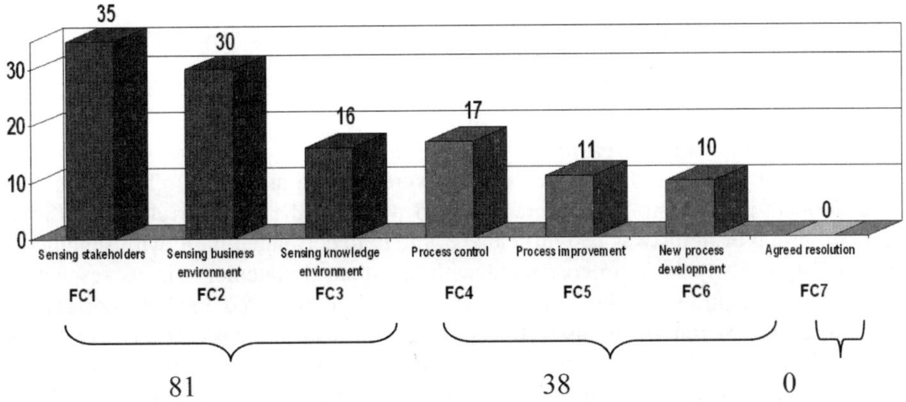

Fig. 6. Number of references to the seven fundamental capabilities across all interviews

Interestingly, the 'appropriate resolution' capability, which reflects decision making, was not mentioned explicitly or implicitly by any of the interviewees. Also surprising is the relatively lower importance of new process development. These points are further elaborated in the discussion section. Analysis of the number of references by interviewee elicited that there were no significant differences among the interviewee references based on any of their organizational characteristics.

4.2 Results of the Survey Data

Table 4 describes the characteristics of the 37 respondents, showing that the majority of respondents were executives, from small companies, delivering pure SaaS applications they have developed, mostly enterprise systems.

The average tenure of respondents in their present role was 5.8 years, and the average duration of an organization in the software market was 12.16 years (STD 13.21), while the average duration in the SaaS market was 4.4 years (STD 3.18). These figures reflect the relative novelty of the SaaS market. 15 out of 37 organizations have provided their SaaS software application since the company's foundation.

Since the survey was delivered electronically to the target population, the resulting sample included respondents from Canada (3), New Zeeland (2), Israel (8), USA (13), India (1), Denmark (1), Spain (1), Ireland (3), the UK (1) and other countries (2).

Table 4. Respondents business affiliation

Characteristic	Characteristic Value (N=37)	
Respondent role	Executives: 23 (62%)	Lower level: 14 (38%)
Company Size	Large (>1000 employees): 5 (8%)	Small (less than 50 employees): 32 (86%)
ISV/SP	Independent software vendors and providers their products in SaaS: 32 (86%)	Service providers, deliver 3rd party software: 5 (14%)
Business model	SaaS only: 24 (65%)	SaaS alongside software products: 13 (35%)
Software type	Enterprise software (i.e. ERP, CRM, Billing, EMR, etc.): 23 (62%)	Non-enterprise software (i.e. accounting, project management, testing, etc.): 14 (38%)

4.2.1 Reliability of the Measurement Instrument

Spearman correlation and Cronbach's alpha were used to assess the reliability of the measurement instrument. Items were removed when (1) the item correlation with the relevant group of items was insignificant (2) the item correlated more with statements in other groups (3) the item correlated with less than 3 statements in its respective group (4) correlation was less than 0.336 which is considered medium correlation (Pallant 2005). Seventeen items were removed as a result of this test (see Appendix 3). As shown in Table 5, Cronbach's alpha after item removal was higher than 0.78 for all fundamental capabilities, which is above the 0.7 threshold required for assuming reliability (Cortina 1993).

Table 5. Measurement items reliability

Fundamental Organizational Capability (FOC)	Cronbach's alpha	Number of valid observations	Number of items
FOC1 Sensing Stakeholders	0.811	36	5
FOC2 Sensing Business	0.787	37	4
FOC3 Sensing Knowledge	0.778	37	5
FOC4 Process Control	0.945	30	12
FOC5 Process Improvement	0.889	32	7
FOC6 Process Development	0.907	32	8
FOC7 Appropriate Resolution	0.900	30	6

4.2.2 Perceived FOC Rankings

We employed a paired-sample t-test analysis to compare the respondents' ratings of the FOCs when asked directly about the strength of each FOC in their organizations, with the indirect ratings based on the simple mean of the ratings of the items. Simple mean was used rather than weighted mean assuming each of the valid items equally represented the FOC.

The direct and indirect ratings of all pairs but Appropriate Resolution were significantly different as seen in Table 6, namely, respondents rated the strength of the FOC differently when asked to directly rate it, compared with the indirect rating calculated via items reflecting each FOC.

Table 6. Paired samples statistics – direct vs. indirect FOC ratings

FOCs	N	Mean		Std. Deviation		t	df	Sig. (2-tailed)
		Direct	Calculated	Direct	Calculated			
Sensing stakeholders	37	5.65	4.91	0.676	1.013	4.665	36	.000
Sensing business	36	5.47	4.99	0.91	0.729	3.755	35	.001
Sensing knowledge	36	5.39	4.56	0.766	0.891	6.772	35	.000
Process control	37	5.11	4.50	1.048	1.046	3.127	36	.003
Process improvement	36	5.47	4.36	0.774	1.132	7.023	35	.000
New process	36	5.14	4.65	0.867	0.980	2.793	35	.008
Appropriate resolution	35	5.20	4.95	1.079	0.982	1.505	34	.142

Interestingly, all direct ratings (but one) were significantly higher than the indirect ratings, suggesting that respondents overestimated the strengths of their FOCs compared to the ratings calculated from items that indirectly measure the FOC. This finding clearly merits further research.

We then recoded the direct ratings of the seven FOCs into a 1 – 3 scale (1,2=1, 3-4=2, 5,6=3) and compared it with the ratings of the importance of the FOCs to the SaaS delivery success using paired-samples t-tests (Table 7).

Table 7. Paired samples statistics – direct FOC vs. FOC importance ratings

		Mean		Std. Deviation				
	N	Importance	Direct Strength	Importance	Direct Strength	t	df	Sig[1].
Sensing Stakeholders	33	2.545	2.939	.564	.242	-4.073	32	.000
Sensing Business Env.	35	2.629	2.829	.547	.453	-2.503	34	.017
Sensing Knowledge Env.	33	2.636	2.879	.489	.331	-2.484	32	.018
Process control	37	2.429	2.771	1.046	.479	-2.652	34	.012
Process improvement	36	2.353	2.882	1.132	.319	-5.022	33	.000
New process dev.	34	2.412	2.735	.557	.448	-2.458	33	.019
Appropriate Resolution	34	2.529	2.735	.563	.448	-2.231	33	.033

[1] Two tailed.

All comparisons showed statistically significant differences between the direct ratings of the perceived strengths of the FOC in the respondents' organizations and the ratings of the importance of the FOCs to SaaS success. As in the previous comparison, the means of the direct ratings were consistently higher than the ratings of the importance of the FOC. This finding corroborates the assumption that respondents tended to over-rate the strength of the FOCs in their organizations.

Next, we examined the order of the FOC rankings by the magnitude of the means, as perceived by the respondents (Table 8), showing significant differences among the three ranking options.

Table 8. Order of the FOC rankings

No.	Direct FOC rankings	Indirect FOC rankings	Ranking by importance
1	Sensing stakeholders	Sensing business env.	Sensing Knowledge Env.
2	Sensing business env.	Appropriate resolution	Sensing Business Env.
3	Process improvements	Sensing stakeholders	Sensing Stakeholders
4	Sensing knowledge env.	New process development	Appropriate Resolution
5	Appropriate resolution	Sensing knowledge env.	Process control
6	New process development	Process control	New process dev.
7	Process control	Process improvement	Process improvement

Consistent with the ranking elicited in the qualitative analysis, the three 'sensing' capabilities were ranked highest when ranked by importance to SaaS delivery success (rightmost column), although the internal order of the capabilities differed. The three intervention capabilities were ranked last, with 'process improvement' closing the list as the least important. However, in contrast to its ranking in the qualitative analysis, 'appropriate resolution' was ranked here in the fourth place after the three sensing capabilities. There were interesting significant differences among the rankings of the 'appropriate resolution' capability.

One way ANOVA analysis employed to assess relationships between respondents' characteristics and rankings of FOCs did not yield any significant difference. This can be attributed to the small number of respondents within each characteristic category, or attest to the random distribution of opinions among respondents. We suggest that future research elaborates on the relationships between traits such as organizational size, country of origin, type of provider, etc. and perceptions about FOCs and SaaS.

Finally, we examined the correlations between the SaaS performance indicators and the FOC rankings, starting with the direct rankings of the strengths of the FOC in the respondents' organizations (Table 9).

Table 9. Correlations between the direct FOC rankings and the five performance indicators

Performance Indicators	FOC1*	FOC2	FOC3	FOC4	FOC5	FOC6	FOC7
Our SaaS customers are satisfied with the product	.361*	.508**	.253	.427*	.362*	.635**	.319
Our SaaS customers are satisfied with the service (timely answers, support, etc.)	.537**	.259	.289	.430*	.312	.698**	.201
The number of SaaS customers are in line with the company's expectations	.392*	.313	.179	.569**	.406*	.359*	.285
The number of SaaS customers which renew contracts are in line with the company's expectations	.343*	.134	.194	.176	.172	.201	.096
The amount of changes and customizations required of the SaaS application is small	.145	.176	.263	.442**	.248	.334	.430*

* FOC1- sensing stakeholders, FOC2 – sensing the business env. FOC3 – sensing the knowledge env. FOC4 – process control, FOC5 – process improvement, FOC6- new process dev. FOC7 – appropriate resolution.

Correlations above 0.5 are highlighted, showing that high correlations existed between customer satisfaction with the product and 'sensing the business environment', and 'new process development'. Customer satisfaction with the service was highly correlated with 'sensing the stakeholders' and with 'new process development'. Lastly, the number of SaaS customers was highly correlated with 'process control'. The indicators related to contract renewal, and to change and customization requests was not highly correlated with any of the seven FOCs.

5 Discussion and Conclusions

This study investigated the relatively novel SaaS model of enterprise software sourcing from the vendor's perspective which has been less studied compared to the more prevalent customer view. We attempted at assessing the vendors' readiness by asking about lessons learned from the ASP failure, by inquiring about their perceptions of SaaS as an innovation, and by gauging their direct and indirect assessment of the strength and importance of capabilities believed to drive SaaS delivery success. These capabilities were elicited from a recently developed model, the Seven Fundamental Capabilities Model.

5.1 Summary of Key Findings

Lessons learned from the past ASP era: based on five interviews with SaaS vendors' executives, who actually represent all local companies that deliver enterprise systems in SaaS mode, the impression is that lessons from the past ASP era were derived but in a limited manner, as just one interviewee affirmed conducting a strategic review of the topic. The others mentioned informal reference to specific problems such as application integration and the adequacy of the financial model. A number of issues were never discussed by any of the interviewees' organizations.

SaaS as an innovation: three interviewees regarded SaaS as an evolutionary innovation, hence reported no major changes in current organizational processes used to deliver software products. One interviewee representing a pure-SaaS vendor (i.e. founded as a SaaS delivery vendor and delivers a SaaS-oriented application) perceived SaaS a revolutionary innovation. One interviewee suggested SaaS was a mixture of evolutionary and revolutionary innovation, and mentioned that marketing, support, and financial processes have been changed.

Capabilities that drive SaaS delivery success: the interviewees ranked the three sensing capabilities highest in importance based on the number of times these capabilities were mentioned in their narrative. These results were corroborated by the ranking of the importance of the capabilities to a SaaS vendor. There was however some inconsistency within this category, as the interviewees regarded 'sensing the stakeholders' as most important, whereas the survey respondents ranked this capability last among the three sensing capabilities. No agreement was evidenced on the rank of the 'appropriate resolution' capability. Among the intervention capabilities, 'process control' was ranked first by both interviewees and survey respondents, yet they differed in ranking the importance of the other two capabilities.

An interesting inconsistency emerged when ranking the capabilities strength in the organizations directly (explicit question) or indirectly (via items that implicitly reflect the capability). Respondents consistently evaluated the strength of the seven capabilities higher when ranked directly compared to the calculated indirect rank. This higher direct ranking persisted even in the comparison between strength and the importance of the capability in the SaaS business. We discuss this gap hereafter.

Finally, only marginal correlation was found between the capabilities and five performance measures indicating SaaS success, with 'new process development' largely ($r>0.5$) correlated to customer satisfaction with the product and with the service. Three other capabilities were also largely correlated each to one indicator. This is also discussed after the limitations are noted next.

5.2 Limitations

Three major limitations of this study should be noted: sample size, qualitative data analysis method, and the model novelty.

The samples providing both qualitative and quantitative data were small and their acquisition method posed several limitations. As mentioned earlier, although we covered all local SaaS enterprise systems providers and aimed at interviewing as senior managers as possible, we cannot ascertain that the interviewees indeed delivered the true strategies of their companies. Hence caution is warranted in interpreting the results.

The small number of respondents to the survey, although suiting the lower bound of response rate achieved under similar circumstances (Deutskens et al. 2004), is also a limiting factor, which allowed using rather weak statistical tools for data analysis. A larger sample size in future research is required to substantiate the results.

The indirect analysis method employed for the assessment of the importance of the capabilities is rather questionable, thus further research in this direction is required.

Finally, as indicated earlier, the proposed model of fundamental capabilities is new and by itself requires further support and substantiation in future research. Due to its use as the framework for the organizational capabilities assessment, the results should be further corroborated for validity by additional research.

5.3 Answers to the Research Questions

Three questions were the focus of this research: SaaS vendors' perceptions about SaaS as an innovation, lessons they have learned from the past ASP phenomenon and implications on their SaaS delivery processes, and their evaluation of the strength of seven capabilities posited to be required for organizational success in general, including in the SaaS industry.

From the interviews we learned that established software vendors, who have recently started to offer SaaS as an additional line of business, perceive it as an evolutionary innovation hence did not implement significant change in their existing business processes. Two pure-SaaS providers regarded SaaS as either revolutionary or mixed innovation. Because there are indications that SaaS is a revolutionary innovation, as discussed later, we believe that the readiness of the interviewed vendors is rather questionable. The fact that most vendors did not conduct deliberate lessons-learned sessions supports our assumption. Lastly, respondents rated their organizational capabilities higher than their ranking of the importance of the capabilities to SaaS delivery success, indicating they believed their organizations were ready for SaaS delivery. However, a calculation of these values from indirect measurements showed consistent lower ranking, possibly indicating lower readiness than explicitly admitted. This gap, if indeed substantiated by further research, is worrying.

5.4 Implications for Research

Although ample research studied the ASP phenomena (Kern et al. 2002; Desai et al. 2003; Ma et al. 2005; Currie et al. 2007; Heeseok et al. 2007), only a handful suggested theoretical frameworks that provided adequate explanation of the ASP failure (Currie 2004). In this study we propose two such frameworks: the evolutionary-revolutionary innovation theory, and the new Seven Fundamental Organizational Capabilities Model.

Drawing on the evolutionary-revolutionary literature (Lyytinen and Rose 2003), there are strong indications that SaaS, as a sourcing option for enterprise-wide applications, is rather a revolutionary innovation since it renders existing IT assets and processes redundant and even burdensome, and because it completely replaces existing solutions. We therefore suggest that the revolutionary innovation framework better explains SaaS diffusion and adoption, and call for future research in this direction. Thus, models explaining and predicting SaaS adoption should include factors relevant to the revolutionary innovation adoption context, for example risk, vendor trustworthiness, compatibility, and organizational change management. As to the vendor side, this study is a first step towards more research on SaaS delivery value chain and supporting processes, aimed at illustrating frameworks addressing SaaS specificities.

The introduction of the novel Seven Fundamental Capabilities Model is another theoretical contribution of this work by itself, in addition to its application to the SaaS vendors' readiness context. The model, if further validated, provides a generic parsimonious yet comprehensive tool to analyze and assess various aspects of organizations and management. We demonstrated the plausibility of the model as a framework for organizational strengths and weaknesses evaluation, yet more research is clearly required to develop valid measurement instruments for the capabilities. Another theoretical challenge is linking the capabilities to performance measures. Thus, future research should examine the causal relationships between the capabilities value pattern and performance. Investigating contingencies affecting these effects are of particular interest, for example, the type of products or services, organizational characteristics and environmental situations.

Another interesting theoretical aspect of the model is investigating organizational strengths and weaknesses via the lens of the process value chain, as suggested in Figure 5. Analysis of this value chain by identifying optimal inputs, processes, and outputs while highlighting the contribution of the seven capabilities to efficient and effective conversion, is a theoretical contribution in general, and, as shown in this study, can be applied to various industries, new or old. Its application to the SaaS industry is a specific contribution to better understand SaaS delivery success.

5.5 Implications for Practice

Although an initial step in this research trajectory, the results perhaps raise several questions as to vendors' readiness for successful SaaS delivery. If further supported, the destiny of SaaS might perhaps resemble this of ASP.

5.6 SaaS as an Innovation

Corroborating the literature (Fenn and Linden 2005; Koenig 2006; MacGregor 2006; TenWolde 2007), SaaS delivery is considered an innovation by the interviewees, without consensus whether an evolutionary (incremental) or revolutionary (disruptive or radical). This assessment of the type of innovation, particularly if found revolutionary, is important because it implies certain measures SaaS vendors need to take in order to succeed. According to the literature for instance, existing organizational assets and processes might hinder revolutionary innovativeness, while these same assets and processes can contribute to success of evolutionary innovation (Abernathy and Clark 1985; Henderson and Clark 1990; Afuah 2003; Popadiuk and Choo 2006). Likewise, market penetration is different for evolutionary or revolutionary innovations (Garcia and Calantone 2002; Voelpel et al. 2004; Philippe and Phillip 2007). If indeed a revolutionary innovation, vendors should adapt their organization's structures and strategies accordingly while departing from existing processes. Failure to do so might weakens their readiness and, hence, their success in delivering SaaS.

Whereas leading software providers such as Oracle, SAP, Microsoft, and IBM were absent from the ASP marketplace, they are now quite active in the SaaS business. This could have been a promising cue because it is believed that the former ASP ecosystem suffered from this absence. However, indications that these vendors perhaps perceive SaaS as an evolutionary innovation, thus try to deliver it using processes similar to the delivery of software products, is worrying. So far, only Saleforce.com was successful in establishing a viable business model for delivering enterprise applications in SaaS model. Indeed, this company was founded as a SaaS provider and claims it to be a revolutionary innovation.

5.7 Subjective Evaluation of the FOCs

Unsurprisingly, the three 'sensing' capabilities were rated highest and most important by all respondents, as could be expected in a service-oriented business. This, however, cannot be unique to SaaS delivery and is likely to be perceived as most, or at least very, important in all modern businesses, particularly sensing the stakeholder which quite often is interpreted as 'sensing the customers'. While the novelty of SaaS clearly requires technological capabilities, as well attention to the competition in order to thrive, 'process control', 'new process development', and 'appropriate resolution' should also be valued by SaaS vendors. The fact that 'new process development' was related to customer satisfaction more strongly than other capabilities lends support to this assumption. Likewise, the finding that all directly-assessed seven capabilities scored higher than the rankings of the indirectly calculated capabilities attests to a potential gap between what should be done and what is actually achieved. It is thus possible that executives perceived their organizations' readiness higher than they really were.

5.8 The Seven FOCs Model

We believe that organizations, in the SaaS market and elsewhere, can benefit from using the Seven FOCs Model as a tool to assess strength and weaknesses while examining the value chain of converting inputs into valuable outputs. The capabilities required in each part of the chain should be evaluated, the results of which should serve to decide on corrective measures and action plans to improve weak capabilities that should be strong, and to preserve strong capabilities. This model can serve as a managerial tool that is generic, fairly intuitive, and holistic.

5.9 Conclusions

The present study can contribute to the body of knowledge about SaaS, as well as to the more general literature about services, where works investigating the vendor perspective are scarce. The implications of the results to theory are in introducing two analysis frameworks, most importantly the introduction of the seven fundamental capabilities theory, adapted to the SaaS context. Of particular interest are the objective and subjective rankings of the seven capabilities to succeeding in the SaaS marketplace, as well as their relationships with various performance indicators.

On the practical side, the results, if further supported, can provide guidance to decision makers in organizations considering becoming SaaS vendors, particularly related to the fundamental capabilities required in order to succeed in this emerging market. Understanding these capabilities will allow such firms to more appropriately allocate their resources towards gaining competitive edge in a relatively new business model. This is more important now than before, since favorable predictions pertaining to the future of the SaaS market are now supported by the interests of leading providers as IBM, Oracle, SAP and Microsoft. The success of Salesforce.com in providing CRM as a service on the one hand, and the efforts of IBM and Salesforce.com to introduce cloud computing platforms to facilitate this mode of software delivery, perhaps indicate a more successful destiny of SaaS compared to its ASP predecessor. However, it is not yet certain that SaaS vendors have truly grasped the novelty of SaaS and are making the adequate preparations. More research in this direction is thus merited.

References

Abernathy, W., Clark, A.K.B.: Mapping the winds of creative destruction. Research Policy 14, 3–22 (1985)

Adams, C., Neely, A.: Prism reform. Financial Management 5, 28–31 (2002)

Adams, J.S.: Inequity in social exchange. Advances in experimental social psychology 2, 267–299 (1965)

Afuah, A.: Innovation Management. Oxford University Press, New-York (2003)

Avlontis, G.J., Papastathopoulou, P.G., Gounaris, S.P.: An empirically- based typology of product innovativeness for new financial services: Success and failure scenario. Journal of Product Innovation Management 18, 324–342 (2001)

Barney, J.B.: The Resource Based View of Strategy: Origins, Implications, and Prospects. Editor of Special Theory Forum in Journal of Management 17, 97–211 (1991)

Becker, S.W., Whisler, T.L.: The Innovative Organization: A Selective View of Current Theory and Research. The Journal of Business (pre-1986) 40(4), 462–469 (1967)

Benbasat, I., Goldstein, D.K., Mead, M.: The Case Research Strategy in Studies of Information Systems. MIS Quarterly 11(3) (1987)

Bennett, C., Timbrell, G.T.: Application Service Providers: Will They Succeed? Information Systems Frontiers 2(2), 195–221 (2000)

Carr, N.G.: The end of corporate computing. MIT Sloan Management Review 46(3), 67–73 (2005)

Choi, T.Y., Dooley, K.J., Rungtusanatham, M.: Supply networks and complex adaptive systems: control versus emergence. Journal of Operations Management 19(3), 351–366 (2001)

Cortina, J.M.: What is coefficient alpha? An examination of theory and applications. Journal of applied psychology 78(1), 98–98 (1993)
Currie, W.L.: A knowledge-based risk assessment framework for evaluating web-enabled application outsourcing projects. International Journal of Project Management 21(3), 207–217 (2003)
Currie, W.L.: The organizing vision of application service provision: a process-oriented analysis. Information and Organization 14(4), 237–267 (2004)
Currie, W.L., Desai, B., Khan, N., Xinkun, W., Weerakkody, V.: Vendor strategies for business process and outsourcing: recent findings from field research. In: Proceedings of the 36th Annual Hawaii International Conference on System Sciences, HICSS 2003 (2003)
Currie, W.L., Joyce, P., Winch, G.: Evaluating Application Service Provisioning Using System Dynamics Methodology. British Journal of Management 18(2), 172–191 (2007)
Daft Richard, L.: Organization theory and design. South Western College Publishing, Cincinnati (1998)
Daft, R.L.: A Dual-Core Model of Organizational Innovation. Academy of Management Journal 21(2), 193–210 (1978)
Day, G.S.: Creating a superior customer-relating capability. MIT Sloan Management Review 44(3), 77–82 (2003)
Desai, B., Currie, W.: Application service providers: A model in evolution. In: Proceedings of the 5th International Conference on Electronic Commerce, ACM International Conference Proceeding Series, vol. 50, pp. 174–180 (2003)
Desai, B., Weerakkody, V., Currie, W.: Market entry strategies of application service providers: Identifying strategic differentiation. In: Proceedings of the 36th Annual Hawaii International Conference on System Sciences (2003)
Deutskens, E., De Ruyter, K., Wetzels, M., Oosterveld, P.: Response rate and response quality of internet-based surveys: An experimental study. Marketing Letters 15(1), 21–36 (2004)
Dewar, R.D., Dutton, J.E.: The Adoption of Radical and Incremental Innovations: An Empirical Analysis. Management Science 32(11), 1422–1433 (1986)
Dosi, G., Nelson, R.R., Winter, S.G.: The nature and dynamics of organizational capabilities. Oxford University Press, USA (2000)
Dubey, A., Wagle, D.: Delivering Software as a Service. The McKinsey Quarterly Web Exclusive (2007)
Dym, R.: Why Software as a service? Helping Our Customers Achieve Compliance (2007) (OpSource retrieved Accessed on, 11/12/2007)
Eisenhardt, K.M.: Building Theories From Case Study Research. Academy of Management. The Academy of Management Review 14(4), 532—550 (1989)
Eisenhardt, K.M., Martin, J.A.: Dynamic capabilities: What are they? Strategic Management Journal 21(10/11), 1105 (2000)
Ekanayaka, Y., Currie, W.L., Seltsikas, P.: Delivering enterprise resource planning systems through application service providers. Logistics Information Management 15(3), 192–203 (2002)
Ekanayaka, Y., Currie, W.L., Seltsikas, P.: Evaluating application service providers. Benchmarking: An International Journal 10(4), 343–354 (2003)
Featherman, M.S., Wells, J.D.: The intangibility of E-services: effects on artificiality, perceived risk, and adoption. In: Proceedings of the 37th Annual Hawaii International Conference on System Sciences (2004)
Fenn, J., Linden, A.: Gartner's Hype Cycle Special Report for 2005 (2005), http://www.gartner.com/resources/130100/130115/gartners_hype_c.pdf (retrieved 1/2/2008)

Fenn, J., Linden, A.: Gartner's Hype Cycle Special Report for 2005. Gartner (2005)

Freeman, R.E.: Strategic Management: A Stakeholder Approach. Pitman, Boston (1984)

Garcia, R., Calantone, R.: A critical look at technological innovation typology and innovativeness terminology: a literature review. Journal of Product Innovation Management 19(2), 110–132 (2002)

Greschler, D., Mangan, T.: Networking lessons in delivering 'Software as a Service'—part I. International Journal of Network Management 12(5), 317–321 (2002)

Heart, T., Pliskin, N.: Business-to-Business eCommerce of Information Systems: Two Cases of ASP-to-SME e-Rental. INFOR 40(1), 23–34 (2002)

Heart, T., Pliskin, N., Curley, K.: Application Hosting as Means for Aligning Business and IT. International Journal of E-Business 5(2), 176–187 (2007)

Heeseok, L., Jeoungkun, K., Jonguk, K.: Determinants of success for application service provider: An empirical test in small businesses. International Journal of Human-Computer Studies 65(9), 796–815 (2007)

Henderson, R.M., Clark, K.B.: Architectural innovation: The reconfiguration of existing product technologies and the failure of established firms. Administrative Science Quarterly 35(1), 9–22 (1990)

Huang, A., Gutierrez, J.C.: Oracle On Demand: Using Technology for Strategic Advantage (2006), Oracle from, http://www.oracle.com/ondemand/collateral/oracle_ondemand_brief.pdf

Kaplan, B., Maxwell, J.: Qualitative research methods for evaluating computer information systems. In: Anderson, J., Aydin, C., Jay, S. (eds.) Evaluating Health Care Information Systems. Springer, New York (2005)

Kashi, G.: Fundamental Capabilities for Organizational Operational Success. Industrial Engineering and Management. Beer-Sheva, Ben-Gurion University of the Negev. Ph.D (2007)

Kern, T., Kreijger, J., Willcocks, L.: Exploring ASP as sourcing strategy: theoretical perspectives, propositions for practice. The Journal of Strategic Information Systems 11(2), 153–177 (2002)

Kern, T., Lacity, M.C., Willcocks, L.: Netsourcing: renting business application and services. Prentice Hall, Englewood Cliffs (2002)

Knight, K.E.: A Descriptive Model of the Intra-Frim Innovation Process. The Journal of Business 40(4), 478–494 (1967)

Koenig, M.: SaaS 2.0: Software-as-a-Service as Next-Gen Business Platform, Executive summary. Saugatech (2006)

Konary, A.: On-Demand Service: Changing the Software Value Model. I D C Analyst Connection (2005), http://www.marketwatch.com/minisites/oracle/IDG_IDC_Orace_OnDemand_Analyst_Connection.pdf (retrieved 1/2/, 2008)

Kusunoki, K., Nonaka, I., Nagata, A.: Organizational capabilities in product development of Japanese firms: a conceptual framework and empirical findings. Organization Science 9(6), 699–718 (1998)

Lixin, T.: Shifting paradigms with the application service provider model. Computer 34(10), 32–39 (2001)

Lyytinen, K., Rose, G.M.: The disruptive nature of information technology innovations: the case of Internet computing in systems development organizations. MIS Quarterly 27(4), 557–595 (2003)

Ma, Q., Pearson, J.M., Tadisina, S.: An exploratory study into factors of service quality for application service providers. Information & Management 42(8), 1067–1080 (2005)

MacGregor, C.: SaaS 2.0: Saugatuck Study Shows Rapid SaaS Evolution to Business Platforms. PRWeb, Press Release Newswire (2006)

Marin, D., Schnitzer, M.: The economic institution of international barter. Economic Journal 112(479), 293–316 (2002)

McLaughlin, L.: Cloud Computing Survey: IT Leaders See Big Promise, Have Big Security Questions (2008), `http://www.cio.com/article/455832/Cloud_Computing_Survey_IT_Leaders_See_Big_Promise_Have_Big_Security_Questions` (retrieved October 17, 2009)

McNee, W.S.: SaaS 2.0. Journal of Digital Asset Management 3(4), 209–214 (2007)

Mota, J., de Castro, L.M.: A capabilities perspective on the evolution of firm boundaries: A comparative case example from the portuguese moulds industry. Journal of Management Studies 41(2), 295–316 (2004)

Myers, M.D.: Qualitative Research in Information Systems. MISQ Discovery 21(2), 241–242 (1997)

Nonaka, I.A., Takeuchi, H.A.: The knowledge-creating company: How Japanese companies create the dynamics of innovation. Oxford University Press, Oxford (1995)

Pallant, J.: SPSS survival manual. Open University Press, Buckingham (2005)

Patnayakuni, R., Seth, N.: Why license when you can rent? Risks and rewards of the application service provider model. In: Special Interest Group on Computer Personnel Research Annual Conference, pp. 182–188 (2001)

Philippe, S., Phillip, A.C.: Acting to see: when disruptive times call for disruptive marketing. European Business Forum (29), 40 (2007)

Popadiuk, S., Choo, C.W.: Innovation and knowledge creation: How are these concepts related? International Journal of Information Management 26(4), 302–312 (2006)

Poppo, L., Zenger, T.: Testing Alternative Theories of the Firm: Transaction Cost, Knowledge-Based, and Measurement Explanations for Make-or-Buy Decisions in Information Services. Strategic Management Journal 19, 853–877 (1998)

Porter, M.E.: What Is Strategy? Harvard Business Review 74(6), 61–78 (1996)

Rabinowitz, G., Kashi, G., Root, A., Gavius, A.: Seven core capabilities of organization (in press, 2008)

Ratnasingam, P.: E-Commerce Relationships: The Impact of Trust on Relationship Continuity. International Journal of Commerce & Management 15(1), 1 (2005)

Rogers, E.M.: Diffusion of Innovations. The Free Press, New York (1983)

Ross, J.W., Westerman, G.: Preparing for utility computing: The role of IT architecture and relationship management. IBM Systems Journal 41(3), 5–19 (2004)

Rulke, D.L., Zaheer, S., Anderson, M.H.: Sources of managers' knowledge of organizational capabilities. Organizational Behavior and Human Decision Processes 82(1), 134–149 (2000)

Saeed, M., Jaffar-Ur-Rehman, M.: Enhancement of Software Engineering by Shifting From Software Product to Software Service. In: First International Conference on Information and Communication Technologies, ICICT (2005)

Schein, E.H.: Organizational culture. American psychologist 45(2), 109–119 (1990)

Seaman, C.B.: Qualitative methods in empirical studies of software engineering. IEEE Transactions on Software Engineering 25(4), 557–572 (1999)

Senge, P.M.: The Fifth Discipline: The Art and Practice of the Learning Organization. Currency (1990)

Sheehan, J.: Understanding service sector innovation. Communication of the ACM 49(7), 42–47 (2006)
Swanson, E.B.: Information systems innovation among organizations. Management Science 40(9), 1069–1092 (1994)
Teece, D.J., Pisano, G., Shuen, A.: Dynamic capabilities and strategic management. Strategic Management Journal 18(7), 509–533 (1997)
TenWolde, E.K.: SaaS 2.0: What Does the Future Hold? OpSource SaaS Summit, IDC (2007)
Turner, M., Budgen, D., Brereton, P.: Turning software into a service. Computer 36(10), 38–44 (2003)
Vassiliadis, B., Stefani, A., Tsaknakis, J., Tsakalidis, A.: From application service provision to service-oriented computing: A study of the IT outsourcing evolution. Telematics and Informatics 23(4), 271–293 (2006)
Voelpel, S.C., Leibold, M., Tekie, E.B.: Wheel of business model reinvention: How to reshape your business model to leapfrog competitors. Journal of Change Management 4(3), 259–276 (2004)
Wall, T.D., Michie, J., Patterson, M., Wood, S.J., Sheehan, M., Clegg, C.W., West, M.: On the validity of subjective measures of company performance. Personnel Psychology 57(1), 95–119 (2004)
Walsh, K.R.: Analyzing the application ASP concept: technologies, economies, and strategies. Communications of the ACM 46(8), 103–107 (2003)
Wang, C.L., Ahmed, P.K., Uxbridge, K.L., Middlesex, W.L., Sunway, B.: Dynamic capabilities: A review and research agenda. International Journal of Management Reviews 9(1), 31–51 (2007)
Waters, B.: Software as a service: A look at the customer benefits. Journal of Digital Asset Management 1(1), 32 (8 pages) (2005)
Wernerfelt, B.: A Resource-Based View of the Firm. Strategic Management Journal 5(2), 171–180 (1984)
Winter, S.G.: Understanding Dynamic Capabilities. Strategic Management Journal 24(10), 991–995 (2003)
Zmud: Diffusion of modern software practices: influence of centralization and formalization. Management Science 28(12), 1421 (1982)

Appendix 1: Semi-structured Interview Instrument

Part 1	Interviewee company profile and positioning
1.1	What software functionalities does the company provide (CRM, ERP, ...)?
1.2	How these are delivered (one package, modules, several packages...)
1.3	Which functionalities does the company consider to launch in a SaaS model?
1.4	a. How would you distinguish between SaaS solutions and the Products; what are the characteristics which enables/do not enable it to suit a SaaS model ?
1.4	b. Which market segment do the software's SaaS and product customers belong to? Why this one?
1.4	c. Does the company have any intentions to re-segment its market by selling the new SaaS SW to an existing segment? Why?
1.4	d. If the SW is provided in SaaS, are they targeted towards new or existing customers who are likely to migrate?
1.4	e. If the SW is provided in SaaS, does the company still provide it in the product model?
1.4	f. How many customers does the company have for each product/service?
1.5	The company has decided to begin providing the software in a SaaS business Model.
1.5	a. Why?
1.5	b. Why now?
1.5	c. Why does the company think it will succeed?
1.5	d. What is the company's vision for the future development of this software?
1.6	Does salesforce.com have any relevancy to the company's decision to provide the software in a SaaS business model?
Part 2	Learning from the past ASP experience
2.1	What is the notion for the new business model? (ASP/SaaS,/On-demand/...) What is the company's definition for this Business model?
2.2	Did the company consider ASP's experience as part of the SaaS assessment prior to choosing to deliver in this business model?
2.3	What are the expected obstacles/risks?
2.4	How is the company planning to overcome them?
2.5	What are the key success factors?
2.6	How is the company planning to tackle the key success factors?
2.7	According to academic literature the following were the major reasons for ASP's failure. How is the company trying to overcome the expected obstacles?
2.7	1. Technical/environmental: connectivity and the internet
2.7	2. Managerial: trust in the model
2.7	3. Managerial: long-term contracts
2.7	4. Managerial: range of applications offered
2.7	5. Managerial: integration of applications offered
2.7	6. Operational: customization
2.7	7. Customers satisfaction from the service

2.7	8. Inadequate financial model
Part 3	SaaS Innovation Perceptions
3.1	Does the company consider the provisioning of the software in a new service business model as innovative?
3.2	What is the company's strategy regarding the innovation type of the SaaS software (revolutionary or evolutionary)?
3.3	Does the company work according to a DOI (diffusion of innovation) model?
3.4	What are the success factors for diffusion of innovation for the potential customer as the company sees them?
3.5	The following factors are considered in academics as the key success factors for diffusion of innovation in organizations. What is the company's approach to serve these factors?
3.5	a. Relative Advantage
3.5	b. Competability
3.5	c. Complexity
3.5	d. Trailability
3.5	e. Observability
3.5	f. Nature of social system
3.6	According to the academic literature, there are five adopter's categories in innovation adoption life cycle: innovators, early adopters, early majority, late majority and laggards.
3.6	a. What is the company's approach for finding these "innovators" and "early adopters and pass the critical phase ("chasm")?
3.6	b. How does the company convince the "innovators" and "early adopters" to purchase/use the software?
3.6	c. Why does the company think that it would be successful?; What are the factors for success in passing the critical phase ("chasm")?
3.7	Does the company locate "*champions*" in the potential customer's organization in order to promote the probability of diffusion?
3.8	What are the company's criteria for considering the diffusion/adoption of the software at a customer's company as successful? How is it measured?
3.9	3.9. Which customers are considered as "serious" customers (diffusion/adoption/routine)? Does the number of services rented count?
3.10	According to academic literature, there are five stages in organization's diffusion of innovation process. Agenda-setting, Matching, Redefining/Restructuring, Clarifying, Routinizing (Rogers, 2003) What is the level of disruption or discontinuity in the customer's organization as a result of adopting the new product?
Part 4	Providing SaaS
4.1	What is the company's approach to software services?
4.2	How does the company see itself as a service provider (rather than a product provider) in the software market?
4.3	Does the company work according to a specific business model in order to become a software service provider?
4.4	Does it affect its value chain and supply chain? How?
4.5	Does the company prepare itself in order to become a software service provider? In general
4.5	a. Marketing
4.5	b. Organizational changes
4.5	c. SLA
4.5	d. 24X7 Call Center / support

Appendix 2: Interview Data Analysis Method

Interviews Analysis Summary						
1.5	The company has decided to begin providing the software in a SaaS business Model.					
1.5.a	Why?					
	Interviewee / Concept	A	B	C	D	E
	Competition	X	X			
	Market need and technology availability (Internet)	X		X		
	Vision related to the SaaS delivery model advantages	X				X

Example of the semi structured interview analysis tool.

Interviews Summary		Seven fundamental capabilities							
Q#	Fundamental Capability / Question	Sensing stakeholders	Sensing knowledge environment	Sensing business environment	Develop new processes	Process control	Process improvement	Agreed resolution	Counting Technique
	Company	35	16	30	17	11	10	0	(# of companies and # of times this capability is referred to)
	X	9	4	9	5	3	3	0	# of times this capability is referred to in this interview
	Y	7	1	10	4	3	2	0	
	Z	8	5	6	3	2	2	0	
	A	6	1	3	2	1	2	0	
	B	5	5	2	3	2	1	0	
1.5	The company has decided to begin providing the software in a SaaS business Model.								# of interviewees to which this capability is relevant in this question
	a. Why?	1	3	4	0	1	0	0	
	b. Why now?	0	1	1	0	0	0	0	
	c. Why does the company think it will succeed?	0	1	1	0	0	0	0	
	d. What is the company's vision for the future development of this software?	0	1	1	3	0	2	0	

The FOC analysis tool – example.

Appendix 3: The Survey Instrument

Respondents were asked to rate statements in parts I – III on a 1 (strongly do not agree) to 6 (strongly agree) scale.

Part I: Direct ranking of the seven fundamental organizational capabilities

1	The organization is attentive to the needs of its SaaS customers
2	The organization is attentive to opportunities and threats created by the business environment
3	The organization recognizes relevant knowledge which exists in its environment
4	The organization meets its objectives in the SaaS market
5	The organization improves its business processes related to activities in the SaaS market
6	The organization successfully develops new processes related to the SaaS market
7	All organizational stakeholders are involved in decision making related to the SaaS market

Part II: Indirect statements reflecting the seven fundamental organizational capabilities

	Sensing the stakeholders
8*	The organization knows the various options of its stakeholders (parties within and outside the organization with whom it interacts directly)
9*	The organization knows what are the transfer costs of its customers in moving to competitors
10*	The organization is not surprised by customer's churn
11	The organization promotes open communication with all types of stakeholders
12	The organization has structured mechanisms for evaluating its stakeholders' needs
13	The organization acts according to feedback from its stakeholders
14	The organization is a preferred organization by its stakeholders
15*	The organization dedicates more attention to its important customers
16	There is an improvement tendency in stakeholders' (internal and external) satisfaction
	Sensing the business environment
18*	The organization reacts in real-time to changes of trends in its business environment
19*	The organization is not surprised by its competitors' moves
20	The organization knows its competitors well
21	The organization is aware of the threats in its business environment
22	The organization is aware of the opportunities in its business environment
23	The organization recognizes the trends affecting its fields of interest
	Sensing the knowledge environment
24	Relevant knowledge which is observed in the environment is assimilated in the organization effectively
25	Knowledge which is introduced into the organization generates effective activities
26*	Knowledge which is introduced into the organization improves processes
27*	The organization is well aware of the knowledge of its competitors
28	The organization is familiar with relevant academic knowledge
29	The organization has monitoring mechanisms aimed at assessing knowledge in its environment
30*	The organization takes part in relevant conferences
31	The organization has a "learning organization" culture
32*	The organization successfully imports important knowledge by using consulting companies

	Process control
33	Every important process in the organization has a success measure
34	Every measure has a specific quantitative target
35	When a standard is not met corrective actions are taken
36	The measures and targets are understood by all those who are evaluated
37	Those being evaluated are involved in setting the standard
38	Corrective actions when targets are not met are a systematic part of processes and procedures
39	Measurement is carried out during the process and not only at its end
40	The measurement process is easy to operate
41	Those being evaluated are given continuous feedback of their performance
42	Measurement results are known to those being evaluated in real time
43*	Measurement results are used regularly in the long term decision making
44*	Organizational measurements and targets are coordinated among different levels in the organization
	Process improvement
45	The organization promotes process improvement
46*	The organization recognizes and respects creativity and innovation
47*	The organization has a culture of learning from mistakes
48	The organization has an infrastructure for promoting improvement activities (i.e. allocates time for improvement, suggestion boxes, improvement teams, etc.)
49	The organization has a mechanism for mapping processes that have a potential for improvement
50	The improvements are in the right areas which will result in organizational improvement
51	The organization has the capabilities and proven methods for process improvement (statistical tools, methods and tools for locating waste)
52	Relevant consulting firms are involved in process improvements
53	The organization actively assimilates process improvements
	New process development
54*	The organization knows how to identify the need for development of new processes
55	New processes support value enhancement for the organization's stakeholders
56*	The organization systematically plans and designs new processes
57*	The customers of new processes give feedback regarding the quality of the new process during its development
58	During development of new processes success measurements are taken based on intermediate targets
59	In case of failing to achieve a goal of a new process, corrective actions are taken
60	Development of new processes is carried out by the relevant people
61	Process development in the organization includes resource planning and control
62	The organization forecasts the financial success of a new process / product / service
63	There is an integration among relevant departments in development of new processes
64	The organization properly monitors the effect of a new process on other organizational processes
	Appropriate resolution
65	The business strategy (which generates competitive advantage), is agreed by all the organization's stakeholders
66	The organizational market strategy is agreed upon by all the organization's stakeholders
67	Important processes within the organization as: collaboration, outsourcing, mergers and acquisitions, are agreed upon by all stakeholders
68	Decisions regarding: budget, pricing, investments and expenses are agreed upon by all stakeholders
69	There is an active negotiation among all the organization's stakeholders in order to define the organization's targets and goals
70	There is an active negotiation among all the organization's stakeholders in order to define the organization's priorities and resource allocation aimed at achieving the organization's targets and goals

* Removed item.

Part III: SaaS performance indicators

71	SaaS customers are satisfied with the product
72	SaaS customers are satisfied with the service (answers, support,...)
73	The number of SaaS customers are aligned with the company's expectations
74	The number of SaaS customers which renew contracts are aligned with the company's expectations
75	The amount of changes and customization of the SaaS application is small

Part IV: Definitions of the seven fundamental organizational capabilities and ranking of their importance to SaaS delivery success on a 1 (not important) to 3 (very important) scale

Capability	Definition
Agreed resolution	The organization's ability to reach an agreed resolution among its stakeholders about input sources, input to output conversion processes, and output allocation for the stakeholder.
Sensing stakeholders	The organization's ability to identify, understand and correctly map the stakeholders' needs and expectations from the organization.
Sensing the business environment	The ability to identify, understand and correctly map relevant organizational business risks and opportunities.
Sensing the knowledge environment	The ability to identify, understand and correctly map opportunities to bring relevant knowledge into the organization
Process control	The ability to achieve a continuously desirable standard in organizational processes.
Process improvement	The ability to increase the output value for a unit input in existing organizational processes.
Develop new processes	The ability to develop new organizational processes in order to increase the output value for a unit input

Evolving Relationship Structures in Multi-sourcing Arrangements: The Case of Mission Critical Outsourcing

Ilja Heitlager[1], Remko Helms[2], and Sjaak Brinkkemper[2]

[1] Schuberg Philis, Boeingavenue 271, 1119PD, Schiphol-Rijk, The Netherlands
[2] University of Utrecht, Department of Information and Computing Sciences, Organisation and Information Group, P.O. Box 80.089, 3508TB, Utrecht, The Netherlands

Abstract. Information Technology Outsourcing practice and research mainly considers the outsourcing phenomenon as a generic fulfilment of the IT function by external parties. Inspired by the logic of commodity, core competencies and economies of scale; assets, existing departments and IT functions are transferred to external parties. Although the generic approach might work for desktop outsourcing, where standardisation is the dominant factor, it does not work for the management of mission critical applications. Managing mission critical applications requires a different approach where building relationships is critical. The relationships involve inter and intra organisational parties in a multi-sourcing arrangement, called an IT service chain, consisting of multiple (specialist) parties that have to collaborate closely to deliver high quality services.

To better understand the evolution of relationships in such an IT chain, we propose a modelling technique for the structure and evolution of the organizational aspects these relationships. Understanding this structure is relevant in discerning how interactions take place during the lifecycle of the outsourcing relationship. To validate the modelling technique we studied a Dutch provider of Mission Critical Outsourcing services, which is ranked independently as a quality market leader. In two international internet banking environments we analyse the evolution of the inter and intra organizational structure. The contribution of this paper is an approach to understanding the evolution of the organizational structure of collaborative multi-sourcing arrangements. Understanding the evolution of these structures is deemed relevant for the further study of successful high quality multisourcing arrangements.

Keywords: Mission Critical Outsourcing, IT Service Chains, Collaboration, Outsourcing Relationships, Organisational Modelling, Design Science.

1 Introduction

Information Technology Outsourcing (ITO) is now a widely dispersed approach for the delivery of IT services and is still a growing phenomenon in the IT industry. It has also received considerable research attention, although commonly treated as a generic phenomenon. Most attention has been paid primarily to the customer perspective and

I. Oshri and J. Kotlarsky (Eds.): Global Sourcing 2010, LNBIP 55, pp. 185–201, 2010.

the external factors of IT service delivery: what to outsource, how to outsource, how to select the suppliers, how to set up agreements, and how to manage the relationship from a customer perspective (Lacity et al., 2009).

Mission Critical Outsourcing (MCO), a niche in the outsourcing arena, is about the management of mission critical applications. These are applications on which business rely 24 hours a day, seven days a week, where any downtime of the IT service has a direct impact on the results of the organisation. Secondly, these applications are used in very dynamic and changing business environments. A characteristic which seems to be in direct conflict with availability. A third characteristic is that these mission critical environments are heavily regulated environments with a plethora of external rules, laws and regulations to which they must comply. Typical examples include trading floors and direct banking environments (Heitlager et al., 2010).

Dominant in research and practise of ITO however is the commodity paradigm: outsourced IT functions are non strategic, better and less expensively fulfilled by external firms. Furthermore the logic of commodity assumes that all vendors offer similar kinds of standardised services. Iff the outsourcing agreement runs unsatisfactorily, this is also primarily related to the external factors, like inadequately defined contracts, unclear demands, or poorly managed relations. To protect customers, multi-sourcing or selective outsourcing strategies have been proposed as a means to reduce risks (Lacity et al., 1995, 1996) (Gallivan and Oh, 1999). By multi-sourcing competition between (preferred) suppliers would control costs and prevent lock-in from suppliers.

Since mission critical applications are so tightly linked with highly dynamic and changing business needs, they are not well supported in the world of standardised commodity service. From our own observations, we found that they require very customised service from specialist service providers. Resulting in multi-sourced IT services (Multi IT Outsourcing or MITO) where customers have explicitly chosen the best-of-breed approach for the provisioning of these services (Oshri et al., 2009). MITO and MCO is about selecting specific multiple parties (in house/outsourced or offshored), with each delivering a part of the IT service. This is either because of a lack of internal capabilities or because of a well-stated strategy to find the best specialists "to do the job".

Best-of-breed multi-sourcing arrangements require parties that know how to collaborate. Consequently, understanding the evolution of the relationship is very important. Since the IT service delivery is provided by multiple parties, the complete service is actually provided by a group of parties, resulting in an IT service chain. Due to the mission critical nature of the IT systems one is forced to look inside the service delivery, and into the development of the collaboration between these parties.

Little attention has been given however to the internal factors of outsourced IT service provisioning: the way service providers, internally and externally, actually collaborate and develop their combined service provisioning to end-customers. We believe that explicit documentation of this structure leads to a clear understanding of how parties are organised and collaborate. This is essential in the ongoing development of a continuous outsourcing relationship, which has already begun from the very first moment customer and provider have indicated an interest.

The purpose of this paper is to focus on one specific element of the service provisioning and to look at the structure of the (interpersonal) relationship. We would like to develop a modelling technique to explicitly study the evolution of the structure of these associations. In this paper we introduce this technique and evaluate the appropriateness based on two real case studies.

In the next section we briefly describe previous research. After this, we discuss the research approach. Subsequently, we introduce the modelling technique and following the introduction of the technique we apply it to two cases studies of MCO deals and then evaluate the technique. In the final section we conclude and outline further research.

2 Previous Research

ITO has received ample attention in the research community, and indeed has some specific characteristics as opposed to outsourcing in general, such as an emphasis on contract and formal processes (Kern and Willcocks, 2000). Different aspects of ITO have received attention from: determinants, rationale, approach, the why and the how. Much of this research has taken a customer perspective and mostly addressed the contractual and formal aspects of the relationship. ITO is considered as a generic phenomenon, a "losers game", even. A phenomenon that has little strategic value and impact on business practise (Lacity et al., 2009), often lacking benefits at all (Cullen et al., 2008; Ertel et al., 2006).

In the outsourcing research literature, however, two schools of thought can be identified with respect to the quality and success of outsourcing: the contractual governance and relational governance. Earlier research has identified that both are equally important and can compensate for each other (Poppo and Zenger, 2002). There is one body of work that studies the configuration of outsourcing relations and specifically mentions the structural aspects of contract, transition and governance structure in the (primarily dyadic) outsourcing relationship (Alborz et al., 2003, 2004; Gong et al., 2007). Factors which we would like to call the 'external factors' of the relationship. Indeed it is our observation that relationships are built by people interacting and not solely defined in contracts. This relationship starts at the first moment of contact and is developed step-by-step as the outsourcing goes through the various phases.

Another body of work studies the relationship quality in isolation, independent of the type of service provided (Beimborn and Blumenberg, 2007; Blumenberg, 2008; Blumenberg et al., 2008). It mentions important aspects of outsourcing relationships, but without taking the evolutionary aspects of organisational structure into account.

The notion of the outsourcing lifecycle has received attention in both theory and practice. Different models with five and even up to nine steps have been proposed (Cullen et al., 2005; Delen, 1999; Tjia and Poot, 2007). These models consider the

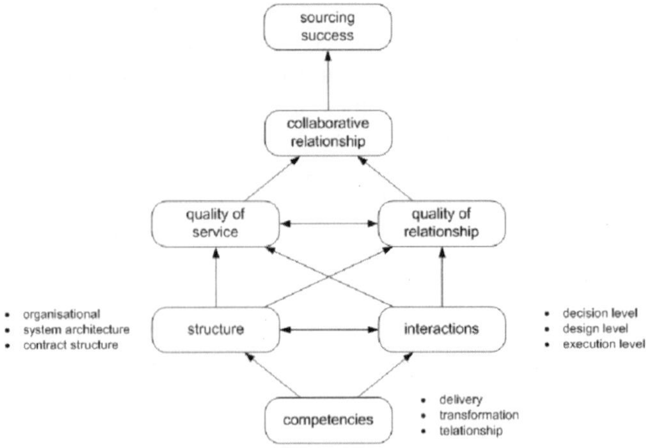

Fig. 1. The research framework to study multi-sourcing arrangements

high level evolution of the outsourcing process from a customer perspective, from the initial strategic decision to the possible backsource or re-insource decision. These models certainly structure the outsourcing decision-making process and describe the main steps to be taken. But what these models do not address is how parties and individuals within the various phases collaborate and interact.

However real emphasis on high quality service delivery in collaborative multi-sourcing arrangements has not, to date, received any attention and justifies our research.

3 Research Method

In our research we study exclusively the collaboration between various IT service providers in multi-sourcing arrangements for mission critical systems and applications. We seek to investigate the performance relationships and research those concepts and building blocks which form the foundation of these relationships. Confronted with many underperforming relationships a lot of the research is often focused on the most common critical failure factors. In our research we take a more positive viewpoint and assume that exceptional performance is not something contingent but that there are general lessons to be learnt (Avital et al., 2006).

We focus on MCO and the components of the service provisioning that comes with it. The three characteristics -high availability, frequent changes and regulated markets - lead to a different focus in the service provisioning from both service providers and customers. Firstly, the demands for high availability and the high impact on the business motivates a very risk-driven approach in which costs to mitigate risks in specific business contexts are more important than user acceptance in standardised environments.

Secondly, the combined characteristics of critical to the business and regulated markets demands very specialised parties, with parts of the complete IT service not unlikely to be fulfilled by multiple best-fit parties. Third and finally, the contrasting requirements of (high) availability and changing environments demands specific service providers capabilities, for example a high share of employees with full context (and understanding) of the customer business and systems.

The study of these kinds of environments leads to an integral model that investigates the collaborative capabilities of a multi-sourced best-of-breed environments of specialist providers, possibly both in-house and external (Cohen and Young, 2006). For this we have developed a research framework visualised in Figure 1. A full discussion of MCO and why it needs a specific research framework can be found in (Heitlager et al., 2010).

The integral research framework will focus on the quality of both the service and the relationship. These qualities are only perceived in interactions at all levels: decision-makers, design level and executioners. From a strategic perspective all the way down to the personal relationship, a factor that has been valued early in collaborative strategic management (Kanter, 1994), but has received little attention in IT outsourcing.

These interactions are structured within the configuration in which the business-IT initiative is set. How well parties setup up these structures is determined by the capabilities parties have.

In the rest of this paper we would like to focus on one precise element, the structure of the relationship. This is the setting in which the interactions take place. Operating in very specific and highly changing environments requires a lot of contextual knowledge of both the business and IT environments. This context is not easily explained, documented or taught, but grows through the individual member's experiences. To understand how organisations design and implement services, the structure of relationships has to be made explicit.

To gain a deeper understanding of the relationship structure and its evolution, we introduce a modelling technique to model this relationship and how it changes over time. Guided by the principles of Design Science research we develop a new artefact for the deeper understanding of these relationships (Hevner et al., 2004). In this paper we introduce the technique, set clear guidelines to evaluate the applicability and test this with two real world case studies. The contribution of this paper is the introduction of this modelling technique, a discussion of its relevance to mission critical outsourcing and the lessons learned. We focus more on the managerial aspects and less on the methodological aspects, as we will develop the foundation and methodology of application in later research.

The purpose of the modelling technique is to gain a clearer understanding of the relationship between people and the organisational units they operate in. To assess the quality of the modelling technique we consider three evaluation criteria:

1. Following the research framework, all relevant parties in decision-making, design and execution must be included.
2. The technique must be able to show intercompany organisational and interpersonal relationships, since it models multi-sourcing arrangements and must address the issues of personal context.

3. The technique must model the evolution over time, since we consider long term relationships.

After introducing the modelling technique we discuss two cases and evaluate the applicability based on these three evaluation criteria.

4 Modelling the Evolution of Outsourcing Relationships

In this section we introduce the modelling technique and discuss some of its details. An example is provided in Figure 2. The modelling technique is designed to capture the relationship, meaning the core interactions that take place, between groups of people in an interorganisational context. Besides this, we consider the evolution over time. For that, we track the evolution over time in rows, not necessarily linked with the formal stages of an outsourcing relationship, but more with the actual evolution over time. As the relationships develop, each row in the drawing will define a clear moment, either pre or post contract. Within an organisation multiple groups can be identified, thereby hinting at the intraorganisational context as well. An outsourcing relationship between organisations undergoes various phases from inception of the outsourcing need all the way up to the well established but growing relationship where additional or even new activities are executed.

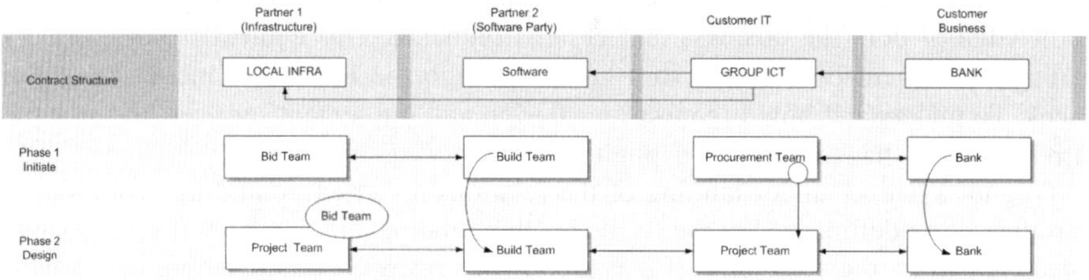

Fig. 2. Example of relational structure diagram

4.1 The Concept of an IT Service Chain

Central to the best-of-breed multi-sourcing arrangements is the grouping of various organisations with complementary services. Each party provides a specific service: infrastructure, application management, functional management, or business operations. Consequently, the complete IT service provisioning is broken up into a selection of explicit providers which we prefer to call the 'IT service chain'.

Following the research framework, we distinguish between three separate levels of interaction within an outsourcing relationship: decision-maker level (basically those that develop and maintain the contract and service level agreements), the design level (architecture, solution definition) and execution level (day-to-day operations). These three levels are reflected in the modelling technique as follows:

The decision-making level is separated from the other two levels in the diagram: the contract and execution structure are two specific elements in the modelling technique. As shown in Figure 2, the contract structure is defined in the header and the execution, with its evolution over time modelled in the main body. To distinguish between the design and execution levels we introduce the execution and consulted groups (with respect to design), i.e. regulators have an impact on the design.

With each distinct moment in time as a row, we actually have swim lanes for the organisations and the various departments/groups. Thereby we introduce the concept of interorganisational structures with inter and intra organisational departments. To summarise we have an IT service chain in a contractual structure (header part) with organisations (lanes or columns). Organisations have departments (the blocks and ovals) and the relational structure evolves over time (rows).

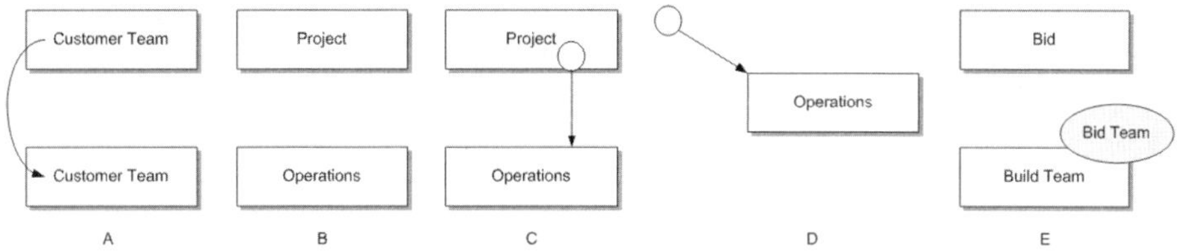

Fig. 3. Five basic transitions

Specific to outsourcing is the transition in which existing services are carried over to the new service provider. And although on the highest abstraction level (and contractual) the relationship is consistent between the various parties/organisations, the relationship is effected by interactions between individuals representing this organisation. If the total relationship moves into a new phase, new roles and people are required and possibly complete service provisioning is transferred from one group to another. Understanding how transitions take place is a prerequisite to understanding how knowledge within teams is dispersed and to predicting when the relationship has to be developed or can "just work for itself".

The relationship goes through various phases and various outsourcing researchers and consultants have defined these phases. These mostly consist of the pre and post contract phases, with a transition in between. Although each phase has its own specific function and own specific activities, possibly executed by different groups of people, from a relationship and trust building perspective they are equally important. Meaning that, each phase adds to the development of the relationship between the various parties. Therefore we have put all phases in one diagram, without formalising these phases and illustrating the evolution of the relationship.

Looking at one particular party or organisation (one swim lane) we can distinguish several organisational changes in each "phase transition", which we will discuss below.

4.2 Evolution of the Relationship

As we stated in the introduction, it is essential in MCO for a team to have both context and knowledge about both the business as well as its own activities. So in the basic transition the team or group stays intact, meaning that the most relevant team members remain in the team, as defined in Figure 3 A. The second type of transition is to have a new team perform the next phase. For example changing from a bid team, doing the sell, to the project team doing the implementation or transition, as shown in Figure 3 B. The third archetypical transition is when new members are added to a specific team for a certain phase, as is shown in Figure 3 C.

There are three basic team transitions, however these transitions are not extensive. Having the modelling technique allows the development of more different patterns of transitions. There are a few variants identified, like a new key player introduced into a team. A key player is a decision-maker at most and an influencer at least, as shown in Figure 3 D. Furthermore we identify the particular case in which a completely new team picks up a next phase but is in close contact with the previous team. In other words the team changes its role, as is shown in Figure 3 E.

4.3 Key Elements of the Modelling Technique

To summarise the modelling technique consists of two main parts: the header with the contract structure and the body with the relationship structure evolution over time. In the body, rows denoting distinct moments in time and columns denoting organisations. For now we have defined two groups: actual teams that execute in day to day operations (rectangles) and groups that are consulted (ovals). The interactions are represented by direct arrows, the transitions over time with arcs. One additional transition is illustrated where the key player (small circle) moves from one team to another or is added to a team.

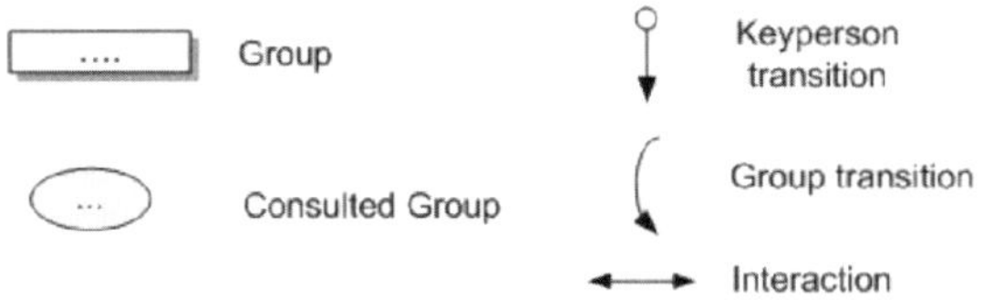

Fig. 4. Legend

In total we have three distinct organisational objects (rectangle, oval and circle) and three arrows (transition, interaction and personal transition) as shown in the legend in Figure 4.

5 MCO Case Studies

Having defined the modelling technique, we continue with the application of two real life case studies to demonstrate the pertinence of the technique. We consider two international outsourcing deals from a Dutch infrastructure provider that operates in the niche of mission critical outsourcing. Both deals are with Dutch large multinational (financial) organisations that have well-developed IT organisations and infrastructures with broad experience of outsourcing.

Both case studies are based on interviews with various members of the team that provided the in-frastructure outsourcing services. In these interviews we have considered the evolution over time of the relationships between the various departments and organisations. The infrastructure provider focuses primarily on service provisioning for mission critical applications and has developed the service capabilities based on the dedicated team model as shown in Figure 5. The service provider observed that most large IT service organisations developed their service around a tiered approach, following the logic of operational excellence, the service is optimised for costs by standardisation.

This approach, built for generic services and the handling of many incidents and requests, the service is organised in first, second and third line support. In the first line, all calls and requests are received and processed, possibly answered based on standard scripts. If handling of the requests is not handled in time the call is, according to procedure, nicely passed to the second line with more skilled support engineers. If however these engineers are not able to resolve the issue they have to pass it to the various experts in their own business units or stovepipes. The issue with this tiered model is that difficult requests and very problematic issues also have to follow this process. Because the skilled engineers have to service many customers, it is hard to maintain context or information about the customer environment. The dedicated team model, the grouping of engineers in a group dedicated to a customer environment, is an approach that values the collaboration and promotes the integration of knowledge between team members. Valuing the collaboration within the organisation and outside the organisation is the background of this research and the rationale for the development of this modelling technique.

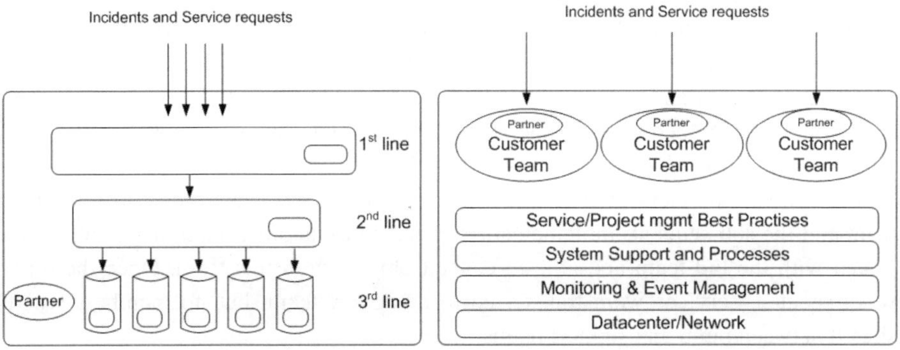

Fig. 5. Two models of service provisioning: tiered model and dedicated team

5.1 Case 1: International Bank

This case study concerns a large bank with a strategy to develop international online banks. An online bank is a retail/consumer bank where all operations are virtual and internet based. A variety of services are offered through the online bank ranging from savings accounts to mortgages. Typical online banks consist of web-based direct banking access, a local marketing department and a back-office unit for banking operations.

Being a bank, different rules and regulations have to be taken into account, ranging from: reports on individual savings accounts; tax office reports; and compliance to national banks in respect of the banking licenses. Because of audit requirements, these regulations have an impact on both system architecture and service provisioning because of audit requirements.

The bank had selected a provider of universal and direct banking software and had implemented the first bank as a pilot at its own datacenter. As part of further expansion and to gain fast and direct access to expertise in web-based applications, the bank predicted a need for external (outsourced) support.

In this situation, there are four organisations involved: the local banking business, the central banking IT department, offering business analysis and functional support, the software vendor and the infrastructure provider. The bank choose to have both the contracts for infrastructure and the software vendor at the central IT department. All design and decision-making, therefore, is centralised at the IT department.

Here we describe the first six phases of the relationship. In the first phase, the bank's IT department started to design the banking solution with the software vendor and the first country where the bank was rolled out. The focus was primarily on functionality. A sufficient pilot infrastructure was set up and the bank's project team provided all support. As this pilot was executed successfully, another solution was developed to support the further expansion into other countries. At that moment an RFI was send out to both traditional and specialist outsourcers.

The outsourcing party that won the bid, won it because it offered a dedicated team approach containing all the skills required for the operations. As opposed to the other bids, it emphasised an operating model where design/build and execution of the service would be provided by the same team. In the model, this is visualised in the transitions of this partner by complete team transitions.

The software partners offered a model in which the bid was executed by the first team and the sub-sequent implementation executed by another team, but tightly integrated with the bid team and able to consult closely with this team. Once the build was executed, services were transferred to a support team, but no members where shared between build and support teams.

The bank's central ICT function basically had two different teams: the project team and the operations team. A new team was formed once the bank went live, with the

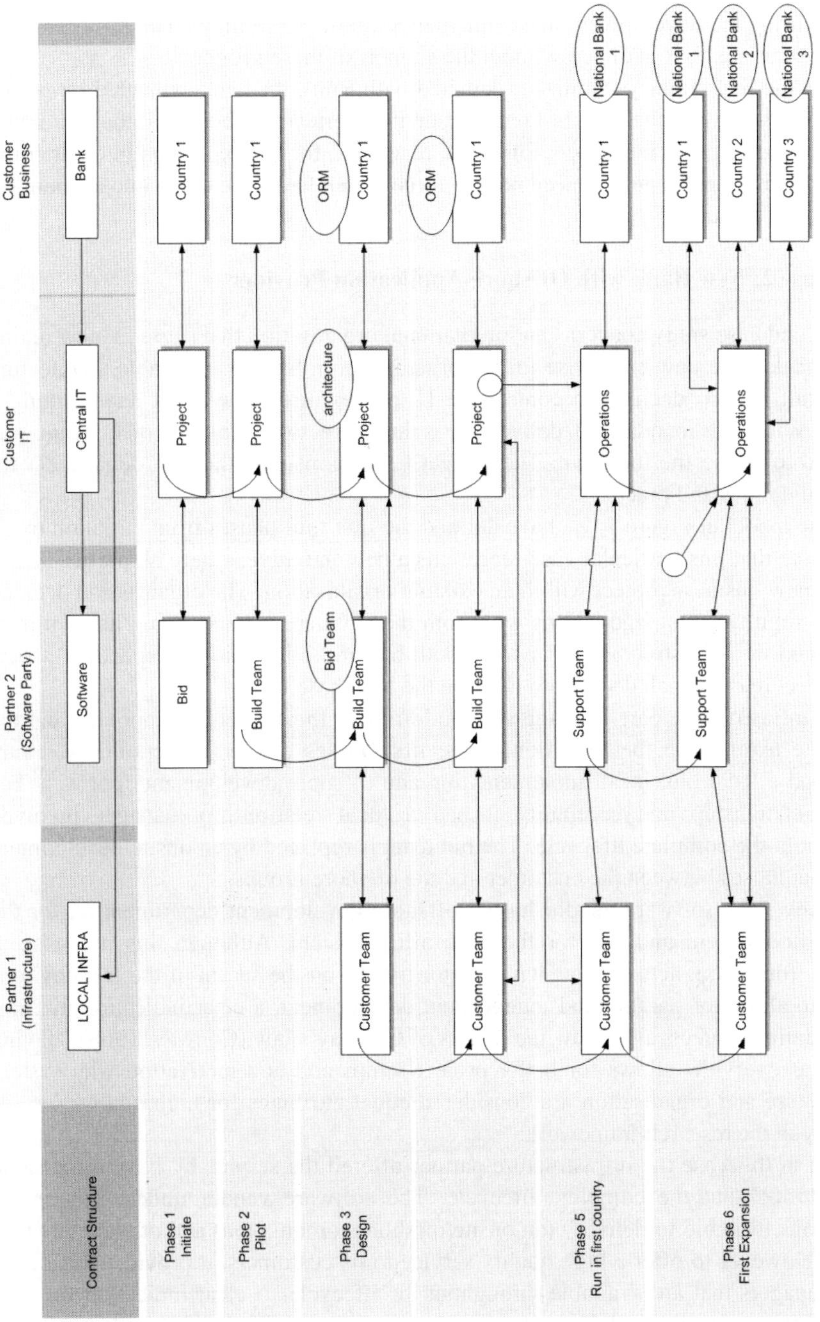

Fig. 6. Relational structure evolution of case 1

top manager and key player remaining after the transition. The bank itself provided the initial architectural support and the operational risk management group was consulted during the development and implementation of the solution. The project would not have initiated or continued without the support of these groups.

After the first country stabilised (depicted with Run), the bank expanded into other countries. However, the bank's IT department experienced personnel changes and a new key player came into place. Finally in phase six, for the expansion in other countries, new rules and regulations came into force which had to be taken into account for the final IT solution.

5.2 Case 2: New Bank with Offshore Application Provider

The second case study concerns an international organisation that started a new online direct bank. As a new enterprise for the organisation it had no applicable architecture to consult. It also decided to control the IT parties directly without any central IT group. With full mandate to deliver the solution, a totally new project team was founded to set up the initiative. The project teams consulted the ICT department for basic guidelines and practises.

In the model in Figure 7, we have defined the first four phases from initiation to 'go live'. Note that this particular case represents a new initiative, where all parties developed a new business project within an existing organisation. The organisation decided to start simultaneous negotiations with both the software vendor, being its own integrator and the infrastructure party. And both began the initiation independently with the project team, which decided to mediate the bid phase.

The infrastructure party had the plan/build/run by the same team approach and the complete team made the transition in the first phases of the project. The software party had a local bid, local implementation and offshore development approach. For direct relationship and continuity it had a local relationship manager involved throughout the complete lifecycle. The bid team is replaced by an onsite development team that liaises between the customer and the offshore groups.

However the software vendor has an offshore development department on for the front-office system and one for the back-office system. Although this might seem trivial information, actually this has a major impact on the set up of the test environments to allow for parallel and independent development, a clear indication that implementation projects also show the affects of Conway's law (Conway, 1968). Having this clear overview allows for better project setups and is a motivation why system architecture and organisation are considered equal attributes for high quality service delivery in the research framework.

Also in this case the infrastructure partner offered the service by having the same team through-out the complete lifecycle. The software vendor underwent regular transitions from bid to delivery (an onsite/offshore combination) and offshore support teams. However to offer a high quality service to its customers, it provides local relation managers that are available throughout the lifecycle. A clear indication for both the infrastructure team and the customers team to start the relationship early on.

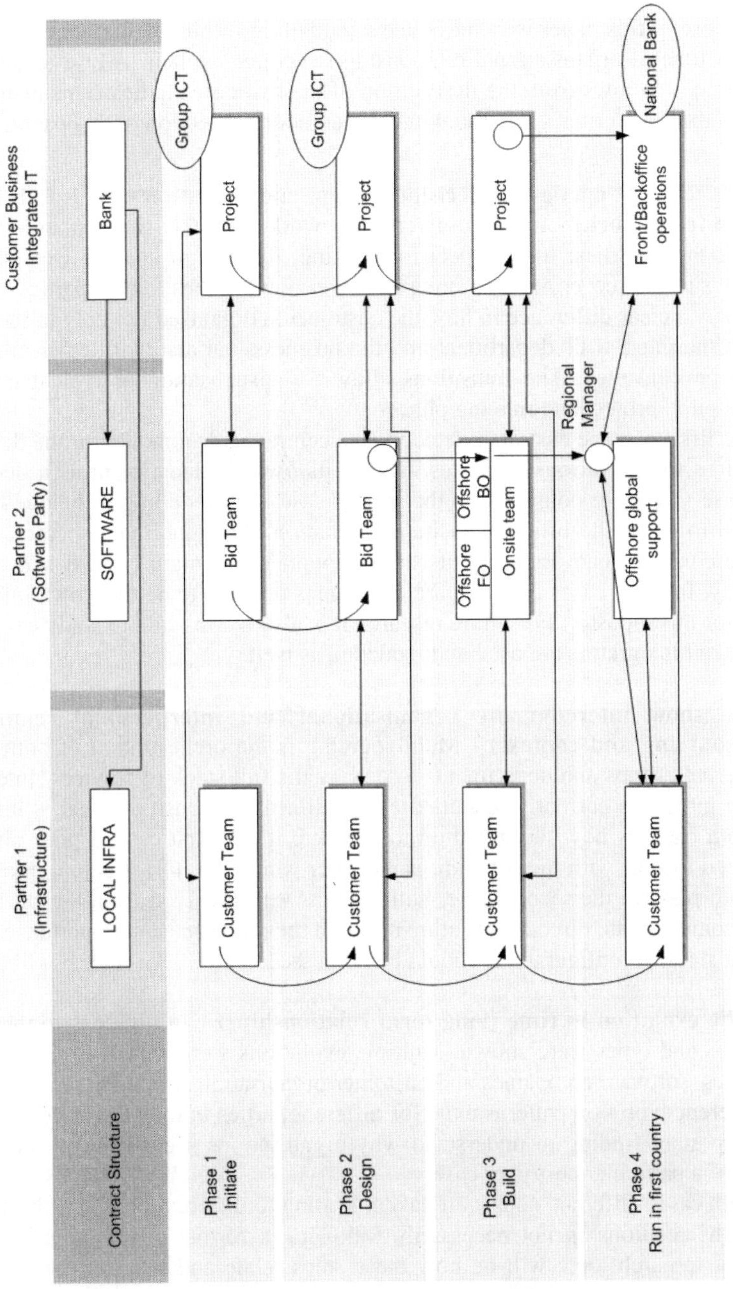

Fig. 7. Relational structure evolution of case 2

6 Evaluation

The purpose of this paper is to introduce a modelling technique that makes the evolution over time of organisational relationship structures explicit. A brief evaluation of the technique follows from the description of the two case studies. This evaluation is based on the three criteria presented in the methodology section of this paper.

Show all relevant parties for decision, design and execution (this is following the research framework) - In the research framework for MCO we emphasise the relevance of three parties: for the decision-making, the design and the execution. The modelling technique provides a complete overview of these three parties. The two cases show a clear difference in how the customer is organised not only in the relation between the internal IT department and the business, but also with other groups that have to be consulted. The transitions allow for visualisation of typical transitions between pilot, project and running phases.

In the first case, the customer decided on a central control model for the delivery of IT services to the various countries, having its own IT department as a decoupling point to service other countries. In the second case, the modelling technique has to be extended to show the offshore/onsite combination. An important aspect is how the offshore company had organised its local support to maintain context and customer proximity. In these cases the software companies decided to be their own integrators, typical for this industry. For future research it is also worthwhile to study cases where independent integrators are used and modelled as well.

Able to show intercompany organisational and interpersonal relationships (multi-sourcing and context) - Multi-sourcing is the orchestration of both internal and external groups and departments to deliver the full stack of services. Interactions between groups is currently modelled as a uniform relationship. What is interesting from both cases is how the initiation took place. In the first case, a pilot phase was introduced to start with the software party, after which the infrastructure organisation came into play. In the second case, both parties were involved from the start but not able to communicate directly. In future research the relevance and importance of these different starting configurations should be addressed.

Show the evolution in time (long term relationships) - In both cases, the various transitions and types were shown. Multiple evolutions were shown for infrastructure companies, software companies and customer organisation structures. Making it clear that different evolution patterns exist for different parties in the IT service chain. This is an important finding in understand why organisations seem to learn and unlearn context of a particular customer case.

In both cases different steps were taken, leading to different phases with the evolution of the relationship not necessarily following a formal phase progressions. An important research topic will be how these steps relate and whether they should be seen as sub-steps or deserve to be identified independently as necessary steps to be taken.

7 Conclusion and Further Research

This paper focuses on the delivery of exceptional services in Information Technology Outsourcing. More specifically it focuses on the niche market of Mission Critical Outsourcing, a niche where best-of-breed configurations between specialist service providers are critical. In particular, that very close interaction between the various people in the different organisational units is essential. In this paper we have started the development of a precise modelling technique to make the structure explicit and understand evolution of these relationships. We have defined the technique and shown its value in discussing two global outsourcing cases.

We believe we should look into how service providers offer their services. Particularly for MCO we have to examine how each service is provided. In our research framework we state that the organisational structure and relationship between the various departments is essential for the delivery of quality service. Instead of solely relying on formal processes and contractual agreements it is critical to learn whom to collaborative with. Modelling the structure and the evolution of this structure is an important aspect in the understanding of, and reasoning about, interorganisational relationships. As a result, we believe this modelling technique contributes to this understanding.

The relevance for practise comes from both knowledge transfer and practical application. The modelling technique allows the expression of relevant factors in relationship building and explains what is relevant to the people involved. In actual usage, it helps to understand where to put the effort and "dedicate resources" to build relationships further. Having a clear overview of the evolution in one picture supports in defining next steps.

The relevance to scholars is that in IT outsourcing, service quality not only depends on contracts and formalities, but also on the development of trust and contextual knowledge in (interpersonal) relationships. The structure of these relationships has not been addressed in the past. With the modelling technique we have laid a foundation for the further study of these relationships and their evolution.

This paper is the starting point and more research is required. The research should focus on three different aspects. For this technique to become more mature it needs more application. Although we focus in our research exclusively on MCO, its application is not limited and should add value in other domains and organisations as well. While maturing the technique it needs more formalisation to provide it with a sound and solid basis. This is also essential in being able to discern patterns of successful or unsuccessful configurations. In the evaluation of the cases some topics have been identified for further research.

This paper is part of a larger research framework. The technique proposed is essential in understanding the relationships. The framework is based on an integrated approach and we believe that the modelling of the structure is essential in developing a deeper understanding of outsourcing relationships. We have high expectations of the merging of this modelling technique with other aspects of IT outsourcing service provisioning as a consequence of the research framework.

References

1. A Model for Studying IT Outsourcing Relationships. In: PACIS 2003, Shanghai, China, pp. 1297–1313 (2003)
2. Alborz, S., Seddon, P.B., Scheepers, R.: Impact of configuration on IT outsourcing relationships. In: AMCIS 2004, Atlanta, GA, USA. Association for Information Systems (2004)
3. Avital, M., Lyytinen, K.J., Boland Jr., R., Butler, B.S., Dougherty, D., Fineout, M., Jansen, W., Levina, N., Rifkin, W., Venable, J.: Design with a positive lens: An affirmative approach to designing information and organizations. Comm. Ass. Inf. Sys. 18, 519–545 (2006)
4. Beimborn, D., Blumenberg, S.: How to Measure Relationships–Merging Alignment and Outsourcing Re-search towards a Unified Relationship Quality Construct. In: AMCIS 2007, Atlanta, GA, USA (2007)
5. Blumenberg, S.: IT outsourcing relationship quality dimensions and drivers: Empirical evidence from the financial industry. In: AMCIS 2008, Atlanta, GA, USA (2008)
6. Blumenberg, S., Beimborn, D., Koenig, W.: Determinants of IT Outsourcing Relationships: A Conceptual Model. In: HICSS 2008. Computer Society Press (2008)
7. Cohen, I., Young, A.: Multisourcing: Moving Beyond Outsourcing to Achieve Growth and Agility. Harvard Business School Press, Boston (2006)
8. Conway, M.E.: How Do Committees Invent? Datamation Magazine (1968)
9. Cullen, S., Seddon, P.B., Willcocks, L.P.: Managing Outsourcing: The Life Cycle Imperative. MIS Quart. Ex. 4, 229–246 (2005)
10. Cullen, S., Seddon, P.B., Willcocks, L.P.: IT outsourcing success: a multi-dimensional, contextual perspective of outsourcing outcomes. In: Second Information Systems Workshop on Global Sourcing: Service, Knowledge and Innovation, Val d'Isere, France (2008)
11. Delen, G.: De pendulumbeweging van uitbesteden - Never outsource a problem (in dutch). IT-Beheer Praktijkjournaal 3 (1999)
12. Ertel, D., Enlow, S., Barr, K.: Managing Outsourcing Relationships: Essential Practices for Buyers and Providers. Technical report, Vantage Partners, Boston, MA (2006)
13. Gallivan, M., Oh, W.: Analyzing IT Outsourcing Relationships as Alliances among Multiple Clients and Vendors. In: HICCS 1999, vol. 32, p. 277 (1999)
14. Gong, H., Tate, M., Alborz, S.: Managing the Outsourcing Marriage to Achieve Success. In: HICSS 2007, p. 239c. Computer Society Press (2007)
15. Heitlager, I., Helms, R., Brinkkemper, S.: Studying multi-sourced IT service chain arrangements: The relevance for Mission Critical Outsourcing. Technical Report, UU-CS-2010-001, Department of Information and Computing Sciences, University of Utrecht (February 2010) (submitted for publication)
16. Hevner, A.R., March, S.T., Park, J., Ram, S.: Design Science in Information Systems Research. MIS Quart. 28, 75–106 (2004)
17. Kanter, R.M.: Collaborative advantage: the art of alliances. Harvard Bus. Rev. 72, 96–108 (1994)
18. Kern, T., Willcocks, L.P.: Exploring information technology outsourcing relationships: theory and practice. J. Strat. Inf. Sys. 9, 321–350 (2000)
19. Lacity, M.C., Willcocks, L.P., Feeny, D.F.: IT Outsourcing: Maximize Flexibility and Control. Harvard Bus. Rev., 84–93 (May-June 1995)
20. Lacity, M.C., Willcocks, L.P., Feeny, D.F.: The Value of Selective IT Sourcing. MIT Sloan Man. Rev. 37, 13–25 (Spring 1996)

21. Lacity, M.C., Khan, S.A., Willcocks, L.P.: A review of the IT outsourcing literature: Insights for practise. J. Strat. Inf. Sys. 18, 130–146 (2009)
22. Oshri, I., Kotlarsky, J., Willcocks, L.P.: The Handbook of Global Outsourcing and Offshoring. Palgrave Macmillan, Oxford (2009)
23. Poppo, L., Zenger, T.: Do formal contracts and relational governance function as substitutes or complements? Strat. Man. J. 23(8), 707–725 (2002)
24. Tjia, P., Poot, M.: Zeven stappen naar succesvolle offshore uitbesteding (in dutch). Informatie (2007)

Adaptability in IT Sourcing: The Impact of Switching Costs

Dwayne Whitten

Texas A&M University, College Station, TX 77845, USA

Abstract. IT sourcing decisions are increasingly becoming more strategic than in the past. As this occurs, firms should maintain a strategy of adaptability in order to mitigate the risks inherently associated with sourcing. A major influence on the adaptability of a firm in the short- and long-term are the switching costs associated with moving an activity from one source to another. As switching costs increase, firms may be "locked in" to one source. Firms should therefore work to decrease the switching costs so that they are more able to move an activity from one source to another if the market changes or an outsourcing relationship sours. Three strategies are presented for lowering switching costs which will ultimately help increase adaptability.

Keywords: Outsourcing, sourcing, switching costs, adaptability, agility, flexibility.

1 Introduction

In the past few decades, considerable research has been done in the area of IT outsourcing. Much of this work has focused on what should be done to achieve outsourcing success. Relatively little work has focused on the area of switching vendors and bringing previously outsourced activities back in-house (backsourcing) (Lacity and Willcocks, 2000). Even less has been done specifically in the context of planning for the possibility of either of these two events. Recent statistics indicate that as many as half of all IT outsourcing agreements are discontinued in favor of backsourcing or switching vendors (Lacity and Willcocks, 2002). Thus, it seems apparent that research should be conducted to learn more about this phenomenon.

One key aspect of this phenomenon is the cost associated with switching or backsourcing and the role switching costs play in inhibiting the ability of a firm to adapt their sourcing strategies. Switching costs are the relationship-specific investments between buyers and suppliers (Farrell and Shapiro 1988). Switching costs also significantly influence managerial decisions. They have been shown to influence the competitive strategies that managers adopt (Eliashberg and Robertson 1988).

Previous research has shown that high switching costs can lead customers to stay in relationships, even though they are dissatisfied (Jones, Mothersbaugh, and Beatty 2002; Morgan and Hunt 1994a; Porter, 1980; Weiss and Anderson, 1992; Willcocks and Lacity 1995). In cases where switching costs were not significant, customers were more agile and reacted by switching vendors (Heide and Weiss 1995; Jones and

I. Oshri and J. Kotlarsky (Eds.): Global Sourcing 2010, LNBIP 55, pp. 202–216, 2010.

Sasser 1995). Thus, previous research has shown that switching costs can hamper a firm's adaptability.

Since it is a reality that firms may switch vendors or backsource, shouldn't they maintain a sourcing strategy that promotes adaptability in order to make the change as seamless and low-cost as possible? The answer to this question was sought in a recent research project surveying application development managers.

The objective of this paper therefore is to investigate switching costs and ultimately their impact on a firm's adaptability. Through a better understanding of the costs, strategies will be presented which can be used to promote adaptability by decreasing the prohibitive costs of switching.

The paper begins with an introduction, followed by a review of the literature focusing on switching costs. Next, the theoretical background is provided along with the hypotheses. The next section describes the quantitative data collection and a description of the analysis and results. Three strategies are then presented which are proposed to increase firm adaptability. Finally, a discussion of the interview process is discussed and a detailed discussion of the strategies is offered.

2 Literature Review

Adaptability, or similarly flexibility, can be defined as the ability to change the extent, nature, or scope of sourcing arrangements (Tan and Sia, 2008). Adaptability is important as firms adjust to meet structural shifts in the marketplace and when firms have a need to change strategies, products, or technologies (Lee, 2006). This ability to adapt is critical in today's ever-changing business environment as firms attempt to position themselves to mitigate uncertainty on the horizon. Many firms view this with strategic importance (Suarez, 1995). A good example of the benefits of being able to adapt is when labor costs increase in a given market (India) and firms subsequently move operations to lower-cost countries (China) or when the quality of service provided by a particular vendor decreases.

Switching costs become important when considering adaptability because the premature termination of an outsourcing relationship can be undesirable due to high switching costs (Ybarra and Wiersema, 1999). Switching costs can be thought of as the overall cost or difficulty of switching (Weiss and Anderson 1992), additional cost and effort in changing suppliers (Ping 1993), an undefined component of termination (Morgan and Hunt 1994) and investments that inhibit change (Nielson 1996). They can also include the perceived economic and psychological costs (Jones et al 2002), perceptions of time, effort and money in changing service providers (Jones et al 2000), onetime costs associated with switching providers (Burham et al 2003), and perceived disutility (Chen and Hitt 2002). Thus, switching costs can include relational and economic cost dimensions. Switching costs have been shown to be an important area in several research streams including interorganizational exchange, economics, marketing, and IT. The interorganizational exchange research defines switching costs as an attachment between transacting parties resulting from previous investments made by the exchange partners (Blau 1964; Williamson 1981). They have also been referred to as investment actions of transacting parties that hinder the termination of the relationship (Jackson 1985). These investments may be in the form of human assets (i.e. expertise), economic assets, and physical assets (i.e. fixed assets, procedures or processes) (Williamson 1981). As a result of increased investments in the relationship, there are stronger allegiances and more difficulty in discontinuing the relationship.

The marketing and economics literatures describe switching costs in a variety of contexts. They have been referred to as one-time costs associated with the termination of the current relationship and securing an alternative (Porter 1980) and also more generally as the disutility related to change (Weiss and Anderson 1992). Switching costs have been described as including psychological cost dimensions as well as physical and economic costs (Jackson 1985).

In the marketing literature, switching costs have been described as managerial perceptions of the costs involved with converting from an independent to a direct salesforce (Weiss and Anderson 1992). These costs have been measured as tangible expenses related to the conversion process including the investments of effort and time. More recent research has shown the importance of switching costs in customer retention models.

The IT literature explores switching cost from an array of perspectives. Chen and Hitt (2002) examine switching costs as a uni-dimensional factor in the personal online brokerage industry as one influence of customer switching behavior. Their findings indicate that switching costs significantly influence switching behavior in the online brokerage context. A broader definition of switching costs is needed though as multiple research streams have identified various aspects of switching costs. Thus, a higher-order switching cost factor may help explain variations in the literature. From a firm perspective, understanding how vendors can inflate the costs of terminating exchange relationships by effectively managing certain types of switching costs (e.g. loyalty, benefits) will lead to more efficient managerial decision-making in the outsourcing context. Whitten and Wakefield (2006) developed a multidimensional switching costs scale and tested it in the IT outsourcing services arena. A description of those scale dimensions follows.

Uncertainty Costs

Uncertainty costs occur when replacing a known level of service with an unknown level gives rise to uncertainty. This is a relational cost described in social exchange theory as the value of an alternative based on expectations rather than knowledge. Managers unknowledgeable about the performance of another provider may hold certain expectations, but the gap between expectations and knowledge represents a risk or cost of switching. As one manager said, "we may not be completely happy with [company name], but we know it could be a lot worse with someone else." This underscores the concern that some companies have with regard to switching from the current provider.

Post-switching Behavioral and Cognitive Costs

Post-switching behavioral and cognitive costs are intangible investments of time and effort related to learning and adapting to new service processes and routines (Jones et al 2002). These costs can be significant, especially in cases where there is unfamiliarity between the client and provider as in the case with switching to a new provider.

Even backsourcing can cause post-switching behavioral and cognitive costs if the internal processes are significantly different than the ones used by the original provider. A manager indicated that "getting everyone on the same page" after leaving the current provider is one of their biggest concerns. "Learning which forms to fill out and who to talk to" added to his concern.

Setup Costs

Setup costs generally precede the actual contracted services or backsourcing operations. These costs may include direct expenses or relate to human resource investments and/or acquisitions of durable assets (i.e. machines, production facilities) (Spekman and Strauss 1986). Setup costs also include relational investments of time and effort to initiate and establish the exchange relationship. The infrequency of contracting may increase transaction costs due to initial 'relationship building' activities (Cheon et al 1995).

Some companies who are in bad financial condition may outsource, and then in the process, sell technology assets to obtain financial capital and then either lay off employees or transfer them to the vendor. This does provide financial benefits in the short run, but makes setup costs for backsourcing particularly high as new assets must be purchased. Even when switching to a new vendor, setup costs related to relationship-building can be significant. One client manager said "The time and effort required to change has always been a limiting factor for us. There is always so much to do to get things going."

Hiring and Retraining Costs

Outsourcing may represent an investment in human capital of a specialized nature as companies often outsource to access the technical talent not available in-house (Lacity and Willcocks 1998). One problem that can exist in the market is finding skilled IT employees (Violino and Caldwell 1998; Murray 2000). Special-purpose knowledge and expertise create human assets that can raise switching costs if alternative providers lack these skills.

No matter whether it is hiring new employees in a backsourcing deal or hiring a new vendor when switching, a certain amount of hiring and retraining costs exist. This can be especially significant in those situations where employees were terminated or transferred at the outset of the outsourcing deal. One company interview said "We were fortunate to be able to rehire some of the people that we originally transferred to [outsourcing vendor], but not all of them came back. We still had to do a lot of rehiring before we could get off the ground."

Management System Upgrade Costs

Backsourcing creates changes in overall management practices and routine operations when new employees are brought into the organization. The costs incurred to upgrade the management system may be monetary outlays to acquire additional system assets or human resources, or may be intangible disbursements of time and effort to integrate the assets. The management of new outsourcing arrangements (switching) may also require upgrades (i.e. systems or personnel) according to the nature of the services.

Lost Benefit Costs
Lost benefit costs represent the loss of both tangible and intangible advantages that accrue and are directly related to continued patronage (Gwinner et al 1998). These benefits and privileges provide an incentive for the client to remain in a service relationship with the provider (Beatty et al 1996).

Search and Evaluation Costs
Search and evaluation costs occur prior to the decision to terminate an exchange contract. The IT outsourcing search process is initiated with a formal RFP (request for proposal) to elicit both internal and external bids (Lacity and Willcocks 2002). These actions represent transaction costs associated with the make-or-buy decision. Both economic and cognitive resources are expended to gather information to evaluate the alternatives. Search costs include the time and effort to locate alternatives (Lacity and Willcocks 2000) and extensive cognitive effort may be required to assess viable alternatives in order to arrive at an informed decision (Shugan 1980).

Sunk Costs
Sunk costs are economic and relational outlays of non-recoverable time, money, and effort invested in the exchange relationship. According to economic theory, considering historic and non-recoverable costs is irrational and only future costs and benefits should be included in decisions (Gaumnitz and Emery 1980; Howe and McCabe 1983; Soman and Gourville 2001). However, sunk costs may represent a psychological cost (Guiltinan 1989) that managers find difficult to ignore and may complicate the decision making process (Jackson 1985; Keil et al 2000).

3 Theory and Hypotheses

Previous research has shown that the presence of high switching costs may lock customers into a relationship in which they are dissatisfied (Willcocks & Lacity, 1995; Morgan & Hunt, 1994). Customers may feel dependent upon a provider if they have little experience with other vendors, thus increasing their uncertainty of switching from the current vendor. The switching costs they fear may be both economic and social.

Two theories, transaction cost theory (TCT) and social exchange theory (SET), provide detail on the importance of switching costs. TCT provides the theoretical foundation for a considerable amount of IT outsourcing research because it provides the economic rationale for entering and exiting interorganizational relationships. TCT describes how transactions represent the exchange of goods or services between parties with economic motivations, thus serving as the basic unit of analysis in organizations (Williamson 1975). TCT describes the economic motivation for a company to either provide a good or service internally or purchase it externally. TCT shows a direct relationship between the transaction cost of outsourcing to one firm versus outsourcing to another vendor or backsourcing. If the total switching cost plus the anticipated transaction cost of switching or backsourcing is relatively low, then the client firm would naturally be expected to terminate the existing outsourcing relationship. This theory is widely used in the outsourcing literature to evaluate the choice of outsourcing or providing in-house IT services (Willcocks and Lacity, 1995; Aubert, Rivard, and Patry, 2004). Since successful interorganizational relationships depend on the efficient and effective management of economic investments, TCT provides an appropriate frame for evaluating the economic cost components in decisions to (dis)continue an outsourcing relationship.

SET describes how a decision-maker might consider the perceived switching costs as well. The perceived costs would include the perception of how well the new provider can provide the service, how good the relationship can be, and if the new provider will perceive the relationship to be important. Thus, one expects that switching costs, actual or perceived, are negatively associated with the decision to end an outsourcing arrangement and conversely, positively associated with the decision to continue in an outsourcing relationship. Support for this proposition has been shown in environments where switching costs were not present. In these situations, customers reacted by switching vendors (Heide & Weiss, 1995). Thus, the following hypotheses are offered:

Hypothesis 1a: Lower switching costs are negatively associated with clients who continue with the same vendor.
Hypothesis 1b: Lower switching costs are positively associated with clients who switch vendors.
Hypothesis 1c: Lower switching costs are positively associated with clients who backsource.

4 Data Collection

Contact data for application development managers was gathered from the Directory of Top Computer Executives (Grover et al., 1996). The survey sample were asked in the cover letter to respond to each survey item in regard to an outsourcing relationship in which they were involved in the past three years. A total of 160 responses were received for a response rate of 26%. A range of industries were represented. Thirty-four percent of the respondents had previously outsourced application development before subsequently choosing to backsource (bring the previously outsourced activities back in-house); twenty-three percent had switched vendors during the course of an outsourcing contract, and the remaining forty-three percent of firms had continued with their application development outsourcing arrangements. Each respondent was involved in the decision to continue or discontinue with the outsourcing contract. The firms in this study were, on average, large, experienced with application development outsourcing (6.8 contracts in the last 5 years), and outsourced a sizeable amount of application development (23.8% of the IT budget). See Table 1.

Table 1.					
	Total # of org employees	Total # of IT employees	% of IT / org employees	Outsourcing contracts in last 5 years	% of IT budget outsourced
Backsource	2878	87	3.0%	5.5	14%
Switch	5543	86	1.7%	8.5	34.5%
Continue	5762	155	2.7%	6.6	27%

5 Analysis and Results

Non-response Bias

Non-response bias was evaluated by first categorizing respondents by their response time. Early responders were categorized as those whose instruments were received in the first 25% of responses, while late responders were considered those whose instruments were received in the last 25% of responses. A comparison of the means of classification and summary variables for the two groups was conducted using one-way analysis of variance (ANOVA). Variables used in the analysis included the total number of employees and IT employees in the organization, the number of years the organization has practiced outsourcing, the number of previous outsourcing contracts the organization has signed in the last five years, and the total dollar amount of the contracts. Each of the comparisons among the groups resulted in insignificant differences. Thus, results indicate that non-response bias has not impacted the data set.

Internal and External Validity

The factor analysis was conducted using AMOS 4.0. Items whose factor scores were less than 0.40 (Hair, Anderson, Tatham & Black, 1998) or had correlated error terms were removed from further analysis following an iterative process to refine the scale (Joreskog, 1993). A total of 13 of 77 items were removed. After these items were removed, the scales were assessed again. The individual item loadings indicate a strong correspondence between the observed variables and their factors with all loadings at or above the 0.40 minimum (Hair et al., 1998).

Goodness-of-fit indices (IFI, TLI, and CFI) were used to determine how well the factor structure fit the data. Goodness-of-fit scores above the generally accepted 0.90 threshold (Bentler, 1992) indicate an acceptable fit of the model to the data. Goodness-of-fit measures are provided in Table 2. All of the indices except TLI (0.89) for the switching costs scale, were above the 0.90 threshold. Table 2 also shows the Cronbach's alpha measure of reliability for each scale. Since scores greater than 0.7 are considered significant (Hair et al., 1998), all of the included scales were determined to be reliable.

Construct validity was assessed using convergent and discriminant validity. Convergent validity is supported by the highly significant loadings ($p < .01$) (Bagozzi, Yi, & Phillips, 1991) and the factor regression coefficients (R^2) being greater than .50

Table 2.					
Factors / dimensions	**Cronbach's Alpha**	**AVE**	**IFI**	**TLI**	**CFI**
SWITCHING COSTS			0.91	0.89	0.91
Management System Upgrade Costs	0.79	.068			
Hiring and Retraining Costs	0.82	0.83			
Uncertainty Costs	0.79	0.53			
Post-Switching Behavioral and Cognitive Costs	0.86	0.64			
Lost Performance Costs	0.87	0.77			
Setup Costs	0.83	0.74			
Search and Evaluation Costs	0.95	0.86			
Sunk Costs	0.88	0.85			

(Hildebrandt, 1987). Discriminant validity is established when measures that should not be related actually do not relate. Discriminant validity can be assessed by calculating the Average Variance Extracted (AVE). AVE represents the amount of construct-related variance captured in relation to the error variance. The average percentage of variance extracted for each construct should be higher than .50 (Hair et al., 1998). This indicates that the variance accounted for by each construct is larger than the variance accounted for by measurement error (Hair et al. 1998). The AVE for all of the included measures exceed 0.50 (Table 2), thus providing evidence of discriminative validity of the measures.

ANOVA and Scheffé's Test

An analysis of variance (ANOVA), significant at the 0.01 level, verified that differences exist among responses between the three groups (those who backsourced, switched, and continued). Scheffé's post-hoc test was then used to investigate all specific mean differences between groups (Hair et al., 1992). Tables 3-8 display the results from multiple comparisons between groups. As seen in the tables, a significant difference exists across all switching cost dimensions between those who switched or backsourced and those who continued with the same vendor with the exception of post-switching costs.

Table 3. Scheffe's Test Results

Pre-switching Costs

DECISION	Subset for alpha = .05	
	1	2
Backsource	2.5765	
Switch	3.0634	
Continue		4.2740
Significance	.241	1.000

Table 4. Scheffe's Test Results

Sunk Costs

DECISION	Subset for alpha = .05	
	1	2
Switch	4.4095	
Backsource	4.4769	
Continue		5.4494
Significance	.966	1.000

Table 5. Scheffe's Test Results

Lost Performance Costs

DECISION	Subset for alpha = .05	
	1	2
Switch	2.7284	
Backsource	2.8525	
Continue		4.2962
Significance	.903	1.000

Table 6. Scheffe's Test Results

Hiring Costs

DECISION	Subset for alpha = .05	
	1	2
Switch	2.3675	
Backsource	2.5294	
Continue		3.5358
Significance	.865	1.000

Table 7. Scheffe's Test Results

Post-switching Costs

DECISION	Subset for alpha = .05	
	1	2
Backsource	3.1274	
Switch		3.7746
Continue		3.9412
Significance	1.000	.810

Table 8. Scheffe's Test Results

Management Costs

DECISION	Subset for alpha = .05	
	1	2
Backsource	2.9990	
Switch	3.3096	
Continue		4.1563
Significance	.638	1.000

Discussion

Based on survey instruments returned from 160 application development managers, it became apparent that firms do make sourcing changes and in the process, the costs of switching weigh in as an important consideration for these managers. With the exception of post-switching costs (Table 7), all of the switching costs were significantly different between the switching and backsourcing groups as compared to the group that continued (Tables 3-8). These results generally support Hypotheses 1a-1c.

This evidence indicates that high switching costs are positively associated with continuing in the same outsourcing relationship. Even though some firms may want to switch or backsource for various reasons, they may be prevented from doing so due to high switching costs. Thus, they may be locked in to that one source for the provision of the service. Other firms which have lower switching costs, and thus can more easily transition to a new source, are able to be more adaptable in their sourcing. This is evident in Figure 1, where firms which continued with their existing contract had higher switching costs. When costs were lower, those firms chose to switch or backsource. Thus, the data supports the proposition that lower relative switching costs can promote adaptability.

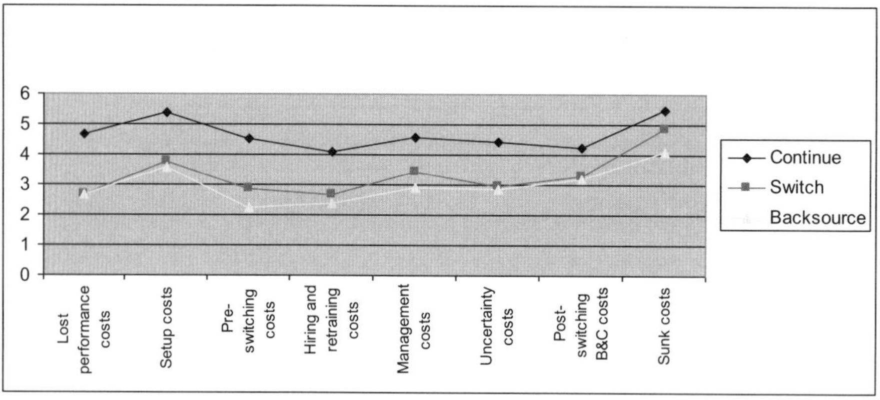

Figure 1

Based on the results which indicate that switching costs can prohibit the ability of a firm to move service provision smoothly, three strategies were developed for firms wanting to develop a strategy of adaptability. The strategies follow:

Strategy 1: Maintain an internal workforce.

Strategy 2: Maintain hardware and software to support operations in-house.

Strategy 3: Maintain relationships with multiple vendors.

6 Interviews

To provide further support for and better describe the three strategies, interviews with three executives responsible for outsourcing contracts were conducted. Each firm was large and headquartered in the U.S. Each executive had been involved with the outsourcing decisions of the firm for at least three years prior to the interviews. Three industries were represented: energy, high tech, and oilfield services. Drawing from the literature and initial findings of this project, a set of semi-structured interview questions were created. Each interview lasted approximately 45 minutes with some follow-up questions via phone at a later date as required for clarity.

All of the respondents agreed that switching costs were an important factor when deciding on the source of service provision and had considered those costs with previous sourcing decisions. Further, by observation, each respondent had at least considered the strategies, although in some cases were unable to implement them due to time or resource constraints.

Following is a detailed description of each of the three strategies, with insights included from the interviews.

Strategy 1: Maintain an internal workforce
Although one of the most cited goals of outsourcing is to decrease costs by reducing the internal workforce, it is not recommended to eliminate or reduce the workforce to near zero. By maintaining internal IT human resources capabilities, backsourcing can take place with relative ease. For example, setup costs, pre-switching costs, and hiring and retraining costs will be kept to a minimum. Further, in order to continue to build internal human resource capabilities, it is recommended to divide some processes into two parts (Lacity and Willcocks, 2001). One part is outsourced while the other is completed in-house, thus allowing the firms to retain and build process expertise. As an example, a large bank in Singapore outsourced the non-sensitive part of network maintenance to IBM while maintaining the sensitive network service in-house (Tan and Sia, 2008). Table 1 shows that for those firms which backsourced, their IT staff to overall firm staff ratio was nearly double that of the firms who switched. Those who switched employed fewer employees relative to firm size. Thus, as the number of IT employees decreases, the ability to more easily bring activities back in-house decreases as well.

The executive from "Energy" indicated that their goal is to maintain personnel in each IT function so that sufficient knowledge is retained within the firm. Although they extensively use outsourcing, considerable in-house effort is sustained. As he mentioned, "We never want to get to a point where we lose all capabilities in one space. The costs of rebuilding that knowledge and talent is too high."

Strategy 2: Maintain hardware and software to support operations in-house
Many firms reduce ongoing costs and bring in additional cash at the start of an outsourcing contract by selling hardware to the outsourcing vendor, especially those firms in financial trouble. While it may be acceptable to reduce the hardware level to a certain extent and not renew certain software contracts, internal capabilities must be maintained so that backsourcing can happen. Without internal hardware and software

capabilities, the setup costs especially can be considerable. This is very similar to Strategy 1 in regards to maintaining in-house abilities.

The executive from "Retail" said "While we have sold off some redundant assets before at the outset of a contract, we don't make it a common practice." "Oil" indicated that their firm had sold computers and other equipment as a result of a previous contract, but they only did that because "the costs of maintaining those assets were too high." One of the benefits of this particular contract was they were able to transfer some older equipment to the vendor which was costly to maintain, while keeping newer equipment in-house which sustained many other projects.

Strategy 3: Maintain relationships with multiple vendors
In many cases, firms contract to one vendor only. While this may afford efficiencies, a better strategy is to work with multiple vendors (multi-sourcing) so that if one relationship fails, your firm has experience with other vendors already. This reduces dependencies and raises competitiveness among competitor vendors (Lacity and Willcocks, 2001). This also makes it much less difficult to switch. In situations where a firm has experience with multiple vendors, the following costs are reduced due to the knowledge of already working with that vendor: lost performance costs, pre-switching, uncertainty, post-switching, among others. Examples of this strategy include British Petroleum using SEMA, Syncordia, and SAIC to perform upstream and downstream accounting and JP Morgan signing a seven-year $2.1 billion contract with four major suppliers (Tan and Sia, 2008). In both cases, these firms were able to possess a good exit strategy with lower switching costs if a change needed to be made.

"Energy" contracts with many outsourcing vendors across a multitude of IT areas. One reason they do this is to try out new vendors with smaller, relatively simple tasks. By systematically working with multiple vendors, they can better assess the vendors' capabilities, etc without being locked into just one. As the executive stated, "We never want to be in a situation where we are held hostage by one vendor. So, we have several vendors we use primarily and occasionally we will try out a new one. This also helps keep the other vendors honest."

In sum, by following these three strategies, firms can reduce switching costs which can ultimately increase their adaptability. As adaptability increases, firms are then better able to react efficiently and effectively to change which can lead to increased competitiveness.

References

1. Aubert, B., Rivard, S., Patry, M.: A Transaction Cost Model of IT Outsourcing. Information & Management 41(7), 921–932 (2004)
2. Beatty, S.E., Mayer, M., Coleman, J.E., Reynolds, K.E., Lee, J.: Customer-sales associate retail relationships. Journal of Retailing 72(3), 223–247 (1996)
3. Burnham, T., Frels, J., Mahajan, V.: Consumer Switching Costs: A typology, Antecedents, and Consequences. Journal of the Academy of Marketing Science 31(2), 109–126 (2003)
4. Chen, P., Hitt, L.M.: Measuring Switching Costs and the Determinants of Customer Retention in Internet-enabled Businesses: A study of the online brokerage industry. Information Systems Research 13(3), 255–274 (2002)

5. Cohen, L., Young, A.: Multisourcing: Moving Beyond Outsourcing to Achieve Growth and Agility. Harvard Business School Press, Boston (2005)
6. Farrell, J., Shapiro, C.: Dynamic Competition with Switching Costs. Rand Journal of Economics 1(19), 123–137 (1998)
7. Gaumnitz, J.E., Emery, D.R.: Asset Growth, Abandonment Value, and the Replacement Decision of Like-For-Like Capital Assets. Journal of Financial and Quantitative Analysis 15(2), 407–415 (1980)
8. Guiltinan, J., Childers, T., Bagozzi, R., Peter, J. (eds.): A Classification of Switching Costs With Implications for Relationship Marketing. In: Proceedings of the AMA Winter Educator's Conference: Marketing Theory and Practice, Chicago, IL, pp. 216–220 (1989)
9. Gwinner, K., Gremler, D., Bitner, M.J.: Relational Benefits in Services Industries: The Customer's Perspective. Journal of the Academy of Marketing Science 26(2), 101–114 (1998)
10. Heide, J.B., Weiss, A.M.: Vendor Consideration and Switching Behavior of Buyers in High-Technology Markets. Journal of Marketing 59, 30–43 (1995)
11. Howe, K.M., McCabe, G.M.: On Optimal Asset Abandonment and Replacement. Journal of Financial and Quantitative Analysis 18(3), 295–305 (1983)
12. Jackson, B.B.: Winning and Keeping Industrial Customers: The Dynamics of Customer Relationships. Lexington Books, Lexington (1985)
13. Jones, M.A., Motherbaugh, D.L., Beatty, S.E.: Switching Barriers and Repurchase Intentions in Services. Journal of Retailing 76(2), 259–274 (2000)
14. Jones, M.A., Mothersbaugh, D.L., Beatty, S.E.: Why Customers Stay: Measuring the Underlying Dimensions of Services Switching Costs and Managing their Differential Strategic Outcomes. Journal of Business Research 55(6), 441–450 (2002)
15. Jones, T., Sasser, E.: Why Satisfied Customers Defect. Harvard Business Review 73(6), 88–99 (1995)
16. Keil, M.J., Mann, A.R.: Why Software Projects Escalate: An Empirical Analysis and Test of Four Theoretical Models. MIS Quarterly 24(4), 631–664 (2000)
17. Lacity, M., Willcocks, L.: An Empirical Investigation of Information Technology Sourcing Practices: Lessons From Experience. MIS Quarterly 22(3), 363–408 (1998)
18. Lacity, M., Willcocks, L.: Relationships in IT Outsourcing: A Stakeholder Perspective. In: Zmud, R. (ed.) Framing the Domains of IT Management: Projecting the Future Through the Past, pp. 355–384. Pinnaflex, Cincinnati (2000)
19. Lacity, M., Willcocks, L.: Global Information Technology Outsourcing: In Search of Business Advantage. Wiley, Chichester (2001)
20. Lacity, M., Willcocks, L.: Inside Information Technology Outsourcing: A State-of-the-Art Report. Templeton Research Paper (2002)
21. Lee, H.: The Triple-A Supply Chain. Harvard Business Review (October 2004)
22. Morgan, R., Hunt, S.: The Commitment-Trust Theory of Relationship Marketing. Journal of Marketing 58(3), 20–38 (1994)
23. Murray, J.: Improving the IT Hiring Rate. Information Systems Management 17(3), 33–35 (2000)
24. Nielson, C.C.: An Empirical Examination of Switching Cost Investments in Business-to-Business Marketing Relationships. Journal of Business & Industrial Marketing 11(6), 38–60 (1996)
25. Ping Jr., R.A.: The Effects of Satisfaction and Structural Constraints on Retailer Exiting, Voice, Loyalty, Opportunism and Neglect. Journal of Retailing 69(fall), 320–352 (1993)
26. Porter, M.: Competitive Strategy: Techniques for Analyzing Industries and Competitors. The Free Press, New York (1980)

27. Shugan, S.M.: The Cost of Thinking. Journal of Consumer Research 7(2), 99–111 (1980)
28. Soman, D., Gourville, J.: Transaction Decoupling: How Price Bundling Affects the Decision to Consume. Journal of Marketing Research 38(1), 30–44 (2001)
29. Spekman, R.E., Strauss, D.: An Exploratory Investigation of a Buyer's Concern For Factors Affecting Co-Operative Buyer-Seller Relationships. In: Backhaus, K., Wilson, D.T. (eds.) Industrial Marketing, pp. 115–133. Springer, Berlin (1986)
30. Suarez, F., Cusumano, M., Fine, C.: An Empirical Study of Flexibility in Manufacturing. Sloan Management Review 37(1), 25–32 (1995)
31. Tan, C., Sia, S.K.: Managing Flexibility in Outsourcing. Journal of the Association for Information Systems 7(4), Article 10 (2008)
32. Violino, B., Caldwell, B.: Analyzing the Integrators. Information Week Online 709, 45–69, 11-16 (1998)
33. Weiss, A., Anderson, E.: Converting From Independent to Employee Salesforces: The Role of Perceived Switching Costs. Journal of Marketing Research 1(29), 101–115 (1992)
34. Whitten, D., Leidner, D.: Bringing IT Back: An Analysis of Application Development Backsourcing and Switching. Decision Sciences Journal 37(4) (2006)
35. Whitten, D., Wakefield, R.: Measuring Switching Costs in IT Outsourcing Services. Journal of Strategic Information Systems 15(3), 219–248 (2006)
36. Willcocks, L., Lacity, M.: Information Systems Outsourcing in Theory and Practice. Journal of Information Technology 10(4), 203–207 (1995)
37. Williamson, O.: Markets and Hierarchies: Analysis and Antitrust Implications. Free Press, New York (1975)
38. Ybarra, C., Wiersema, M.: Strategic Flexibility in Information Technology Alliance: The Influence of Transaction Cost Economies and Social Exchange Theory. Organization Science 10(4), 439–459 (1999)

The Role of Contracts and Informal Relations in the Governance of IT Outsourcing Processes

Giovanni Vaia and Aurelio Tommasetti

University of Salerno, Via Ponte don Melillo, 84084 Fisciano (SA), Italy

Abstract. This paper aims to give a contribution to represent and comprehend the characteristics of the relationships between customers and providers in the specific context of IT services supply; furthermore it provides its peculiar perspective on the relationship between the formal *governance*, which is mostly realized through the use of contracts, and the informal relations based on trust and *commitment* between the parties. Moreover, the current study underlines that within contexts which are strongly based on the uncertain evolution both of market and technology, the *governance* of IT outsourcing processes needs the development of complex informal relationships in support of the contracts. The study shows how it is possible to absorb the effects of the market and technology uncertainty within the IT outsourcing contracts. Moreover, the research shows how the use of dynamic contracting together with an explicit attention to the social processes can lead to remarkable operative and strategic benefits.

Keywords: IT outsourcing, IT outsourcing contracts, relationships between customer and provider, outsourcing governance, IT services.

1 Introduction

Today, providers of IT outsourcing[1] services (ITOS)[2] and their customers face new challenges in managing and innovating business IT services, due to a very strong technological dynamism and ongoing market evolution. The two latter factors contribute to create a situation of growing uncertainty for both hardware and software solutions and the services related to them.

---

[1] "IT outsourcing is broadly defined as a decision taken by an organisation to contract-out or sell the organisation's IT assets, people and/or activities to a third party provider, who in exchange provides and manages assets and services for monetary returns over an agree time period" (Kern and Willcocks, 2002).

[2] Scholars identified different ways to classify the IT outsourcing services. For instance Aubert et al (1996) classify the functions of the information systems (IS) in system operation and software development; instead Arnett and Jones (1994) offer a bigger classification identifying the system integration systems, facility management, contract programming, software support, network maintenance, minicomputer maintenance, mainframe maintenance and workstation maintenance. Grover et al. (1996) divide the Outsourcing IT in application development and maintenance, end-user computing support, system planning and management, purchasing of applications (software).

I. Oshri and J. Kotlarsky (Eds.): Global Sourcing 2010, LNBIP 55, pp. 217–232, 2010.

The IT market growth and development mostly depends on how much IT services providers satisfy customers' needs. A large part of these needs will stem by new technology implementation and by the expansion of business processes with technology-based solutions. Benefits of initiatives as such would be essential: they would be an important contribution for IT services to become a strategic resource for businesses because they would offer an effective support to the strategic change, to innovation and to performance improvement. (Oshri *et al.*, 2009; Weill *et al.*, 2002; Martinsons, 1993).

IT suppliers are called to promptly adapt themselves to business evolution. Research of flexibility and strategic change are critical targets in highly complex technological and market contexts. Up to now, such complexity and strategic uncertainty have been managed thanks to solutions of vertical disintegration of IT activities. This kind of solutions have been preferred to hierarchical integration ones. IT services providers are called to replace their customers in running IT services which are characterized by very high complexity levels, strong uncertainty and difficult integration with the customer processes. As a result, IT business outsourcing has been experiencing an increasing trend since the Nineties.

In 2008 IT outsourcing business has settled down between 220 and 250 billion dollars, with an increase of 6-9% foreseen for the next years (Willcoks *et al.*, 2009).

In this context, ITOS providers are asked to deeply comprehend customers' business processes and to develop a strong skill to adapt their offer of technologies according to changing models and to the business needs. This market demand implies a change in outsourcing relationships and justifies a specific focus on the analysis of the management of customer–provider relationship. The suppliers become "strategic partners" of their customers: they are involved and integrated in IT management and development processes, pushing towards a harmonious and cooperative relationship based on trust and commitment[3] (Goo et al,2009, Poppo & Zenger, 2002). For this reason, the implementation and management of an outsourcing relationship offer many opportunities to both the parties involved but, at the same time, complicate the costumer – supplier relationship governance.

The aim of this paper is to analyse the *management toolkit* for the relationship governance in IT outsourcing processes within the Italian context, relating two variables: market and technology. Particularly, through the presentation of five empirical cases from the customer and provider's side, the paper analyses the capability of formal control (contracts) and the relational governances[4] (trust and commitment) (Poppo and Zenger, 2002) to conduct and control the supplying relation with reference to different business and technological contexts.

After resuming main theoretical approaches which describe IT outsourcing relationships (section 2), the paper focuses on the empirical analysis and its main results

---

[3] The concept of trust is represented by benevolence, integrity, honesty feelings and it reflects the expectations of a side whose own needs, demands will be satisfied by the behaviours of the other one (Zaheer and Venkatraman, 1995). The commitment, instead, can be defined in terms of lastingness (desire to continue the relation) input (disposition to invest in the relation, both in monetary terms and working effort), coherence (trust in the stability of the relation) (Noteboom, 1997; Kumar *et al.*, 1995).

[4] The relational governance refers to the observance of the obligations, promises, and expectations and it is realised thanks to trust and social recognition (Goo *et al.*, 2009).

(sections 3 and 4); it finally shows some implications for future management and research (section 5 and 6).

2 The Research Problem

An ongoing debate in IT outsourcing literature relates to the management aspects of IT outsourcing and, particularly, to the activities concerning the *execution* of IT services provider contract, emphasizing the identification processes of the object of exchange and the definition of specifications (for instance, the choices to *make* or *buy*) rather than the contracts implementation aspects (Mahnke, 2001).

Transaction Costs has influenced mostly this approach (Williamson, 1975; Barthélemy, 2001; Lacity and Hirscheim, 1993). From this perspective, many researches underlined the main role of contracts in order to have a successful outsourcing processes management (Saunders *et al.*, 1997; Lacity and Willcocks, 1996).

As pointed out, the evolving technological background and a stronger uncertainty about the evolution of business processes surely contribute to a growth of the informative asymmetry between the customer and the ITOS supplier and to the resulting increase of information management and transaction costs.

Nevertheless, the market of IT outsourcing is growing more and more, as underlined previously. Its growth is often independent from highly specific activities (as in the case of the development of new applications) and thus they are needful of a strong and frequent cooperation between the parties, hence involving high transaction costs. This incoherence between theory and practice is confirmed by several researches (Barthélemy, 2001; Earl, 1996) which underlined how the IT outsourcing projects' failures in relationships are often caused by the incapability of the customers to manage the relation through the contract only. Customers are unable to evaluate *ex ante* provider's tenders and competences, *ex post* to evaluate their performances (Willcocks *et al.*, 1995).

Literature from the last few years underlined the need to use a perspective in analyzing the supplier's relations based on the role of the informal/social relations (Poppo and Zenger, 2002). Willcocks and Choi (1995), for instance, state that the more the IT services are outsourced, the more long-term relations last and the focus is on results and trust rather than on the contract. Theories with strong social/relational connotation (Lee and Kim 1999; Macneil, 1980; Aiken and Hage, 1968), reorganize their contractual dimensions when they state that inter-organizational relations in outsourcing are relations based on exchange and on social interactions in which the *core exchanges* are contractually defined (and in which exchanges allow to analyse the behavioural dimensions which develop among the individuals by the time).

Kern and Willcocks (2000) summarise the literature about this issue and identify the context, the contract, the interactions and the behaviour of the parties as key dimension of the relation. They underline how the economic action leads IT outsourcing processes and that ITO processes are at the same time also dipped into social relations.

Nevertheless, studies which focus on the relationship between formal and relational governance are controversial. On one hand if some researches show that the mechanisms tied to the relational governance replace the need of contracts (Gulati,

1995), on the other hand (Ghoshal and Moran, 1996), evidences from studies within the same trend (Goo *et al.*, 2009; Poppo and Zenger, 1998, 2002), show that the contract and trust and commitment can be considered as complementary tools and not as alternative governance ones.

This study, entering this trend, offers empirical evidences to better explain the relation between formal governance and relational governance as far as IT service supply is concerned.

3 Description of the Study

We collected the empirical material of this article interviewing 10 companies with the aim to observe 5 customer-supplier relations. Later, we will focus on a description of the customer context and on the IT services[5] provided. The empirical study is based on the observation of contracts and of the formal documents concerning the service provided on the interviews given by the parties involved.

In particular, the study of contracts focused on the analysis of definition, structure and monitoring of the *Service Level Agreement* (SLA)[6]. These latter can be considered as the most important aspects of the contract because they describe the services/products supplied, the service levels the customer expects to receive, the monitoring metrics, the management of changes, etc.

The interviews had both the role of a better definition of the contracts contents and of the evaluation of informal aspects characterizing the customer-provider relations. As stated in Table 1, suppliers have been mainly interviewed. Nevertheless, where possible, the resulting data were compared through interviews to several subjects belonging to both the customer and the supplying company, and through observations coming from the contracts and the records supplied (Eisenhardt, 1989; Pettigrew, 1990; Yin, 1994).

During interviews conducted with a semi-structured approach, we tried to find out about the conditions of the *relation* set up (the number of suppliers called to produce a bid for the service, the rules during the preliminary phase of contract (Richardson, 1993), the use of techniques such as *target costing* and *profit sharing,* generally identified as a tool to support the cooperation between the parties (Nishiguchi, 1994; Sei, 1996), the nature and the modalities with which the *informative exchange* takes place and the role played by variable elements as *trust* (Noteboom *et al.*, 1997) and *commitment* (Scanzoni, 1979).

---

[5] An IT service can be defined as a system of functions correlated with a deliver of an IT system in support of one or more areas of business. The service can constitute a synthesis of hardware, software and systems of communication, as in the processes and organisational roles, but perceived by the user an independent entity and coherent, like for example electronic mail, a CRM system, internet applications. This implies an integrated and coherent management of the infrastructure and the applications. This vision of IT implies that the performance and the availability of every single component are meaningful if they are evaluated according to the performance and the availability of all the components which arrange the supply chain of the final service to the user.

[6] To deepen the SLA structure see Goo *et al.*, 2008.

Table 1. Synthesis of interviews

	N People interviewed	*Roles of people interviewed (customer and provider side)*	*Period of interviews*	*Length (h)*
Case 1	10	IT Manager, Delivery Manager, Project Manager, Account Manager,	2006-2008-January 2010	20
Case 2	5	Account Manager, Project Manager	2008-January 2010	7
Case 3	4	IT Manager , Project Manager, Operation Manager, Account Manager	October-December 2008 November-December 2009	10
Case 4	3	IT Manager, Infrastructure Specialist, Consultant	January 2010	5
Case 5	12	General Manager, IT Manager, Account Manager, Personnel involved in operations	September-October 2009	20

4 Empirical Evidences

4.1 Characteristics of Customers and IT Outsourcing Services Provided

The choice of companies was based on the evaluation of the services provided, on their relevance in the IT sourcing context and on the heterogeneity of business and technological contexts, in order to offer a different viewpoint on the variables which directly or indirectly influence the choices of governance. Table 2 offers a synthesis of the characteristics of both the customers and suppliers' companies and of the IT services supplied.

The first case observed (C1) concerns of an international company in the telecommunication field which provides both wire and mobile services, and one of its IT outsourcing services supplier which is constantly listed among the first 15 companies in the Fortune list.

The business services of the customers company range from telephone and data services to outsourcing services of information systems mainly for small and medium companies, such as networking management, business continuity, data centre and security services.

The IT management of the customer, organized in eight functional units and two staff units, guarantees the development and the management of infrastructures and information systems for the business and for TLC operations; it guarantees also enterprise solutions, coordination of the development activities of the enterprise IT platforms and the planning of solutions for security.

As far as the outsourcing relation is concerned, the two companies consolidated their relation in 2003 with the signature of a contract to provide services for five years and for a total amount of 225 million euros. In particular, the contract concerned the work station management of the customer, including services of first and second level Help Desk (it consists on collection and resolution of problems, managing trouble tickets, and/or the possible recover of a normal working state of some hardware installed, such as PC and peripherals), maintenance actions due to anomalies collected and unsolved by the Help Desk, aiming at the restoration of software bugs; IMAC services (Install, Move, Add, Change) (i.e. on-site activities of PC and peripherals installation, hardware and software update, the displacement of equipments and lay-out activities); logistic services and asset management (i.e. collect, store, pre-installation activities of hardware and software at the warehouse and delivery and settlement of the assets by the users; the service includes the management of the customers tracking and warehousing systems).

The second case (C2) concerns an important insurance company with more than 350 branches in Italy. The company offers insurance for circulation and travelling, complementary health insurance, etc.

The IT department supports the business with several services to run car insurances and register customers; release of online life policies; e-mail domain; central antivirus safety; safe access to internet; support for office automation and desktop management.

This is the second case where the supplier is a big multinational player, who started to provide his services in 2001, with a contract renewal in 2004.

The outsourcing project stemmed from the need to improve the quality of IT services through a centralization of faulty processes management, through a higher level of performance in proactive resolutions and thanks to a better control of performances and IT costs.

As in the previous case, also in this case the outsourcing services provided for the company headquarter and for over 350 branches, concerned not only IMAC services but also help desk services, as well as the hardware and software assistance on workstations.

The customer company in the third case (C3) is one of the most important companies in the fashion and luxury sector worldwide. Through subsidiary companies and branches, the Group works with a structure of distribution which reaches more than 100 Countries, with 40 showrooms and more than 10.000 stores. More than 1.400 of these distribution points are mono-brand stores managed by third partners and 284 are directly managed stores.

During the last 6 years their IT area was transformed, in order to be a real useful factor for the business.

This transformation process is leading the IT area towards a corporate dimension with the aim to offer services in any region thanks to the support and the proposition of innovative technologies and processes, quick implementation of proper information systems, application and technological services and the guarantee of operation continuity.

In this context, the IT area is implementing a huge project of investments to update its own Information Technology platforms, aiming at reaching an integrated and optimised management of the business processes.

Also in this case services provided regards the workstation management, business and infrastructure applications management, hardware and operative system management.

Our analysis focused both on the contracts and on the relation with the customer's former supplier, which started in 2004 and ended in 2009, and both on the contract and the relation with their new provider.

The fourth case (C4) concerns a company which works in the pharmaceutical research field. The company, with about 150 employees, whose 90% are researchers, is characterized by a creative multidisciplinary and stimulating environment. Their projects aim at developing drugs which are able to modify the course of illnesses in patients.

Their IT technology is made of highly up-to-date platforms able to manage and to analyse data in order to identify, select and optimise small molecules of high quality which possess the necessary characteristics to become a successful drug. Services bought by the customer concern hardware maintenance, storage, software development and maintenance.

The fifth case (C5) is about a company specialized in supplying systems and telematic services for insurance and automotive market. The Italian company expanding to international markets, represents a best practice in the worldwide background of telematic services extending up to the market sectors of mobility (mobile telematic systems) and data transmission.

The supplier is an important Italian IT service supplier company with about 650 employees and with a turnover of 60 million euros. It is oriented to business integration solutions, enterprise solutions, application management services both of process and infrastructure.

The supplier deals with outsourcing management of application services (for instance data extraction from data warehouse), or of evolutionary maintenance (for instance bug resolutions), as well as with the development of new applications (for instance the development of a new application for data reporting supplied by the mobility system).

Table 2. Synthesis of the characteristics of the customer and provider's companies

	C1	C2	C3	C4	C5
Sectors	TLC	Insurance	Fashion	Pharmaceutical	Services
Products/Services	Voice and data, outsourcing of Information systems for SME	Car insurance, life insurance	Clothing and Accessories	Pharmaceutical research	Infomobility, telematics
Provider Characteristics	600 employees, 60M € revenues	2600 employees, 1000M € revenues	700 employees, 190M € revenues	N/A	650 employees, 70M € revenues
Contract length	From 2003 to date	2001 renewed in 2004 to 2008	2004-2008. New provider from 2009 (1 year contract)	N/A	N/A
IT Outsourcing Services	Workstation Management , Help Desk HW/SW Maintenance	Workstation Management , Help Desk HW/SW Maintenance	Workstation Management , Help Desk HW/SW Maintenance	SW purchasing, customisation and maintenance, storage services	SW development and maintenance
Business Processes Dynamism	Low	Low	Medium/ High	High	High
Technology Dynamisms	High	High	High	High	High
Criticality of IT services	Low	Low	Medium/ High	High	High

The selected case studies offer a very wide range of market status and technology. The choice of these case studies was actually made in order to observe inductively the changes in the governance of the relationship due to a change in the conditions of business and information technology.

Indeed, from an exploratory analysis of the first two cases we observed an increasing trend to use relational elements in the governance of the relationship when the business processes change over time and an evolution in IT services becomes necessary.

This process brought us to examine our hypotheses in different contexts. With regard to technology, the evolution of business needs usually occurs when there is a change in the services characteristics, but we also noticed a change in technology, disconnected to changes in business processes. Just as in the case of technology updating and tuning.

Although the mutual relationship between technology and business changes is of great interest, it is not examined in this study. A variable for further examination is the criticality of IT services for the supply of business processes. This latter has been considered as an aspect of strong characterization in the observed cases, but it is necessary to further investigate its real capacity of influencing the choice of governance solution.

The aim of this study was to verify if and how changes in business and technology requirements are managed and incorporated into contracts and if the two types of governance become alternatives in situations of strong variability.

Especially, in C1 and C2 cases the context of business is stable, in the way in which the necessity of the business/users don't experiment fast changes.

In both these cases technology is continually evolving, both for standard updates and for developments which improve existing performances or which introduce new functions. Although in these two cases the conditions of business and technology are assimilated, including IT outsourcing services, the use of the governance tools is different.

Case studies C3, C4 and C5 present a more dynamic context both in business and in technology. In these three cases, the IT service providers offer consultancy often finalized at the development of *ad hoc* projects, where it is difficult to define *ex ante* requirements, customer's needs and all eventual outputs. This is also the case in which there is a higher criticality of IT services to guarantee the continuity of the customer's business process.

4.2 The Role of Contracts in C1 and C2

Many similarities emerge from the empiric observation about the "structure" of the supply contracts. A different orientation also emerges, concerning the "use" of the contract as governing tool of the supply relation.

The contract is the main managing tool of the supply relation between the customer and the provider for the C1 and C2 cases mostly. This means that the main contractual terms are formally conveyed to all the people involved in the services (last consumers, services and management processes managers, customer and supply area) and they become a basis to manage the processes and the interactions between the actors.

Moreover, the contract becomes the benchmark to manage the disputes and strained relations between the actors/parties.

. . the contract is our datum-point to manage the relation with the customer (Account Manager, C2)

Detailed contracts follow a plan outlined by the literature already[7], as regards their structure. All the contracts define the aims and the contents of the service levels, and the roles and the responsibilities of the involved actors in the outsourcing process. Setting the limits of the collaboration means the implementation of the standard processes for the IT services management (for instance the ITIL- IT Infrastructure Library) and standard metrics, in most cases. That allows to transfer the details of the operative procedures defined within the management processes, the policy, the roles and responsibilities, the management reporting, escalation path of senior (hierarchical) levels for the disputes and/or conflicts management, using a shared and understandable language. Moreover, they set performance criteria, based both on "end-to-end" service levels guaranteed by the provider (metrics), and define the measurement criteria of processes supported (KPI). This allows to check the observance of the costs and the qualitative levels defined and this allows to solve the disputes through processes defined by the contract. The system of penalties is linked to this measurement system. But it seems to lose its sanctionative nature because the customers prefer do not damage the relation with their clients on one hand, while they use it to assimilate the risk linked to the uncertainty about some variables of the supply on the other one. In fact the customers cannot define the dimensioning and the characteristics of the supply system before. The penalty becomes a *risk sharing* tool *ex ante. Ex post*, the presence of penalties allows an implicit "redefinition" about prices of the services, when there are some disservices and a loss of business for the customer. The provider has in the pipeline the possibility to pay penalties considering previous performances and experiences. But he increases the level of the offered services in order to win a tender for a supply though he knows the mechanism of the penalties (the difficult of the customer to evaluate ex ante the "feasibility" of the service offered by the provider makes possible this opportunistic approach. But it is offset by the penalties). So the penalty reduces the price of the supply of the service when there are some disservices. About the C1 case, there are not the elements tied to the possibility of managing a change and so modifying the contractual terms with clear negative consequences on the capacity to manage destructured and innovative activities by the parties. It is possible to identify two different approaches though both C1 and C2 rely on the analysis of the contracts.

The first approach is characterised by a **static management of the contract,** we called **"traditional classic contracting".** The provider tries to respect the levels of the predetermined service pursuing to improve the volume of the income through the management of a greater number of tickets on one hand, and pursuing to avoid penalties on the other.

In this case the definition of precise performance measures and monitoring methods, used in order to reduce the opportunism of the provider, becomes a limit on the long term, because of the incapability of the provider to understand the needs of the customer and translate them in dynamic and performing services. As underlined by the interviews in C1, this kind of approach results more successful when both the

---

[7] For deepening the structure of the contracts see Goo *et al*, 2008.

business and technological processes of the customer are steady. For instance, you can consider the ordinary maintenance services on work station within a company which produces bottles. In this case the customer will tend to reduce the management costs of own systems and to render the outsourcing process the most favourable possible by the provider monitoring and the application of penalties, if it will be necessary.

The second approach (C2) is characterised by a **dynamic management of the contract ("dynamic contracting")**. It is more appropriate to the business and technological characteristics. There are two examples of this kind of approach: the *Service Credits* and the *Weighed Dynamic Measures*. As regards the first case, when the services are less than the agreement and the provider runs into the penalties he can stop their payment if he works to supply services with a qualitative/quantitative level not inferior to the Service Level Objectives agreed; if the provider supplies services under the Minimum Level of Service, he will pay fixed penalties. So the customer gives the provider a "trust credit" on the medium-long term, avoiding to penalize a lower performances of the provider which could depend on events due to incidental situations. As regards the second case, the provider is stimulated, through weighed performance measures, to reorganize the effort on targets more crucial at a given moment, conditioning the decisions of outsourcing and consolidating the trusty relation in the long period. So the performance measures and the linked penalties are "weighed" with indexes which express the level of importance of an IT service at a given moment.

Then the contract becomes an exchange process projected in the future, where the exchange is repeated several times or the relation extends throughout different periods. The contract does not ever specify what it is necessary to do any time exactly, but it often defines only the aims to achieve and the procedures to follow (or the methods of revision of the main parameters which regulate the contract); the necessary adjustments due to events produced during the relation are regulated time by time, considering the whole development of the relation until the event (these adjustments often concern the amount rather than the price). Finally, the contract guarantees the observance of most contractual terms rather than the legal system, with the fixed incentives and any following agreements.

4.3 The Role of the Informal Governance in C3, C4 e C5 Cases

While the C1 and C2 seem to confirm the central role of the contracts in the IT outsourcing governance, the C3 C4 and C5 cases show a different scenario. The contract has no relevance for these customers. Customers mainly govern the relation according to the trust. This one increases thanks to a friendly and empathic relation, affinities and ethical principles. In these cases the parties try to establish relations based on familiarity and sympathy in order to develop a positive exchange in the course of time. The motivations are the difficulties to express the needs of the users at an international level and most of all the changes of technology, with a good degree of certainty (Hill, 1990). Customers understand the need to reduce the informative asymmetries (also tied to an incomplete control of any technological domain) and with these one the possibility of disputes and opportunism. In this case, the customers have a strong need to start everlasting learning and informative exchange processes, in order to be supported since the technological design stage.

It has been three months since we began working with the new outsourcer and we still haven't signed a contract! (Project Manager, C3)

Finally, a rigidly observed contract provokes damages rather than benefits/advantages (IT manager, C4)

Trust becomes the essential driver to manage the relation, where the contracts observe this approach, appearing little structured[8]. The customers consider this one a successful choice for two reasons:

- the need to offer a continuity to the business;
- the difficulty in defining ex-ante the requirements of a new IT service undergoing rapid growth.

For instance, in C4 the continuity of the experiments in laboratory is crucial for the company, cause an disruption could create a nullification of the previous testing and a consequent loss of time and economic resources engaged; instead, in C5 the requirements of business are redefined continually, the innovative services of the company are the result of the ideas of the management and the aims and the technological requirements are not so clear.

As the parties sign the contract, they put it aside and they do not take it out again/this one is closed in a drawer and it never get out from there...(IT manager, C4)

Trust allows to found the relation on rules characterised by flexibility and ability to adapt in order to manage the technological and business uncertainty, to start processes of knowledge exchange, to focus the growth of systems according to the real need of the company and the structural capabilities. These **relational aspects help to pass the limits of the formal contract concerning the ability to adapt** (Ken and Willcocks; Sull and Spinosa, 2007). They help to predispose customer and provider to an everlasting change of the relation in order to meet new requests of services, through a pathway of joined learning. The result of this approach is the systematic contact between customer and provider in order to improve both quantitative and qualitative aspects of the service. In C3, C4 and C5 cases the relation between customers and providers is friendly and it also expresses a desire to go on growing through capital investments (for instance in pre-feasibility studies) and human resources. Moreover, it starts *knowledge sharing* processes. A real time knowledge exchange is crucial in this sector where changes concerning software implementations reflect on other software and hardware systems. The exchange of information allows to plan the resolution in a proactive way of the recurrent problems concerning the infrastructure on one hand, the growth of systems according to the real needs of the company and the structural capabilities on the other one. Instead, the process of development of trust is not supported by sharing processes of rules and values which are often quoted in literature. The most important contractual aspects are the clauses/terms of management of the disputes and their resolution. The reason of this interest is based on the fact that the dynamism business and technologies pushes or could push towards disagreements

[8] Only in C3 it has been observed a well structured contract as in the previous cases. The customer presumes to calculate and regulate the relation in detail within a good contract which is not used as governing tool of the relation practically.

about the aims and the opportunistic behaviour. The management procedures of these disputes become crucial. Literature confirms that the more the processes and the activities to resolve the disputes are explicit, the more their resolution is coherent (Dant and Schul, 1992).

5 Discussion and Conclusions

The case studies show that it is better to adopt a complex set of relational and governance tools when the object of the supply is an IT service, whose characteristics are highly linked to business processes of the customer. The research underlined a relation between the governance chosen and the characteristics of the business and technology. The results of the research confirm that the contract, as a governance tool, has some limits where the levels of uncertainty of the business and technology increase. Rapid changes of the business needs, due to an accelerated growth and/or diversification of the markets, push to manage the relation in a proactive, informal, flexible way. The contract emerges as a successful tool where the business (C1 and C2) is (relatively) steady. But it is necessary to add elements of flexibility and dynamism to the contract, for example credits of the service, management plans of the future demand, management plans of innovation and improvement of the service, when the uncertainty increases. It is also necessary to found the relation on the social relations mainly, where the ability to adapt to the technological and business changes represents a trusting evidence for the customer. Formal governance and relational governance seem to be extremes of a continuum in unstable and uncertain situations (they work as substitutes). However, we observed a high complementariness and a strong mutual aid in intermediate situations. In particular, the contract offers a significant reinforcement of the trust, according to the results of previous researches (Goo et al, 2008; Poppo and Zenger, 2002; Klein, 1996; Willcocks and Choi, 1995; Fitzgerald and Willcocks, 1994; Baker et.al, 1994). Rating procedures of the performances, oriented to optimize the output rather than the sanctions, cause the success of the relation strengthening the trust since the start up, as the case of the credits of the service or the weighed dynamic measures. That creates a "virtuous" circle where the provider has the possibility to regain the relation and the trust of the customer, even if there is a temporary failure. So any kind of assessment becomes a tool to start improvement actions (quantitative – KPI – and qualitative periodic meetings). It emerges that the assessment can be considered not only a redefinition mechanism of the contract but also a "trust building" mechanisms. This one plays a crucial role where the contracts are incomplete and they cannot play a crucial role about the coordination of the relation. Instead a second factor is linked to the ability to establish some successful mechanisms of communication. In particular, the rules and the processes defined by the contract in terms of changing management, future service demand and improvement plans/actions, influence the trust very much. As observed in C2, the frameworks of process as ITIL help to transfer the details of the operative procedures defined within the management processes, the policies, the rules and responsibilities, the management reporting, the escalation pathways, with a shared and understandable language. Another aspect concerns the prearranged creation of a method to manage the disputes. As observed in C4, the perception to have defined a fair and right procedure for both the parties, offers room to develop a positive relation based on the trust. In brief, the contract proved the main governance tool of the relations when there is little uncertainty, the business requirements and the technological change are steady. Dynamic contractual solutions emerged as effective. As the technological change is marked, the procedures for a risks and *reward* sharing include the uncertainty linked to the development of supply service. There again findings show that the outsourcing relations can led to significant benefits where the risk exposure can be controlled by close informal relations. The management of the uncertainty, of the technology's dynamism and of the business processes is managed by relational *governance* based on the trust, which seems substitute the contract (concerning its dynamic and flexible expression too). A strict contractual control can involve a vicious cycle of suspects and recriminations. So it can stifle the relation, reducing the capabilities to define the expectations and future demand of services. Reading of the cases some criticalities emerge. They are not managed by both the customers and the providers and they give some ideas to improve the practice. C1 case shows that the provider could be adopt an opportunistic behaviour in technological change situation, and he could not meet the real needs of the customer. The contract is not able to prompt in itinere the actions and reactions of the counterpart towards the joined aims through management and control processes (Willcocks, Fitzgerald, 1994), even if it can be considered the main governance tool. As regards this point, both a difficult and a will to reconsider the contract emerged from the interviews including elements of higher flexibility. Instead in C4 and C5 cases an abandonment of the contract and a consequent advantage of the trust could create an uncontrolled increase of the demands of the customer damaging the provider. So "vicious" processes start in which everlasting activities of negotiation could lead significant negative effects both about the behaviour of the actors and the operative success of the relation. Moreover the development of the trust is not an immediate process. We observed that there are not managing procedures of development of the customer-provider relations which consider their complexity, and their strategic role as well. These "trust building" mechanisms play a crucial role where the contracts are little structured and they can not play a crucial role in organizing the relation. The use of these tools should support and enrich a bigger integration of the key business processes in the *supply chain* (Lambert *et al.*, 1998). For instance, we did not observe *target costing* and *profit sharing* techniques. The benefits are not shared when there is a reduction of the costs (to the advantage of the customer), or an improvement of the productivity (to the advantage of the customer and/or provider). As anticipated, only in C2 case, there are dynamic techniques of redefinition of the contract which allow to organize the activities and the performances on the strength of needs and achieved results (see the following sections). The right mix of contractual elements and trust building procedures gives the possibility to achieve some benefits from the outsourcing process and to organize the efforts in a more successful and effective way, in different situations of uncertainty.

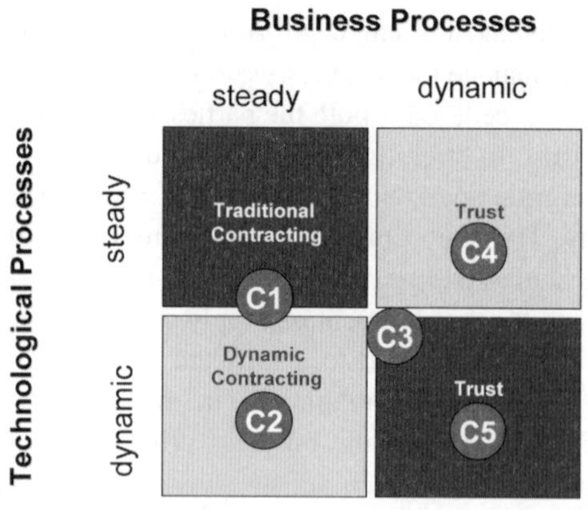

Fig. 1. Governance typologies and impact factors

6 Limits

Cases chosen have allowed the inductive analysis of the variation of the use of governance mechanisms together with the changing business conditions and technology. It means that the variety of the cases did not allow the reiteration of the "test" and so the validation of the starting assumptions in order to get stronger generalizations. Moreover the trust is a variable which can be influenced by different contingent factors, for instance the size. Further, the object of the supply is another variable which influences the governance choices and its relation with the uncertainty should be deepened, as literature shows widely. These limits push us to verify the typology of the governance and influencing factors in cases with same characteristics. They push us to enrich the model on the strength of the different categories of supply.

References

1. Aiken, M., Hage, J.: Organizational interdependence and intra-organizational structure. American Sociological Review 33(6), 912–930 (1968)
2. Arnett, K.P., Jones, M.C.: Firms that choose outsourcing: a profile. Information & Management 26, 179–188 (1994)
3. Aubert, B., Rivard, S., Patry, M.: A transaction cost approach to outsourcing behaviour: some empirical evidence. Information & Management 30, 51–64 (1996)
4. Baker, G., Gibbons, R., Murphy, K.J.: Subjective performance measures in optimal incentive contracts. The Quarterly Journal of Economics 109(4), 1125–1156 (1994)
5. Barthelemy, J.: The Hidden costs of IT outsourcing. MIT Sloan Management Review 43(3), 60–69 (2001)
6. Dant, R.P., Schul, P.L.: Conflict resolution processes in contractual channels of distribution. Journal of Marketing 56(1), 38–54 (1992)
7. Earl, M.J.: The risks of IT outsourcing. Sloan Management Review, 26–32 (Spring 1996)
8. Eisenhardt, K.M.: Building Theories from Case Study Research. Academy of Management Review 14(4), 532–550 (1989)

9. Ghoshal, S., Moran, P.: Bad of practice: A critique of the Transaction Cost Theory. Academy of Management Review 21(1), 13–47 (1996)
10. Goo, J., Huang, D.C., Hart, P.: A path to successful IT outsourcing: Interaction between Service-Level Agreements and commitment. Decision Science 39(3), 469–506 (2008)
11. Goo, J., Kishore, R., Rao, H.R., Nam, K.: The role of service level agreement in relational management of Information technology Outsourcing: An empirical study. MIS Quarterly 33(1), 119–145 (2009)
12. Grover, V., Cheon, M.J., Teng, J.: The effects of service quality and partnership on the outsourcing of information systems functions. Journal of Management of Information Systems 12(4), 89–116 (1996)
13. Gulati, R.: Does familiarity breed trust? The implications of repeated ties for contractual choices in alliances. Academy of management Journal 38(1), 85–112 (1995)
14. Kern, T., Willcocks, L.: Exploring information technology outsourcing relationship: theory and practice. Journal of Strategic Information Systems 9, 321–350 (2000)
15. Klein, B.: Why hold-ups occur: The self-enforcing range of contractual relationships. Economic Inquiry 34(3), 444–463 (1996)
16. Kumar, N., Scheer, L.K., Steenkamp, J.B.: The effects of perceived interdependence on dealer attitudes. Journal of Marketing Research 32(3), 348–356 (1995)
17. Lacity, M., Hirschheim, R.: Information Systems Outsourcing. Wiley, Chichester (1993)
18. Lacity, M., Willcocks, L.: Interpreting information technology sourcing decisions from a Transaction Cost Perspective: Findings and Critique. Accounting, Management, and Information Technologies 5(3), 203–244 (1996)
19. Lambert, D.M., Cooper, M.C., Pagh, J.D.: Supply Chain Management: Implementation issues and research opportunities. International Journal of Logistics Management 9(2), 1–19 (1998)
20. Lee, J.N., Kim, Y.G.: Effect of partnership quality on IS outsourcing: Conceptual framework and empirical validation. Journal of Management Information Systems 14(4), 29–61 (1999)
21. Macneil, I.R.: The new social contract: An inquiry into modern contractual relations. Yale University Press, New Haven (1980)
22. Mahnke, V.: The process of vertical dis-integration: An evolutionary perspective on outsourcing. Journal of Management and Governance 5, 353–379 (2001)
23. Martinsons, M.G.: Outsourcing information systems: A strategic partnership with risks. Long Range Plannning 26(3), 18–25 (1993)
24. Nishiguchi, T.: Strategic Industrial Sourcing. Oxford University Press, New York (1994)
25. Nooteboom, B., Berger, H., Noorderhaven, N.G.: Effects of Trust and Governance on Relational Risk. The Academy of Management Journal 40(2), 308–338 (1997)
26. Oshri, I., Kotlarsky, J., Willcocks, L.P.: The Handbook of Global Outsourcing and Offshoring. Palgrave Macmillan, United Kingdom (2009)
27. Pettigrew, A.M.: Longitudinal Field Research on Change: Theory and Practice. Organization Science 1(3), 267–292 (1990)
28. Poppo, L., Zenger, T.: Testing alternative theories of the firm: transaction cost, knowledge based, and measurement explanations for make-or-buy decisions in information services. Strategic Management Journal 19, 853–877 (1998)
29. Poppo, L., Zenger, T.: Do formal contracts and relational governance functions as substitutes or complements? Strategic Management Journal 23(8), 707–725 (2002)
30. Richardson, J.: Parallel sourcing and supplier performance in the Japanese automobile industry. Strategic Management Journal 14, 339–350 (1993)

31. Saunders, C., Gelbelt, M., Qing, H.: Achieving success in information outsourcing systems. California Management Review 39(2), 63–79 (1997)
32. Scanzoni, J.: Social exchange and behavioural interdependence. In: Burgess, R.L., Huston, T.L. (eds.) Social exchange in developing relationships. Academic Press, New York (1979)
33. Sei, T.: Is technical innovation all? A hidden meaning of social relationships behind the product development stage in the Japanese automotive industry. In: Nishiguchi, T. (ed.) Managing Product Development. Oxford University Press, Oxford (1996)
34. Sull, D.N., Spinosa, C.: Promise-based management: The essence of execution. Harvard Business Review 85(4), 78–86 (2007)
35. Weill, P., Subramani, M., Broadbent, M.: Building IT Infrastructure for Strategic Agility. MIT Sloan Management Review 44(1), 1–11 (2002)
36. Willcocks, L., Choi, C.: Co-operative Partnership and "Total" IT Outsourcing: from contractual obligation to strategic alliance? European Management Journal 13(1), 76–88 (1995)
37. Willcocks, L., Fitzgerald, G.: A business guide to outsourcing IT: A study of European best practice in the selection, management and use of external IT services. Business Intelligence (1994)
38. Willcocks, L., Griffiths, C., Kotlarsky, J.: Beyond BRIC: Offshoring in non-BRIC countries: Egypt – a new growth market. The London School of Economics and Political Science (2009)
39. Willcocks, L., Lacity, M.: Strategic sourcing of information systems. Wiley, London (1998)
40. Willcocks, L., Lacity, M., Fitzgerald, G.: Information technology outsourcing in Europe and the USA: Assessment issues. International Journal of Information Management 15(5), 333–351 (1995)
41. Williamson, O.E.: Markets and Hierarchies. Free Press, New York (1975)
42. Yin, R.K.: Case Study Research. Sage Publications, London (1994)
43. Zaheer, L.G., Venkatraman, N.: Relational governance as interorganizational strategy: An empirical test of the role of trust in economic exchange. Strategic Management Journal 16(5), 373–392 (1986)

Living Labs: Arbiters of Mid- and Ground-Level Innovation

Esteve Almirall and Jonathan Wareham

ESADE - Ramon Llull University,
Av. Pedralbes 60-62 Barcelona, Spain

We perform a comparative case analysis of four working Living Labs to identify their common functions. Theoretically, we ground our analysis in terms of how they function, their processes of exploration and exploitation, where they work in the innovation strata, how new socially negotiated meanings are negotiated and diffused. Our research highlights four novel insights: first, Living Labs function at the low and mid level innovation strata; second, Living Labs are technologically agnostic; third, Living Labs use context based experience to surface new, socially constructed meanings for products and services; and finally, Living Labs are equally focused on exploration and exploitation.

1 Introduction

Much has been written about the gap between Research and Innovation, many times raising notable interest in the business press as well as public policy (Moore 1991). The so-called "European Paradox" (E.C. 1995, Dosi et al. 2005), or the inability of European nations to transform their leadership in research into commercial successes in the marketplace is an example of this. The European Commission has identified pre-commercial public procurement as an instrument in helping to cover this gap (E.C. 2008, E.C. 2006). However, applied R&D and prototyping are characterized by a high degree of uncertainty in the potential commercial success of the proposed solution, driving potential entrepreneurs and investors away (E.C. 2006). This is where both the gap and the lack of financial support are located – a gap often covered by venture capital (Bos, 2008).

A number of initiatives in the E.U. (E.C. 2007), E.U. member states (Dekker 2008) and other countries like Canada (SDTC 2007), aim to address this gap by using pre-commercial procurement as an instrument to match products and consumer expectations and creating a test ground that can generate an initial demand (E.C. 2006).

Meanwhile, a new institution has been emerging in Europe, aiming to address the very same concerns- Living Labs. Living Labs are driven by two main ideas: a) involving users early on in the innovation process, and b) experimentation in real world settings, aiming to provide structure and governance to user participation in the innovation process (Almirall & Wareham, 2008). A typical Living Lab looks like a collaborative project engaging companies, academia, government and technological centers, where users are involved in nascent development stages and successive iterations are validated in real life environments. Living Labs have grown in the last two

I. Oshri and J. Kotlarsky (Eds.): Global Sourcing 2010, LNBIP 55, pp. 233–249, 2010.

years to a network of institutions comprising 129 members, not only in Europe, but also in Brazil, South Africa, Mozambique, China and Taiwan.

An important concept in Open Innovation is the role and prominence of intermediaries (Chesbrough, 2006) which include well-known organizations such as Innocentive, Nine Sigma or InnovationXchange. Intermediaries have been classified so far, as agents, brokers or marketplaces (Chesbrough, 2006). We argue that Living Labs are also intermediaries and perform roles as facilitators of user involvement, and in some cases, orchestrators of the whole innovation process.

Given our limited experience with Living Labs, this research seeks to examine some of their best practices and methodologies, exploring to what extent they can contribute to close the gap between Research and Innovation. Thus, in our study, we address the following research questions:

1) How do Living Labs capture and incorporate the contribution of users in the innovation process?
2) How do Living Labs do support exploration and explotation?
3) In what kinds of innovation do Living Labs contribute? How?
4) Do Living Labs focus on incremental or radical innovations?
5) Do Living Labs focus on the evolution of products and services or the interpretation and negotiated meaning of the services?

The paper is organized as follows. First we review the literature related to our topic. Second we introduce the research approach, followed by a description of the methodologies being employed together with brief case stories illustrating their use and an in-depth analysis on the light of the research questions. Finally we discuss implications in the context of Open Innovation and innovation policy. Generalizable propositions relating to the function of Living Labs are formulated to guide future research.

2 Literature Review

There are numerous strands of theory that might be relevant when exploring the functions of a relatively nescient phenomenon such as Living Labs. We chose our theoretical focus based on the assumption that Living Labs represent a novel approach as innovation intermediaries in product development and validation, and relevant theories should embrace areas in which Living Labs are divergent from more traditional, deterministic R&D paradigms.

Users have been identified in a number of roles in crossing the gap between research and innovation. Maybe the most obvious of them is their role as a source of invention and ultimately innovation (von Hippel 1988, 2005). As semi-partitioned spaces that cultivate user-lead insights, Living Labs are fundamentally infrastructures that surface tacit, experiential and domain based knowledge to codified knowledge. Boisot and Li (2006) and Boisot et al. (2007) describe knowledge as either experiential, narrative, or abstract symbolic, representing categories on a continuum where knowledge is either uncodified and concrete (experiential), or codified and abstract (abstract symbolic). Narrative knowledge has some intermediate level of structure, but not to the degree to where it can be considered validated or objective.

According to the iSpace theory (Boisot et al. 2007), knowledge follows a social learning cycle where it begins from a state of experiential, undiffused and uncodified personal knowledge, and moves to a state as codified and abstract proprietary knowledge. This evolution is the domain of much traditional R&D and problem solving work. Under certain circumstances, knowledge can be further diffused into the public domain, losing its proprietary status or property right protection and becoming part of the public knowledge sphere. This transition can either be intentional by commercialization, or unintentional because of piracy, leakage or social diffusion. After time, public knowledge becomes adequately assimilated or absorbed into the general consciousness such that it is considered common sense. Diffused and absorbed common sense knowledge is re-employed in the scanning processes that underlie experiential knowledge, thereby completing the social learning cycle. Given the large emphasis on context based experimentation in Living Labs, this stream of thinking offers valuable insights into the processes that underlie their knowledge cultivation methods.

Another relevant, well-known stream of theory is the role of risk taking in entrepreneurial activities. Frank Knight (1921) established the paradigm of Knightian uncertainty versus risk. For Knight, it was important to differentiate between risk, where outcomes are unknown but quantifiable in known ex-ante probability distributions, and uncertainty (ie. Knightian uncertainty), which is, by definition, unquantifiable or immeasurable.

Knightian uncertainty has become an important concept in the literature on entrepreneurship and venture capital, as it is often argued that one of the important functions of VCs is to absorb Knightian uncertainty, where related institutions (e.g. traditional banks) would have a tendency to work with quantifiable risk. These early stages of product development and innovation characterized by Knightian uncertainty are frequently equated with March's (1991) seminal definition of exploration. March introduced two fundamental concepts of organizational operation and strategic renewal: "exploration includes things captured in terms such as search, variation, risk-taking, experimentation, flexibility, discovery and innovation. Exploitation includes things such as refinement, choice, production, efficiency, selection, implementation and execution," (March 1991, p. 71). To suggest that Living Labs only function at the level of exploration and not exploitation may confer unwarranted compression on the concepts. Although, as March argues, exploration is variation-seeking, risk-taking, and experimentation oriented, exploitation is variety reducing and efficiency oriented (March 1991), the fact of the matter is that almost two decades of research based on this thinking has lead to limited consensus on their exact definitions or theoretical utility (Li et al. 2008).

However, Bhidé (2009) extends concepts of explorations and Knightian uncertainty to develop a concept of "venturesome consumption", a process in which businesses and users experiment with and explore novel manners of integrating existing basic research into new products and services. Specifically, he refers to solving the technical challenges of commercialization; bringing the product to market through viable sales channels, platforms and supporting product ecosystems. He differentiates between high-, mid-, and ground-level innovation types. High-level innovation refers to the building blocks or raw material of common products or services (micro-processors, silicon or coffee beans). Mid-level innovations are the intermediate products or modules that are vital components of the product (motherboards, bean roasting expertise), where ground-level innovations are the knowledge or products that directly result in the consumption experience (laptop computer or cup of espresso). His general thesis is a response to the alarmist rhetoric that the wealthy western economies are losing their innovation edge to low cost but highly educated BRIC countries. He suggests that, while this may be true for many high-level innovations that do traverse national boarders quite easily, this is not the case for mid- or ground-level innovations, as they are often best conducted close to, and in tight collaboration with, potential consumers in their local markets or settings. Regional economics aside, the framework is of interest because it suggests that the consumer-lead innovation domain in which Living Labs function focuses on mid- and ground-level innovation. This has several implications. First it suggests that Living Labs are instances of "*venturesome consumption – the willingness and ability of intermediate producers and individual consumers to take a chance on and effectively use new know-how and products – (which) is as least as important as its capacity to take on high-level research*" (Bhide 2009 pg. 16). Here, resonance of Knightian uncertainty and Marchian exploration is clear. Secondly, that the innovation domains are highly defined by local contexts; their discoveries and insights are most relevant in regional markets, yet decreasingly valuable on an international scale. However, globalization greatly increases the potential for replicability of these insights.

A final strand of research relevant to Living Labs is Design-Driven innovation. Design thinking attempts to cross the gap between a great idea and a great product by tapping into the users' needs, feelings and sensations by having a more exact understanding of what users explicitly feel or do when they use a particular product or service (Brown, 2008). At a primary level, design thinking places user experience and cognition at the forefront of study through well established tools such as usability testing, ergonomics, and both low- and high-tech ethnography. Fully focused on human psychology and perception, design thinking awards user emotions, rather than the product design, the highest status in the innovation hierarchy. It is most commonly associated with design firms such as IDEO or the recent D-School initiative at Stanford University (Brown 2008). An understanding of the user as a partner who is an "expert of his/her experience" and where the designer and the researcher supports him by providing tools for ideation and expression (Sleeswijk et al 2005; Sanders and Stappers, 2008) is at the core of the Living Labs approach (Mirijamdotter et al, 2006) which also shares tools and methods from design thinking.

However, at a deeper level, Verganti (2008) suggests that much design-driven innovation can also take an opposite trajectory. Through a deep understanding of the broader social trends and technology evolution, design-driven innovation can attempt to radically change the emotional and symbolic content of products by redefining the meanings and languages associated with them in a very deterministic manner. His proffered example is the Wii platform - how what was previously a gaming and entertainment platform has been renegotiated as a serious in-home exercise platform for an otherwise uncultivated market segment. In order to renegotiate the social meaning or vision of a product, designers must direct their attention toward the external interpreters of these meanings; that is, artists, schools, suppliers, distributors, other industries and the media. In other terms, design-driven innovation is less a function of understanding serendipitous user experimentation and experience, but rather about the purposeful interaction with the arbiters of product languages and socio-cultural meaning.

Initially, the relation to Living Labs may appear less clear. As partitioned arenas for user experimentation and exploration, the relationship to design thinking and user experience is obvious. But it may also be plausible that Living Labs function as subtle yet powerful platforms that enable the renegotiation of social meanings; purposefully or accidentally. This idea connects with related work in economic geography that highlights social practice as providing locus and meaning to Innovation (Tuomi, 2002); as an enabler of innovation (Florida, 2005; Saxenian, 2006); and more recently as a source of competitive advantage through the willingness and ability of businesses and consumers to effectively use products and technologies derived from scientific research early on in its life cycle in venturesome consumption (Bhidé 2008).

3 Research Design

Despite the fact that the European Network of Living Labs (ENoLL), comprises close to 130 different organizations from around the world, their existence is fairly recent. In part because of its novelty and in part because of the lack of a precise definition of the term, under the Living Labs denomination we can find a diversity of practices, organizations and projects with varying levels of maturity. As a consequence, we choose to focus a recent set of practices carried out by one of the organizations through a sufficiently large time span, that could bring some insight on the roles of both users and the Living Lab involved in the process, making possible to assess its dynamics and the benefits captured by firms and public organizations involved.

3.1 Sample and Data Collection

We employ a multiple case-study methodology is the most appropriate for both the field and the research questions formulated in the present study. This exploratory method is best suited for investigating new and poorly understood processes, focusing on the "what" and "why" questions (Eisenhardt, 1989), being specially appropriate for research into new topics and new technologies (Shane, 2000; Stake, 2000; Mcdermott and O'Connor, 2002).

In this respect, the present research took advantage of the active participation and involvement of one of its authors in both the European Network of Living Labs (ENoLL) and the Foundation i2Cat.

For the selection of cases, we based our choice in two criteria:

1) Projects regarded as highly successful and perceived with a significant degree of innovation and high social value.
2) Cases where the involvement of users and the role of the Living Lab were highly salient.

Six cases were selected, from three different domains: health, media and industry: Opera Oberta and Cultural Ring in media, Teleictus, Eye Health in health and Industrial Ring and CatLab in industry. For each case, in-depth interviews using a semi-structured interview guideline were conducted with project leaders, Living Lab members, users and representatives of the firms involved. These industries were contrasted with secondary data such as project documentation, project websites and public presentations of the projects.

Table 1. Selected Cases and number of Interviews per sector

Case	Description	# of Interviews
Media		
Opera Oberta	High Definition IP broadcasting of live Opera	3
Opera Learning	Synchronous HD Opera courses	3
Health		
TeleIctus	Remote diagnosis and treatment of Ictus	3
Eye Health	Remote diagnosis of eye related diseases	3
Industry		
Industrial Ring	Internet2 network connecting an industrial cluster primary in the automobile sector	4
CatLab	Catalonia Living Labs project	3

In total, 19 interviews were collected and recorded, lasting each one between 1 and 2 hours. Additionally, these cases were framed in the Catalan Living Labs project – i2Cat, of which one of the authors was deeply involved for more than 2 years being its coordinator and representative in the ENoLL, European Network of Living Labs.

4 Research Findings

4.1 The Hosting Organization: i2Cat

i2Cat is a Foundation established as a public private partnership constituted by three universities, around ten private firms and the Secretary for the Information Society of the Catalan regional government. Currently, four specific clusters are active: media, infrastructure, health and learning.

The objectives of i2Cat are twofold. On one side traditional basic and applied research has a prominent status, especially due to the participation of three major technological universities. However, a great deal of effort is devoted to more exploratory innovation. These practices found their match when the European Network of Living Labs started its activities. i2Cat was one of the founding members, and with the support of STSI (Catalan gov. funding agency for the Information Society) started an initial program to coordinate Living Labs activities in Catalonia. This program crystallized in the launch on October 2007 of CatLab – the Catalan Network of Living Labs, comprising eight organizations performing Living Labs activities together with the Catalan government.

4.2 Opera Oberta and Opera Learning

Opera Oberta (Opera Oberta, 2001) explored the use of high definition video-conferencing and high speed Internet in the context of live Opera. The driving force behind the project the Opera Theater Liceo in Barcelona. The overall project consortia included technology providers like Thomson Multimedia (cameras and equipment), Barco (projection), Video Digital (MPEG2 coding), telecom operators (Telefónica and Menta), public infrastructure networks (Cesca, i2Cat, Red Iris, Terrassa City Hall) together with commercial exhibitors (Cinesa Diagonal) and a network of universities where Opera performances were retransmitted.

On December 18, 2001, the opera "La Traviata" was transmitted in HDTV using an HDSI link at 1.5Gb to a large movie theater in Barcelona (Cinesa Diagonal), while the same signal was broadcasted through SDI at 270Mb in multicast to a network of 4 universities around Catalonia.

Building on the success of this first experience, the project continued with additional retransmissions and evolved in three main directions. The first one was *Opera Learning* that extended this effort until 2004 with regular programming of university elective opera courses done through HD on-line video conferencing. The second line of evolution was its transplant beyond opera to other artistic manifestations. Cultural Ring (Cultural Ring, 2003-2008), linked a dozen of Catalan centers and encompassed around twenty groups that regularly used the scientific high speed Internet2 network deployed in Catalonia for art interaction. Finally the third line was its use for concrete Opera events that have become traditional in Catalonia, one of them is "Opera-on-the-Beach", performed annually.

Pre-commercial Gap

The main challenge in broadcasting opera and other forms of cultural art lie not in the technological readiness, but in connecting the dots that make the implementation of this technology real. This involves steps that range from legal aspects such as securing the digital rights of the performances to technological ones such as connecting cameras and broadcasting equipment to an IP network, or readiness in terms of infrastructure deployment by being able to use a high speed network large enough for the project to finding viable services and business models able to sustain the project.

Opera Oberta & Opera Learning created and validated some of these services, basically direct synchronous opera transmission and educational services based on HD videoconferencing. This task was beyond the reach of any single entity, but required contributions of many actors; the uncertainty of viable business models made it very unlikely that this project could emerge from traditional entrepreneurial - venture capital mechanisms or sponsored by large companies.

Benefits captured by both companies and public institutions were diverse. For example, Technotrends gained substantial expertise in HD video-conferencing, Telefónica and Red-Iris (the Spanish scientific network used as a backbone) were not only to gain expertise in handling high priority/ high bandwidth traffic and in fine tuning networks, eliminating many bottlenecks and incidences. The Opera Theater ended up with one of the largest HD Opera recordings and obtained public awareness.

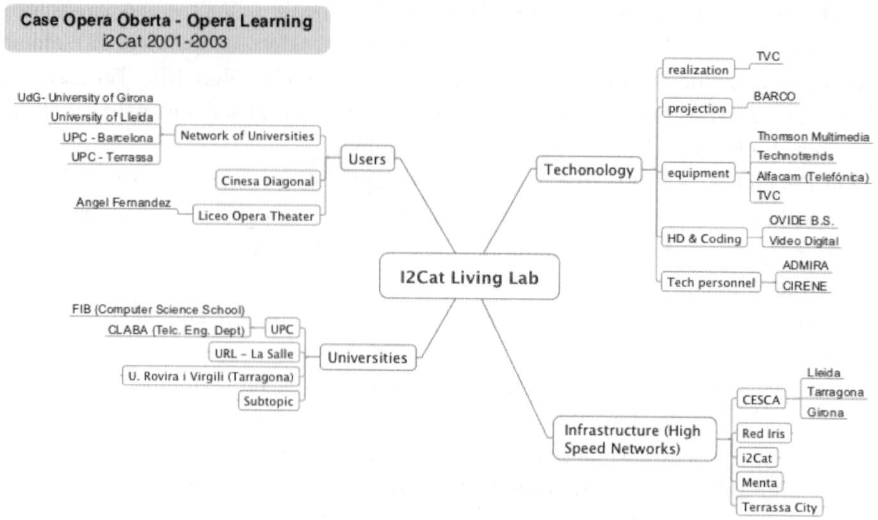

Fig. 1. Participants in Opera Oberta – Opera Learning

The Contribution of Users

In terms of taking advantage of the technology, we can distinguish between upstream and downstream users.

On one side we can find Liceo Opera Theater. In the value chain it played the role of content providers. On the other side we can find the network of universities and the movie theater, Cinesa Diagonal who were the final recipients of the service.

As end consumers of the content, the universities incorporated the content into their curricula. As these courses dealt with live production and simultaneous broadcasting, a great deal of modifications had to made to classroom infrastructures and curricula design, but also improvements to the audio quality, a requirement that was not directly obvious to the technical designers of the platform.

The role of the Living Lab organization

The first role of the Living Lab consists in creating and innovation arena and involving the relevant actors and technologies. The second role is orchestrating and coordinating the experimentation while facilitating the identification of reachable targets. A third role and probably the most distinctive of Living Labs, is mediating between users and the other actors. Finally, this case demonstrates how Living Labs function as connectors and brokers, establishing and orchestrating collaboration where relationships were otherwise nonexistent.

4.3 Teleictus

Teleictus (Teleictus, 2007) is the brain child of Dr. Ismael Cerdà working in Vic General Hospital and addresses the problem of having 7/24 expertise in diagnosing and treating strokes. The project implements HD video conferencing system together with a tool for sending CT images (MIO from C2C – http://www.c2csis.com) and the MEDTING platform (http://medting.com) for sharing clinical stories, linking a reference hospital (Hospital Vall Hebron in the initial test) with a satellite hospital (Vic General Hospital in the initial test), together using high speed internet for the diagnosis and continuous monitoring of patients.

Given state of the art experience in stroke telemedicine (Demaerchalk et al., 2009), Teleictus was developed independently, exploiting many advantages of integrating off the shelf state of the art video-conferencing systems.

Surprisingly, one of the first discoveries was that the high speed connection was not really a requirement, rather, the high importance of the activation protocols and the mechanisms of coordination between partners and emergency room personnel were critical issues.

This example was not an isolated, but one that exemplifies a general trend in the project where technical aspects became less relevant, and the fit between technology and organizational procedures became focal. It was mid and low level knowledge in the hands of users what ensured this fit. Therefore, the initial plans for building sophisticated new equipment were discarded in favor of the integration of off-the-shelf commercial solutions. Building on that success, more than 100 patients have been already treated with the system that is now expanding to a second phase comprising more than 20 satellite hospitals and some reference centers. A third phase covering the whole Catalonia is already planned.

Pre-commercial Gap

Even if providing a solution for this problem may seem easy from a technical point of view, a number of factors can prevent that companies embark in this endeavor. Among them we should cite:

1) The perceived risk derived from dealing with a single client in a territory, in that case the Catalan Public Health System.
2) The need for acceptance in a community where procedures are highly codified such as the medical sector.
3) The lack of availability of an adequate infrastructure.

Therefore solving the pre-commercial gap in this case means solving a number of additional problems beyond the technical ones.

1) The availability of a high speed network.
2) The development or the plausible expectation of an initial demand able to cover for the development.
3) Ensuring that the solutions fits and into a medical protocol widely accepted and is in line with the standards and restrictions of the hospitals addressed.

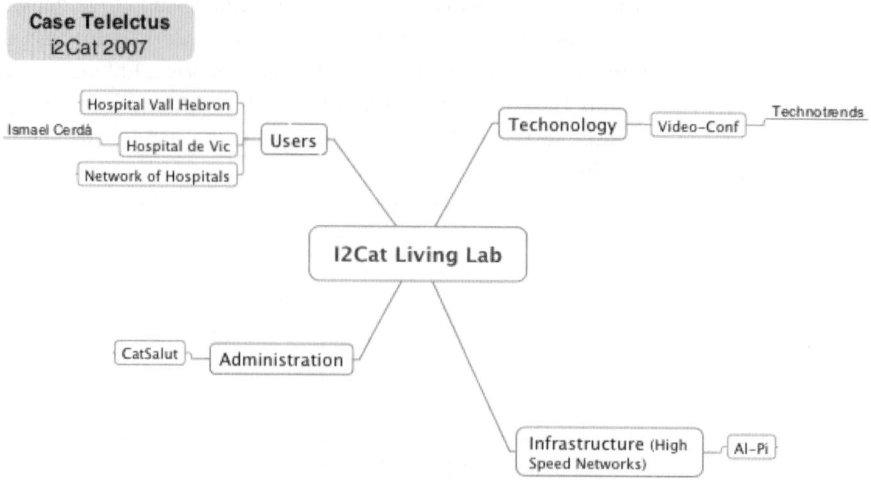

Fig. 2. Participants in the first phase or Tele-Ictus

The Contribution of Users

The contribution of users to the project was twofold. On one side we can find the role of a "lead user" in the figure of Dr. Cerdà, who from his position in a public hospital greatly contributed to the project with an entrepreneurial attitude.

On the other side, we can find that the solution was shaped not only with the collaboration of doctors from both hospitals, but with the active participation of nurses and personnel from the computer departments of both institutions. Examples of their contribution in that second area can be found in the activation protocol, the physical placement of the instrumentation, the administrative circuit and in general portfolio of collaborative procedures hospitals and departments.

The Role of the Living Lab organization

Again, lowering the risk associated with innovation by selecting participants and providing an arena where technological proposal could be operationalized was the key element for the success of the project.

4.4 EyeHealth

EyeHealth aims to solve the problem of providing expert assistance in ophthalmology to rural family doctors located in distant areas. In this case, the project was initiated by a private company: Ilo ophthalmology. Ilo provides expert diagnostics in ophthalmology to both private users and doctors. Because Ilo is located in Lleida (north of Catalonia – Spain) a group of medical doctors in the Pyrenees was selected for co-developing the project that is now active as a service.

The output of the project consisted in a system for acquiring, managing and processing ophthalmologic information, together with their images. The system is accessible by Internet. It works as follows. When a patient with a vision complaint reaches a family doctor enlisted in the project, he can make a choice of taking an image of the retina of the patient, with a special easy-to-use instrument, and introduce it to the system. This image is later on evaluated by a specialist who, if needed, can enter in a dialogue with the doctor to further discuss the diagnostic.

Fast trials and the experience gained were also determinative to the evolution of the project. As an example, the importance of the connectivity aspects through the process. If in the beginning the need for a high speed connection was visualized as a requirement, as the project evolved, the evidence of the trials and the users present suggested that a completely disconnected service could also work, providing increasing benefits in effectiveness because of its asynchronous nature allowing the grouping of technical expertise and the equipment to serve different locations.

Pre-commercial Gap

In this case, two main factors prevented the entrance of a commercial company or the start of a public service in this territory. First, uncertainty about the technology, about the level of acceptance by the Catalan Public Health System and family doctors and about the validity of the operational and business model. And second, the need to ensure an initial demand.

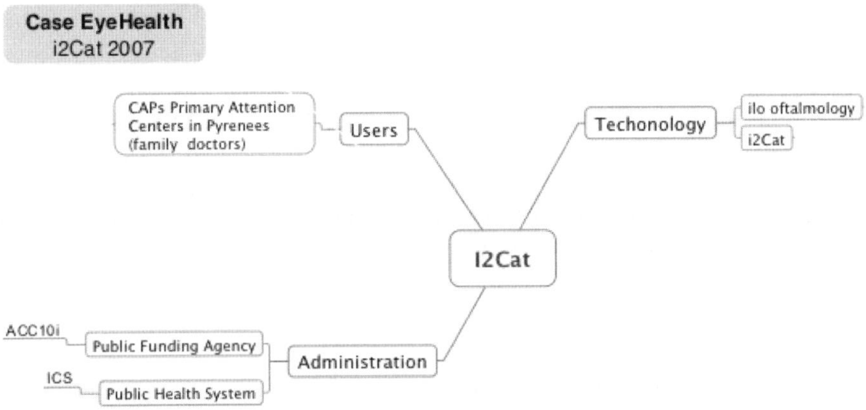

Fig. 3. Participants in EyeHealth

The Contribution of Users

One of the collective discoveries was the fact that on-line connections were not really needed in most of the cases. This finding allowed the use of flying equipment that worked off-line and moved from location to location in a fixed route, maximizing this way its use.

The role of the Living Lab organization

The four main roles that we were discussing in previous cases: enlisting different actors, orchestrating the process, facilitating the technology and mediating with users are present here too. However, compared to the cases discussed before, this one is more focus in a concrete solution and its implementation allowing more and faster interactions in its development.

4.5 Industrial Ring

The Industrial Ring (Anella Industrial, 2008) is the youngest and probably the most ambitious project in our sample. Building on the success and the experience gained with the Cultural Ring, it aims to explore the benefits and services that high speed Internet connectivity can bring to large manufacturing companies.

Its inception is similar to the rest of projects previously discussed. A lead user, in this case a professor of the Engineering School (Emili Hernández) in charge of students' projects and heavily involved with the automobile industry, enlisted i2Cat and both begin to put the project into motion.

Its first incarnation is in the automobile sector, connecting auto companies (Seat-Volkswagen and Nissan), component suppliers (Gestamp, Ficosa), testing services (Applus-Idiada, Iteuve), engineering and integration companies (T-Systems, Sener, Ansys and Esi) with the two supercomputing centers of Catalonia (Cesca and BSC-CNS) through the participation of telecommunication providers (Albertis and Al-Pi). The main applications are services for large file transmission (typically CAD files are larger than 1GB) and remote car testing providing immediate results for telemetry and the integration for High Definition videoconferencing and monitoring.

Pre-commercial Gap

In a case similar to Opera Oberta, we can see how the lack of a widespread infrastructure prevents the birth of initiatives aimed at its use. However, in that case this factor goes together with the perception of a low and scattered demand because of the target group focuses on companies and professionals rather than the general public.

Finally there was also a perception of an undefined and unclear business model in an environment dominated by free services.

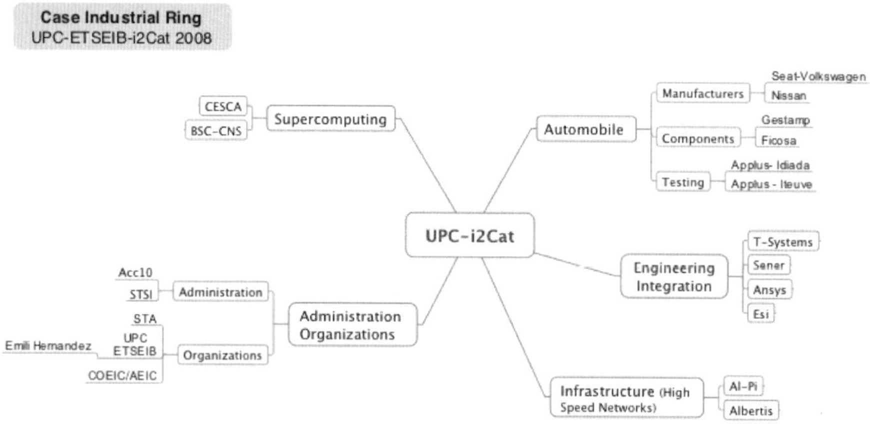

Fig. 4. Participants in the Industrial Ring

5 Analysis

5.1 RQ1 User Contributions

As we have documented, users contribute in Living Labs in a variety of ways. Using high speed Internet for transferring huge CAD files or providing remote telemetry services, such is the case of the Industrial ring, is a direct translation of lead-user needs. Another example EyeHealth were direct connections were replaced for temporary storage and batch processing.

However, the most common case of identification, codification and incorporation of knowledge in the hands of users can be found when dealing with tacit knowledge. Tacit knowledge is present and its codification is in fact present in all cases. A clear example of this is the incorporation of knowledge about placement of equipment in Teleictus or also in the search for a business model that could fit a complex project where a public health system with central and satellite hospitals is involved with private companies.

There is also a third type of knowledge in the hands of groups of users, especially lead users. This is domain specific knowledge. Again we can find many examples of the use of domain specific knowledge. Opera Oberta, because of its specificity probably provides the most clear cases. This is the case of the need of raising the quality of the music channel in spite of the one of the video or many specific issues about placement of the equipment and loudspeakers or insights about contents programming or diffusion.

Due to the iterative process inherent to Living Labs, we can find many similarities to iSpace theory described by Boisot (2007). In almost all cases we can find how users translate uncodified knowledge by validating it in experimental situations. From here, the results are codified and diffused into the network of actors which, in our study, was the Living Lab networks. Accordingly, we formulate the following propositions.

Proposition 1a. Living Labs observe user-lead practice in diffuse social contexts.

Proposition 1b. Living Labs identify and codify tacit and practice based knowledge.

Proposition 1c. Living Labs diffuse tacit and practice based knowledge into ad hoc innovation networks.

5.2 RQ2 Exploration and Exploitation

The type of risk associated with exploration is probably the most evident because of its magnitude. This type of risk can be divided into technological, personal and market risk.

Technological risk relates to both technology availability and suitability for the intended task. Here we can find in all the cases how Living Labs reduce this risk. Almost all cases presented are based on the use of pre-commercial, research oriented platforms for experimentation. Such is the case of Opera Oberta, Opera Learning, Industrial Ring and Telecictus that use totally or partially the Catalan Internet2 network.

Personal risk is also a limiting factor, its assumption is a characteristic of the entrepreneur. Living Labs can mitigate of this risk by creating an innovation arena that mostly takes the form of a project financed by European, National, regional or directly by the funds of the Living Lab.

Finally, Living Labs also contribute to reduce the risk associated to user acceptance. They do this by creating an initial demand for products and services drawing on public procurement or on the capacity of the partners involved. This initial demand is a necessary condition for developing the product in real life environments and reverts once the project has finished in an steady flow of demand that covers the early stages of product development. Probably the most significant case, among the ones revisited in this paper, is the one of Teleictus, because this initial demand and the later support and adoption by the Catalan Health System is allowing its deployment through the whole Catalonia, but all projects equally enjoyed this benefit.

By contrast, exploitation is the process of selecting, implementing and validating successively refined prototypes in real life environments. If we examine with detail the cases presented we can observe that all of them relate to complex multi-stakeholder environments where coordination costs and business models are not obvious. In the case of TeleIctus and EyeHealth, we can find the mix of a highly complex public health system together with private companies. Likewise in Opera Oberta and Opera Learning and in the Industrial Ring we find the need of reliance in a public sponsored Internet2 platform made up with segments of dark fiber belonging to municipalities.

Living Labs, because of their neutrality as organizations that come mostly from research or technological centers, are in a privileged situation to manage and provide governance to this type of projects. This is especially evident when contrasted with an start-up that will certainly be discouraged by the difficulties in capturing value and finding a model for governance. Hence, propositions 2 highlight the role of exploration and exploitation.

Proposition 2a. Living Labs perform exploration by assuming Knightian risk, experimentation and discovery.

Proposition 2b. Living Labs perform exploitation via refinement, selection, implementation and execution.

5.3 RQ3 Innovation Types and Levels

Bhidé (2009) argues that innovation levels can be high, mid, and low–level. High level innovation is basic research and easily transportable across national contexts, where mid- and low-level innovation constitute context defined adaptations that facilitate the adoption and use of new products and services.

This analysis fits well into our Living Lab cases. There we find exercises dealing mostly with low level innovation, where business models, customer adoption, interfaces, and other facets of the local social context were far more significant than the basic technologies.

For example, in the case of Opera Oberta & Opera Learning, the challenge was more in coordinating the experimental network of dark fiber; convincing the partners, finding a suitable business model that could first maintain the project; and thereafter implementing existing technology (high - definition video-conferencing) into a novel context. A similar case was in TeleIctus, with the variation of the need for component integration between high-definition video-conferencing, tele-monitoring and tele-diagnostic, together with the existing systems in the Catalan Public Health network. Similar cases can be presented for the Industrial Ring or EyeHealth. Accordingly, propositions 3 are presented.

Proposition 3a. High Level innovation is highly portable across international contexts, where mid and low level innovation is localized, geographically and spatially bound.

Proposition 3b. Living Labs operate and mid and low level innovation strata.

5.4 RQ4 Incremental or Radical Innovation

The evidence of the cases presented also show a mix of radical and incremental innovations. In Opera Oberta - Opera Learning high speed Internet is used for distributing live Opera contents to several theaters and potential home viewers. We can think of it as a radical departure from the established system of on-site performance. In the other extreme, the use of high speed networks to transport huge files and remote telemetry is probably better situated as an incremental innovation in practice, together with the cases of TeleIctus and EyeHealth.

Even if the size of the sample is limited, we can witness how its distribution is skewed towards incremental innovation. This may also be consistent with the real world, where incremental innovations are more prevalent overall.

A different way to characterize this process is portraying it as a process of fit, where innovations seek their fit in a precise context at social, interaction and manifestation of business value through an iterative process. We can probably all agree that this process of fit is neither exclusive of radical nor incremental innovations. In fact, both types of innovations can benefit from it.

Proposition 4. Living Labs are agnostic as to whether innovation is technologically incremental or radical.

5.5 RQ5 Product Evolution or Interpretation of Meaning

Boisot et al (2007) argues that experiential knowledge is codified and diffused through and social lifecycle of knowledge. This social validation process, resulting from testing hypothesis in real life environments and reusing them if successful is a key element of Living Labs. Tuomi (2002) highlights meanings from products and services as a social construction coming from practice. Hence, the social validation of knowledge can occur both in the accepted realm of a product's meaning, but also a new, renegotiated definition that emerges either accidentally or purposefully (Verganti 2008).

Probably the most salient evidence of this process in the Living Labs sample occurs in novel uses that open the door of new practices. In the cases described, we can find some clear examples of this process, such as the reinterpretation of Opera Oberta as a learning tool involving a large network of Spanish and South American Universities, or the use of EyeHealth as a platform for the advancement and education of rural doctors in ophthalmology. In both cases, meanings are completely redefined not only as a result of random events or serendipity, but also situated in purposeful interaction processes. Accordingly, our analysis suggests that that living Labs are equally aligned towards both accepted social meanings as well as the generation of new interpretations.

Proposition 5a. Living Labs perform context-based experimentation in order to generate local modifications within existing socially negotiated meanings.

Proposition 5b. Living Labs perform context-based experimentation in order to generate new socially negotiated meanings for products and services.

6 Discussion and Conclusion

A cross case analysis of Living Labs has found that the function in closing the pre-commercial gap by manifesting initial demand for products and services as well as orchestrating the actions of disparate actors in order to gain critical mass for the creation of a product or service. They observe, codify and diffuse tacit knowledge based in specific social settings. They also facilitate both exploration and exploitation at mid- and low- innovation strata. Finally Living Labs are agnostic to whether their innovation are incremental or radical, and work both within existing social meanings, as well as to renegotiate them.

As a novel, emergent concept, delineating Living Labs against other forms of innovation intermediaries remains challenging. Clearly, future empirical work can add to the theoretical precision, as well as greater understanding of their predominant methods and relative advantages.

References

Almirall, E., Wareham, J.: Living Labs and Open Innovation: Roles and Applicability. The Electronic Journal for Virtual Organizations and Networks 10, 21–46 (2008)

Bhidé, A.: The Ventursome Economy – How Innovation Sustains Prosperity in a More Connected World. Journal of Corporate Finance 21(1), 8–23 (2008)

Blank, S.: Retooling Early Stage Development. Podcast-Entrepreneurial Thought Leader Lecturer, Stanford Technology Ventures Program, http://ecorner.stanford.edu/authorMaterialInfo.html?mid=2048 (accessed on December 29, 2008)

Boisot, M., MacMillan, I., Han, K.S.: Explorations in Information Space: Knowledge, Agents, and Organizations. Oxford University Press, Oxford (2007)

Boisot, M., Li, Y.: Organizational versus Markets Knowledge: From Concrete Embodiment to Abstract Representation. Journal of Bioeconomics 8, 219–251 (2006)

Bos, L.: Pre-Commercial Procurement. European Commission: Strategy for ICT Research and Innovation Unit, http://ec.europa.eu/information_society/tl/research/priv_invest/pcp/documents/pres_lieve_bos.pdf (accessed on December 29, 2008)

Brown, T.: Design Thinking. Harvard Business Review 85, 84–95 (2008)
Chesbrough, H.: Open Business Models: How to Thrive in the New Innovation Landscape. Harvard Business School Press, Boston (2006)
Dekker, C.: Pre-Commercial Procurement in the Netherlands. European Commission: Strategy for ICT Research and Innovation Unit, `http://ec.europa.eu/information_society/tl/research/priv_invest/pcp/documents/pres_carla_dekker.pdf` (accessed on December 29, 2008)
Demaerchalk, B.M.: Stroke Medicine. Mayo Clinic Proceedings 84, 153–164 (2009)
Dosi, G., Llerena, P., Sylos, M.: Science-Technology-Industry Links and the European Paradox: Some Notes on the Dynamics of Scientific and Technological Research in Europe. LEM Papers Series 2005/02, Sant'Anna School of Advanced Studies, Pisa, Italy (2005)
E.C.: Green Paper on Innovation. European Commission, Brussels (1995)
E.C.: Pre-Commercial Procurement of Innovation. Expert Report, `http://ec.europa.eu/information_society/tl/research/key_docs/documents/procurement.pdf` (accessed on December 29, 2008)
E.C.: Pre-commercial Procurement, `http://ec.europa.eu/information_society/tl/research/priv_invest/pcp/documents/commpcp.pdf` (accessed on December 29, 2008)
E.C.: Pre-Commercial Procurement, `http://ec.europa.eu/information_society/tl/research/priv_invest/pcp/index_en.htm` (accessed on December 29, 2008)
Florida, R.: Cities and the Creative Class. Routledge, New York (2005)
Knight, F.: Risk, Uncertainty, and Profit. University of Chicago Press, Chicago (1921)
Mirijamdotter, A., Stählbröst, A., Sällström, A., Niitamo, V., Kulkki, S.: The European Network of Living Labs for CWE- User-centric Co-creation and Innovation. Exploiting the Knowledge Economy: Issues, Applications and Case Studies 3, 840–847 (2006)
Moore, G.A.: Crossing the Chasm. Harper Business Essentials, New York (1991)
Sanders, E.B., Stappers, P.J.: Co-creation and the new landscapes of design. CoDesign 4(1), 5–18 (2008)
Saxenian, A.L.: The New Argonauts – Regional Advantage in a Global Economy. Harvard University Press, Cambridge (2006)
SDTC Sustainable Development Technology Canada, presentation – overview, `http://www.sdtc.ca/en/news/SDTC_Overview.pdf` (accessed on December 29, 2008)
Sleeswijk Visser, F., Stappers, P.J., van der Lugt, R., Sanders, E.B.N.: Contextmapping:
Experiences from Practice. CoDesign 1(2), 119–149 (2005)
Stake, R.: The Art of Case Study Research. SAGE Publications, Thousand Oaks (2000)
Tuomi, I.: Networks of Innovation: Change and Meaning in the Age of the Internet. Oxford University Press, Oxford (2006)
Verganti, R.: Design, Meanings, and Radical Innovation: A Metamodel and a Research Agenda. Journal of Product Innovation Management 25, 436–456 (2008)
von Hippel, E.: The Sources of Innovation. Oxford University Press, New York (1988)
von Hippel, E.: Democratizing Innovation. MIT Press, Cambridge (2005)

Realising the Real Benefits of Outsourcing: Measurement Excellence and Its Importance in Achieving Long Term Value

Ilan Oshri[1] and Julia Kotlarsky[2]

[1] Rotterdam School of Management, Erasmus University, Rotterdam, The Netherlands
[2] Warwick Business School, University of Warwick, Coventry, The UK

Abstract. These days firms are, more than ever, pressed to demonstrate returns on their investment in outsourcing. While the initial returns can always be associated with one-off cost cutting, outsourcing arrangements are complex, often involving inter-related high-value activities, which makes the realisation of long-term benefits from outsourcing ever more challenging. Executives in client firms are no longer satisfied with the same level of service delivery through the outsourcing lifecycle. They seek to achieve business transformation and innovation in their present and future services, beyond satisfying service level agreements (SLAs). Clearly the business world is facing a new challenge: an outsourcing delivery system of high-value activities that demonstrates value over time and across business functions. However, despite such expectations, many client firms are in the dark when trying to measure and quantify the return on outsourcing investments: results of this research show that less than half of all CIOs and CFOs (43%) have attempted to calculate the financial impact of outsourcing to their bottom line, indicating that the financial benefits are difficult to quantify (51%).

There is no doubt that client firms need to improve their ability to measure the benefits of outsourcing. These benefits go beyond the one-time cost saving. They strongly relate to the firm's competitive advantage and therefore often represent the key success factors (KSFs) in a particular industry. We identify seven lessons that will guide executives to achieve better results from their outsourcing engagements. The starting point for any client firm is to understand the context of its outsourcing activities followed by the planning of its outsourcing strategy according to its resources and capabilities. Once an outsourcing strategy has been devised, a clear benchmark should be designed and clearly communicated to stakeholders involved. Setting up such a benchmark will allow the firm to then more carefully identify the service provisions expected from the vendor.

However, value is a dynamic concept that changes over time. Therefore, client firms should revisit the value generated from outsourcing relationships over time and as the rules of competition in their industry change.

The last three lessons concern building outsourcing capabilities within the client firm. This will be achieved by making the CIO a strategist, shaping the retained organization according to present and future needs and by fostering outsourcing learning capabilities and close relationships with vendors.

I. Oshri and J. Kotlarsky (Eds.): Global Sourcing 2010, LNBIP 55, pp. 250–270, 2010.

As some vendors continue to specialise and to develop domain knowledge, we believe that client firms should adopt a learning approach in engagement with their suppliers. Put simply, if a client firm is to become a sophisticated outsourcing consumer, it has to learn how to closely work with its suppliers in order to avoid making mistakes as well as learn how to maximize the returns from its outsourcing arrangement.

Keywords: Sourcing trends, sourcing strategies, decision making.

1 Current Trends in Outsourcing

The global IT outsourcing (ITO) market has increased each year since 1992. Back in 1989, global ITO was a \$9 to \$12 billion market. In 2008, the global ITO market was estimated to be worth between \$220 to \$250 billion[1]. The business process outsourcing (BPO) market in 2008 was less than the ITO market, but grew at a faster rate. The estimate for the ITO market – over the next five years, is that it will grow by 6-9% per annum while mainstream BPO expenditure is likely to grow worldwide by 10% to 15% a year, from \$140 billion in 2005 to potentially \$230 billion plus by 2013. BPO expenditure will be in areas such as the human resource function, procurement, back office administration, call centres, legal, finance and accounting, customer facing operations and asset management[2].

With the growing volume of ITO and BPO, there are some forces that shape the outsourcing landscape. Cost-cutting is still the dominant driver for outsourcing; however, other factors are becoming more prominent such as access to talent, achieving business transformation and innovation. Alongside this, clients are becoming more 'outsourcing savvy'. Such clients expect to achieve real impact on their business through outsourcing. Long-term outsourcing contracts are becoming the norm with the expectation that large vendors will be able to provide end-to-end services across multiple business towers (e.g. HR, Finance, Procurement). Depending on their size and geographical spread, vendors become more specialised in certain areas of business processes with only few large players that can offer end-to-end services. Knowledge process outsourcing is gaining momentum as Brazil, Russia, India and China (BRIC) and emerging countries move up the value chain. Captive centre activity has intensified, with some clients setting up captive centres in either near-shore or offshore locations, others looking to divest their captive centres and some terminating offshore operations. Lastly, both clients and vendors have been putting more efforts into socially responsible sourcing and green IT.

There are also changes in the geographies of outsourcing. While India will continue to dominate the ITO and BPO scene, China will emerge as an alternative,

---

[1] Willcocks L.P, Griffiths C., and Kotlarsky J.K. (2009) Offshoring in non-BRIC Countries: Egypt- a New Growth Market, LSE Outsourcing Unit Report.

[2] Willcocks, L.P., M. Lacity. 2009. *The Practice of Outsourcing: From ITO to BPO and Offshoring*. Palgrave, London.

though it will still struggle to achieve scale in Western European and North American markets. Near-shoring will emerge as a strong trend in which some countries will become preferred outsourcing destinations such as Central and Eastern Europe (CEE) servicing Western Europe, the Caribbean to the USA and Canada, and North Africa to France and Spain. Outsourcing successes and disappointments will continue as both clients and suppliers struggle to deal with a highly dynamic set of possibilities[3]. The present downturn in the economy is certainly putting additional pressure on clients to realise cost savings from outsourcing as well as from vendors to demonstrate the value offered through an outsourcing proposition. Several reports from 2008 and 2009 have already indicated that the scope of outsourcing has increased since start of the economic downturn has started. At the same time, several commentators have warned against short term expectations to see quick and significant return on outsourcing investment. Yet, the trend is clear: client organisations will seek a clear Return on Outsourcing Investment, which is timely, transparent and that is in line with the firm's business objectives. It is the quest to develop a systematic approach to measure value from outsourcing arrangements that client organisations face. Below we look into these aspects in great detail.

2 About This Research

This research, conducted by Warwick Business School in collaboration with Cognizant, focuses on understanding the real benefits of outsourcing beyond a one-time cost saving alone. The study goes beyond this objective by trying to understand the underpinning factors behind client firms' inability to systematically measure the benefits offered through outsourcing and by examining the strategic role that key players can play in achieving this goal.

The ideas presented in this paper are based on original research conducted at Warwick Business School (UK) and carried out by Dr. Ilan Oshri and Dr. Julia Kotlarsky. The researchers conducted semi-structured interviews and held discussions with experts in the field of outsourcing, including CIOs and CFOs from leading multinationals with headquarters based in Europe, such as ABN AMRO, Maersk, Shell and Phillips. These firms are considered to be some of the most sophisticated outsourcing clients and their practices have become a benchmark for many others. The ideas in this paper are also based on a quantitative survey, which was carried out in partnership with research organisation Vanson Bourne. The quantitative survey sampled 263 CIOs and CFOs across the UK (52%) and other European countries such as France, Germany, Denmark, Sweden, Switzerland and Benelux (Belgium, Netherlands and Luxemburg), comprising 48% CFOs and 52% CIOs at companies with revenues from $500m up to over $6bn (71% over $1bn) from financial services, manufacturing, logistics, retail, utilities, telecom and other sectors.

[3] Willcocks, L.P., C. Griffiths, J. Kotlarsky. 2009. Beyond BRIC. Offshoring in non-BRIC countries: Egypt – a new growth market. The LSE Outsourcing Unit report.

3 CIO and CFO Perspectives on Outsourcing

In this section we reflect on the insights gained from the survey and the numerous discussions we have had with experts in the field of outsourcing. In particular, we discuss:

- which functions are outsourced
- how critical these functions are to the business
- outsourcing models
- the drivers to outsource
- confidence in offshore providers
- the benefits expected from outsourcing
- the methods to quantify returns on outsourcing
- the role of the CIO
- outsourcing in difficult times
- future outsourcing trends.

3.1 Functions Outsourced

Clearly with ITO still growing fast, IT and IT-enabled business processes are still the most popular candidates for outsourcing. With the commoditisation of computer and data-transmission technologies over the last decade many firms are now relying on specialised third party vendors to carry out work on their behalf. Among the vast range of services outsourced, IT application maintenance is on the top of the list, being outsourced by 76% of companies surveyed, followed by IT development projects (outsourced by 53%) and IT and technology consultancy (50%). More specifically, among the various IT application maintenance activities, IT infrastructure support (e.g. network management, server and hardware maintenance) and data-centre management are the most commonly outsourced (by 54%). Second most popular area to be outsourced is ERP maintenance, upgrades and implementations of applications such as Oracle, Peoplesoft or SAP (by 41%), as illustrated by Table 1.

Activities that involve sensitive or confidential information (e.g. Finance and Administration, HR, Payroll and CRM that uses clients' and employees' confidential data) or those that are related to core business and marketing activities (e.g. data warehousing and business intelligence systems) are less popular for outsourcing. While many of these processes are relatively easy to codify and transfer to a third party[4] (Aron and Singh 2005), it is also a strategic decision by many companies to keep these processes in-house for security reasons or to move them offshore to captive facilities where a higher degree of control can be exercised at a lower cost.

---

[4] Aron, R., J.V. Singh. 2005. Getting Offshoring Right. *Harvard Business Review* **83**(12) 135-143.

Table 1. Areas of business being outsourced (CIO and CFO perspectives)

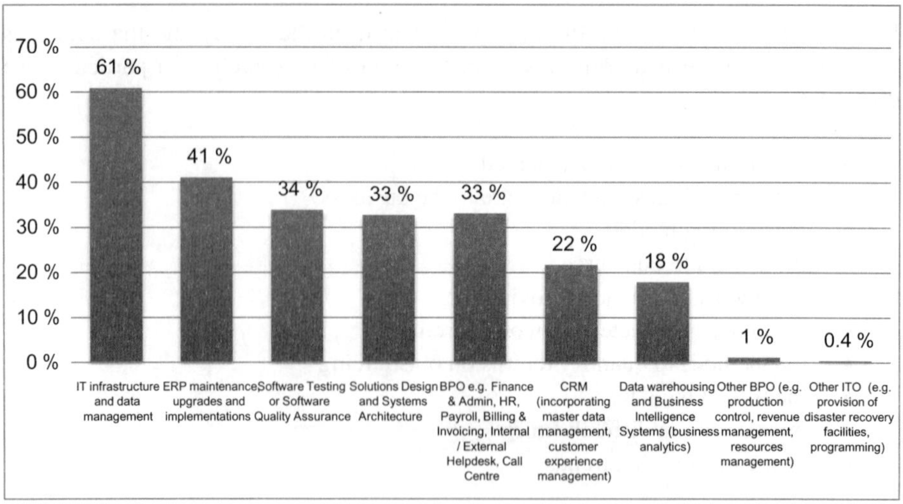

3.2 The Criticality of Outsourcing to the Business

While 33% of all respondents view outsourced business arrangements as critical or very critical to their business, there are different perceptions among the CIOs and CFOs surveyed in this study. 39% of CIOs believe that outsourcing is critical to their business while only 27% of CFOs thought so (see Table 2). The explanation for these differences is simple. CIOs, who typically act as the initiators and sponsors of an outsourcing arrangement, see the immediate impact on the organisation, in particular when the organisation is changing its strategic approach towards the IT function to focus on building the retained organisation, which are the roles and the people filling these roles in the client organization who will remain onboard to make sure the deal is successful. Under such circumstances, the criticality of the outsourcing activity to the business is high as most firms find themselves having a growing dependency on their outsourcing partners. CFOs tend to look at outsourcing through a cost-saving lens, which does not always materialise in the short term, and in some cases would never do. One CIO commented on the CFO's view of outsourcing:

> *CFOs always expect short term cost savings. They are looking at the short term. If you outsource this year then the CFO will ask you: 'What were the cost savings this year, bottom line?'*

Clearly, such differences in perceptions raise the question: what is the role of the CIO in conveying a clearer message to the executive board about the real value in outsourcing? We discuss this aspect in great detail in the section 'The Role of the CIO'.

3.3 Outsourcing Models

Many clients who have had experience with outsourcing for several years have by now learned that working with multiple suppliers often helps to keep them on their toes with regard to their cost, quality, and business transformation offerings. At the same time, managing multiple suppliers requires advanced sourcing management capabilities and in-house learning capabilities that not all firms can afford to build and maintain. Those clients, therefore, often choose a selective sourcing approach. Some outsource some business functions to two to three 'best of breed' suppliers (based on domain or geography). Others might choose a 'supplier panel' approach that involves a panel of 'preferred suppliers' that constantly compete for contracts throughout the outsourcing arrangement. More sophisticated clients will outsource end-to-end services across multiple business towers to a single vendor, in what is now known as a 'bundled services' outsourcing arrangement. Each outsourcing model has its advantages and challenges. And there is a development path in which clients move along the outsourcing learning curve and gradually become outsourcing savvy. In this journey, clients first develop their sourcing management capabilities and their learning abilities to adapt and change according to market conditions and their internal needs. Some believe the selective-sourcing model will become one of the dominating models in the near future. Within this outsourcing model, the most popular services to be outsourced to more than one vendor are IT infrastructure and maintenance (by 25% of respondents) and IT and technology consultancy (17%).

3.4 Key Drivers of Outsourcing

While the common belief is that cost-cutting is the key strategic driver for outsourcing, the results of this research show that access to skills not available internally is perceived by CIOs and CFOs to be more important in 2009 (61%). The second driver is cost reduction (41%) and access to innovative processes and practices (also 41%) (See Table 2). Clearly, there is a shift in the way client organisations see the strategic drivers behind outsourcing. CIOs and CFOs are now focusing on the need to access talent and innovative ideas as a source of competitive advantage. In this regard, vendors with extensive domain knowledge developed through work with multiple clients are perceived as knowledge-bases of ideas and innovations. Cost advantage is achieved by such vendors through the location of some of their delivery centres in either near-shore or offshore locations. These results also show that the benefits expected to be delivered from outsourcing are not the one-off type. Seeking innovation and accessing talent imply that client organisations perceive their vendors as partners to the long-term development of business strategy through the support and improvement of services and products. In this scenario the vendor becomes a true partner in improving the client's competitive advantage through cutting edge ideas and costs cutting. Another key strategic driver that came out from the interviews is flexibility. CIOs argued that outsourcing has allowed them to quickly scale up or down operations in response to market demand without having to bear the costs involved. This key driver has become critical during the present downturn as firms need to respond quickly to changes in markets. One CIO stated:

Our vendor is much more able to scale up staff than we can. I would need to think twice before hiring staff. But I can ask my vendor: "Can you scale up the number staff working for us in the next couple of weeks to 200 because we have a new project?" That's agility!

Table 2. Key drivers of outsourcing CIO and CFO perspectives

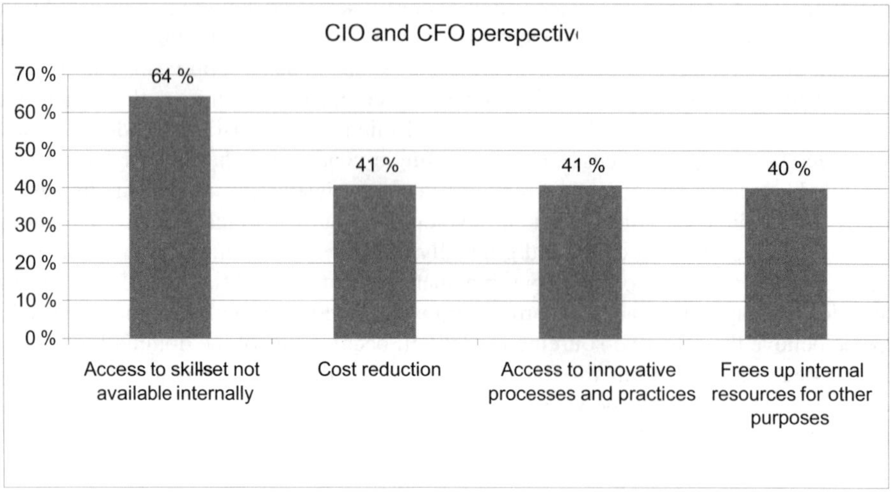

3.5 Confidence in an Offshore Provider

Firms that are contemplating outsourcing high-value knowledge-intensive work to offshore providers should consider numerous risks. For this reason some firms mitigate such risks by setting up their own captive centres in offshore locations. The drive behind such a move is to maintain control over critical activities while reducing costs. However, as many firms realise, the concept of the captive centre - a subsidiary of the parent firm that provides services from offshore location - still requires massive investment and management attention to make it successful, simply because the concept of the captive centre is changing. For example, some firms (successfully) divested their offshore investment (e.g. British Airways) while others had to close down their service centres (e.g. Dell). The risk associated with offshoring work to a third party provider also depends on the nature of the task. Repetitive tasks that can be easily codified are promising candidates for offshoring through a third party provider. Tasks that include components of tacit knowledge with high degree of dependency on other services are less favourable for offshoring. Yet in recent years we have witnessed the emergence of Knowledge Process Outsourcing (KPO) in which high value work that requires significant domain expertise is increasingly outsourced to offshore vendors. The central theme of KPO is to create value for the client by providing business expertise rather than process expertise from offshore locations. The results of the survey

Table 3. Time to achieve ROI

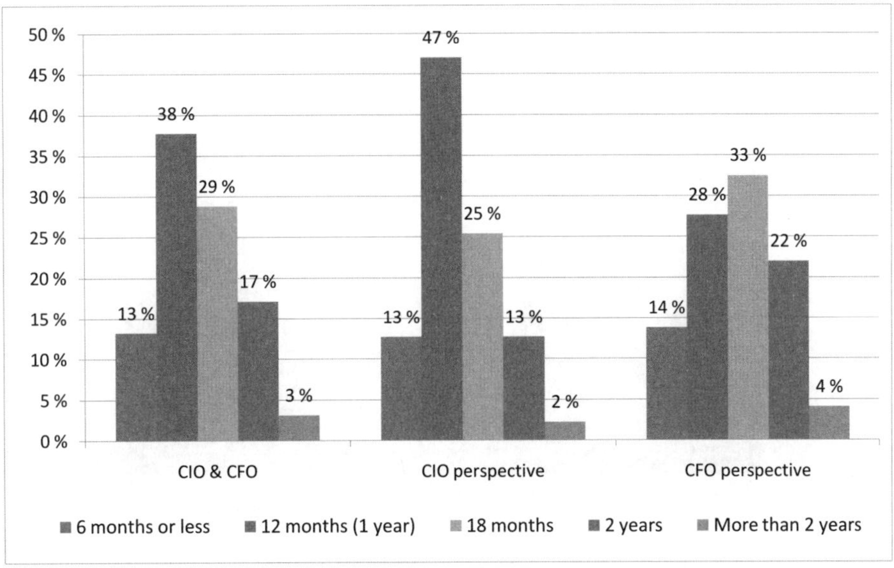

show that CIOs and CFOs have high confidence in offshoring work to a third party provider in particular in the area of IT development (63%), and to a lesser extent in the areas of IT maintenance (47%) and BPO (44%). These results demonstrate the level of maturity that the surveyed firms have developed in preparing their repetitive (IT maintenance) and knowledge processes (IT development and some BPOs) to outsourcing. One of the most straight-forward practices in this regard was expressed by one CIO:

> *We don't believe in "ship it and then fix it". We believe in "fix it first and then ship it". So we fix our processes first and then we ship then to our vendors.*

3.6 Return on Outsourcing Investments

With large scale, lengthy outsourcing contracts becoming the norm, there is a question regarding the expected time clients should achieve an impact on their business through outsourcing. C-level executives we have interviewed claimed that the real impact can be achieved only after two years. The reason being is that it usually takes about six months to set up the outsourcing relationship (e.g. client to vendor transition), after which the vendor becomes more involved in the client's line of business to improve current services, offer innovations and demonstrate a return on the investment in outsourcing.

Table 4. Response to the following question: Do you think the business value of your organisation's outsourcing arrangements can be assessed beyond the one-time cost savings for each project?

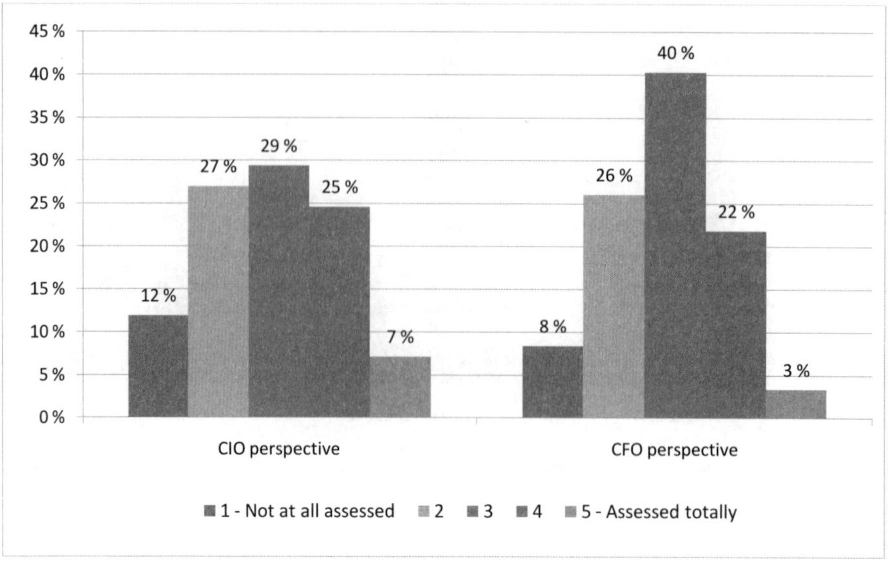

The results of the survey show that both CIOs and CFOs prefer to demonstrate a return on outsourcing investment within up to one year (51%). Interestingly, 60% of the CIOs would like to demonstrate such ROI while only 42% of the CFOs believe that it can be achieved within one year or less. Majority of CFOs (33%) expect to see ROI within 18 months. Clearly, pressed by the economic downturn, CIOs and CFOs are seeking to utilise outsourcing as a means through which returns can be demonstrated quickly. One CIO warned against this approach saying:

> *[...] you will see CIOs now desperate as they are looking for a quick outsourcing deal to get their cost down, which is wrong. It is absolutely wrong because if you just do it for lower cost, then I would say to you: 'don't go into outsourcing because you will be disappointed because the costs will go up.'*

However, with outsourcing contracts becoming more complex, often involving multiple suppliers and several areas of the business, ROI can be a tricky concept to analyse and properly calculate. Clearly, when clients expect vendors to join them in their journey to achieve competitive advantage, there will always be a challenge to realise the ROI at any given time. The results of the survey support this observation with only 39% of the CIOs and CFOs believing that the financial contribution of their outsourcing activities can be assessed. Furthermore, as more and more outsourcing

Table 5. Response to the following question: How confident are you in this quantification?

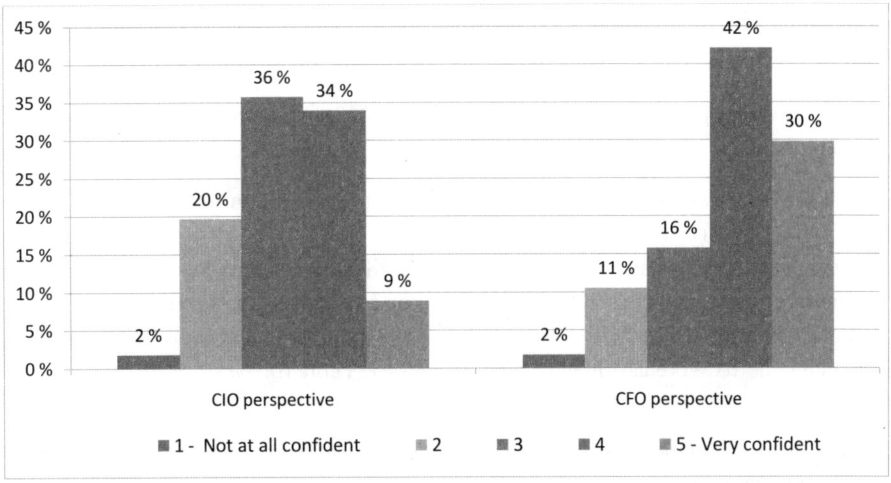

contracts are about high-value activities which often involve intense and ongoing collaboration in the form of a joint venture between the client and the vendor, translating benefits from outsourcing activities into financial terms is becoming ever more challenging to achieve. Only 28% of the CIOs and CFOs surveyed believed that their organisations can assess the business value beyond the one-time cost savings of the project (see Table 4).

3.7 Quantifying the Returns on Outsourcing Investments

Some sophisticated vendors have perfected their performance management systems by developing metrics that capture and quantify any activity carried out by their staff. In this way, these vendors secure their margins and avoid the ‘winner’s curse’ syndrome (Kern et al. 2002). On the other hand, most clients tend to mainly rely on Service Level Agreement (SLAs) as a mean to assess their satisfaction from outsourcing arrangements. One CIO described their approach to assess satisfaction from outsourcing arrangements:

> *We try to simplify it. It’s too much over the top. We have everything we outsourced on service level agreements and we have a pretty good matching system.*

Quantifying the indications provided by SLAs seems to be a challenge. 37% of the CIOs and CFOs in our survey never tried to quantify the financial benefits from their outsourcing arrangements. Additional 20% of the CIOs and CFOs in the survey did not know whether such an attempt was carried out in their organisation. Of those CIOs and CFOs who quantified the financial benefits from outsourcing arrangements (113 respondents), 43% of them were not confident in the way they have measured such returns (see Table 5). One of the respondents commented on this question saying:

> *That is the problem. You know what it costs but you don't really know what the value is.*

Not surprisingly, according to the survey, CFOs are more confident in the way they quantify such returns than CIOs.

When asked: Why have you not tried to quantify the financial contribution of your outsourcing arrangements? 51% of the CIOs and CFOs in our survey said that such financial benefits are difficult to quantify, and 41% of the CIOs and CFOs thought that such benefits were assumed to be positive (see Table 6).

Table 6. Response to the question: Why have you not tried to quantify the financial contribution of your outsourcing arrangements?

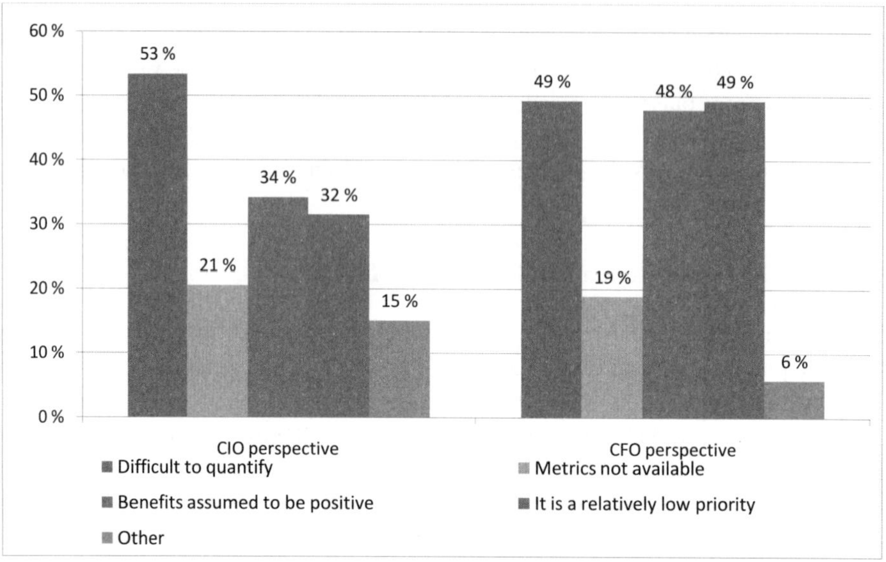

3.8 The Role of the CIO

Outsourcing arrangements of IT development and business processes are critical for the competitiveness of most firms. The CIO and the retained organisation are expected to act as the connecting link between the business strategy and markets through the smooth execution of the sourcing strategy. For this reason, it is imperative that the CIO will be able to bring the business case to the executive board and act as a change agent within the firm to achieve business transformation and innovations through outsourcing partnerships. However, according to our survey, 64% of the CFOs do not think that CIOs succeed in communicating the financial benefits from outsourcing arrangements. This raises a question regarding the maturity and sophistication of the retained organisation in some firms, where the CIO is incapable of communicating the business case of outsourcing to the executive board and demonstrate the financial benefits to be gained. One CIO reflected on these results by giving an example:

> *[...] in my network when I discuss with other CIOs and I ask them, "How are you doing on your business case?" They said, "What do you mean business case?" I then say: "You need something to describe against a report. If you don't start with a business case, if you don't start with clear objectives, how are you going to report it"?*

The results also show that some of the critical strategic benefits from outsourcing are perceived by CFOs to be poorly communicated to the executive board by CIOs, such as business transformation and impact on competitive advantage. The fact that many of the CIOs are not members of the executive board magnifies this problem as the message that the CIO would like to send to the executive board through the CTO or another C-level Office to whom the CIO is reporting to, may get 'lost in translation'.

3.9 Outsourcing in Difficult Times

As the global economy is still battling the downturn, CIOs and CFOs are taking some actions to shelter their firms from the storm. CFOs are looking for costs reduction across the board. Also, there are indications that firms are hesitant regarding new outsourcing projects, delaying their decisions to better times, while some CIOs attempt to re-negotiate the terms of some of their large scale on-going outsourcing projects. One CIO commented in the survey:

> *We would want to increase and improve the delivery of services from outsourcing, but will "hold-off" in the short-term.*

About 40% of our respondents indicated that they pulled work back from outsourcing providers or slowed the growth of outsourcing initiatives. Among those who have pulled work back from outsourcing providers or slowed the growth of outsourcing initiatives (105 respondents), the main reasons for doing so were unclear value for money (78%), high vendor management costs (46%) and lack of governance (38%), as shown in Table 6. Poor quality (17%) was not considered a key factor to back-sourcing work or slowing the growth of outsourcing initiatives. Clearly, client firms perceive value creation as a critical element in developing long-term relationships

Table 7. Causes of cutback or slowdown of outsourcing

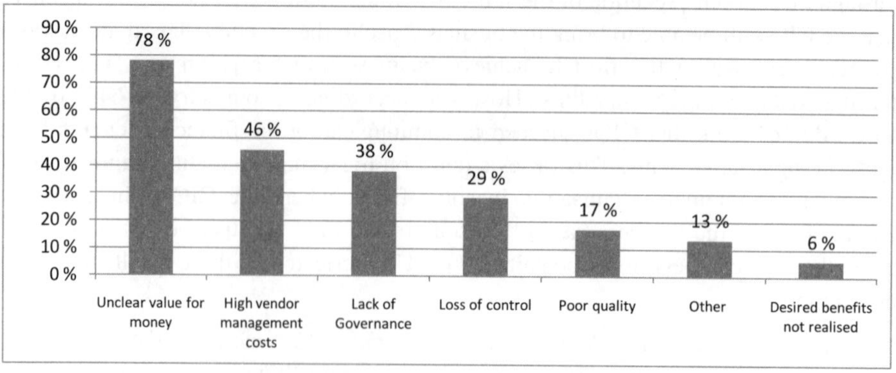

with outsourcing partners. To develop such partnerships between vendors and clients, the benefits of outsourcing should be transparent, timely, easy to communicate and in line with the key success criteria of the business.

3.10 Economic Downturn and the Impact on the Labour Force

Firms seeking to improve their financial position during an economic downturn often consider outsourcing as one possible route. While some firms would have indeed preferred outsourcing as a route to improve their financial position, these firms could be forced to hold to their staff and refrain from contracting work out to low-cost highly skilled work force. One CFO summarised this aspect well, arguing that:

Outsourcing has worked very well for us, but maintaining jobs is the priority.

There are several aspects in the European context that provide an explanation for this approach. These vary from protective labour law to public resentment towards sending jobs overseas. In some countries, for example France, the labour law is protective, therefore making redundancies or outsourcing very difficult. One French CFO commented in the survey:

The French want to preserve their jobs, so outsourcing is likely to suffer.

A similar approach is pursued in Germany. A German CFO commented in the survey:

In Germany, companies are having to keep staff in jobs so outsourcing is not currently popular.

The survey provided support to this approach. CIOs and CFOs indicated that they will be inclined to freeze salary rises first (74%), then reduce person-hour (37%) and only then reduce headcount (32%), as shown in Table 8.

Table 8. Response to the following question: In the current economic environment which of the following moves are you contemplating for your business?

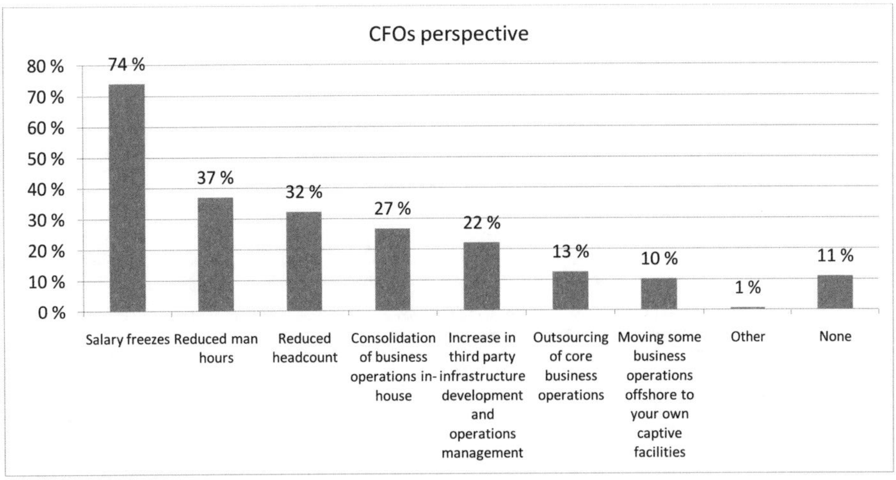

3.11 The Future of Outsourcing

Is outsourcing a trend or the onset of fundamental transformation of crucial business arrangements? Many believe that we are on the verge of a major transformation in which sourcing will play a significant role. In this regard, the ability to work with a network of suppliers will become part of the firm's core competence and will therefore redefine what is core and what is non-core for the firm. Sixty per cent of CIOs and CFOs believe that their firms will increase or maintain the same level of outsourcing activities as before. This clearly shows that firms believe in the value that outsourcing can deliver and in the impact that outsourcing can have on the firm's competitive advantage.

There are several particular areas where firms anticipate to continue outsourcing in the future - most notably in IT infrastructure and data management (41%), IT and technology consultancy (38%) and ERP support and implementation (25%) (See Table 9).

New sourcing models and trend

With new advances in Information and Communication Technologies (ICTs), mobile and nano-technologies and the recent improvement of IT infrastructure in India, China, and most CEE countries, we have witnessed the emergence of new sourcing models that rely on remote service provisions and remote access to computing resources. In particular, we are seeing more services offered in a Software-as-a-Service

Table 9. Functions to be outsourced in the future

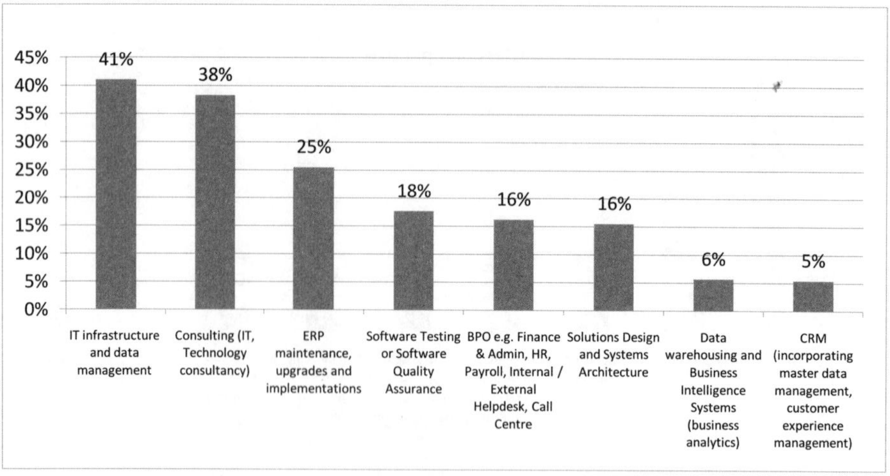

(SaaS) fashion. SaaS is a business model of software deployment where an application is hosted as a service and provided to customers across the Internet (i.e. Web-based application). Forty three per cent of the CIOs indicated that they are likely to explore this service in the next three years (see Table 10). Thirty nine per cent of the CIOs will very likely explore Remote Management Services (e.g. infrastructure and network management). Other emerging sourcing models, such as business process utility, information utility and cloud computing are also of interest but at much lesser extent.

Table 10. CIOs perspective on which services firms will be using in the future

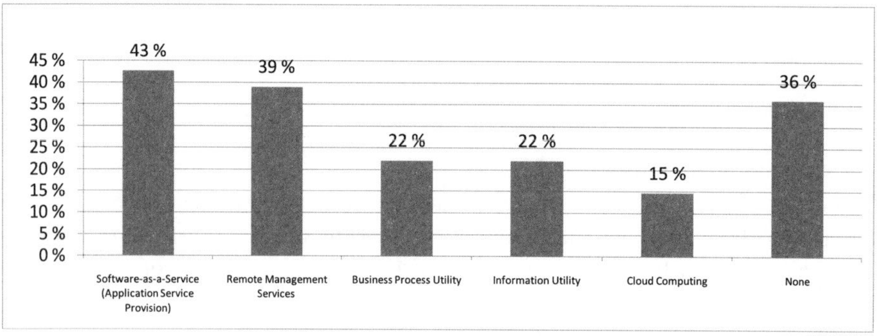

4 The Road to Realising Real Benefits from Outsourcing: Seven Lessons

Any firm would like to clearly present the benefits from its outsourcing arrangements. However, many firms will eventually realise that they don't know what exactly they have gained and at what price. The simple reason for that is: the journey to realising your benefits from outsourcing arrangements cannot allow any shortcuts. Being in a position to realise the real benefits from outsourcing requires a step by step approach. First, the context of the outsourcing activity should be understood and analysed. Part of that is realising the drivers, internal resources and expectations. Based on the context of the outsourcing activity, the firm should now make decisions on how and where to outsource (e.g. nearshore or offshore). This will be the firm's outsourcing strategy. Once the drivers and strategy have been figured out, it will now be imperative to understand the benchmark that would best suit the firm's outsourcing arrangement. Figuring out the benchmark to use in the outsourcing arrangement would not mean that the firm has realised the value gained from its outsourcing arrangement. Value can and will change over time and as the outsourcing arrangement matures and evolves. For this reason, value should be reassessed throughout the outsourcing arrangement to allow adjustments in value creation between the parties involved. At the same time, the firm will need to ensure the development of three critical organisational resources. These are the retained organisation; the firm's learning capabilities; and the role the CIO is playing. We now describe each lesson in detail.

Lesson 1: Figure Out the Context of the Outsourcing Activity

A good starting point is by understanding why the firm would like to outsource a service and what resources are available to successfully carry out an outsourcing project. We observed a couple of common mistakes in this regard: a bandwagon effect in which firms outsource because the competition does so (also known as 'me too' strategy) or firms outsource 'a problem'. These are the wrong reasons to outsource a service. The consequences of such an approach can be dire, with a combination of potentially major difficulties to understand and benefits to realise from this outsourcing arrangement.

Instead, firms should follow a systematic approach to analysing the context of the outsourcing activity. There are several criteria that a firm should examine. Some are about the service and some are about the firm's resources and capabilities. Simply ask yourself the following questions:

- What is the firm trying to achieve by outsourcing?
- How critical is the service to my competitive advantage?
- How dependent is the service on information or other inputs from the firm?
- How difficult is it to codify and monitor work considered for outsourcing?
- How precise are the metrics?
- How mature is the firm in managing outsourcing arrangements?

Fig. 1. A Step-by-Step Framework to Realise Outsourcing Benefits

Answering these questions should give you a clear understanding of the drivers to outsource, your internal resources and your expectations. A service that is a source of competitive advantage should be kept in-house. Realising the benefits of an embedded service that is difficult to codify be challenging as it increases operational risks. Likewise, outsourcing processes that are difficult to monitor (e.g. R&D, supply chain coordination); in particular when the firm does not have precise metrics to evaluate quality is not recommended[5]. In these cases, the firm should examine its maturity level in outsourcing. A high degree of outsourcing maturity and sophistication will allow the firm to devise methods that overcome some challenges and help to mitigate some operational and structural risks.

This is only the first step but lays the foundations for moving on to the next step: your outsourcing strategy!

Lesson 2: Figure Out the Outsourcing Strategy

The outsourcing strategy will dictate the complexity of the outsourcing arrangement and therefore the ability to realise its benefits. Our advice to firms is simple: choose

[5] Aron and Singh (2005) op.cit.

an outsourcing strategy that the firm's resources and capabilities can cope with. By doing so, you will be able to assess and realise the benefits gained from your outsourcing arrangements.

Surprisingly, many firms experiment with sourcing models that are beyond their organisational capabilities. For example, in recent years many firms experimented with multi-vendor sourcing arrangements. We noticed that not so many firms can actually realise the benefits offered by the multi-vendor outsourcing model. It takes advanced sourcing capabilities to effectively and efficiently manage a single vendor in a particular business function, let alone multiple vendors that coordinate several transformation programs across several business functions. To be successful in this model, a firm needs highly developed outsourcing management and learning capabilities to realise the benefits delivered by each vendor as well as achieve value from having multiple sources of skills involved. Another example is the outsourcing of a range of services within a particular business function (e.g. HR) to a single vendor. While the client might perceive this as a straightforward outsourcing arrangement in which the benefits should be easily realised as there is only one vendor involved, the client will in fact need to develop sophisticated outsourcing capabilities that will allow realising the benefits from synergies between outsourced services. We have learned that most clients have failed to realise this promise.

Lesson 3: Figure Out the Benchmark

Many firms rely on Service Level Agreements (SLAs) as the main mean through which value from an outsourcing arrangement can be realised. SLAs are critical in any outsourcing arrangement; however, they don't give the entire picture and in some case SLAs can be misleading. Firms that rely on SLAs to realise the benefits from outsourcing arrangements are basically monitoring service performance, which can be meeting the service provisions; however, offer little transformation. Therefore, the challenge for firms is to realise the impact of outsourcing on the business and not on the service performance. For this reason, firms must figure out the benchmark to use when measuring real benefits. The benchmark is usually a key success factor (KSF) in that industry. In one industry it could be the time to market of a new product while in another industry it will be quality. Once a benchmark has been identified, SLAs can be drafted to correspond with the provisions that generate a competitive edge. This will promise that the key effort of the client and the vendor is to improve the firm's competitive advantage through business transformation that is monitored through a set of SLAs.

Lesson 4: Realise What is Value Over Time

Value is a dynamic concept. The desired value to be delivered from an outsourcing arrangement set by the client and vendor in the beginning of the project is destined to change over time. Few firms are aware of this and even fewer take steps to mitigate this risk. Clearly, by not sensing the changes in value over the outsourcing project life, tensions and disagreement are likely to emerge between the parties, which will eventually erode the benefits from the outsourcing arrangement. At the same time, the dynamic nature of value does not mean that clients are entitled to redefine their expectations every week. There should be a joint approach to address this challenge.

The first step is therefore to develop sensing mechanisms for changes in value. Sensing mechanisms are best supported through shared learning between the client and the vendor. The more shared learning opportunities are created between the client and vendor teams, the more likely that value as a dynamic concept will be monitored. Our research found that value is best sensed when the outsourcing arrangement is based on relational value. Under such circumstances, efforts are put into the development of the supply network relationships by responding to the changing nature of value.

Lesson 5: Make your CIO a Strategist

Many CIOs, as we have learned in our research, do not 'speak' the 'business language'. Most of them are not executive board members. Many of them have emerged from the IT/IS ranks and often had little exposure to and involvement in shaping the firm's business strategy. In recent years some argued that in fact the role of the CIO is now less strategic, mainly because IT cannot anymore be considered as a source of competitive advantage. However, in the last fifteen years, the CIO has led outsourcing projects and transformed the way services are designed and delivered. The boundaries of the firms have been redefined and sources of innovations have been reconsidered. Clearly, nowadays the CIO is, if anything, more strategist than ever and its role within the firm is destined to grow. However, to cope with such changes the CIO needs to learn. They need to learn the 'business language' spoken at the executive board. They need to learn to design and argue a strong business case of an outsourcing arrangement at the strategic, operational and financial level. They need to learn to focus on business improvement processes rather than service improvement processes and on business transformation rather than IT improvements. Their role within the organisation should be more central, with a direct influence on decisions made at the board level. A CIO then should become a central figure and a driving force in implementing Lessons 1-4, 6 and 7, as depicted in Figure 1 above.

Lesson 6: Build the Retained Organisation

The CIO alone will not be able to transform the firm and deliver value from outsourcing arrangements; however, the CIO can and should build the retained organisation to act as a change agent that examines and monitors value delivery[6]. Most firms consider the retained organisation as the minimum resource needed to support IT function continuity. The mistake in this approach is the focus on IT function continuity. Instead, the retained organisation should be perceived as the resource that drives firm's transformation and innovation. For example, in many outsourcing arrangements the client transfers staff to the vendor. A common mistake by CIOs is that they tend to

[6] Willcocks, L.P. and A. Craig (2008) " The Outsourcing Enterprise. Building core retained capabilities." Logica Whitepaper.

keep the bright and talented across the various areas of skills. Instead, a CIO should transfer bright and talented staff to the vendor in those areas of skills that the vendor is expected to take leadership, for example application development. At the same time, the CIO should build new expertise within the IT function to ensure that the focus of the IT function is on continuity, transformation and innovation. But the retained organisation includes other capabilities, such as *relationship building*, which concerns the wider communication between business and IT communities. It involves helping users understand the potential of IT for the creation of value, helping users and IT experts collaborate, and ensuring users' ownership and satisfaction. For most firms this is a major challenge simply because the tremendous difference in culture between "techies" and "users". Role holders with this capability have to facilitate a shared purpose and constructive communication among people engaged in the business and the IT function[7]. Without this capability, the retained organisation will enable IT function continuity, but will fail to demonstrate the benefits of business transformation.

Lesson 7: Invest in Outsourcing Learning Capabilities

One of the most critical capabilities that outsourcing clients need to develop is learning. And still, clients tend to take a narrow approach to learning by focusing on learnt lessons from a single outsourcing arrangement and often paying little attention to building a learning capability across multiple outsourcing arrangements[8]. Furthermore, clients often apply all their resources to ensure that vendors meet the service provisions while ignoring opportunities to learn from their vendors. Just consider the vast experience acquired by a vendor over time in a particular industry. Also consider the growing specialisation of vendors in a particular industry or technology mainly achieved through the knowledge acquired by centres of excellence (CoEs). Experts from these CoEs have dealt with multiple outsourcing arrangements, reviewed numerous contracts, negotiated benchmark and SLAs metrics and work together with various clients to make these arrangements a success[9]. Furthermore, some leading vendors have perfected their knowledge management systems to ensure that their learning capability supports multiple engagements in an efficient manner (e.g. reuse of concepts). And yet, clients, as we learned, refrain from consulting with these experts. It is still the notion of 'us' and 'them' that inhibits learning between clients and vendors.

Removing these learning barriers requires vision and courage. If a firm is to become a sophisticated outsourcing player, it has to learn how to learn from its vendor firstly to avoid mistakes we have seen make again and again by inexperienced clients and, secondly, to improve the benefits that can be gained from an outsourcing arrangement.

---

[7] Willcocks and Craig (2008) op.cit.

[8] Oshri, I., J. Kotlarsky, L.P. Willcocks. 2007. Managing Dispersed Expertise in IT Offshore Outsourcing: Lessons from Tata Consultancy Services. *MIS Quarterly Executive* **6**(2) 53-65.

[9] Oshri et al (2007) op.cit.

About the Authors

Dr. Ilan Oshri is Associate Fellow at Warwick Business School. He is also Associate Professor at Rotterdam School of Management (The Netherlands) and Associate Fellow of the LSE Outsourcing Unit. He is the co-author of five books including The Handbook of Global Outsourcing and Offshoring, Outsourcing Global Services, Knowledge Processes in Globally Distributed Contexts and Standards-Battles in Open Source Software. His work was published in numerous magazines and journals including The Wall Street Journal, MISQ Executive, Communications of the ACM, IEEE Transactions on Engineering Management, European Journal of Information Systems, Journal of Information Technology, Management Learning, Journal of Strategic Information Systems and others. Ilan is a regular speaker in international conferences and a keynote speaker in corporate events and seminars. He is the European Editor of JIT and also the co-founder of the Global Sourcing Workshop. (www.ilanoshri.com)

Dr. Julia Kotlarsky is Associate Professor at Warwick Business School. She is also Associate Fellow of the LSE Outsourcing Unit and holds visiting position at Vrije University Amsterdam (The Netherlands). Her academic and consultancy work revolves around managing knowledge, social and technical aspects of globally distributed software development teams, IT outsourcing and offshoring. Julia is a regular presenter in international conferences and conventions. She published her work in numerous journals including the *Wall Street Journal*, *Communications of the ACM*, *MISQ Executive*, *European Journal of Information Systems*. She is co-founder of the Annual Global Sourcing Workshop now in its fourth year and co-author of several books including "Knowledge Processes in Globally Distributed Contexts" (Palgrave, 2008), "Outsourcing Global Services: Knowledge, Innovation and Social Capital", Palgrave (2008) and "The Handbook of Global Outsourcing and Offshoring" (Palgrave, forthcoming 2009). (www.juliakotlarsky.com)

Author Index

Printing: Mercedes-Druck, Berlin
Binding: Stein + Lehmann, Berlin